THERE IS NO SUCH THING AS A NATURAL DISASTER

THERE IS NO SUCH THING AS A NATURAL DISASTER

Race, Class, and Hurricane Katrina

edited by Chester Hartman and Gregory D. Squires

Routledge
Taylor & Francis Group
New York   London

Routledge is an imprint of the
Taylor & Francis Group, an informa business

Routledge
Taylor & Francis Group
270 Madison Avenue
New York, NY 10016

Routledge
Taylor & Francis Group
2 Park Square
Milton Park, Abingdon
Oxon OX14 4RN

© 2006 by Taylor & Francis Group, LLC
Routledge is an imprint of Taylor & Francis Group, an Informa business

Printed in the United States of America on acid-free paper
10 9 8 7 6 5 4 3 2 1

International Standard Book Number-10: 0-415-95487-8 (Softcover) 0-415-95486-X (Hardcover)
International Standard Book Number-13: 978-0-415-95487-7 (Softcover) 978-0-415-95486-0 (Hardcover)

Library of Congress Cataloging-in-Publication Data

There is no such thing as a natural disaster : race, class, and Hurricane Katrina / edited by Chester Hartman and Gregory D. Squires.
    p. cm.
    Includes bibliographical references and index.
    ISBN 0-415-95486-X (hb) -- ISBN 0-415-95487-8 (pb)
    1. Hurricane Katrina, 2005--Social aspects. 2. Hurricane Rita, 2005--Social aspects. 3. Disaster relief--Social aspects--Louisiana--New Orleans. 4. Disaster relief--Social aspects--Gulf States. 5. Marginality, Social--Louisiana--New Orleans. 6. Marginality, Social--Gulf States. 7. People with social disabilities--Government policy--Louisiana--New Orleans. 8. People with social disabilities--Government policy--Gulf States. 9. Human services--Louisiana--New Orleans. 10. Human services--Gulf States. I. Hartman, Chester W. II. Squires, Gregory D.

HV6362005.L8 T44 2006
976'.044--dc22
                                2006023824

Visit the Taylor & Francis Web site at
http://www.taylorandfrancis.com

and the Routledge Web site at
http://www.routledge-ny.com

Contents

Foreword

MARY FRANCES BERRY

Events surrounding the Gulf region have revealed the best and worst features of life in the United States. Perhaps this is inevitable in such a cataclysmic event that redefined the totality of life in an entire region and captured the attention of so much of the nation for so long. Hopefully, the more favorable dimensions of our culture that have been revealed will prevail, and there is reason to hope this will be the case.

Immediately after Katrina, and the flooding that wreaked even greater havoc, struck New Orleans, thousands of families sent money to the Red Cross and many other relief organizations. Baton Rouge, Houston, and communities around the country literally opened their doors to evacuees. Universities invited students from Tulane, Loyola, Dillard, Xavier, Southern, and other Gulf area schools to attend their classes. Church groups helped families relocate in the South and all regions of the nation. But occasional looting also followed in the wake of the storm, as seems inevitable following tumultuous events ranging from hurricanes to national sports championships. Developers are poised to exploit real estate opportunities that may well grow out of the current chaos as many poor and working families lose their homes. The utter failure of government relief efforts reminds us all how critical sound infrastructure and efficient public services are for the conduct of all phases of life, ranging from simply getting to school or work in the morning to the more profound challenges of raising children and creating prosperous businesses in safe and clean communities.

As the recovery slowly proceeds, at least the outlines of a better New Orleans and a stronger Gulf region — if not more vibrant communities around the nation — are being drawn. Even traditionally conservative commentators have expressed the importance of not recreating the segregated, high-poverty neighborhoods that characterized much of New Orleans and metropolitan areas in the U.S. generally. Diverse voices are expressing the rightful proposition that rich and poor alike must be able to return to their communities if they want to do so, while also aiding those who have decided their futures lie elsewhere. Many noncompetitive government grants are going to well-connected lobbyists, but there are many others demanding that local residents have a meaningful voice in recovery efforts.

Within a few months of Katrina, Rita, and Wilma, and the flooding and evacuation of much of New Orleans, fears were already being raised that the nation was beginning to lose interest. No doubt other events will soon capture our imaginations. But as the pages of this book reveal, this story will not go away. It shines a clear light on where we have been and, more importantly, where we can go. Hopefully, the leadership of key public and private organizations, community advocates, and area residents will come together to realize what can be accomplished when our better instincts prevail.

Acknowledgments

We appreciate the help and contributions at various points provided by Jan Chadwick, Gail Christopher, Peter Dreier, Teri Grimwood, Phyllis Mann, and Victor Wallis. Most especially, we are grateful to David McBride and Stephanie Drew at Routledge, whose support (and patience) have been remarkable.

We also wish to acknowledge the extraordinary work being done in the Gulf area by so many dedicated people and organizations. In recognition of that, we have chosen, symbolically (and we hope materially), to donate all royalties from the sale of this book to one such group, Emergency Communities (http://www.emergencycommunities.org/), which provides meals, medical care, legal advice, education, and safe spaces — involving people who come from both within and outside the stricken community — as part of the recovery and rebuilding process.

Chester Hartman
Gregory D. Squires

CHAPTER 1

Pre-Katrina, Post-Katrina

Editors' Introduction

The water- and wind-driven devastation that wracked New Orleans and the entire Gulf Coast region during and after the 2005 hurricane season is virtually without parallel in recent U.S. history. A staggering 2 million people were displaced (Hsu 2006). In the wake of Katrina and Rita came a series of events that were also without parallel. Illustrations include:

- Credible accusations of dereliction, even financial improprieties, on the part of national sacred cows such as the Red Cross and the Humane Society, leading to firings, resignation of the Red Cross president, criticisms by international Red Cross organizations, and official state and federal investigations (Strom 2005, 2006; Salmon 2006a, 2006b; Nossiter 2006). FEMA workers too have been accused of bribery (Lipton 2006c).
- Foreign aid coming to us, not from us—and then mishandled. United Arab Emirates was the leader, contributing $100 million (Lipton 2006b). (Cuba, on the other hand, proposed to send medical personnel and equipment, which offer the State Department ignored.)
- Pets taking center stage: Many flood-endangered folks, the elderly in particular, refused evacuation when they learned from government workers that they could not take their pets—in effect, their family—with them. In response, full-page ads, with pathetic photos, later appear in the *New York Times* and the *Washington Post*. The Humane Society of the United States cleverly entitled them

1

"No Pet Left Behind" in their attempt to generate support for a Senate bill, The Pets Evacuation and Transportation Standards (PETS) Act.

- A mandating of moratoriums (albeit ephemeral) on mortgage foreclosures and evictions—an intervention in the housing market virtually unheard of since Depression days.
- Absentee voting problems (only partially resolved) on an unprecedented scale for the April 22 New Orleans primary and May 20 run-off elections.
- The limitations of insurance coverage, as insurance companies flee coastal areas and the federal flood insurance program goes into the red to the tune of $23 billion as a result of post-Katrina claims (Treaster 2006; Treaster and Dean 2006).
- The Iraq war comes home, as a strapped U.S. military, bogged down in the Middle East, is unable to send National Guard, reservists, or active personnel to help out in the many ways the federal government has supplemented state and local resources in the past.
- Police officers simply walking away from their jobs, in many cases prioritizing the needs of their own families.
- Incidents of racism/exclusion/NIMBYism that still have the power to shock: On August 31, 2005, police in the West Bank city of Gretna blocked a bridge from New Orleans, preventing large numbers of African-American evacuees from escaping the deluged city (Hamilton 2006).

But of course the most salient and ongoing story is one of poverty and racism—all those dramatic, pathetic shots, on television and in the papers, showing who the prime victims were, their helplessness, suffering, and abandonment. While this was no surprise to the community organizers, journalists, academics, and others who deal with these issues every day, for all too large segments of America this was seen as a "wake-up call" (Turner and Zedlewski 2006; Brookings Institution 2005; Pastor et al. 2006; Dyson 2006). Speaking from New Orleans just a few weeks after the storms, President Bush asserted: "Poverty has its roots in racial discrimination, which cut off generations from the opportunity of America.... We have a duty to confront this poverty with bold action.... Let us rise above the legacy of inequality." Conservative *New York Times* columnist David Brooks, while mislabeling the events as a "natural disaster," recognized that they "interrupted a social disaster" (Brooks 2005).

It is the pre-Katrina and post-Katrina worlds that this collection of essays addresses. What created the pre-Katrina world? What should the post-Katrina world be? How might we get from here to there? And since Katrina is in fact a shorthand for a set of economic, social, and political conditions that characterize most of metropolitan America, what lessons and models does this provide for the nation as a whole? Ironically, we might say that in some sense we are fortunate that New Orleans is the focus: One can hardly imagine equivalent national attention had the locus been Spokane, Toledo, or Utica.

Pre-Katrina New Orleans, like most major U.S. cities, was characterized by extreme levels of poverty and racial segregation. The local poverty rate has long been high, and poor residents have been heavily concentrated. New Orleans' poverty rate in 2000 was 28%, compared to 12% for the nation. The number of high-poverty census tracts (tracts where 40% or more of the residents are poor) grew from 30 in 1980 to 49 in 2000. The number of people living in these tracts increased from 96,417 to 108,419. Consequently, among US cities, New Orleans had the second highest share of its poor citizens (38%) living in such neighborhoods in 2000. In addition, the black poverty rate of 35% was more than 3 times the white rate of 11%, and 43% of poor blacks lived in poor neighborhoods (Jargowsky 1996, 2003; Brookings Institution 2005; Wagner and Edwards 2006). And New Orleans has long been highly segregated. According to two common indicators of racial segregation—the Index of Dissimilarity and Isolation —New Orleans is one of the 10 or 15 most racially segregated among the nation's 50 largest metropolitan areas. As a Brookings Institution report (2005:5,6) summed up the situation: "By 2000, the city of New Orleans had become highly segregated by race and had developed high concentrations of poverty.... [B]lacks and whites were living in quite literally different worlds before the storm hit."

But where New Orleans stands relative to other metropolitan areas is almost beside the point. Big cities throughout the U.S. all contain large numbers of poor people, many neighborhoods of concentrated poverty, and highly segregated housing patterns. Why is this? What are the consequences? Oddly enough—and even though nothing from his personal history or his followup actions reflects such understanding and analysis—George W. Bush got it right: We need to understand the history and the legacy of inequality, and why generations of Americans have been and continue to be cut off from opportunity (Massey and Denton 1993; Briggs 2005).

Racial disparities and poverty are not the result primarily of individual actions. They are the cumulative result of a long history of institutional arrangements and structures that have produced current realities. We can start with the 250 years of African-American slavery and the longer-term effects that status had on wealth creation, family life, and white attitudes toward—as well as treatment of—blacks. Following the secession by eleven southern states (including Louisiana) and a bloody civil war that ended the secession, the defeated states (selectively) asserted a claim of "states' rights" as a means of limiting federal intervention. Afterwards, a century of legal segregation throughout the South—overturned by the Civil Rights Movement and several court rulings—ensued, with less formal barriers at work in other parts of the country. Even progressive federal policies, in particular, those introduced in the New Deal period, were racially discriminatory. The social security system categorically excluded two occupations, courtesy of Southern members of Congress: farmworkers and domestics. Not coincidentally, these were occupations dominated by racial minorities, particularly African Americans. Federal housing programs provided minimal home ownership assistance to minority households and reinforced patterns of residential segregation. The GI Bill following World War II similarly provided relatively little education and housing assistance to minorities, compared to the massive benefits whites secured from this program. Even when African Americans received these federal benefits, they were still effectively denied by educational institutions, housing providers, and employers (Katznelson 2005; Williams 2003; Brown et al. 2003).

But, of course, this is not "just history"—and in any case history has clear and powerful continuing impacts. "Redlining" by lending institutions is still all too common. School conditions for black and white students are very different, and, *Brown* notwithstanding, K-12 schools are resegregating all over the country. Housing and employment discrimination, often hard to pinpoint and prove, is rife. Exclusionary zoning regulations, racial steering by real estate agents, federally-subsidized highways, and tax breaks for home owners as well as suburban business development prop up the system. Racial health disparities abound. The criminal justice system—incarceration rates, sentencing patterns, the laws themselves—reflects extreme racial disparities (Massey and Denton 1993; Mauer 2006; Smelser et al. 2001; O'Connor et al. 2001). Need we go on? Concentrated poverty and racial segregation severely reduce opportunity of all types. As sociologist Douglas Massey, co-author of the classic *American Apartheid*, observes: "Any process that concentrates poverty within racially isolated neighborhoods will simultaneously increase the odds of socioeconomic failure" (Massey 2001:424).

And, so, in New Orleans, those with means left when they knew the storm was coming: They had access to personal transportation or plane and train fare, money for temporary housing, in some cases second homes. Guests trapped in one luxury New Orleans hotel were saved when that chain hired a fleet of buses to get them out. Patients in one hospital were saved when a doctor who knew Al Gore contacted the former Vice President, who was able to cut through government red tape and charter two planes that took them to safety. This is what is meant by the catch phrase "social capital"—a resource most unevenly distributed by class and race. Various processes of racial segregation have resulted in middle- and upper-income whites being concentrated in the outlying (and in New Orleans, literally higher) suburban communities, while blacks have been concentrated in the central city, where the flooding was most severe.

A related key issue is the failure to maintain critical public services, including the infrastructure (e.g., levees in flood-prone areas) on which low-income and minority residents depend to a far greater extent than middle- and upper-income families. In the Katrina case, officials long knew the protective levees surrounding the city were inadequate, leaving it vulnerable to precisely the type of disaster that occurred on August 29. But whether it is the levees in New Orleans, the bridges in the San Francisco Bay Area, or the public schools in almost every city, such public services are generally viewed as expenses that need to be minimized rather than essential investments to be maximized for the purpose of enhancing the quality of life in the nation's cities. In its *2005 Report Card for America's Infrastructure*, the American Society of Civil Engineers (2005) concluded: "Congested highways, overflowing sewers and corroding bridges are constant reminders of the looming crisis that jeopardizes our nation's prosperity and quality of life." Assessing 12 infrastructure categories, the Society gave the nation a "D" for its maintenance efforts, noting there had been little improvement in recent years and asserting an as yet unfunded $1.6 trillion investment need over the next five years. The consequences have not been and will not be race- or class-neutral. Low-income people and people of color are disproportionately dependent on public transportation to get to work and to shop; on local police to keep their neighborhoods safe; and on emergency services of all types. They have fewer private resources to serve as cushions in times of stress—not only outside forces like hurricanes but personal disasters such as sudden unemployment, unexpected illness or injury, or other vagaries of modern life. As James Carr, Senior Vice President of Research for the Fannie Mae Foundation, observed, if the city of New Orleans had been a more diverse community it may well have had the political clout to secure the levees long ago (Carr 2005).

The clear "bottom line" is that, while there still is plenty of racist behavior by individuals, incompetence by FEMA and other public and private bureaucracies, corruption on the part of government contractors and their partners in the public sector (Eaton 2006), and other forms of malfeasance and misfeasance, by far the most potent force in creating these extreme disparities is institutional racism—"color-blind racism," as it is often termed—something that most black people understand and experience, but most white people do not. Consequently, it should have been no surprise when Katrina hit New Orleans that the areas damaged were 45.8% black, compared to 26.4% in undamaged areas, and that 20.9% of the households in damaged areas were poor, compared to 15.3% in undamaged areas. And if nobody is allowed to return to damaged areas, New Orleans will lose 80% of its black population, compared to just 50% of its white population (Logan 2006).

New Orleans and the Gulf Coast region generally, like virtually all metropolitan areas in the U.S., experience many costs of racism, concentrated poverty, and uneven development. These forces may well shape, and hinder, redevelopment efforts in and around New Orleans as well as other communities seeking paths to prosperity for their citizens.

This volume delineates the contours of development (or lack thereof) and offers a window into a different world. Inequities associated with race, class, gender, and other socially constructed markers are not inevitable. They reflect the conscious choices made by political and economic decision-makers and implemented by public and private institutions. Different choices are available in a post-Katrina world. Our book is about some of those choices.

∼

The essays we have commissioned for this book present a broad-brush picture of the impact of Katrina and Rita, in New Orleans and beyond. (In many instances, the authors use the term Katrina as a shorthand that refers to Katrina, the subsequent Hurricane Rita, and the flooding and wind damage that followed both events; as well, "New Orleans" is often a shorthand expression meant to cover the broader areas of Louisiana, in addition to Mississippi, Alabama, and Texas.)

An insightful historical context is offered by Michael Powers, of the Center for American Progress and the George Washington University department of history, on the impact of and responses to disasters of equivalent notoriety in our nation's history: the Chicago Fire of 1871, the 1906 San Francisco Earthquake, the 1930s Dustbowl, and Hurricane Andrew in 1992. His historical lessons stress the importance of a comprehensive revitalization approach to recovery, rather than simple rebuilding; involvement of the affected persons in their own recovery; the importance of oversight and accountability; the need for ecological balance; and the appropriate division between private- and public-sector responsibilities.

Alan Stein, former head of the Louisiana Division for the City of New Orleans Public Library and Special Collections, and Gene Preuss of the University of Houston history department offer some rich direct reporting on the hurricanes' impact via the valuable tool of oral history. Their essay illustrates the major tragedies, minor inconveniences, and the totality of disruption that still confront those who were in Katrina's path.

john powell and his colleagues at the Ohio State University Kirwan Institute for the Study of Race and Ethnicity emphasize the role of structural racism for understanding the disaster, as well as racially-conscious guidelines for a transformative recovery. Their central point is that racism is as much a product of systems and institutions as it is a manifestation of individual behavior, and that such structural arrangements produce and reproduce racially disparate outcomes as well as reinforce racist attitudes.

Two frequently overlooked, under-recognized subpopulations—women and the elderly—are the subject of essays by, respectively, Heidi Hartmann and Avis Jones-DeWeever of the Institute for Women's Policy Research and Margaret Gullette of Brandeis University's Women's Studies Research Center. As these two chapters demonstrate, the vulnerability that women and the elderly face every day throughout the country—often with life-and-death implications—became starkly evident in the wake of these storms.

The critical issue of housing is treated by Sheila Crowley of the National Low Income Housing Coalition and by Robert Zdenek and his colleagues at the Alliance for Healthy Homes. The chapters cover the unprecedented extent of destruction (of both privately- owned as well as public and assisted housing) and the government's largely botched efforts at relocation and replacement housing. They also trace the attempts to salvage, rebuild, and reoccupy New Orleans' damaged homes. FEMA's on-again/off-again use of hotels and motels as temporary replacement housing; the "FEMA-ville" trailer parks and their vulnerability to repeat storms; the problems of finding landlords willing to accept housing vouchers; and the especially ugly presence of NIMBY-ism as well as housing discrimination based on race are all laid out in detail—detail that doubtless will change in the future (Nelson and Varney 2005; Filosa 2006; Korosec 2005; Wilgoren 2005; Lipton 2006a).

Two of the city's critical public services comprise the next set of essays: the damage to and response by the New Orleans Department of Health, by Evangeline (Vangy) Franklin, the City's Director of Clinical Services and Employee Health; and the impact on and skewed recovery of the city's already highly troubled school system, by Michael Casserly of the Council of the Great City Schools. Health services were badly disrupted and displaced just at the time they were most needed. Higher rates of illness among evacuees have been reported, especially among children. Mental health problems are rife, with a notable rise in suicides. Decomposed bodies are still being found, adding to the still incomplete toll of storm-related deaths. And toxic waste problems doubtless will persist and show up—Agent Orange-like—in years to come. (Dewan 2006a, 2006b; Redlener

2006; Nossiter 2005; Connolly 2005; Cass 2006; Hsu and Eilperin 2006; Barringer 2005; Cole and Woelfle-Erskine 2006; Saulny 2006b). Electronic storage and transfer of medical records is an essential needed reform. On the schools front, the disruption was enormous, as tens of thousands of K-12 students wound up in different school districts and different states, disrupting their curriculum and teacher/student relationships. A great many of them missed months of formal education (Dewan 2006c). A major change in the New Orleans public school system has been a shift to charter schools, a controversial move and one that has been pushed as a more general goal by market-oriented advocates in the education reform field (Saulny 2006a).

Two chapters treat economic development and the city's efforts to restore commercial activity. Robert Whelan of the University of New Orleans College of Urban and Public Affairs assesses the pre-Katrina economic environment and rebuilding plans, and John Taylor and Josh Silver of the National Community Reinvestment Coalition provide an assessment of the critical need for involvement of private-sector financial institutions in the rebuilding process. Pre-Katrina New Orleans suffered from fundamental economic problems—a large poor population lacking basic skills, the absence of a diverse economic base, uneven access to credit, and a general lack of opportunity and dynamism. There is a clear need for greater attention to economic development, done in a regional context—all of which requires greater vision on the part of political and business leaders.

The role and importance of local community organizing is the subject of the essay by Wade Rathke and Beulah Labostrie of ACORN (the Association of Community Organizations for Reform Now). Keeping in touch with the farflung evacuee population, encouraging their continued involvement in voting (in the April-May city election) and planning for the city's future is the key organizing task. Who will come back, to what sections of the city, whether there will be a "right of return," how safe the city will be from future storms—all depend on bringing people together and empowering them.

In the final chapter, Peter Marcuse of Columbia University's urban planning program describes various models of urban planning and their variable potential impact on the recovery process. He recognizes the danger that the white elite will take over the recovery process and plan for a smaller city with fewer poor and African-American residents. He calls for a more democratic planning and decision-making process, equity in the distribution of costs and benefits, and a powerful role for government. The enormous failures around Katrina—documented in numerous official reports and hearings, with more doubtless to come—should not be taken as lessons that government doesn't work. Government works when those who believe in it and place responsible, capable people in positions of authority make it work; and there is no substitute for capable, responsible government for dealing with disasters of all types. The notion of "failed states" needs to be challenged, and fixed (Cohen 2005). Marcuse identifies The Hurricane Katrina Recovery, Reclamation, Restoration, Reconstruction and Reunion Act of 2005, submitted by the Congressional Black Caucus, as by far the best existing concrete proposal, and adds his suggestions for improvements to that effort.

An entire community and region of the country must be rebuilt. But in many respects the challenges in New Orleans reflect those in metropolitan areas all around the nation. If the totality of destruction and reconstruction confronting the Gulf is unique today, virtually all communities are struggling to provide decent housing, create family-supporting jobs, build and run decent schools, create a fair criminal justice system, invent comprehensive public health care systems, revitalize wide-ranging cultural institutions, and so much more. The citizens of New Orleans seem prepared to face these challenges. Hopefully, the public, private, and nonprofit institutions will be up to the task.

We end with this observation by three academics:

> The experience of African Americans in New Orleans can serve as the "miner's canary," as Lani Guinier and Gerald Torres argue. Similar to the way in which canaries alerted miners to the specter of poisonous air, the fates that befall people who are disadvantaged by inequalities based on, for example, race, class, and gender are signifiers of society-wide inequalities. If policymakers and the public heed the lessons of Katrina and make efforts to address the structural and institutional sources of American inequality, perhaps the brunt of future disasters will not be borne by those who are least able to endure their costs (Frymer, Strolovitch, and Warren 2006).

Sober words.

Chester Hartman and Gregory D. Squires
July 2006

An orthographic note: With regard to terminology on race and racial categories, we opt to let each author use whatever is her or his word, punctuation, capitalization preference; such usage embodies issues that, for many, have levels of meaning well beyond mere style, and we chose not to impose any arbitrary single format or rule.

References

American Society of Civil Engineers. 2005. *2005 Report Card for America's Infrastructure.* Reston, VA: American Society of Civil Engineers.

Barringer, Felicity. 2005. Toxic Residue of Hurricane Stirs Debate on Safety. *New York Times.* December 2.

Briggs, Xavier de Souza, ed. 2005. *The Geography of Opportunity: Race and Housing Choice in Metropolitan America.* Washington, D.C.: Brookings Institution Press.

Brookings Institution. 2005. New Orleans After the Storm: Lessons from the Past, a Plan for the Future. Washington, D.C.: The Brookings Institution.

Brooks, David. 2005. Katrina's Silver Lining. *New York Times.* September 8: A-29.

Brown, Michael K., Martin Carnoy, Elliott Currie, Troy Duster, David B. Oppenheimer, Marjorie M. Shultz, and David Wellman. 2003. *White-Washing Race: The Myth of a Color-Blind Society.* Berkeley: University of California Press.

Carr, James H. 2005. Comments at conference on Predatory Home Lending: Moving Toward Legal and Policy Solutions. John Marshall Law School, Chicago, September 9.

Cass, Julia. 2006. For Many of Katrina's Young Victims, The Scars Are More Than Deep. *Washington Post.* June 13.

Cohen, David. 2005. The Aftermath of Hurricane Katrina: Coming to Grips with US Failure, in John Brown Childs, ed., *Hurricane Katrina: Response and Responsibilities.* Santa Cruz: New Pacific Press, 134–142.

Cole, Oskar and Cleo Woelfle-Erskine. 2006. Rebuilding on Poisoned Ground. *Color Lines,* Spring: 26–28.

Connolly, Ceci. 2005. Katrina's Emotional Damage Lingers. *Washington Post.* December 7.

Dewan, Shaila. 2006a. Storm Evacuees Found to Suffer Health Setbacks. *New York Times.* April 18.

_____ 2006b. In Attics and Rubble: More Bodies and Questions. *New York Times.* April 11.

_____ 2006c. For Many, Education Is Another Storm Victim. *New York Times.* June 1.

Dyson, Michael Eric. 2006. *Come Hell or High Water: Hurricane Katrina and the Color of Disaster.* New York: Perseus Books.

Eaton, Leslie. 2006. In Louisiana, Graft Inquiries Are Increasing. *New York Times.* March 18.

Filosa, Gwen. 2006. Housing Discrimination Hits the Web: Post-Katrina Ads Cited in Federal Complaints. *Times-Picayune.* January 3.

Frymer, Paul, Daa Z. Strolovitch, and Dorian T. Warren. Katrina's Political Roots and Divisions: Race, Class, and Federalism in American Politics. *Understanding Katrina: Perspectives from the Social Sciences.* February 1. http://understandingkatrina.ssrc.org/FrymerSrolovitchWarren/

Hamilton, Bruce. 2006. Bridge Standoff Still Under Scope: Gretna Faces Lawsuit for Stopping Evacuees. *Times-Picayune.* January 4.

Hsu, Spencer S. 2006. 2 Million Displaced By Storms. *Washington Post.* January 13.

Hsu, Spencer S. and Juliet Eilperin. 2006. Safety of Post-Hurricane Sludge Is Disputed. *Washington Post.* February 23.

Iceland, John, Daniel H. Weinberg, and Erika Steinmentz. 2002. *Residential Segregation in the United States: 1980-2000.* Washington, D.C.: U.S. Government Printing Office.

Jargowsky, Paul. 2003. Stunning Progress, Hidden Problems: The Dramatic Decline of Concentrated Poverty in the 1990s. Washington, D.C.: The Brookings Institution.

_____. 1996. Poverty and Place: Ghettos, Barrios, and the American City. New York: Russell Sage Foundation.

Katznelson, Ira. 2005. *When Affirmative Action Was White: An Untold History of Racial Inequality in Twentieth-Century America.* New York: W.W. Norton & Company.

Korosec, Thomas. 2005. Survey Finds Bias in Evacuee Housing: 66% of White Callers Got Better Deals in Houston and 16 Other Cities. *Houston Chronicle.* December 27.

Lipton, Eric. 2006a. Trailers, Vital After Hurricane, Now Pose Own Risks on Gulf. *New York Times.* March 16.

_____. 2006b. Hurricane Relief From Abroad Was Mishandled. *New York Times.* April 7.

_____. 2006c. FEMA Workers Accused of Bribery. *New York Times.* January 26.

Logan, John R. 2006. The Impact of Katrina: Race and Class in Storm-Damaged Neighborhoods. Working paper, Brown University, Spatial Structures in the Social Sciences.

Massey, Douglas S. 2001. Residential Segregation and Neighborhood Conditions in U.S. Metropolitan Areas. In *America Becoming: Racial Trends and Their Consequences*, edited by Neil J. Smelser, William Julius Wilson, and Faith Mitchell. Washington, D.C.: National Academy Press.

Massey, Douglas S. and Nancy Denton. 1993. *American Apartheid: Segregation and the Making of the Underclass.* Cambridge, MA: Harvard University Press.

Mauer, Marc. 2006. *Race to Incarcerate.* New York: The New Press.

Nelson, Rob and James Varney. 2005. "Not in My Back Yard" Cry Holding Up FEMA Trailers: Emotional Tone of Opposition Hints at Role and Stereotypes of Race, Class. *Times-Picayune.* December 26.

Nossiter, Adam. 2005. Hurricane Takes a Further Toll: Suicides Up in New Orleans. *New York Times.* December 27.

_____. 2006. F.B.I. to Investigate Red Cross Over Accusations of Wrongdoing. *New York Times.* March 31.

O'Connor, Alice, Chris Tilly, and Lawrence D. Bobo, eds. 2001. *Urban Inequality: Evidence from Four Cities.* New York: Russell Sage Foundation.

Pastor, Manuel, Robert D. Bullard, James K. Boyce, Alice Fothergill, Rachel Morello-Frosch, and Beverly Wright. 2006. In the Wake of the Storm: Environment, Disaster, and Race After Katrina. New York: Russell Sage Foundation.

Redlener, Irwin. 2006. Orphans of the Storm. *New York Times.* May 9.

Salmon, Jacqueline L. 2006a. Red Cross, Humane Society Under Investigation. *Washington Post.* March 26.

_____ 2006b. Counterparts Excoriate Red Cross Katrina Effort. *Washington Post.* April 5.

Saulny, Susan. 2006a. U.S. Gives Charter Schools A Big Push in New Orleans. *New York Times.* June 13.

_____. 2006b. A Legacy of Storm: Depression and Suicide. *New York Times.* June 21.

Smelser, Neil J., William Julius Wilson, and Faith Mitchell. 2001. *America Becoming: Racial Trends and Their Consequences.* Washington, D.C.: National Academy Press.

Strom, Stephanie. 2005. President of Red Cross Resigns; Board Woes, Not Katrina, Cited. *New York Times.* December 14.

_____ 2006. Red Cross Fires Administrators in New Orleans. *New York Times,* March 25.

Treaster, Joseph B. 2006. Home Insurers Embrace the Heartland. *New York Times.* May 20.

Treaster, Joseph B. and Cornelia Dean. 2006. Yet Another Victim of Katrina: Federal Flood Insurance Program Is Itself Under Water. *New York Times.* January 6.

Turner, Margery Austin, and Sheil R. Zedlweski. 2006. After Katrina: Rebuilding Opportunity and Equity into New New Orleans. Washington, D.C.: The Urban Institute.

Wagner, Peter and Susan Edwards. 2006. New Orleans by the Numbers. *dollars & sense* 264 (March/April): 54–55.

Wilgoren, Jodi. 2005. Vouchers in Their Pockets, Evacuees Find It Hard to Get Keys in Hand. *New York Times.* October 28.

Williams, Linda Faye. 2003. *The Constraint of Race: Legacies of White Skin Privilege in America.* University Park, PA: The Pennsylvania State University Press.

CHAPTER 2

A Matter of Choice
Historical Lessons for Disaster Recovery

MICHAEL P. POWERS*

As the federal, state, and local governments consider the appropriate goals, policies, and programs for the recovery effort in the wake of Hurricane Katrina, they would be well served to learn the lessons offered by previous disaster responses. While there is no contesting Katrina's catastrophic nature, the devastation it caused is not without historical parallel. The past is littered with examples of natural events and manmade disasters that collide violently with society. Following each disaster, citizens and their government faced the daunting task of reconstructing decimated physical and socioeconomic infrastructure, much like the task that now faces the Gulf Coast region. Also comparable is the disproportionate hardship placed by these disasters on those disadvantaged by class, race, and ethnicity. As such, careful review of the responses to previous disasters holds the potential to yield instructive lessons to those coordinating the current recovery effort.

The following is an examination of various aspects of the long-term rebuilding and recovery efforts that followed previous disasters equivalent in scale to Hurricane Katrina. The events covered include the Chicago fire of 1871, the San Francisco earthquake and fire of 1906, the Mississippi

* A special thanks to Allida Black, whose knowledge, support, and advice were invaluable.

flood of 1927, the Dust Bowl and Great Depression of the 1930's, and Hurricane Andrew in 1992. The goal is neither to provide a comprehensive analysis of any recovery effort nor to suggest the application of specific components of previous efforts, many of which occurred more than 50 years ago. Rather, the objective is to draw from the previous successes and failures valuable overriding principles for long-term recovery efforts; to recommend broad goals for the recovery efforts in the Gulf Coast based on these principles; to evaluate selected actions to date in relation to these goals; and to make recommendations toward the fulfillment of those goals. In addition, special attention will be paid at each stage to the impact of the rebuilding and recovery efforts on low-income individuals and ethnic and racial minorities, as they have proven historically to be more vulnerable than others to the effects of disasters.

Chicago Fire

By 1871, Chicago was intimately familiar with fires, experiencing major ones in 1839, 1857, 1868, and 1870 (Smith 1995). In the previous year, the city averaged two fires a day, and the week prior to the Chicago fire saw 20 such blazes (Helmer 1996). The one that began on October 8, 1871, however, far outstripped the rest. Driven by gale winds, drought conditions, and the predominance of wood structures, the conflagration ripped through Chicago until lack of fuel and a fortunate rainstorm brought it to a halt. When the smoke cleared, 2,100 acres of the city were virtually demolished. The fire destroyed 18,000 homes and businesses, leaving more than 100,000 residents homeless and 300 dead. Total damages were estimated at $200 million, roughly a third of the city's total valuation (Pauly 1984). The financial impact was compounded by the failure of nearly all local fire insurance companies, which were the primary provider for the portion of working-class residents that could afford any insurance (Sawislak 1995).

Following the immediate rescue efforts, Mayor Roswell B. Mason empowered the Chicago Relief and Aid Society to handle the collection and distribution of aid for the relief and recovery effort. Comprised largely of Chicago's commercial elite, the likes of George Pullman and Marshall Field, the men guiding the charitable society were "steeped both in spirit of capitalism and the Protestant ethic" (Smith 1995:69). Thus, they rejected the traditional method of benevolent charity in favor of "scientific charity," whereby aid was given only to help those suffering temporary setbacks regain self-sufficiency, as opposed to permanently supporting the "chronic poor" (Sawislak 1995:88–100). The design and execution of the recovery effort reflected the composition and beliefs of the Society, as well as illustrating that policy can be structured to encourage a return to self-sufficiency, that the private sector does not always produce results that help those affected by disasters, and that oversight and accountability are needed to protect the interests of lower-income groups.

Given the Society's views, employment became a key focus of the recovery plan. To enable an efficient return to work, the relief organization established an Employment Bureau to connect employers in need of labor with men searching for work, to provide replacement tools to tradesmen who lost theirs to the fire, and to pay women to sew needed clothing and bedding. Within a week, the Society implemented a rule denying aid to any and all able-bodied men unless they could not attain employment through the Employment Bureau, which, according to the Society, rarely ever happened (Sawislak 1995).

While this practice achieved some success, the private sector's desire for cheap labor undermined its ability to move poor victims to self-sufficiency. The Great Rebuilding, which saw the entire city virtually rebuilt in 18 months, indicates how fast and broadly labor was employed. However, seeking to reduce their costs, businessmen actively courted laborers from across the United States and Europe, leading to the influx of 30,000 to 40,000 workers in the year following the fire. Such pressures depressed wages while increasing rents 30% to 40%, inhibiting the ability of the poor and working classes—comprised largely of immigrants—to achieve the self-sufficiency trumpeted by the Relief and Aid Society. At the same time, Society members with lumber interests lobbied successfully against a reduction in lumber tariffs, which would have reduced the cost of rebuilding low-income wood homes (Sawislak 1995).

The widespread bankruptcy of local fire insurance companies represents another situation where the private sector response failed to adequately help those affected by the fire, especially members of the middle and working classes. Lax regulations allowed many local companies to employ bad financial practices and to ignore risk, in some cases issuing "a policy for anyone who could afford the premium" (Sawislak 1995:78). Whereas those with more assets to protect, and more money to pay in premiums, received full or near-full settlements from more reputable Eastern and European companies, working-class policyholders often received pennies on the dollar, if anything (Sawislak 1995). As a result, vulnerable residents were left without funds to rebuild their homes or to restore their small businesses, through no fault of their own. Neither the government nor the Society took any action to prevent the insolvency of these companies.

Perhaps the most striking aspect of the long-term effort was the Relief and Aid Society's extralegal nature, which shielded it from oversight and accountability. Given *carte blanche* by Mayor Mason, the Society created a branch to provide "special relief," outside of the normal aid mechanisms.

The program's provision of aid "reflected the belief …that the plight of the poor and unwashed deserved less sympathy than that of the rich (or formerly rich) and refined" (Smith 1995:75).[1] Since there was no external review or appeals process, those discriminated against had no way to seek redress (Smith 1995). Furthermore, as members of the Society were not elected, their decisions were insulated from outside influence.[2] This caused particular harm to members of the working class, who had no representation in the Society and for whom the ballot was often their only means of influence.

Though it would be hard to classify the recovery effort as successful from the vantage point of poor and working-class Chicagoans, it did accomplish much of what the members of the Relief and Aid Society desired. As businessmen, they wanted to see Chicago rebuilt quickly and for as little as possible, which it was. As moralists, they believed that the rich and upper-middle-class deserved more help than the poor, which "special relief" helped provide. Finally, they wanted everyone to work, which largely occurred, but the connection they made between employment and self-sufficiency was fundamentally false. All said, the effort largely achieved that for which it was designed. It just was not designed with the interests of poor and working-class immigrants in mind.

The San Francisco Earthquake and Fire

Early in the morning of April 18, 1906, a 7.8 magnitude earthquake rocked San Francisco. The quake caused particular destruction to the "made land" sections of the city, where the unconsolidated earth amplified the vibrations, toppling buildings and bursting water mains (Regents of the University of California 2006a).[3] While the effect of the earthquake alone would have been terrific, the fires that erupted as a result of breached chimneys and gas lines compounded the devastation. Aided by the close proximity of buildings, the lack of adequate water supply, and the predominance of wood construction, fire plagued the city for three days, leveling 2,800 acres and more than 28,000 buildings, 90% of which were made of wood. Roughly a quarter of a million San Franciscans became refugees (Platt 1999; Fradkin 2005).[4]

Like Chicago, the city's elite businessmen headed the long-term relief and rebuilding effort. Using their ties to the Washington administration, influential businessmen such as Edward Harriman persuaded Theodore Roosevelt to designate the Committee of Fifty, a self-appointed citizens' committee dominated by business interests, to be the sole recipient of contributions. Somewhat predictably, the Committee tied the well-being of the city's residents to the status of commercial business. Thus, the emphasis of the recovery was the quick re-establishment of pre-crisis business, which in turn led to the rebuilding of the pre-crisis city.

On a broad scale, the rebuilding effort failed to correct the fundamental structural deficiencies that compounded the level of destruction. From the damage caused by earthquakes in 1865, 1868, and then in 1906, geologists knew well that the areas of "made land" with loose, unconsolidated foundations were more susceptible to violent shaking. Ignoring this risk, businessmen promptly rebuilt "bigger, better and higher in the same places" (Fradkin 2005:239). Similarly, some engineers and scientists called for reform of the building code to protect against repeat fires. Among other things, they suggested cutting avenues, widening the streets, and requiring all buildings in the fire limits zone (a designated area obligated to meet higher standards for prevention of fire) to use only incombustible materials. Business interests defeated such efforts, using the logic that "what San Francisco needs is the cheapest building possible in which business can be done" (Fradkin 2005:243). Ultimately, business' shortsightedness trumped the real concerns for safety.

The careless rebuilding process doomed San Franciscans to similar fates in the future. Since 1906, major fires have broken out numerous times among San Francisco's "tightly packed blocks of wood homes," including one in 1959 that razed 36 buildings (Regents of the University of California 2006b). In 1989, a 7.1 magnitude earthquake struck the Bay Area. Despite the epicenter being located more that 50 miles from San Francisco, the quake caused extensive damage in the same "made land" areas that crumbled in 1906.

The 1906 recovery effort also fell short in that those most in need received relatively little aid. Explicitly aware of the need for labor to rebuild the city, the committee in charge of housing quickly erected semi-permanent camps to house the displaced so they would be able to work. Unfortunately, the effort failed to reach large, and more destitute, segments of the population. By mid-June, of the 43,000 persons still homeless, only 18,000 were living in official relief camps. The other 25,000, representing some of the poorest residents from the worst-hit areas, received little or no help through the official relief effort. Instead, many of these people fashioned housing from the rubble of ruined buildings and relied on the charity of individuals and less well-funded charitable organizations (Fradkin 2005).

Part of this problem stemmed from the design of the committee, which, like the Chicago Relief and Aid Society, had no representation for the poor and no mechanism for accountability. Convinced that efficiency was the top priority, the Citizens' Committee routinely refused to be pressured into what they regarded as inefficient giving. In the first week, the Red Cross cut off food supplies to an encampment of 800 people because the cost of transportation was viewed as too high. This approach spelled bad news for poor immigrants like the elderly Irish women who slept on floors, unable to access cots that the relief effort possessed (Fradkin 2005).

The driving force behind the San Francisco recovery was the belief that the well-being of the city depended on the well-being of business. In addition to being conveniently self-serving, the assumption precluded reforms that would have improved the city's long-term safety. The control of the recovery effort by economic elites, Philip Fradkin writes, ensured that "the relief effort would be incredibly efficient, relatively honest, and blind to the needs of the poor and minorities" (2005: 205). As in Chicago, the outcomes in large part reflected the goals.

Mississippi Flood

Heavy rainfall from August 1926 through the summer of 1927 elevated concerns that the manmade levees lining the thousand-mile course of the Lower Mississippi River would not be able to contain a potential flood. On April 16, the main levee in southeastern Missouri gave way, followed by subsequent breaches in 144 additional locations. The ensuing floodwaters covered more than 1.6 million acres of land inhabited by 930,000 people in seven states, damaging more than 160,000 homes and utterly destroying 41,487. In current value, the damage done to crops and livestock exceeded $1 billion (Kosar 2005). Not until four months after the breaking of the first levee did all the water drain from the land (Barry 1997).

Breaking precedent, President Coolidge appointed Secretary of Commerce Herbert Hoover, whose fame derived from his World War I relief efforts, to coordinate the government's work with the Red Cross. Yet this commitment of federal resources to disaster relief did not equal a radical commitment to federal aid. While Hoover was widely heralded for the coordinated, efficient, and rapid response, his unwillingness to involve the government directly in large-scale relief efforts, his deference to local authority, and possibly even his presidential aspirations hampered the rehabilitation process. One bright spot in the recovery was the adoption of more suitable methods of flood control that began to recognize the need to accommodate nature.

The revitalization work Hoover undertook, although well designed, did not provide aid sufficient to get members of the lower economic class back on their feet. As flood victims left the camps, they were to receive enough "feed, seed, tools, clothes, basic furnishings to start again" (Barry 1997:388). Hoover also provided home economists and agricultural extension agents who taught refugees how to sew, can vegetables, raise poultry, and practice good hygiene. The plan failed to achieve its goal not only because the aid provided fell far short of what would real-istically be needed to start from scratch, but also because local Red Cross officials often ignored the stated policy that "all aid be given directly to sufferers" (Barry 1997:388).[5] In response to such claims, Hoover named a Colored Advisory Commission, made up of 18 blacks, to investigate the charges. The commission found that local officials often gave ten-ants' rations to plantation owners, who either kept them or sold them to the tenants; that black landowners were denied rations; and that plant-ers were known to beat tenants who tried to leave the plantation. Rather than laud the commission for its oversight and address the problems, Hoover had the findings censored and rewritten to suppress damaging accusations (Barry 1997).

On the scale of major initiatives, the recovery from the Mississippi flood was more notable for what it lacked than for what it possessed. The recovery effort lacked any reforms that addressed the structural inequities abundant in a land where the tenant farming and sharecrop-ping systems kept blacks perpetually in a cycle of "debt and dependence" (Spencer 1994:171). Hoover acknowledged the system's engrained weak-nesses, writing that the region suffered from a "background of bank-rupt economics" (Barry 1997:384). In response, Hoover floated the idea of creating a land resettlement corporation, designed to develop 20-acre plots from foreclosed plantations and sell them to individual farmers, complete with the housing, equipment, and animals necessary to run a small farm (Lohof 1970). The resettlement plan, nominally available to both blacks and whites, could have dramatically altered the landscape of the Delta region and enabled black tenant farmers to break free of depen-dence on white landowners.

While there is no guarantee that the land resettlement plan would have succeeded, the actions taken in the relief effort specifically, and often ille-gally, reinforced the subjugation of black laborers. Concerned with los-ing the labor supply, plantation owners and local relief officials used black relief camps "as holding pens designed to ensure the retention and pres-ervation of the Southern labor force" (Spencer 1994:172). At every camp in Mississippi, National Guard troops forcibly detained blacks, allowing them to leave only if they held a special pass. When the waters receded, planters were allowed to reclaim their workers (Barry 1997). These and similar actions clearly indicated that those leading the recovery effort intended to reconstruct the tenant farming society along with the racial and economic inequality that accompanied it. Hoover accepted this, stat-ing: "The national agencies have no responsibility for the economic system which exists in the South," a statement in stark contrast to the concept of the land resettlement plan (Spencer 1994:172).

Hoover's only real attempt at rehabilitation was an initiative intended to increase access to credit. The program called for business leaders to buy stock in newly created state reconstruction corporations. The capital would then be used to provide loans, which the corporations would then sell at a discount, using the proceeds to provide still more loans. Intrinsic in this plan was the requirement that the solution be founded primarily in private industry. However, even after strong-arming reluctant business leaders for the initial funds, few were able to access the loans. John Barry explains in *Rising Tide* (1997: 375):

> Credit involved risk. Private capital demanded either collateral enough to mitigate that risk or return enough to compensate for it. The devastated areas could not pay a high return, and the planters had no collateral, since they had already mortgaged their land to plant the crop destroyed by the waters.

The program had a negligible effect, reaching only 5% of Hoover's expectations. Despite a $635 million federal budget surplus, Coolidge and Congress failed to provide support to make the program more accessible (Barry 1997).

On the issue of river control, the 1927 flood altered the underlying theory regarding man's relationship with nature from one of domination to one of accommodation. Prior to the flood, the Mississippi River Commission, which Congress had authorized to control all aspects of river policy, held the position that levees alone were the appropriate method for preventing floods. As such, they sealed the river off from its natural outlets and reservoirs, despite vociferous objections from leading scientists. The flood proved the levees-only theory incontrovertibly wrong. From this point, those charged with flood control abandoned attempts to dominate the river, instead choosing to manage the river in a way that prevented large-scale destruction of society. To the levees were added a series of reservoirs, floodways, cut-offs, and spillways meant to divert water from the river in a managed way and prevent another such large-scale flood, which they did until the Great Flood of 1993 tore through (or over) more than a thousand levees, causing almost $20 billion of damage (Johnson et al.).

With the exception of flood control, Hoover's reluctance to take governmental action resulted in little long-term aid being provided to those affected by the flood, most notably black sharecroppers. In addition to neither involving the government in land resettlement nor using government resources to increase access to credit, Hoover's deference to the authority of local whites limited his ability to equitably provide even the most basic relief.

The Dust Bowl and the Great Depression

In the early 1930s, the United States found itself in the throes of both a manmade crisis and a devastating ecological disaster. The combination of the Great Depression and the Dust Bowl created circumstances of severe dislocation, chronic unemployment, and ecological devastation. In the Dust Bowl, a four-year drought punished nearly 100 million acres of land in Colorado, New Mexico, Kansas, Texas, and Oklahoma, leaving the dirt dry and powdery. The extensive removal of sod for commercial wheat-planting left little vegetation to hold the dirt. As dry winds blew across the region, they eroded the topsoil, creating massive dust storms. By 1938, 10 million acres in the Dust Bowl had seen the removal of at least five inches of topsoil, and the average acre of cultivated land lost 408 tons of dirt (Worster 1979). At the same time, the manmade crisis that was the Great Depression left the national employment picture equally grim. By 1933, more than 15 million Americans had lost their jobs and steel plants operated at 12% of capacity (Leuchtenburg 1963). The situation was seemingly so hopeless that the national suicide rate rose 25% from 1929 to 1932 (Badger 1989).

More than any prior relief effort, President Roosevelt's response relied upon direct government action. Responding to the public call for government help in the face of crisis, FDR answered with the "bold, persistent experimentation" he advocated during his campaign (Roosevelt 1932). While FDR was willing to intervene and help people, he believed that cash payments without work acted as a "narcotic, a subtle destroyer of the human spirit" and as such were to be avoided as much as possible (Roosevelt 1935). He also recognized how his mandate for action could be used to address underlying issues such as poor education, low skill level, insufficient infrastructure, and ecological devastation, while also meeting millions of people's immediate need for income. His actions were guided by a desire to put people to work in a way that benefited both the country and themselves.

In the Dust Bowl, FDR sought to revamp the agricultural system. Though nature had caused the drought, man's overcultivation of the land had caused the decimation of the soil. Recognizing that individuals direly needed help and that the land was rapidly losing its value for farming, FDR undertook a plan to keep all lands currently in the public domain there in perpetuity and to selectively purchase exceedingly unproductive and abused land so that it might be added to the public domain, where the soil could be replenished and the ecosystem balanced. Initially hoping to purchase 75 million acres, the project acquired just over 11 million, which now hold national parks, wildlife preserves, and grasslands. The third step, which would have given ordinary farmers the power to restrain commercial agriculture, failed to gain traction for long enough to make any impact (Worster 1979). As such, the federal government intervention did achieve a modicum of success in protecting land from further abuse, but failed to implement a larger strategy.

To address the massive unemployment, FDR relied on a mix of programs with different designs, the common element being the use of federal dollars to employ men to do necessary tasks. The Civilian Conservation Corps (CCC), which employed young men in military-supervised forestry and conservation projects, and the Civil Works Administration (CWA) were federally-controlled programs. In contrast, the Public Works Administration (PWA) and subsequently the Works Progress Administration (WPA) funded large-scale public works projects deemed essential by state and local governments.

Together, these programs both provided much-needed employment and produced an astonishing list of accomplishments. The four programs combined paid wages to millions of Americans. These wages vastly raised the standard of living for poor and middle-class families struggling even to afford the necessities of food, clothing, and housing. At the same time, the programs built or improved hundreds of airports, tens of thousands of schools, and hundreds of thousands of miles of roads. Toward the improvement of overall education, the CWA provided 50,000 teachers for rural schools and adult education, while the CCC educated 2.5 million young men through fundamental literacy courses, academic courses, and vocational training (Salmond 1965). The New Deal programs also comprised a chief source of infrastructure investment, with the PWA alone helping to build 70% of all new school buildings and 35% of all hospitals and public health facilities between 1933 and 1936, in addition to such mammoth infrastructure projects as the Hoover, Grand Coulee, and Tennessee Valley Authority dams as well as thousands of miles of railroad tracks (Leuchtenburg 1963).

The relevant point of these programs is that they went beyond simply recreating the nation as it stood prior to 1930. The wages paid raised the standard of living for millions of Americans affected by the Great Depression while also addressing factors that would improve the long-term economic prospects of individuals and the nation. This should not be construed to mean that the New Deal programs were universally successful or that they ended the Depression, but that the increased employment benefited millions of Americans and addressed underlying deficiencies, while at worst not hindering the recovery.

Hurricane Andrew

When Hurricane Andrew smashed into South Florida on August 24, 1992, it left its mark as the most destructive hurricane on record in the United States. The Category 4 hurricane brought with it sustained gusts of 142 miles per hour that wiped out nearly 30,000 homes and damaged more than 100,000 others. The more than 100,000 Floridians living in mobile homes in the affected regions suffered disproportionate damage. In Dade County alone, Andrew destroyed 97% of the 10,000 mobile homes. This spelled particular trouble for low-income individuals and the elderly, many of whom relocated to manufactured housing after being priced out of the conventional housing market (Steinberg 2000). Estimates of the total property damage range from more than $25 billion to $30 billion, of which $15.5 billion was insured (Platt 1999).

The government response, as is common in the modern era of relief and recovery, consisted of a vast array of initiatives and programs addressing topics ranging from short-term changes to the building code to long-term land-use issues related to hazard mitigation. Two noteworthy aspects were the state government's approach to the crisis in the insurance market and its pilot project, which combined the need for quality affordable housing and a reduction in CO_2 emissions, which may be indirectly related to the severity of the hurricanes that batter the region (Randerson 2006; Bustillo 2005).

The massive amount of insured losses from Hurricane Andrew drove ten insurance companies out of business, while others threatened to drop 1.2 million policies (Deslatte 2004). The government not only provided millions of dollars to cover the liabilities of failed companies, but also severely limited the percentage of policies that insurance companies could cancel (Godschalk et al. 1999). Ensuring payment to policyholders specifically helped those with low and moderate incomes whose homes suffered the greatest destruction, 95% of which were insured (Comiero 1998). This protected individuals who had acted responsibly, ensuring that they had money to rebuild their homes.

The state government also created a fund designed to prevent exits from the insurance market. Backed by fees assessed on all property and casualty insurance policies, the fund covers a portion of insurance losses above a set threshold. In 2004, the fund paid insurers $2.1 billion to help cover roughly $17.5 billion in claims (Deslatte 2004). The program reduces the risk that insurance companies will fail in the face of massive destruction and, in turn, protects policyholders.

As one of many steps to address global warming and the need for quality affordable housing in the wake of Hurricane Andrew, the local government partnered with Habitat for Humanity and various corporations to build a sustainable low-income housing development. Jordan Commons broke ground in 1995 on a 187-unit community development designed to help meet the state's commitment to reduce CO_2 emissions through its pedestrian-friendly design, use of solar energy, energy-efficient appliances and design, and maintenance of green space (Godschalk et al. 1999). In addition, the community's planners worked with the National Association of Home Builders to design houses that could withstand hurricane force winds far better than typical housing.

The homes at Jordan Commons, like all Habitat homes, are designed to help low-income families become secure homeowners by reducing the financial risk. Habitat defrays the direct cost of building through the use of donated and volunteer labor, corporate sponsorship, private contributions, and government grants. The cost to the homebuyer is further reduced through the no-profit sale of the home and the provision of no-interest financing. Finally, aware of the limited financial capacity of low-income families, future home owners augment their monetary payments with "sweat equity," contributing hundreds of hours of labor to the building of their homes or other Habitat homes. As a result, low-income families are able to join the ranks of home ownership at Jordan Commons for only $400 a month (Salasky 2001). Though the project is ongoing and thus judgment as to its overall success or failure is premature, the methods used to mitigate financial risk are both clear and logical.

These two elements of the broader long-term recovery effort demonstrate three important principles. First, government action can effectively protect vulnerable persons from market forces. Second, man's interaction with nature, whether through CO_2 emissions or the quality of housing, can influence the extent of destruction caused by natural events. Finally, low-income families can secure home ownership, providing there exists the appropriate political will.

Principles for Recovery and Rebuilding:

1. **Revitalize, do not just rebuild** — While catastrophic natural events are not under man's control, the underlying physical and socioeconomic factors they reveal are. Disasters, though terrible, offer an opportunity to correct these problems. Unfortunately, history shows that many regions devastated by disaster rebuild in a way that codifies these factors. In San Francisco, the city structure was rebuilt in virtually the same manner, which left it susceptible to future fires and earthquakes. In Mississippi, Hoover failed to act on his idea for a land resettlement corporation and thus failed to alter the sharecropping/tenant farm system that plagued

blacks in the Delta. Of the examples described above, only the New Deal programs mentioned made substantial progress in improving the long-term outlook for individuals and society by targeting the underlying issues of low skills, poor education, and inadequate infrastructure. This principle of revitalization particularly benefits minority and lower-income groups for two reasons: (1) it reduces the probability of similar tragedy occurring, which, as has been demonstrated, would almost invariably hit the poor and racial and ethnic minorities hardest, and (2) these groups are more likely to be victimized by existing structural flaws, whether they are high unemployment, bad health, unsafe housing, poor skills, or lack of education.

2. **Involve affected persons in their own recovery** — As disasters often separate large masses of people from employment, there tends to be a surplus of labor for recoveries. These pools of labor can and should be employed in the recovery, as they were in the programs of the New Deal and the rebuilding of Chicago. Doing so not only provides a much-needed service, but also income for those affected so that they can begin the path to self-sufficiency. Furthermore, there tends to be a strong need for low-skill jobs, which often aligns with the general skill level of the most vulnerable victims. However, Chicago's Great Rebuilding demonstrates that employment, though helpful in putting people on the path to recovery, is not necessarily sufficient.

3. **Conduct oversight and provide accountability** — Whether the source is public or private, a huge inflow of monetary and material aid has accompanied each disaster discussed. Experience has shown that those with fewer means are unlikely to have representation in the decision-making with regard to the distribution of relief. Consequently, they are more likely to be wronged in the formation of specific policies or in their execution. In Chicago, the unelected Relief and Aid Society discriminated against members of the working class and poor in the disbursement of "special relief," while in the Delta local Red Cross officials violated Hoover's order and gave tenants' rations to their plantation owners. Oversight and accountability are necessary to influence the way in which relief is provided and to ensure that such policies are appropriately carried out.

4. **Carefully consider ecological balance** — Nature's disasters are only disasters because of the way in which these natural events negatively impact human society. Thus, every such disaster should be cause for careful consideration of the relationship between

human society and naturally occurring events. This transpired following the Mississippi flood in 1927, yielding a vastly improved, though not perfect, system of flood control, whereas in San Francisco, businessmen and city officials gave no second thought to rebuilding on the "made land" areas, resulting in a repeat of the massive destruction when the Loma Prieta earthquake hit in 1989. The ability and willingness to correct relationships between man and nature that are out of balance has serious implications for the future.

5. **Take action to address issues and crises that the private sector cannot adequately handle** — Though resilient, the private sector does not always produce results that help those affected by disasters. Examples of this include the widespread failure of the insurance companies following the Chicago fire, the shortfall of Hoover's credit plan in the Delta region, and large-scale unemployment in the Depression. When government fails to act in such instances, it effectively places full responsibility for what happened on individuals, despite their lack of culpability. This is particularly harmful for those in lower income classes who tend to be less able to weather the whims of market forces. Conversely, when government acts quickly to address these issues, as did Florida's government following the insurance crisis caused by Hurricane Andrew, it can mitigate the damage done to individuals, enabling them to rebuild their lives.

Revitalizing the Gulf Coast

The guiding principle in the effort to rebuild New Orleans and the Gulf Coast region should be revitalization. While the death and devastation wrought by Hurricane Katrina cannot be undone, the physical and socioeconomic flaws exposed by the storm can be fixed. This recovery represents the rare opportunity that blacks in the Delta thought they had in 1927, the opportunity to "wash away the old account" (Barry 1997:383). Previous relief and recovery efforts have squandered such opportunities, instead building these flaws back into the system. There is no doubt that an effort to transform the region will be extremely difficult, but building on past experience, it is possible. The tools to undertake such an effort are present: between $100 and $200 billion in federal funds, tens of thousands of volunteers, support both from major corporations and major labor unions, and the participation of countless charitable organizations. The full and correct utilization of these resources carries the potential to truly revitalize the Gulf Coast.

Below are recommendations based on previous disaster recoveries on how to build a better, stronger region. These recommendations are not meant to represent a complete account of the steps needed to rebuild and recover, but rather to outline overarching goals for which to strive, to evaluate selected current efforts in relation to these goals, and to make proposals for the accomplishment of these goals going forward, all within the context of helping those who are most vulnerable.

Goal 1: Utilize employment opportunities to help those affected move to self-sufficiency and improve their employment prospects while accomplishing necessary reconstruction work

History shows that rebuilding efforts that actively involve those affected by disaster are capable both of accomplishing much-needed reconstruction tasks and enabling a move to self-sufficiency. The New Deal programs greatly upgraded the country's infrastructure while moving millions of Americans off the dole. However, previous recoveries also show that in crises, the private sector's actions do not always coincide with the best interests of the affected persons. In Chicago, business' cost concerns led it to promote immigration that undermined the ability of workers to attain self-sufficiency, while poor insurance practices wiped out many working-class families. Therefore, a successful relief effort should not expect that rebuilding jobs will naturally go to locals or that having a job will automatically make individuals self-sufficient, but rather should take steps to actively pursue these ends.

In the Gulf Coast, the government should act to ensure the preferred hiring of current and former residents of the affected regions. Since the private sector cannot necessarily be relied upon to provide this function, the federal, state, and local governments must. Various proposals for achieving preferred hiring have been put forward, including the use of proactive intermediaries to provide job placement assistance for residents, the extension of tax credits for federal contractors that hire locals, the creation of a Neighborhood Reconstruction Corps, and the requirement that those contractors and businesses receiving government support make public all anticipated employment opportunities (Holzer and Lerman 2006; Pennington 2005; CLASP 2005). A successful program should also place special emphasis on bringing those previously unemployed into the labor force.

To help realize the long-term goal of revitalization and self-sufficiency, the recovery effort should implement policies and programs to increase education, skill level, and job training. As the rebuilding effort moves beyond debris removal, more and more higher-skill jobs in the construction, health care, and tourism fields will emerge. The CCC education program and the agricultural extension agents in Mississippi show that the recovery effort can be used to increase job training and improve skills. Successfully doing so in the Gulf Coast would allow residents with previously limited prospects to capitalize on opportunities within these soon-to-be-growing industries. Like the effort to employ locals, various plans exist to promote worker training in the Gulf region, such as the extension of tax credits to companies that train and promote locals, the establishment of fast-track apprenticeship programs, the creation of "Skills Academies" around specific relevant occupational clusters, and the granting of preferences to companies that provide training in awarding reconstruction-related contracts (Holzer and Lerman 2006; Pennington 2005; CLASP 2005). Training programs like these have the potential to dramatically increase income, enable a move to self-sufficiency, and raise the quality of life for thousands in the Gulf Coast region.

So far, the recovery effort has failed to meet these goals. In the Gulf Coast, as in Chicago, the private sector's desire to cut costs has led to the use of immigrant labor. The documented and undocumented immigrants who have provided much of the labor in the initial phase of the recovery are preferred by industry, because they often work, in violation of the law, for less money, receive less adequate benefits, and are less likely to sue or file claims against abuse.[6] A corollary reason for the failure has been the lack of housing near the areas where work is available due to immigrant workers occupying an already depleted housing stock, as in Chicago, and the remote location of temporary housing. Whereas in San Francisco the Committee of Fifty deliberately provided housing close to the areas that needed to be rebuilt, former residents of the Gulf Coast are spread throughout every state in the country. With regard to job training, no single program has been adopted and promoted, and funding has yet to reach any substantial levels (Holzer and Lerman 2006).

The ideas and capacity to involve locals in their own recovery and improve skills and job training exist. What will determine the degree to which these aims are accomplished is the government's will. Going forward, the government should increase its commitment to involving local residents in the rebuilding effort and to improving their long-term job prospects; provide housing near areas where work is available; and conduct serious oversight into the violations of labor laws that make immigrant labor less costly.

Goal 2: Protect those vulnerable to private-sector actions and market forces

The state and federal government should act to ensure that vulnerable individuals are not subjected to overwhelming market forces. History shows that the degree of suffering experienced by people recovering from disasters is inversely correlated with the actions of the government or relief agency to protect them from market forces. In Chicago, the government did nothing in the face of the widespread failure of insurance companies. Likewise, in the Delta, the federal government's deference to private industry prohibited farmers from accessing much-needed credit. As a result, many direly in need of help were left to fend for themselves. Conversely, following Hurricane Andrew, the state government of Florida acted decisively to protect those whose insurance companies failed, enabling them to rebuild. In the Gulf Coast, those facing default on their mortgages because of displacement and unemployment, especially those with low incomes, deserve government attention. If a crisis emerges and the government does not act, the result will be to decrease low-income home ownership and very possibly increase the number of people homeless or dependent on long-term, state-provided relief, such as public housing or vouchers.

To address these issues, the federal government declared a 90-day moratorium on foreclosures on FHA-insured mortgages and mortgages insured under Department of Agriculture programs, and announced that HUD will provide mortgage assistance to as many as 20,000 households with FHA-insured mortgages. While these measures are a good start, they fail to provide sufficient relief. The 90-day moratorium has long since passed, and thousands of Gulf Coast residents are still without jobs, limiting their means to pay a mortgage. Also, the latter relief is contingent on people having "access to funds from insurance proceeds, loans or personal resources to complete the repairs; and, are currently employed or are very likely to return to work within a short period of time" (HUD 2005). These criteria are severely limiting, since the most vulnerable are least likely to be able to draw on personal savings, unemployment remains a huge problem, and many in the poorest areas lacked flood insurance—in turn, partly a function of the fact that FEMA had designated many areas a low flood risk, and thus lenders did not require flood insurance (Popkin et al. 2006). Furthermore, the assistance is only for those whose houses were damaged, meaning those whose homes escaped the flood but are unable to pay their mortgage because they have been dislocated from their employment do not qualify.

The government should extend the moratorium on foreclosures until it has established an effective program for employing local residents and develop a plan to extend assistance to a larger group of vulnerable people.

Goal 3: Promote and foster improved housing options for low-income families

In the Gulf Coast region, the recovery must emphasize the creation of housing options for low-income individuals that are financially accessible and that break the patterns of concentrated poverty that characterized the housing sector prior to Hurricane Katrina. As is the case throughout the United States, housing costs in the Gulf Coast placed extreme financial pressure on low-income individuals, many of whom paid more than half of their income towards housing (Popkin et al. 2006). In addition, the options available for such individuals led to economic segregation and areas of highly concentrated poverty, commonly accompanied by an array of social ills.

Past experience teaches that recovery efforts have the capacity to increase low-income home ownership in a financially sound manner and to thoroughly revamp a failing system. In the Jordan Commons housing development noted above, low-income families successfully entered home ownership with little financial risk through the effective use of corporate sponsors and donated labor in an environment devoid of the profit motive. Though never fully implemented, FDR's plan to rejuvenate the land in the Dust Bowl illustrates the opportunity presented by a large-scale disaster to fundamentally alter and revamp a failing system. With this in mind, those guiding the recovery should strive to improve the housing options available for low-income owners and renters so that they are both truly affordable and not located in areas of concentrated poverty.

In the Gulf Region, federal, state, and local governments should work with the ready and willing charitable homebuilding organizations, corporate sponsors, and volunteer labor to fund and build safe, affordable homes. Increasing stable home ownership among low-income families would bring important economic and social benefits to the devastated region. Not only has home ownership proven to be a sound financial investment, but it is associated with societal goods, such as higher levels of community participation, better academic results in children, and lower crime rates (Shew and Stelzer 2004). To enable financially stable home ownership, those leading the recovery effort must be committed to obligating the resources, navigating the many obstacles, and overcoming opposition from private-sector interests.

Those leading the recovery should also make a serious commitment to promoting mixed-income housing. Families and individuals living in areas of concentrated poverty, of which there were many in the Gulf Region, are typically unable to improve their social or economic status, and are often faced with elevated rates of crime, health problems, unemployment, and children dropping out of school. Achieving economically and racially integrated housing would serve to mitigate these issues and improve educational achievement among children of low-income families (HUD 2003).[7] Recently, there have been efforts by governments to promote mixed-income housing, the most common mechanism being the provision of some form of benefit to developers of moderate- and higher-income housing who agree to reserve a percentage of the development's units for low-income persons. However, these programs have taken considerable criticism on two general points: First, the programs being manipulated in ways that displaced satisfied low-income residents to the benefit of profit-seeking developers; and second, that the programs resulted in a net loss of low-income housing (Stone 2006).[8] To avoid these pitfalls, any policy or program implemented must be crafted to serve the low-income population first and must contain vigorous oversight.

To date, federal, state, and local governments have done little to promote secure home ownership for those with limited resources or to begin a revitalization of housing options for the poor. While Habitat for Humanity should be commended for its various homebuilding efforts in the Gulf Coast, their charitable capacity is hardly equal to the task at hand. Though President Bush proposed an initiative for urban homesteading for low-income individuals, nothing has come of it. In the meantime, the federal government has awarded $25 million in "sweat equity" grants for affordable housing programs, including Habitat, in which the homebuyers actively participate in the construction of their home (HUD 2006). Unfortunately, none of these grants is specifically tied to the Gulf Coast region. As for the development of mixed-income housing, no plan to significantly alter the housing system has emerged.

The government should pursue and fund a coordinated public-private partnership with charitable homebuilding organizations, corporate sponsors, and volunteers to increase stable home ownership among low-income families. It should also target "sweat equity" grants to the Gulf Coast. Finally, it should develop and fully commit to a plan that promotes mixed-income housing in a way that is not injurious to the low-income population.

Goal 4: Reduce the likelihood of such events occurring in the future

The economic and emotional destruction wrought on the Gulf Coast from Hurricane Katrina and the resultant flooding is beyond description. As such, common logic prescribes that before the city is rebuilt, careful consideration of how to prevent another such disaster should be undertaken. Failure to do so in the past almost inevitably resulted in a repeat of the disaster, such as San Francisco experienced when the Loma Prieta earthquake devastated the same "made land" areas as did the 1906 earthquake. When positive changes are made, as in the Delta following the 1927 flood, the probability that such as disaster will be repeated is significantly reduced.

As such, a combination of elected federal, state, and local officials, community members, and experts holding various viewpoints should convene to consider all the implications of rebuilding. They should address such issues as whether flooding was caused by flaws in the levee or a fundamental flaw in the theory of using levees; whether rebuilding and improving the levees is sufficient to prevent a recurrence of this disaster; and whether or not it is advisable to prevent the rebuilding and habitation of certain areas in order to minimize the impact of a potential future breach. Their findings should form the basis for rebuilding, rather than retracing the blueprint that led to this disaster.

To date, this discussion has not taken place in any coherent manner.

Summary

Of all the lessons from history, the clearest is that the recovery following a catastrophe is first and foremost a function of the priorities and commitment of those controlling the effort. For the most part, past recovery efforts succeeded in accomplishing their goals. When those heading the recovery effort sought to judiciously protect the most vulnerable members of society, they did so. Likewise, recovery efforts that advocated a return to the status quo did just that. From the historical examples examined, it appears that the true priorities of those leading the recovery effort are a primary, if not the primary, determinant of the outcomes achieved.

If priorities largely dictate outcomes, then many of the "failures" cited previously are only failures as a result of the lens through which they are viewed, in this case the lens of low-income individuals and racial and ethnic minorities. The Relief and Aid Society's discrimination against poor and working-class immigrants is only a failure if you believe that members of the same society deserve equal treatment, regardless of creed or class. The armed detention of blacks in the Delta is only a failure if you believe that the right to free movement is more important than the retention of the southern labor force. Hoover's inaction with regard to the resettlement program is only a failure if you value changing a system that subjugates one group of people to another more than you value the concept of limited government. The rebuilding in San Francisco is only a failure if you value the safety of a city over the rapid resumption of business. Conversely, FDR's employment programs are only successful if you value an improved standard of living for millions of Americans over the idea that the most desirable government is necessarily the smallest.

History has taught that the recovery from Hurricane Katrina will be largely a reflection of the values and commitment of those tasked with restoring the region. The revitalization of Gulf Coast will not occur organically; it will take more than moonlit speeches and photo-ops, it will take hard work and unrelenting commitment. More important than how many billions of dollars are being spent is how those funds are being used and who is benefiting from them. Are relief funds being used to train previously homeless residents so that they can regain self-sufficiency, or are they lining the pockets of CEOs and shareholders of large out-of-state corporations that profit off the use of immigrant labor? Are the funds being used to reinvent the character of low-income housing, or are they being sunk into the same defunct system? The answers to these and similar questions are not predestined; they are choices to be made. The degree to which the aforementioned goals are achieved will be the truest measure of the priorities of those leading the effort.

References

Badger, Anthony J. 1989. *The New Deal: The Depression Years, 1933-40*. Chicago: Ivan R. Dee.

Barry, John M. 1997. *Rising Tide: The Great Mississippi Flood of 1927 and How It Changed America*. New York: Simon & Schuster.

Bustillo, Miguel. 2005. Disaster Costs Spark Global Warming Debate. *Los Angeles Times*. July 3.

Center for Law and Social Policy (CLASP). 2005. Employment and Training in the Response to Katrina: Some Principles for Ensuring Access to Jobs and Training. http://www.clasp.org/publications/workforce_final.pdf.

Comiero, Mary. 1998. *Disaster Hits Home: New Policy for Urban Housing Recovery*. Los Angeles: University of California Press.

Deslatte, Aaron. 2004. Florida Hurricane Catastrophe Fund under fire. *Pensacola News Journal*. December 11. http://www.pensacolanewsjournal.com/news/special/insurance/stories/st006.shtml.

Fradkin, Philip L. 2005. *The Great Earthquake and Firestorms of 1906: How San Francisco Nearly Destroyed Itself*. Los Angeles: University of California Press.

Godschalk, David R., Timothy Beatley, Philip Berke, David J. Brower, Edward J. Kaiser, Charles C. Bohl, and R. Matthew Goebel. 1999. *Natural Hazard Mitigation: Recasting Disaster Policy and Planning*. Washington: Island Press.

Helmer, Bessie Bradwell. 1996. The Great Chicago Fire and the Web of Memory: The Great Conflagration. Chicago Historical Society and Northwestern University. http://www.chicagohs.org/fire/conflag.

Holzer, Harry J. and Lerman, Robert I. 2006. Employment Issues and Challenges in Post-Katrina New Orleans. The Urban Institute, February. http://www.urban.org/UploadedPDF/900921_employment_issues.pdf.

HUD. *See* U.S. Department of Housing and Urban Development.

Johnson, Gary P., Robert R. Holmes, Jr., and Loyd A. Waite. The Great Flood of 1993 on the Upper Mississippi River—10 Years Later. United States Geological Survey. http://il.water.usgs.gov/hot/Great_Flood_of_1993.pdf.

Kosar, Kevin R. 2005. Disaster Response and Appointment of a Recovery Czar: The Executive Branch's Response to the Flood of 1927. Congressional Research Service. October 25. http://fpc.state.gov/documents/organization/55826.pdf

Leuchtenburg, William E. 1963. *Franklin D. Roosevelt and the New Deal, 1932-1940*. New York: Harper & Row.

Lohof, Bruce A. 1970. Herbert Hoover, Spokesman of Humane Efficiency: The Mississippi Flood of 1927. *American Quarterly* 22 (3): 690–700.

Pauly, John J. 1984. The Great Chicago Fire as a National Event. *American Quarterly* 36 (5): 668–683.

Pennington, Hilary. 2005. New Start New Orleans: Good Jobs for a Better Gulf. Center for American Progress, October. http://www.americanprogress.org/atf/cf/{E9245FE4-9A2B-43C7-A521-5D6FF2E06E03}/CAP_RESPONSE_TO_KATRINA2.PDF.

Platt, Rutherford H. 1999. *Disasters and Democracy: The Politics of Extreme Natural Events*. Washington: Island Press.

Popkin, Susan J., Margery A. Turner, and Martha Burt. 2006. Rebuilding Affordable Housing in New Orleans: The Challenge of Creating Inclusive Communities. The Urban Institute, January. http://www.urban.org/UploadedPDF/900914_affordable_housing.pdf.

Randerson, James. 2006. Global warming blamed for increasing force of hurricanes. *The Guardian.* March 17.

Regents of the University of California. 2006a. The 1906 San Francisco Earthquake and Fire: Buildings Sank Like Quicksand. Bancroft Library. http://bancroft.berkeley.edu/collections/earthquakeandfire/exhibit/room02_item03.html.

Regents of the University of California. 2006b. The 1906 San Francisco Earthquake and Fire: New Building Codes for New Buildings. Bancroft Library. http://bancroft.berkeley.edu/collections/earthquakeandfire/exhibit/room05_item01.html.

Roosevelt, Franklin D. 1932. Oglethorpe University Commencement Address, Oglethorpe University. May 22.

Roosevelt, Franklin D. 1935. State of the Union Address.

Salasky, Julia. 2001. A New Lease on Life: University Habitat for Humanity volunteers hammer away Spring Break for charity. *The Cavalier Daily.* March 21. http://www.cavalierdaily.com/CVArticle.asp?ID=7843&pid=701.

Salmond, John A. 1965. The Civilian Conservation Corps and the Negro. *The Journal of American History* 52 (1): 75–88.

Sawislak, Karen. 1995. *Smoldering City: Chicagoans and the Great Fire, 1871–1874.* Chicago: University of Chicago Press.

Shew, William and Irwin M Stelzer. 2004. External Benefits of Homeownership. Hudson Institute. February. http://www.fanniemae.com/commentary/pdf/022704.pdf.

Smith, Carl S. 1995. *Urban Disorder and the Shape of Belief: The Great Chicago Fire, the Haymarket Bomb, and the Model Town of Pullman.* Chicago: University of Chicago Press.

Spencer, Robyn. 1994. Contested Terrain: The Mississippi Flood of 1927 and the Struggle to Control Black Labor. *The Journal of Negro History* 79 (2): 170–181.

Steinberg, Ted. 2000. *Acts of God: The Unnatural History of Natural Disaster in America.* New York: Oxford University Press.

Stone, Michael. 2006. Social Ownership. In *A Right to Housing: Foundation for a New Social Agenda*, edited by Rachel G. Bratt, Michael E. Stone, and Chester Hartman. Philadelphia: Temple University Press.

U.S. Department of Housing and Urban Development (HUD). 2003. Community Planning and Development. Mixed-Income Housing and the HOME Program. http://www.hud.gov/offices/cpd/affordablehousing/library/modelguides/2004/200315.pdf.

———— 2005. HUD announces mortgage assistance for disaster victims: $200 million initiative designed to rebuild lives and communities. *News release. December 5.* http://www.hud.gov/news/release.cfm?content=pr05-164.cfm.

———— 2006. HUD announces nearly $25 million in "sweat equity" grants to help families build their own American dream: More than 1,500 affordable homes to be built with SHOP grants. News release. February 23. http://www.hud.gov/news/release.cfm?content=pr06-021.cfm.

Worster, Donald. 1979. *Dust Bowl: The Southern Plains in the 1930s.* New York: Oxford University Press.

Endnotes

1. For discussion of the discrimination against the working class in the provision of special relief, see Sawislak 1995:100–106).
2. For example, the Society chose to discontinue aid to 800 families deemed of the "chronic poor" in the winter of 1872, despite the strident objection of some members of the local government and the existence of $600,000 of unspent funds, which the Society eventually kept for its own coffers (Sawislak 1995:119).
3. "Made land" refers to the areas of San Francisco that are former marshes. To create a surface that could be built on, huge amounts of sand and other debris were dumped into the marshes until a firm dry surface was achieved.
4. Fire alone accounted for up to 90% of the buildings destroyed (Fradkin 2005:240).

5. In Arkansas, the value of goods given to those leaving camps averaged $27, more than $50 short of the estimated amount needed to replace a family of four's clothing, furniture, and effects (Barry 1997:371, 388).

6. Though contractors are supposed to pay the prevailing wage to workers regardless of their legal status and provide valid documentation for their workers, the Gulf Coast is littered with examples to the contrary.

7. The socioeconomic status of a school's pupil population has been consistently established as the primary determinant of academic performance (HUD 2003).

8. Studies suggest that the loose definition of "severe distress" in the HOPE VI program, which provides for the redevelopment of "severely distressed" public housing, has caused the demolition of public housing in favor of privately-owned, mixed-income developments, not because of the physical condition of the buildings, but because of a market for profitable higher-income housing (Stone 2006).

CHAPTER 3

Oral History, Folklore, and Katrina

ALAN H. STEIN AND GENE B. PREUSS

The hurricane season of 2005 reached historic proportion in the sheer number of tropical storms and hurricanes, people displaced, homes and businesses destroyed, jobs lost, and lives lost to Hurricanes Katrina, Rita, and Wilma. The Associated Press overwhelmingly voted the Gulf Coast hurricanes as the number-one story of 2005 (*Dallas Morning News* 2005). The growing number of town meetings, conferences, and congressional subcommittees that have convened to hear the testimony and stories of both the disaster itself and the condemnations of the slow response of local, state, and national relief efforts provide an overwhelming amount of oral history material.

Dyan French Cole told the members of the House Select Committee investigating the response to Hurricane Katrina, "I have witnesses that they bombed the walls of the levee, boom, boom!" Cole, a community activist known to many of New Orleans' 7th Ward residents as "Mamma D," was among several witnesses to address the Committee in early December 2005. Other witnesses told U.S. Representatives of the harsh treatment they received from U.S. military personnel, who kept refugees penned behind barbed wire, refusing requests for health care and first aid. "They set us up so that we would rebel, so that they could shoot us," another woman complained. "At one point they brought in two truckloads of dogs and let the dogs out" (Myers 2005; Hodges 2005). Another woman was even more emphatic: "We was treated worse than an animal. People do leave a dog in a house, but they do leave him food and water. They didn't do that. And that's sad." She explained her frustration:

I'm from New Orleans, Louisiana and I was caught into the storm. I never thought New Orleans would have done us the way they done us. I didn't realize what was going on until maybe the third day after I was trying to get out of that place—they would not let us out. I was on top of the Interstate, the Interstate in front to the Superdome and some guys came along in an Ozone Water truck and picked up a lot of people and we got near as far as getting out. They turned us around with guns. The army turned us around with guns. Policemen. And I realized then that they really was keeping us in there. And you want me to tell you the truth, my version of it? They tried to kill us. When you keep somebody on top of the Interstate for five days, with no food and water, that's killing people. And there ain't no ands, ifs, or buts about it, that was NOPD [New Orleans Police Department] killing people. Four people died around me. Four. Diabetes. I am a diabetic and I survived it, by the grace of God, but I survived it. But they had people who were worse off than me, and they didn't make it. Old people. One young woman couldn't survive it because of the dehydration. So I mean, this is what you call NOPD murder. Murder. That's what I call it. What else would you call it?

(Alive in Truth 2005b)

Certainly, historians writing about the effect of the hurricanes and the historical significance of the 2005 hurricane season, the damage visited on the Gulf Coast, and the changed lives of the people of New Orleans and the American South will assess and analyze the oral testimony, but how should we respond presently? Mamma D's story of levee bombings are among the stories circulating that lend credence to the growing belief that racism and a lack of concern for victims in poorer sections of the Crescent City influenced the government's reaction to the hurricane's victims. For historians, oral history methodology helps with conducting, collecting, and evaluating personal narratives that can shed the light of experience on a path increasingly darkened by the overwhelming number of accounts that emerge on a daily basis.

What is Oral History and How Does it Preserve Community?

This chapter explores the uses of oral history in documenting and interpreting Katrina. Simplistically stated, oral history is the application of modern technology to history's most ancient technique of gathering historical material: using a recording machine to preserve both the questions to, and answers of, eyewitnesses or participants in selected aspects of history. For centuries, stories and traditions were passed orally from one generation to the next. One of the stories that emerged from the massive tsunami of 2004 that killed hundreds of thousands is the account of how relatively few died on the Indonesian island of Simeulue. Residents remembered the stories their grandparents told them of the "semong"—big waves—that followed earthquakes.

Oral history became a tool of significant historical inquiry and documentation in both the literate and nonliterate worlds, but it was with the development of recording technology and the ability to capture the actual voices of narrators that the practice became more popular and legitimate. During the Great Depression, the Federal Writers' Project employed writers and folklorists to document the stories of ex-slaves, immigrant families, famines, and floods.

While the field was legitimized in 1948 by the creation of the Columbia University Oral History Program, it was not until the 1960s and the development of the new social history that the oral history movement came into its own, as it focused on the lives and experiences of "ordinary people," popularized by the works of Studs Terkel. History "from the bottom up" became favored by social historians and activists who viewed oral history in the community as an empowering process for interviewer and narrator alike: It brought to light the voices of those who had been silenced by the dominant historiography due to race, gender, and class biases.

Aided by the world of television and digital media, oral history is a way of documenting urgent events and insights that otherwise might not be recorded. The numerous Katrina projects cited in this chapter illustrate how evacuees are active participants in their own historical drama. Through rich audio-video interviews, their life stories present enormous opportunities for uses, from pedagogy to research. But they also present profound challenges: How reliable are the interviewers and the oral sources? How will the interviews be accessed in their audio and video form? When should we even begin collecting "urgent" oral history of a catastrophe? Finally, how do we interpret what we are collecting?

When Should We Begin Collecting Oral History?

Oral historians, a multidisciplinary group that includes folklorists, anthropologists, sociologists, and historians, have worked for many years with testimony, family stories, and oral accounts like those arising from the ruined areas of the Gulf Coast region. The techniques and methodologies oral historians have developed may help unravel the tangle of confused, horrific, and contradictory testimony from evacuees and survivors displaced by the hurricanes.

An important question oral historians wrestle with — unlike their journalism colleagues — is when to begin collecting the narratives. How our media responded is at the same time reflective of our interest in catastrophes and the media's need for ratings, but there is human compassion as well. *USA Today*'s Peter Johnson wrote, "The human side of Katrina—tales of agony and misery that thousands of Katrina's victims still endure a month after the storm—also has gripped many reporters, who want to stay on the story indefinitely" (Johnson 2005).[1] Reporters covering the 9/11 terrorist attacks and the Shuttle Columbia accident expressed similar sentiments. How should the oral historian respond? The gut-level instinct is to grab a recorder and get "in the field" as soon as possible. But historians, like journalists, are always concerned about maintaining an objectivity concerning their research and writing. Most historians achieve this "historical distance" by writing about the past, not contemporary events.

The discussion about Katrina oral history projects became one of the year's leading discussions on H-ORALHIST, an H-NET discussion list (www.h-net.org/~oralhist/), with oral historians divided in their opinion. The subsequent discussion begged the question: When do current events become history? Historians usually prefer the temporal distance presented by the past. "I have never come nearer to contemporary history than a perspective of 25 years," Barbara Tuchman wrote (Tuchman 1996). On September 8, 2005, Holly Werner Thomas wrote: "It may be too soon to ask, but it seems important that the stories of the refugees from Hurricane Katrina be told. Does anyone have any information about a possible oral history project regarding the hurricane and its aftermath?" (Thomas 2005). One respondent admitted that he felt vexed about beginning to collect narratives too rapidly. After rushing to the refugee center located in Houston's Astrodome to collect oral history of this disaster, he admitted, "Yet when I arrived, I found myself wondering if we should allow some time for reflection" (Preuss 2005; K'Meyer 2005). Would rushing in to collect oral histories while people were still displaced, sheltered in auditoriums, churches, and public buildings be adding more traumas to their lives? "People will need time to settle down, time to reflect, and time to put their lives back together before they will be able to discuss how the disaster affected them.... They are still 'in the midst' of their story." He worried that rushing in and conducting interviews too close to the traumatic incident would be "working at the intersection of grief and history," as two public historians described their interaction while working with 9/11 survivors (Gardner and Henry 2002).

Columbia University Oral History Research Office Director Mary Marshall Clark argues, "If projects can be well-organized, funded well enough, and there is an archive willing to accept tapes and transcripts and to disseminate them when the time comes—it is possible to begin early." Getting an early start could also be important not only to historians, but to survivors it might also be "important in some cases, as it was with many we interviewed after 9/11 who experienced relief in knowing that someone was willing to listen to personal accounts of horror" (Clark 2005).

Another dilemma facing oral historians and others working with people whose lives were shattered by disasters and tragedy is maintaining a professional distance. How involved should one become? Public historians working after the September 11 tragedy in New York explained that they confronted this dilemma. How to collect historical information for the future, and still provide for the needs of the present? (Scudder and Gulick 1972) Mary Marshall Clark described the importance of interviewing soon after an event in order to avoid the problems of contaminating individual memories with those of others, or a larger "public narrative." While conducting interviews for Columbia's September 11, 2001 Oral History Narrative and Memory Project, Clark reported that many interviewees expressed confusion about the meaning and significance of the attacks. There were multiple interpretations based upon the interviewee's ethnicity, sex, and culture. Clark and her colleagues found themselves asking, "Is this history yet? Is it memory? And …. Is it therapy?" (Clark 2003)

Clark goes on to describe the challenges of doing Katrina-related oral history projects:

I have a perspective on the questions raised about documenting Katrina. It's in part philosophical perspective, which is based on understanding how important oral history can be to those who tell. My perspective is this: I think it is both "never too soon" to tell, and "never too late" to tell. The story of Katrina and the failure of the relief effort [as well as] the impact on African Americans and others and the poorest of the poor is still unfolding. Oral histories of Katrina will involve not only the event and its immediate aftermath but its still unfolding legacy: the story of the largest displacement of people since the Civil War and maybe the largest displacement of children ever.

These stories of displacement and resettlement, the decisions about how and whether to return, the redefinition of home, etc. are all stories that can be documented over time, and should be carefully planned so as to respect the human struggles that will be involved. We found with 9/11, though, it can't compare to Katrina in most ways, as the complete destruction and devastation of every kind of support is so much more extreme, that people who were displaced from their homes/lost jobs/were disrupted in major ways couldn't really focus on the oral history process. So we never pushed them to describe the difficulties that were ongoing unless they chose to describe these specific struggles themselves.

(Clark 2005)

How Involved Should One Become When Collecting "Urgent" Oral History of a Catastrophe?

In the spirit of "never too soon to tell," volunteers began conducting oral history research within weeks of the Katrina crisis, even as the crisis event unfolded. Most notably is the "Alive in Truth: The New Orleans Disaster Oral History and Memory Project" (www.aliveintruth.org), run by an all-volunteer group of interviewers/recorders, transcribers, translators, therapists, donors, and community members. The project began in early September 2005 outside the Austin Convention Center, which sheltered some 6,000 New Orleans evacuees, mostly African-American residents who were trapped in the city after the storm. It is one of the first projects to utilize a "life history" approach, focusing on the entire life of the interviewee, not only their hurricane-experience stories:

> I'm from the 7th Ward, and I was raised in New Orleans. I was raised and born in New Orleans. I worked as a babysitter. Went to school there, finished the 10th grade. Went to Warren Easton High School. At the age of 17, I decided to go to Job Corps, but so far I didn't make it there, so I wound up getting pregnant with my first daughter, which is named Dionnka T.

(Alive in Truth 2005a)

This kind of bottom-up approach also helps evacuees find their voice. By interviewing residents from New Orleans' Lower Ninth Ward, the project seeks to document individual lives, restore community bonds, and uphold the voices, culture, rights, and history of New Orleanians.

Some members of the Oral History Association expressed concern over Alive In Truth's volunteers because they become directly involved as advocates for the interviewee. Interviewers have driven narrators to sign up for Medicare, to access warehouses of clothing and furniture, and to file FEMA claims. In the meantime, volunteers continue to encounter people who do not have furniture, who are missing family members and are unaware of resources to help locate them. In many cases, the volunteers encounter survivors with untreated medical conditions who are not in contact with preliminary case management services. Volunteers are prepared to help evacuees find social services for help or to accompany them to FEMA information centers. In the minds of some oral historians, the Alive in Truth interviewers are too close to the problems, and so their personal "bias" will intrude on the interview, since the interviewer takes an activist role by empathizing with the narrator who is contributing his or her story to the project.

Alive in Truth Project Director and former New Orleanian Abe Louise Young has been a Research Fellow for the Jewish Women's Archive, for The Project in Interpreting the Texas Past, and for the Danish-American Dialogue on Human Rights. She describes the importance of active oral history in shaping public policy by networking with other organizations—grassroots, nonprofits, oral history, human rights, state and national, people of color-led groups—in order to connect with a broader social change movement. She also believes that the legacy of Alive in Truth will be in preserving "the archive of accounts [that have] achieved rapid dissemination, educating and informing various constituencies: this is evidence of the broad scope possible with multiple media liaisons, a vision of justice, and belief in the speakers" (Young 2005). In February 2006, Young also introduced an interpretative photography exhibit documenting Katrina at the Carver Library in East Austin, Texas. Entitled "Surviving Katrina: Sharing Our Stories," it was one of the first oral history exhibits documenting the experience of Katrina evacuees. Through text and photographs, it tells the story of six New Orleanians and their experiences coming to Austin.

The project collected over 60 interviews that are, on average, one to two hours long. They are recorded on minidisk, and excerpts are placed into MP3 format (playable and accessible on the web). Young has contributed the interviews to the U.S. Human Rights Network reports, as well as the Katrina Task Force, established at the Ben L. Hooks Center for Social Change at the University of Memphis.

How Do We Interpret What We Are Collecting?

In response to the critical issues laid bare by Hurricane Katrina and its aftermath, the Open Society Institute (OSI) offered a fellowship competition for projects exposing the persistent problems of poverty, racism, and government neglect. OSI, part of the George Soros Foundations Network, recognized the importance of documenting the hurricane aftermath by creating the Katrina Media Fellowships in 2006, a one-time award (averaging $15,000–$35,000) for journalists, photographers, and documentary filmmakers who are using sound recordings collected from oral history interviews for media production. Along with OSI, other national and state arts and humanities councils have supported oral history research projects in the past, but there exists a greater sense of urgency for funding these special projects, a fact recognized by the Oral History Association (OHA), the national organization of oral history professionals headquartered at Pennsylvania's Dickenson College.

The increases in recent disasters and tragedies have forced oral historians to reevaluate the timely collection and interpretation of "urgent" interviews. The OHA is primarily concerned with the slow response time from foundations for funding meaningful interpretative projects. It recognized the importance of emerging crises in oral history research by creating an Emerging Crises Oral History Research Fund in 2006. The fund is primarily designed to provide a more expedient source of funding and a quick turnaround time for oral historians to undertake "crisis research" as well as field work in the United States and internationally (Oral History Association 2006).

While Katrina has provided an opportunity for gathering documentary photography and oral history recordings, the real challenge has been the dissemination of the digital data. The digital revolution meant that crucial aspects of information can be organized, searched, extracted, and integrated with relative speed and accuracy, leading historians like Roy Rosenzweig into the age of digital history. Rosenzweig (co-author of the prize-winning multimedia CD-ROM *Who Built America?*) is the founder and director of The Center for History and Media at George Mason University and Executive Producer of The Hurricane Digital Memory Bank (HDMB), which uses electronic media to collect, preserve, and presents the stories of Hurricanes Katrina, Rita, and Wilma. The George Mason Center (http://chnm.gmu.edu) and the University of New Orleans, in partnership with the Smithsonian Institution's National Museum of American History and other partners, organized this project. Funded by the Alfred P. Sloan Foundation, HDMB is an ongoing effort by historians and archivists to preserve the record of these storms by documenting first-hand accounts, on-scene images, blog postings, and podcasts (Hurricane Digital Memory Bank 2006).

A project partner with the HDMB is the University of Southern Mississippi Center for Oral History and Cultural Heritage. They are engaged in a large-scale "Hurricane Katrina Oral History Project" that will seek to capture the larger human experience of this landmark event. To date, this project includes a partnership with scholars in six states (South Carolina, Louisiana, Tennessee, Utah, Virginia, and Arizona) trained in oral history. The Center is conducting over 1,000 interviews to capture the breadth of the experiences of those impacted, including emergency management officers, local officials, residents, volunteer relief workers, and those displaced by the storm. Other partner projects include:

The Photojournalists of Hurricane Katrina: An oral history and
book project featuring a dozen of the photojournalists who
covered New Orleans and the Mississippi coast post-Katrina. The
project will include unpublished photographs and personal narratives of the aftermath of the storm, allowing these journalists
to relate a powerful story through a blend of words and images.

Archivists and Hurricane Katrina Project: Working with archivists and libraries along the Mississippi Gulf Coast, this project
will use focus groups and individual interviews to assess the
disaster preparedness of historical and cultural institutions.
This initiative will examine existing protocols, how these were
implemented, and identify issues that need to be addressed in
planning. The outcome of the project will be to develop and disseminate documented, workable procedures to fulfill community
information needs of archival processes when disaster strikes.
This project is a partnership with Solinet, Mississippi Library
Commission, and the School of Library and Information Science
at The University of Southern Mississippi.

Hurricane Katrina and the Coastal Vietnamese Community: One of
the most at-risk communities following the storm are the coastal
Vietnamese. This project, working with humanitarian relief
agencies along with local churches and temples, strives to capture the stories of these members of the Gulf Coast community,
many of whom lost everything in the storm. Through gathering
the personal narratives of the Vietnamese, this project offers a
unique opportunity not only to affirm the strength of their community but also to share with them as they rebuild.

Mississippi Nurses and Hurricane Katrina Project: An effort to
interview nurses who worked during the immediate pre- and
post–Katrina period on the Mississippi Gulf Coast and in the
Hattiesburg area. Nurses, as frontline caregivers, were the ones
at the "point of care," attempting to improvise and prioritize care
as they could. These stories are critical to capture, for, as time
goes by, many of these nurses who are already in a state of flux
are becoming harder to identify and locate.

Hurricane Katrina Exhibit: A partnership with the Mississippi
Sound Historical Museum to develop a museum exhibit at their
facility in Gulfport, MS. The exhibit will feature oral narratives,
photographs, and artifacts in one of the first efforts by a cultural
institution to place the storm in historical perspective.

One documentary project that has applied to the OSI fund is entitled "People Power: Citizen Responses to Hurricane Katrina." It is a photo-driven, electronic media project that will tell the dramatic stories of how Louisianans responded with bravery, improvisation, and humanity to save lives, evacuate survivors, and continue to care for those affected by the hurricane and subsequent flooding. Each person interviewed will provide a case study to gauge the recovery process, access to resources and information, and their personal well-being. The narrators will represent the diversity of people living in southern Louisiana pre-Katrina. Their stories will shed light on the complexities of the social inequalities and shared histories of this region. The project combines photography, recorded interviews, and written stories to stimulate debate about the effectiveness of civil society's response to the disaster. These sound and image packages are disseminated through an interactive website designed for the project; weekly spots on community radio stations; state and national magazines; and a photography exhibition. The project website will be linked to the WWOZ website (www.wwoz.org). WWOZ is a world-renowned New Orleans community radio station and cultural hub for New Orleans.

Dr. Lance Hill is the Executive Director of the Southern Institute for Education and Research at Tulane University. Hill worked as a community activist and labor organizer for 20 years before embarking on an academic career. From 1989 to 1992, he served as the Executive Director of the Louisiana Coalition Against Racism and Nazism (LCARN), the grassroots organization that led the opposition to former Klansman David Duke's Senate and gubernatorial campaigns. Hill is a consultant and appears in the New Orleans Documentary Project, produced by Organic Process Productions. The film uses oral histories to interview "characters" like Lewis Taylor, a retired farmer and fisherman, and to document the impact of uprooting communities as well as the effect this will have on future land development and gentrification plans for the area. The film (and planned book) examines controversial issues of governmental power, such as the use of eminent domain and privatization.

Oral history can be used as a tool in collecting social history and folklore. Folklorists must confront "tall tales" or urban myths. Can memories always be trusted? How do we respond to stories so fantastic that they tax credulity, even when they come from dispassionate sources? For example, Tulane historian Douglas Brinkley witnessed Federal Emergency Management Agency (FEMA) officials prohibiting private citizens and people in unauthorized trucks from trying to aid others. Rescuers pulled people from the water, he reported, but medical aid was absent; instead, FEMA officials stood idly by. Brinkley's new book, *The Great Deluge: Hurricane Katrina, New Orleans, and the Mississippi Gulf Coast*, draws upon hundreds of oral history interviews and arrives at the conclusion that it was not a natural disaster at all but a failure of government—"one that, through breached levees and massive government incompetence, the country brought upon itself" (Brinkley 2006).

A coalition of Louisiana- and Mississippi-based scholars (coordinated by Maida Owens, director of the Louisiana Folklife Program) has developed two projects designed to empower evacuees and help contribute to public policy decisions. One program is entitled "In the Wake of the Hurricanes: A Coalition Effort to Collect Our Stories and Rebuild Our Culture" (Louisiana Division of the Arts 2006).[2] Folklorist Susan Roach, an English professor and folklorist at Louisiana Tech University in Ruston, began talking to other folklorists around the state. Roach teamed up with Shana Walton, former associate director of Tulane's Deep South Humanities Center, in applying for a National Endowment for the Humanities grant to help pay interviewers and hire unemployed hurricane survivors to conduct interviews. They model their program on the New Deal Writers' Project, which paid unemployed writers and artists to do interviews and life histories with ex-slaves and survivors of the Dust Bowl. Together, they have recruited about 100 people, from Mississippi to California. Sponsored by the American Folklife Center at the Library of Congress, these projects involve seven universities and faculty throughout Louisiana.

Walton had conducted several interviews at a New Orleans-area shelter shortly after the hurricane struck, but realized that it was too soon after the event. Because of the chaos and stress, it was not the best place to do formal interviews or field work. She then began collecting oral histories for her project on Little Black Creek, a FEMA Camp in rural Mississippi. It is one of dozens of temporary housing camps established by FEMA to house people displaced from New Orleans and the Gulf Coast after the hurricanes. The project is based on relief work and oral histories with camp residents between November 2005 and January 2006, giving an overview of demographics of the approximately 200 camp residents; how their individual trajectories led them to be in a FEMA camp; their assessment of the local and federal government; the biggest challenges facing them; and the attitudes of most toward returning to where they lived before the hurricane. Walton also documents the emergence of community in the camp, and the long-term view from the residents' perspective. Interviews show that camp residents are not only displaced from their homes, but also isolated from reliable sources of information about the rebuilding or from having any input in the process. This overview will be generally compared with others whose research looks at residents who lost their homes but have returned to the city and those who have chosen to relocate.

A similar effort is underway in Texas. As Houston's post-hurricane population swelled by 250,000, Carl Lindahl, a folklorist and English professor at the University of Houston, started conducting several interviews with evacuees, eventually expanding it into a project entitled "Surviving Katrina and Rita in Houston," with his colleague Patricia Jasper, a folklorist with over 20 years of experience. Their goal is to create as many as 3,000 narratives by teaching volunteers how to interview evacuees, because, as he explained, "We've found that a person who has gone through this is a much better interviewer than those who have not. I found the survivors to be heroes rather than victims." He added that the project will not stress the "traumatizing effects" of the storms themselves, nor dwell on the "horror stories," but instead will focus on the "cultural richness" in Houston's community, pointing to the influx of Louisiana evacuees after the 1927 Mississippi River flood that created a section of the city called "French Town" (Shilds 2005).

"Narrating Katrina Through Oral History" (a project sponsored by the Albert Gore, Sr. Research Center at Middle Tennessee State University) is the title of a new initiative under the direction of Lisa Pruitt. Teams of student interviewers from Middle Tennessee State University, working under Pruitt's direction, are conducting oral history interviews with individuals who were forced to evacuate to middle Tennessee from coastal Louisiana, Mississippi, and Alabama before, during, and after Hurricane Katrina. The students are also interested in interviewing volunteer responders from the middle Tennessee region. Several thousand people relocated to middle Tennessee, either temporarily or permanently. Furthermore, hundreds of people from middle Tennessee have traveled to the Gulf Coast as volunteer responders. The overall goal of this project is to create a documentary record of the experiences of as many of these people as possible through the medium of oral history. Tapes and transcripts of the interviews will become a permanent part of the Middle Tennessee Oral History Collection at the Gore Center. Teams of student interviewers will ask participants to describe their experiences evacuating, staying in shelters or with family or friends; re-establishing their lives in middle Tennessee (whether temporarily or permanently); their perceptions of media coverage of the events; their evaluation of various agencies and organizations that responded to the disaster and with whom they had direct experience; and their hopes for their own futures and the future of the affected region. Volunteer responders will be asked to describe their motives for volunteering; the logistics of volunteering; the details of their work; their perception of the scope and impact of the disaster; their perception of media coverage; their perception of the performances of various agencies and organizations involved in responding with whom they had direct contact; and their feelings about the experience of volunteering in response to a major disaster.

The Historic New Orleans Collection (HNOC), a museum and research center located on the dry ground of the French Quarter, found itself in the epicenter of the deluge and established oral history projects with the first responders from the New Orleans Police Department and the New Orleans Fire Department. The interviews with NOPD and NOFD members, entitled "Through Hell and High Water," focuses on the period between August 29, when Katrina made landfall, and September 15, when President Bush gave his address to the nation in front of the St. Louis Cathedral. It was difficult to gain the trust and cooperation of the departments due to the intense media scrutiny of the event. The breakdown of the social structure of the city is a focus of the NOPD interviews, as are the tensions between personal and professional responsibilities as well as interaction with the citizens who remained there. But memories of both departments' past hurricane preparedness plans were also discussed. How these plans were implemented during the hours before the storm, and how they unraveled during it and its aftermath is a major theme of the project. Within the NOFD interviews is the documentation of the rescue operations of about 25 firemen, who, based on their own memories of Hurricane Betsy in 1965, took it upon themselves to bring their own recreational boats to the NOFD pre-storm staging areas on the upper floors of downtown hotel parking garages, and began boat rescue operations immediately following the storm. It is estimated that in the days following the storm, these 25 boats rescued between 12,000 and 15,000 people who were stranded on rooftops or trapped in attics. In addition to the interviews, HNOC has collected approximately 1,000 images taken during this two-week period by members of both the NOFD and NOPD.

Phyllis E. Mann coordinated the volunteer criminal defense attorney efforts in Louisiana to assist evacuated prisoners. She described her experiences in an article for *The Advocate*, the Louisiana Association of Criminal Defense Lawyers newsletter. "There has been so much bad this month in Louisiana," she recalls, and then "there has been so much good" (Mann 2005a). In her own "oral history," she relates the stories she heard from people in jail cells:

The first stories we heard were from men evacuated out of the many Orleans Parish Prison buildings. They received their last meal on Sunday night—it was a cold sandwich. During the night, the power began to go on and off as the Hurricane began to make landfall. Inside the jail, it was dark and the air soon became hot and stale. Without electricity, the controls for the cell doors, dormitory doors, and main doors were inoperable—everyone was trapped. Guards had been required to stay in Orleans during the storm and had been encouraged to bring their families to the jails, so there were children in those buildings also. And the guards were stretched to the breaking point—worrying about their own safety, worrying about the safety of their families, and not doing quite so much worrying about the safety of the people locked inside the cells.... The people who were locked inside were so very much like you and I and especially like our children. There was one young man who had been arrested for reading Tarot cards without a permit.... There were college age folks who had come to New Orleans for a good time, but had the misfortune of getting a little too drunk just a day or two before a hurricane. There were young women who were pregnant; ... middle-aged soccer moms who just had not gotten around to paying that speeding ticket; an older grandmother who was visiting her grandchildren and overstayed her visa from Jamaica; and then there were the poor of New Orleans who were arrested for sleeping on the street ... and the stories go on and on. What all of these people had in common... is that they were all trapped together, inside of a building with no lights, with no air, and they had no food to eat or water to drink .... These are the stories that have broken our hearts.

(Mann 2005b)

How Can We Learn From the Mistakes?

The debate over oral histories has often focused on the issue of historical accuracy. Like the dramatic accounts of the bombing of the New Orleans levees that Mamma D remembers in the aftermath of Hurricane Katrina, other witnesses and officials have denied deliberate acts of destruction and malevolence. Instead, they note that the levees were bombed during the Great Mississippi Flood of 1927 and suggest that perhaps the collective memory of these two events long separated chronologically were somehow merged in the memory of the witness. Validation is a common phenomenon oral historians face. While some reminiscences might not be factually accurate, they are accurate in the psyche of the interviewee.

Captain Francis J. Arnona, Jr. was a ship-docking captain for Crescent Towing and Salvage in New Orleans. Two months before Katrina, he had been through tropical storm Cindy. He had a different impression about the collapse of the levees. He confirmed this in an oral history interview he gave at the Gore Center:

Basically, New Orleans did well. Yeah, there was a lot of wind damage and all from the storm. A lot of windows, the roof on the Superdome was blown off. But, as far as the storm, that didn't cause it. That problem came when the levees breached ... after the fact. Now, seems to me ... they have levee boards down there and, you know, that's run by politicians again. Well, if those levees breached, there was a reason they breached. And they're supposed to be monitoring those levees and shoring them up constantly, but they got a little sitting back on their haunches, "Oh, we're all right. We're all right." Well, guess what? It wasn't all right ....

All they are is dirt and they stick a little slab of concrete on them. That's all they are. I'm going to tell you—a lot of those levees, there were so many broke loose barges and boats drifting around. They hit those levees, they cracked the cement, you know. And they said, "Oh, St. Bernard [Parish] and all got flooded because the levee gave away back there." But, if they ever looked real close, there was a barge sitting on the other side of the levee in somebody's front yard.

One woman who left New Orleans and was interviewed in Austin tells a story where her fear, exaggerated by exhaustion, played tricks with her imagination:

We wanted to stay. We thought maybe the water was going to go down. We didn't know it was that damaged. You know, all over the city because for days we couldn't get out, you know, go nowhere, 'cause of the flood. So they took us, we got on the bus, took us to a bus, took us to the Louis Armstrong airport, and flew us here to Austin. Mm-hm.

'Cause I seen so much, so much happening, hearing so much happening; I was devastated. I was walking in the water, trying to find a way, you know, to get out? And I couldaa sworn I felt a body, or something; somebody's body wrapped around my leg! But I know it couldn't 'a been true! [laughing]

(Alive in Truth 2005a)

Careful analysis has provided several explanations for the problems in relying upon multiple versions of oral testimony. Psychologists term the tendency for hostages to identify with their captors "Stockholm Syndrome," and interviews with former prisoners of war, kidnapping victims, and torture survivors reveal that some victims do not assess any personal blame upon the perpetrators. Historian Alessandro Portelli explains that for some people, certain "climatic moments" overwhelm their ability to place these events into perspective; instead, they are "wholly absorbed by the totality of the historical event of which they were a part." For them, these events become epic stories in their memories (Portelli 1991).

Another method historians have used to overcome the conflict between narrative and documentary evidence is to compare oral traditions with the commonly accepted scholarly version of history. James G. Blight, a cognitive psychologist who is professor of international relations at the Watson Institute at Brown University, has pioneered what he terms "Critical Oral History." Critical oral history seeks to reevaluate historical events by bringing together academic scholars, leading actors and policymakers in the event, and historical documents, in an attempt to arrive at a fuller understanding of how the historical event in question developed. By combining documents, scholars, and participants, Blight explains, the goal is to "learn to collaborate in an effort to get a more comprehensive picture of the historical reality during whatever events we are studying" (Chronicle of Higher Education Colloquy Live 2002).

In the aftermath of Hurricane Katrina, many have criticized the treatment African-American Louisianans received. Among the dozen or so hurricane research projects listed on the Louisiana Folklife Website is one offering a social and environmental interpretation of events, entitled "Katrina Narratives of African-Americans is in an Unprecedented Diaspora: A Social and Environmental Oral History Project," coordinated by Dr. Dianne Glave from Tulane University's Bioenvironmental Research Department (which relocated to Atlanta following Katrina). Glave's proposal re-enforces the need for oral historians to expand on the news media's impressionistic reporting. She believes oral history interviewers share responsibilities with news media:

In the aftermath of Hurricane Katrina, the fragmented and harrowing pieces of many narratives of African Americans who were trapped in the Superdome, Convention Center, and their flooded homes have emerged on television and the internet. Some evacuated immediately while others were forced to wait many days to be rescued; most migrated to points across the United States; and many are now attempting to return to the Gulf region. As a result, the news media has opened an insightful dialogue across the United States and throughout the world concerning race, racism, and class. Scholars now have an opportunity to add to this exchange of ideas—not merely replicating the news—as a catalyst for analyzing the historical context for this natural disaster by looking at African influences, the Middle Passage, enslavement, freedom, migration, the Civil Rights movement and more. Out of this tragedy, I propose an oral history project that would give the Katrina narratives by African Americans scope, adding to what is in the news [by] emphasizing the social and environmental implications.

(American Folklife Center 2006)[4]

Ninety-year-old folklorist Stetson Kennedy infiltrated the Ku Klux Klan during the 1940s and exposed it in a series of documentary books like *Southern Exposure* (still doing business as an investigative magazine). As the director of the Florida Writers' Project Folklore unit in the 1930s, Kennedy worked with Zora Neal Hurston to gather Negro folklore, interview ex-slaves, and expose slave-labor conditions throughout the South. Kennedy wasted no time in making his voice heard in support of the African Americans who were trapped inside the Superdome. Watching the catastrophe unfold on CNN angered Kennedy, who would later write, "It is up to every American to assess, according to his or her conscience, our individual and national shame for what happened before and after Katrina" (Kennedy 2005). He wondered what the men, women, children, infants, aged, and infirm victims of Katrina did to deserve such "bestial" treatment in the Superdome and elsewhere. "Absolutely nothing," he concluded:

Much like the victims of the Holocaust, theirs was the misfortune of being the wrong kind of people. They were poor and, for the most part, dark-skinned. When Katrina took aim at New Orleans, they were included out of preparations for evacuation. And when push came to shove, and everybody else had gotten out, they were left stranded and abandoned in the tsunami of debris and excrement. And all that the great city, state, and nation offered them was to go to the Superdome. What happened to them after they got there will forever be burned into the memory of mankind, thanks to television, even though it lacked the guts to give us more than a glimpse of the horrors going on inside. In a matter of days, America stood stripped naked in the eyes of the world for what it is (you name it). When catastrophe strikes, it's not the women and children first, but the Haves—and Devil take the Have-Nots.

But the world watched, and help never really got there until it was too late—not that it was not available. America has the public and private wherewithal to supply and/or evacuate any number of people anytime anywhere (anybody remember The Berlin Airlift?) So, why not the Superdome and why not Charity Hospital? (Evacuating posh Tulane Hospital presented no problem.) Why not all the folks drowning and starving in their homes and on the streets? The problem was not really how, but who—who would be responsible for them once they had been saved?

With the backdrop of a devastated city, it was all too obvious that whoever took them in would be stuck with them for a very long time—perhaps even forever. Evacuating Japanese-Americans from our Pacific Coast during WWII was quite different. We wanted them out of there, ostensibly for reasons of security, and none of us objected, because Uncle Sam would be feeding them behind barbed wire out in the desert for the duration, and meanwhile, some of us could take over their homes and businesses. No such incentives in New Orleans.

Was racism/bigotry an added factor on top of the economic tab? This observer was reminded of the time, a half century earlier, when a shipload of one thousand Jewish refugees from Nazi Germany sailed up and down the coast of America, hoping in vain for us to take them in. No nation in the world would open its doors, so most of them ended up in the ovens. It was shame on us then and shame on us now.

Narratives and public statements reflect deep-seated resentment against years of poverty and discrimination. There is even fear that as communities rebuild, the discrimination will persist. Sibal Holt is the first African American and first woman to head the Louisiana AFL-CIO. She expressed her concerns to an interviewer about the social transformation and gentrification of poor communities devastated by the storm:

A socially engineered community is what's being done here! They want to engineer what the community should look like. That is wrong! I don't care what anybody else says, that is wrong and that is not paranoia speaking. From the Governor on down they're talking about who should be allowed to come back. They gave certain people one way tickets out of this state, ok? Well some of this money may be able to be used to give them a ticket back into this state. This is their home. But let's be real, what people are booking on is that if these people aren't able to come home within a year, [then] they're going to get settled somewhere else. But what areas of New Orleans and Louisiana are we talking about? The French Quarter, Uptown, and the Garden District—we're talking about the casino areas—what does that sound like to you? Did you hear any names of any predominately African-American poor communities that they're talking about? Now I'm not going to say that they're never going to get to them—but it won't be tomorrow, trust me.

(Mead 2005)

Conclusions

What will the "new" New Orleans look like? Who rebuilds and who does not? The answers to questions such as these will pique the attention of social commentators, politicians, community activists, and historians long into the future. Sibal Holt reflects the concerns shared by many displaced workers from the Gulf Coast:

> Because New Orleans is perceived as a black city—clearly there are about 68–69 percent but the rest in that city are whites. If you would have watched the media during Hurricane Katrina you would have thought there were no white folks evacuating because all you saw was black .... Therefore, when it came time to get these people out there were those who said, you know they're just a bunch of poor people, you know .... So race did play a very heavy factor. Didn't you wonder when you saw all these black folks going to the shelter where are all the white people [were]? ... And even now in terms of the return, the right to return to the place where you were born, where your children were raised, where your home was structured, rather than allow these people to come home and put them in trailers they've put all kinds of Hispanics from not only out of the state but out of the country—who cannot speak a word of English in a lot of instances. But they would rather have them in the city, cleaning up and making what little dollars there are to be made rather than bring these people who have a right to return, who are trying to earn a living and rebuild their homes, and their communities, and their schools. Yeah, race plays a very heavy part in this.

> **(Mead 2005)**

Although most of the media stories focus on the negative effects of the disaster, some interviewees have redoubled their inner strength, through faith, family, or the prospect of starting over in a new community:

> God was good, God blessed us. He really did, He blessed us. And right now, I could see that he did this for a reason. You know, to change lives. 'Cause so much was going on, in New Orleans, so much. Killing, drugging, and you know, corruption in the cops. You know, children getting killed, bystanders. You know, just, just, just full. It's something you wouldn't imagine. You know? But from New Orleans to [Austin] is a big different world. It's a whole different world, the people here are beautiful, wonderful. They're so nice, everywhere you turn. You turn your back, everybody speaks to you. You know, they're concerned, like they care about you. It

makes you feel so good, that you still got people, you know, around that cares about you. It doesn't matter the race, or nationality, or anything. Beautiful.

(Alive in Truth 2005a)

Holt's concerns remind us of the importance of perspective: How we deal with one disaster will teach us lessons that will help us prepare for the future.

> And all these issues have been brought up but we need to keep them in the face of America because people easily forget, we forget so easily, but what has been happening down here in New Orleans and Louisiana is nothing new—people chose not to see it before. Katrina has brought out some of the ugliest things in this state, and that's the embarrassment—that the outside world has seen it. Katrina has brought out how our government treats the poorest of its poor—and that's an embarrassment. Katrina has brought it out, you know. I hope that all of America, that their hearts are touched, their conscience is raised and we need to do right by all our citizens because it's Louisiana today but there could very well be an earthquake in California tomorrow, or it could be a tornado in Oklahoma, you know. It could be anything, mudslides or snowstorms, where they would feel the same type of tragedy, not necessarily a hurricane but the devastation of that tragedy. Would you want the people of your state to be treated the way they treated the people in New Orleans?

(Mead 2005)

Using oral history will help prepare not only for future Katrinas, but future race and class divides. The past connects us to the present, and to the future; it is part of that human need for immortality of some sort. How investigators, lawmakers, and the public wade through the mountains of oral witness to evaluate what went wrong during and after Katrina will inform their decisions as they make plans for future responses.

How Americans weave this tragedy into their collective history and the lessons we take from the disaster will preoccupy the minds of pundits, historians, and both political and community leaders for generations. However, the impact of Hurricane Katrina is not limited to Louisiana, Mississippi, and the Gulf Coast. "Katrinaland" has become a national and international phenomenon that has struck both the nation and the world.

References

Alive in Truth. 2005a. Lynette T, interview September 20, 2005. Accessed January 20, 2006. http://www.aliveintruth.org/stories/lynette_t.htm.

_____ 2005b. Clarice B., October 12, 2005. Accessed January 20, 2005. http://www.aliveintruth. org/stories/clarice_b.htm.

American Folklife Center, Folkife Program. 2006. List of Hurricane Research Projects. Accessed 20 January. http://www.louisianafolklife.org/hurricane_projects.html.

Brinkley, Douglas. 2006. New Orleans: Diary of A Disaster. 132. *Vanity Fair* 132. June. Excerpted from *The Great Deluge: Hurricane Katrina, New Orleans, and the Mississippi Gulf Coast*, William Morrow, an imprint of HarperCollins, May 2006.

Chronicle of Higher Education Colloquy Live. 2002. Critical Oral History as a 'Scholarly Tool.' October 17. Accessed January 18, 2006. http://chronicle. com/colloquylive/2002/10/blight/.

Clark, Mary Marshall. 2003. The September 11, 2001, Oral History Narrative and Memory Project. In *History and September 11th*, ed. Joanne Meyerowitz. Philadelphia: Temple University Press, 125.

_____ 2005. E-mail message to H-Oralhist. Re: Katrina OH Project. September 14. Accessed at http://h-net.msu.edu/cgi-bin/logbrowse.pl?trx=vx&list=h-oralhist&month=0509&week =c&msg=fipOoibMC7xz4lboKrUTSg&user=&pw=.

Dallas Morning News. 2005. Hurricanes' Havoc Overwhelming Choice as Top '05 News Story. December 22.

Gardner, James B. and Sarah M. Henry. 2002. September 11 and the Mourning After: Reflections on Collecting and Interpreting the History of Tragedy. *Public Historian* 24 (Summer): 41.

Hodges, Leah. 2005. Testimony before the Select Bipartisan Committee to Investigate the Preparation for and Response to Hurricane Katrina. December 6. Accessed December 20. http://katrina.house.gov/hearings/12_06_05/hodges_120605.rtf.

Hurricane Digital Memory Bank. 2006. May 15. Accessed at http://www.hurricanearchive.org/.

Johnson, Peter. 2005. Media Mix: Katrina Could Forever Change How TV News Covers Storms. *USA Today*. September 25. Life section.

Kennedy, Stetson. 2005. Shame on Us! Op-Ed piece for the *New York Times*. Unpublished manuscript. September 3.

K'Meyer, Tracy E. 2005. Katrina OH Project e-mail message. September 13. Accessed at http:// h-net.msu.edu/cgi-bin/logbrowse.pl?trx=vx&list=H-Oralhist&month=0509&week=b& msg=bgZiWbA%2bLBxeRfPRAfGLZw&user=&pw=.

Louisiana Division of the Arts. 2006. In the Wake of the Hurricanes: A Coalition Effort to Collect Our Stories and Rebuild Our Culture. Accessed 20 January. http://www.louisianafolklife.org/katrina.html.

Mann, Phyllis E. 2005a. E-mail message to Chester Hartman. November 29.

_____ 2005b. Hurricane Relief Aid. *The Advocate: Louisiana Association of Criminal Defense Lawyers* 2, no. 4 (Fall): 3, 50–51.

Mead, Jerry. 2005. *Labor Express Radio*. Hurricane Katrina Reveals the True Race & Class Divide in U.S. Society: An Interview with Sibal Holt, President of the Louisiana AFL-CIO. December 21. Accessed at http://www.laborexpress.org/page7.html.

Myers, Lisa. 2005. Were the Levees Bombed in New Orleans? MSNBC. December 7. Accessed December 20 from http://www.msnbc.msn.com/id/10370145.

Oral History Association. 2006. Emerging Crises Oral History Research Fund. May 15. Accessed at http://www.dickinson.edu/organizations/oha/org_aw_ecoh.html.

Portelli, Alessandro. 1991. *The Death of Luigi Trastulli and Other Stories: Form and Meaning in Oral History*. Albany: State University of New York Press, p. 46.

Preuss, Gene B. 2005. E-mail message to H-Oralhist, Katrina OH Project. September 13. Accessed at http://h-net.msu.edu/cgi-bin/logbrowse.pl?trx=vx&list=H-Oralhist&month=0 509&week=b&msg=A%2bY3nNiWmbdMejZ5qoPGTQ&user=&pw=.

Scudder, John R. Jr. and Barbara Gulick. 1972. History's Purpose: Becker or Ortega? in *History Teacher*, Vol. 5, No. 4 (May), pp. 41–45.

Shilds, Gerard. 2005. Project to Record Storm Stories. *The Baton Rouge Advocate*. November 6.

Thomas, Holly Werner. 2005. E-mail message to H-Oralhist, Katrina OH Project. September 8. Accessed at http://h-net.msu.edu/cgi-bin/logbrowse.pl?trx=vx&list=H-Oralhist&month =0509&week=b&msg=kevhqGOTlW8fCdHxg0DZkg&user=&pw=.

Tuchman, Barbara. 1996. Distinguishing the Significant from the Insignificant. In *Oral History: An Interdisciplinary Anthology*, ed. David K. Dunaway and Willa K. Baum, 2nd ed. Walnut Creek: AltaMira, p. 96.

Young, Abe Louise. 2005. Alive in Truth. Accessed January 20 from http://www.aliveintruth. org/a_pages/our_process.htm.

Endnotes

1. Author John R. Tisdale wrote in *The Oral History Review* that "the journalist and the oral historian, however, are concerned with leaving information in a physical format to be studied later. Both are concerned with recording information, both are concerned with accuracy, and both rely on the interview as the primary source of information and credibility." John R. Tisdale, "Observational Reporting as Oral History: How Journalists Interpreted the Death and Destruction of Hurricane Audrey," *The Oral History Review*, Summer-Fall 2000 v27 i2 p41.

2. According to Maida Owens in an email to co-author Stein, her organization had the first of four anticipated budget cuts in 2005-06. State government will greatly be affected by the hurricanes, and learned society meetings will not likely be supported at all. Even travel expenses to the American Folklore Society will not be supported, forcing staff to take vacation days to attend. No changes are anticipated in the 2006 budget.

3. For more information please contact Gore Center Director Lisa Pruitt (lpruitt@mtsu. edu) or Project Coordinator Sarah Elizabeth Hickman (seh2r@mtsu.edu).

4. In the wake of Hurricane Katrina, cable news networks experienced huge spikes in ratings. See "Eyes On the Storm," in *Broadcasting & Cable* 135, no 36 (September 5, 2005): 6.

CHAPTER 4

Towards a Transformative View of Race

The Crisis and Opportunity of Katrina

john a. powell, HASAN KWAME JEFFRIES, DANIEL
W. NEWHART, AND ERIC STIENS

"You simply get chills every time you see these poor individuals ... so
many of these people ... are so poor and they are so black, and this
is going to raise lots of questions for people who are watching this
story unfold."

Wolf Blitzer on CNN, September 1, 2005[1]

Immediately after Hurricane Katrina ravaged New Orleans and the Gulf
Coast, journalists and laypeople struggled to find the words to express
their outrage over the situation. In a very real way, the devastation wrought
by the storm challenged normative perspectives on race and class in this
country. The disturbing images of poor African Americans struggling to
survive in an abandoned city and the inadequate response of the government forced uncomfortable thoughts into the national consciousness. Suddenly, race and class mattered, and mattered more than most people were
prepared to acknowledge. When a national dialogue began, however, it
was clear that existing vocabulary was incapable of explaining what everyone was seeing. Like Wolf Blitzer, many people were left stumbling over
the links between race and class, and left trying to figure out why Katrina's
destructive force disproportionately impacted African-American and poor
communities (Berube and Katz 2005). Katrina raised many questions for

everyone who watched the story unfold. How we answer these questions is vitally important.

Soon after the levees broke, politicians and pundits tried feverishly to ease our discontent. They assured us that nature is colorblind, and that the government response, although clearly inadequate, was not a result of racial animus. We were told that class and poverty, rather than race, were the keys to understanding the crisis. Conservatives even went so far as to drape poverty in the rhetoric of welfare-as-dependency, arguing that government assistance had created a culture of victimization. Progressives, for their part, talked about the absence of an adequate safety net to deal with persistent poverty. Yet, questions about *why* African Americans are more likely than whites to be poor, and why poor African Americans are more likely to live in areas of concentrated poverty, are questions that were neither asked nor answered (Muhammed et al. 2004). The mainstream media did make some effort to engage the issue of race, but the resulting discussions either suffered from a reliance on racial stereotypes or failed to move beyond race-based human interest stories. There was little critical discussion of how historical patterns of segregation contributed to the racial layout of the city, and how structures worked together to produce racial disparities and economic inequality.[2]

For far too long Americans have been trapped in an individualistic mode of thinking about race and racism that requires there to be a racist actor in order for there to be a racist action, and that separates race and class into distinct categories. As the full extent of the damage to New Orleans became clear, the nation as a whole struggled to make sense of the situation by filtering visual images and sound bites through the dominant individualistic framework. Consequently, people asked: Is President Bush a racist or simply incompetent?[3] Were so many poor African Americans affected by the storm because they were poor or because they were black, or was it because of their culture? Would the response to Katrina have been different had New Orleans been mostly white? How could so many things have gone wrong in a country that prides itself on responsibility and opportunity?

Unfortunately, thinking about racism narrowly as a product of individual intent is not particularly helpful. Not only does it tend to be divisive because the conversations that follow often center on assigning blame and finding culpability—rather than on change—but it also diverts attention from the function of structures and institutions in perpetuating disparities, while simultaneously locating racism in the mind of individuals. Furthermore, it limits thinking about the negative effects of structures on non-whites, even though there is strong evidence that suggests that were it not for racialized structures most Americans would be substantially better off (Barlow 2003). Thus, broadening how we think and talk about race is critically important for making sense of today's world. Doing so also raises critical questions about the shrinking middle class, our anemic investment in public space, the meaning of merit in a purported meritocracy, and the promises and failures of our democratic experiment—all of which concern every American. Once we are able to discuss race and racism in these broad terms, we will be able to construct a response not only to the damage wrought by Katrina, but also to that which occurs across the country every day.

Katrina was a nightmare for the Gulf Coast, but it also created a unique opportunity to rebuild the Gulf Coast region in a way that transforms pre-existing, long-lasting structural arrangements. More specifically, it created an opportunity for reexamining the connections between race and class, and deciphering precisely how race has been inscribed spatially into our metropolitan areas. In short, it has provided a rare chance to discuss the links between race, equity, justice, and democracy.

Race, as a transformative tool, can and should be applied to more than just the rebuilding effort in New Orleans. Racialized poverty, segregation, and the decaying infrastructure of our central cities are common problems plaguing urban areas nationwide. Used properly, race allows us to examine how institutional failings affect everyone, and enables us to re-imagine a society where democracy and democratic ideals are not constricted and undermined by structural arrangements.

In this chapter, we propose a model for understanding race-class linkages and how racial disparities are reproduced in the United States through structural arrangements that benefit only a few. Although racial disparities are evidence of structural racism, and underscore the fact that our democracy is not functioning as it should (if people truly had collective control over the decisions that affect their lives, would they voluntarily put themselves into areas of concentrated poverty and substandard schools?), drawing attention to these realities is not our primary goal. We do not simply want to eliminate racial disparities. More than that, we want to challenge the structures that are creating them and rebuild new structures to replace them that will produce better life chances for all of us.

We suggest an alternative not only for thinking about what we saw on the Gulf Coast, but also for what we would be able to see every day in our cities if only we had the eyes to see and the words to describe the interactions between race, class, and structures. Thus, we aim to provide a new vocabulary for expanding the discussions about race and class that have arisen in living rooms and boardrooms across the country, and to offer suggestions for what a racially just and equitable response to Katrina might look like.

Through our collective actions and inactions we have created an interconnected web of structures that not only perpetuate group-based inequalities, but distribute meaning as well. Once in place, these arrangements appear to have a logic and momentum of their own, creating a cycle that seems as inevitable as it is vicious. We do not believe, however, that this reflects the natural order of things. Post-Katrina, we saw a collective stirring of compassion and discontent by the country as a whole for our current unjust arrangements. The massive outpouring of donations and volunteer hours by people who seemingly had no self-interest in the crisis, for example, signified that our country cared in some way about what was happening in New Orleans. Our collective conscience has been piqued, and we hope to engage this compassion in a productive way here.

We recognize, however, that the term racism is laden with political and cultural baggage, primarily because it assumedly assigns blame and wrongdoing. Thus, in order to be useful as a transformative tool, as we propose here, the term must be divorced from its association with individual actors or racist actions. Undoubtedly, those who believe that the U.S. has moved beyond racism, or who blame racism on the moral failing of some individual, will label our project misguided. At the same time, those who have been injured by racism might object to our unwillingness to find an individual or group at fault. While we agree with the latter that racism cannot be addressed without locating and naming the cause, we believe that individualized explanations of racism are simply inadequate.

We also acknowledge the difficulty many people have with the concept of white privilege. The idea violates the American sense of individuality and suggests that whites have received something they did not earn legitimately. In addition, many whites believe that it is a way to shift responsibility for the failures of people of color onto them. Many of them are struggling to make ends meet, given rising health care costs, declining job security, and dwindling pensions, and simply find the idea of white privilege untenable. How can they be privileged while struggling to get by themselves? We assert that both this privilege and this assault are real. However, racial meaning makes it difficult to see that this assault is coming not from non-whites, but from a particular set of socioeconomic systems, a particular expression of corporate globalization, and a democratic experiment that has not yet come to full fruition.

Class and Race: Patterns of Damage, Patterns of Response

When the levees were topped and New Orleans began to flood, the mainstream media continued to fixate on the destructive force of Katrina's winds to the exclusion of everything else, including race and racism. The media presented an endless array of equations for calculating and assessing potential storm damage, but none of these formulas included race as an input variable. Even after the floodwaters forced thousands of the city's black residents onto rooftops, and compelled thousands more to wade through waist-deep toxic sludge to reach higher ground in the Central Business District, no one mentioned it.

The lack of an explicit focus on race and racism did not mean that they were absent from the public discourse. One of the dangers of not discussing race openly when it is clearly present is that we are likely to discuss it in a subterranean manner that allows stereotypes, fear, and racial meaning to emerge without being challenged. Consequently, during the Katrina crisis, race was a part of practically every conversation, but it was implicit rather than explicit. The city's black residents, for example, were often described as victims of a storm rather than survivors of a terrible calamity. To be a victim is to be helpless, but to be a survivor is to possess courage and creative skills. The former denies agency, while the latter acknowledges it. Similarly, black survival behavior was treated as criminal behavior, while similar acts by others were celebrated. African Americans searching for food, water, childcare necessities, and basic medical supplies were selfish looters, but doctors, police, and white tourists doing the same were selfless heroes. In a like manner, the city's black residents were dubbed refugees rather than evacuees as they sought safety and shelter in nearby towns and cities as though they were not citizens of this country.

That racial stereotypes and meaning plagued initial Katrina coverage is not a surprise. The mainstream media has never been known for advanced thinking on matters involving race. Neither is it a surprise that early on the media avoided discussing race explicitly. At first, the major news outlets skirted the issue because they deemed it irrelevant. Poor blacks represented the overwhelming majority of those trapped in the city, not because they were black but because they were poor, and as poor people they did not have sense enough to heed pre-storm evacuation warnings. Also, the mainstream media, like most of white America, views discussions of racism as divisive and seeks to avoid such conversations in mixed company whenever possible.

The endless parade of forlorn black faces and desperate and angry black voices emanating from the city, however, made it obvious even to the most skeptical observer that race was a part of the unfolding story. Less obvious, though, was whether or not racism was involved. Consequently, when the mainstream media finally broached the subject, it did not seek to discover how racism contributed to this catastrophe, but only whether it was a factor. Of course, the racism that the media searched for once it began looking was limited only to individuals.

Pundits and reporters on both the right and the left concluded quickly and confidently that racism played no role in the disaster. After all, Mother Nature is colorblind. Katrina did not target New Orleans because it was 68% African American, but rather because the city just happened to be in the path of the hurricane.[4] People, not storms, create racism, and there was absolutely no evidence that anyone had engaged in a willful act of purposeful discrimination. Had not the city's black residents received the same advance warning as everyone else? In addition, no one forced them to stay put, and on top of that, the city was run by black elected officials. How could racism be a factor if the mayor and the police chief are African-American?

Meanwhile, African Americans, both inside and outside the disaster zone, struggled mightily to explain what they knew intuitively and experientially to be true. But in their efforts, they too ended up talking about racism strictly in personal terms. Like hip-hop artist Kanye West, they tended to point to President Bush and the incomprehensibly slow pace at which he marshaled federal resources to respond to the crisis. But the same people who dismissed racism balked at this insinuation. Conservatives conceded that the administration's response was inadequate, but argued that it was merely a function of bureaucratic ineffectiveness, while progressives attributed it to the President's personal ineptitude. Besides, President Bush never said anything racist about the city's black residents, nor did he order federal personnel to treat them any differently than others affected by the storm.

Those who rejected racism as a contributing factor to the disaster, as well as those who knew it was involved, somehow focused so much of their attention on identifying or dismissing the racist behavior of individuals, including that of the President, that the overall discourse on the role of race and racism lacked substance. For the most part, there was no discussion of the myriad ways race informed the social, economic, and political factors that converged long before Katrina made landfall to make New Orleans ripe for a disaster that would hit the city's black residents the hardest. Generally, just about everyone failed to discuss local patterns of residential segregation. They ignored the fact that grossly disproportionate numbers of African Americans lived in neighborhoods that were below sea level. Some pointed out that African Americans comprised 98% of the Lower Ninth Ward, but said little if anything about how this came to be (Greater New Orleans Community Data Center 2005a). Similarly, some noted the sickeningly high poverty rate among the city's black residents, but said nothing about how racialized poverty contributed to the crisis. Neither the concentration of subsidized housing, nor the lack of car ownership among poor blacks—which made it impossible for many African Americans to flee New Orleans because the city's middle-class-oriented evacuation plan was predicated on people leaving in their own vehicles—were mentioned. Racialized disinvestment in schools, public health, and other critical institutions in the core city, which impacts the suburbs as well, has existed for decades, but unlike the wind and the water, it garnered little attention. We do not believe that anyone intended to strand poor blacks in New Orleans. But it was predictable, given that we tend to regard poor people differently than we do others.

The inability of Americans, both white and black, conservative and progressive, to analyze the Katrina disaster in a way that would have rendered visible the central role of structural racism in the disaster resulted from the narrow way in which we tend to understand racism. The normative conceptualization of racism is that it is a deliberately harmful discriminatory act perpetrated by people who possess outmoded racial beliefs. It is the aberrant behavior of white supremacists and is easily identified by the discriminatory intent of perpetrators. Furthermore, it is static. It is an offense committed by a particular person at a specific moment in time. Racism happens, and then it ends.

Racism, however, is as much a product of systems and institutions as it is a manifestation of individual behavior. Indeed, structural arrangements produce and reproduce racial outcomes and can reinforce racial attitudes. The normative conceptualization of racism as primarily a psychological event, therefore, is inadequate and incomplete. Above all else, it fails to consider the ways institutions work together to perpetuate racial disparities (powell 2006). It is hardly surprising, then, that in the discourse on the Katrina crisis, almost no one acknowledged that the connections between public and private institutions over space and time limited the resources and opportunities of the city's black residents and conspired to place them directly in harm's way.

Focusing on individual acts of racism is not irrelevant, but it is not enough. How society frames racism dictates its response to it or lack thereof. Thus, broadening the normative conceptualization of racism is essential to promote racial justice. At the moment, the predominance of the inadequate explanation has created space for conservatives to advance their strategic agenda. By arguing that the city's black residents were vulnerable to the destructive force of Katrina because of their dependency on the welfare state, they have tried to use this logic for the ideological agenda of continuing to dismantle the welfare social state. By pointing to the inadequate federal response as evidence of the inherent weakness of big government, they have attempted to win support for the position that the state is not the proper organ to respond to our needs. Instead, they offer faith-based organizations and a "pure market response" reminiscent of pre-New Deal social arrangements. By decrying looting and the inability of local law enforcement to protect property, they have sought to enhance the position of a police state and to loosen gun control restrictions. By personalizing racism and then denying its existence, they have eliminated racism as a factor to be considered in their plans to rebuild the city.

Although African Americans are not immune from thinking of racism in terms of psychological deviance and abnormal individual behavior, this perspective resonates most strongly among whites because it spares them from having to think critically about their own racial privilege. What's more, it frees whites of culpability in the persistence of racial disparities and releases them from any obligation to do something about institutionalized racism.

Viewing racism narrowly is nothing new. In fact, it dates back several generations, but it was not until the civil rights era that it became the dominant paradigm of racial understanding. By the mid-1960s, whites outside the South conceded that *de jure* segregation was unjust and acquiesced to black demands to make it unlawful by supporting the Civil Rights Act of 1964. At the same time, they acknowledged that prejudice existed in the North, but believed deeply that racism was a Southern problem and that its most insidious manifestation was the irrational, violent behavior of unenlightened southern hayseeds, from members of terrorist organizations, including the Ku Klux Klan, to southern lawmen, such as Birmingham's Bull Connor.

This myopic approach allowed the country to reject the expressive ideology of racism while continuing to support public polices and institutional arrangements that perpetuated racial disparities but made no direct mention of race. The national presumption became that racism does not exist unless one can prove that a racist actor caused it. The persistence of racial disparities, therefore, had nothing to do with racism and everything to do with the failure of the racial other to take full advantage of the unlimited opportunities that were available to all. Whites who benefited from these structures were not privileged, but innocent people who had earned what they had acquired, and, unlike racial minorities, were deserving of national respect. The formal end of Jim Crow was seen as proof positive that racism, except for the occasional bigot, was all but dead.

The crisis created by Katrina has created an opportunity for moving beyond the individualistic framework commonly used in this country to understand not just race but also class in this country. Much like racism, class is often thought about in terms of individual behavior. It is widely believed that people are mired in the lower class because of some personal social defect such as laziness. The only depersonalized social force that is ever mentioned is bad luck. This broader conversation, therefore, is not just important to people of color, but to all Americans. The structural arrangements that create racial disparities, a widening wealth gap, and a shrinking middle class affect everyone.

Often, when we use the word class, we are referring to socioeconomic status, which is useful primarily as a descriptor for individuals or families. A more structural view would allow us instead to view class as a complex position within a nested set of social and power relationships (Mahoney 2003). This is especially important as language around class is used to distort and realign people's interests. One example of this is the use of the term "middle class," which is employed in this country to describe a family making $30,000 a year, living in a rapidly declining, first-ring suburb, with little job security or savings, as well as a family making $150,000 a year, living in a rapidly growing exurb with strong public schools and an expanding job base. Clearly, there are different economic interests here, and different connections to opportunities.

Furthermore, race and class have long been intertwined in the United States to an extent not seen in most other countries. In America, racial concerns have always had a powerful effect on the meaning of class, just as class interests have been a defining factor in the construction of race and racial meaning. Chattel slavery did not exist in any other nation during the years of significant working-class formation. The existence of slavery at a time when servitude was seen as incompatible with the ideals of liberty was a stimulus for a racialized ideology. Race exclusion and white suffrage were significant ways in which white workers responded to fears arising from changes wrought by industrialization. Although poor blacks and poor whites had much in common, white workers secured voting rights while blacks were increasingly excluded from the political sphere. Thus, even when poor whites have low economic and social status in comparison with other whites, their status concerns have the capacity to doom prospects for interracial collective action and even working-class unity. This problem has confounded class-based political organizing in the U.S. for more than two centuries.

Historians Eric Foner and David Roediger observe that the formation of class in this country occurred in opposition to enslaved African Americans and later to freed men and women. This helped to create a hyper-attachment to a link between race, poverty, and dependency. It also created a sense of white solidarity that helps explain the weak sense of class solidarity that exists today (Alesina and Glaeser 2004; Foner and Roediger 1989). The influence does not stop there. Many of our critical institutions built into their original design structures to protect white supremacy, including slavery, even at the expense of whites.[5] As a result of the simultaneous development of racial and class consciousness, class tensions have consistently been relieved through racial baiting. At times, whites have benefited, such as when whites gained suffrage rights. Overall, however, and particularly during the last 70 years and especially regarding social citizenship, whites' life chances have become more limited as a result of our racial history than they otherwise would have been. By convincing non-elite whites that wealth redistribution policies favor minorities, race has been used to chisel away at progressive measures. Some poor whites are willing to vote against redistribution that would favor them because their racial animosity seeks to prevent African Americans from receiving the same redistributive benefit. Economists Alberto Alesina and Edward Glaeser (2004:134) note that "proponents of the welfare state generally attempt to draw distinctions between economic classes. Racial, religious and ethnic divisions distract from those distinctions and reduce the ability to forge a common class-based identity." They estimate that the impact of racial fractionalization on welfare spending may explain about 50% of the gap between the United States and Europe in funds used for welfare.

It is vital that we pay attention to entrenched racial disparities because they manifest the failings of our democracy. Legal scholars Lani Guinier and Gerald Torres (2002) point out that the racially marginalized are not unlike the canaries used underground by miners to warn them of impending danger. Racial disparities are leading indicators of trouble, and just like canaries gasping for air, the marginalized are signaling that this democracy is in trouble because injustices are reproducing themselves and structural arrangements are benefiting a few at the expense of the many. Without a doubt, the greatest burdens in this country are shouldered by poor people of color, but they are not the only ones who are suffering. The uneven way we fund schools harms white students as well as students of color. The way our institutions perpetuate and increase wealth disparities has shrunk the middle class. Slashing social safety net programs in the name of increasing personal responsibility has added millions of people to the ranks of the working poor. Consequently, we can use the Katrina crisis as a launching pad not only for investigating the way we think and talk about race in this country, but also for developing a new discourse on race and class that highlights how the public and private are related, how democracy and structural arrangements that produce disparate outcomes are incompatible, and why institutional inequality concerns us all. In this way, our discussion about race can become transformative; instead of dividing people, it can bring them closer together in a collective reimagining of a just society.

How Space is Racialized

In a conversation about the aftermath of Hurricane Katrina, Congressman Charles Rangel, a Democrat from New York, stated that "George Bush is our Bull Connor" (Clyne 2005).[6] Yet, for all of the administration's mismanagement of Katrina, it is not at all easy to accept that personal racial animus was the cause, just as it is not clear that individual racism causes white voters to reject public school funding, prompts metropolitan governments to pass exclusionary zoning ordinances, or results in public transportation systems falling into decline. Yet these are exactly some of the ways that a segregated society walls off poor people of color from areas of opportunity.

We need to ask how and why segregation is maintained. The answer to how can no longer be found in explicit arrangements of *de jure* segregation, but instead in the impacts of a variety of structural arrangements. The creation and *re*creation of black ghettos in the United States is no mystery. It has been examined in depth by authors such as Douglas Massey and Nancy Denton (1993), and by some of the contributors to this volume. We can trace the ghettos back to race-specific practices by governmental agencies, including the FHA, and to uneven tax allocation, zoning laws, transportation spending, and the increasing devolution of power to ever-smaller jurisdictions (Ford 1995; Massey and Denton 1993; Rusk 1999; Schill and Wachter 1995). The degree to which this discussion is largely "off the table" is not a function of the relative difficulty of pinpointing the origin of the conversation, but rather reflects the degree that individual agency has been privileged at the expense of collective action and social structures.

Answering why segregation persists to this day is somewhat more complicated. Part of the reason is because it fosters racialized poverty and opportunity. While poverty is certainly a phenomenon that crosses racial and geographic lines, the overwhelming face of poverty in this country is urban-dwelling and African-American. Segregation also helps us *race* society. It continually helps recreate the social categories to which we commonly ascribe racial meaning. White space, or the outer-ring suburbs, plays an important role in maintaining an increasing fragile white privilege. So too does the existence of ghettos. Michel Laguerre (1999) argues that in order to have ethnic minorities, one must have minoritized space. This space, he says, allows the dominant group to "naturalize" the idea of uneven development among various groups. The dominant group can then use space as a separator to keep non-dominant groups in a "subordinate position" (Laguerre 1999:106). This separation will appear to be incidental or organic in the same way that our structures seem natural (Bonilla-Silva 2003). Thus, divestment from urban areas (53% of African Americans live in central cities) has had radically disparate racial effects, even in the absence of overt racial intent (Bullard and Wright 2005). Consequently, areas of racialized poverty are accepted as natural, as if they have always existed, and will always exist.

Residential segregation has produced "white space." But white space is tremendously unstable. As globalization expands in a post-Jim Crow era, and as the identity of a particular space comprised of individuals who are "white" comes under assault, "white space" means less and less. Many whites are averse to being labeled racist, but they also refuse to surrender forms of privilege, such as access to preferred residential space. What needs to be propelled forward is the idea that space racialization affects us all. Barlow (2003) examines how modern white space was created in the form of suburbs after World War II. Support for this space came from the elites. In the 1960s, with the end of Jim Crow and the growing economy, as well as the Civil Rights Movement, the boundaries of the suburbs became more porous. This reflected not only a change in space, but also a change in the meaning of white space and whiteness.

Racism itself has also changed. Although the color stigmatization of black persists, and with it racialized attitudes, contemporary racism is more based on hoarding than explicit animosity. Yet white privilege overwhelms working-class common interests that might encourage workers to seek multiracial and multinational unity. On the other hand, a white worker also has a real material interest in preserving his or her privileged access to jobs, political power, citizenship, social services, education, and housing, among other things. Globalization is unleashing forces that are creating crises not only in poorer nations of color, but also within the United States. As globalization takes its toll, the national economy is increasingly bifurcating, between jobs that require little skill and education and those that require college or postgraduate degrees. The "college premium," or the average amount a college graduate earns over a non-college-educated worker, was 31% in 1979. By 1993, it had jumped to 53% (Barlow 2003). This trend reflects the fact that low-skilled jobs can be transported overseas at a greatly reduced wage rate. Moreover, although real wages have been stagnant, the cost of health care, education, retirement, and housing has risen exponentially, further stressing the middle class. A debate has sprung up about the nature of outsourcing in our country. Middle-class workers are working longer and harder, but feel as though they are standing on a melting ice cube.

The dominant politics of this era has sought to galvanize middle-class voters by appealing to their fear of falling into the lower wealth strata. From anti-immigrant policies, to attacks on civil rights policies such as affirmative action, the high-profile war on drugs, to the expansion of prisons, the use of the death penalty, and the war on terrorism, politicians have become highly skilled at creating dangerous foes to attack and contain. Creating a climate of fear has shored up the ideologically popular perception of the white middle class as honest and hard-working. Claims that "immigrants" are taking away their jobs and using their social services have served as convenient explainers for the declining standards of living. In short, global pressures mean that an increasing number of Americans feel left out of the social order because they no longer have access to stable jobs, home ownership, and college education. As Americans begin to question whether or not they can achieve the goals of a middle-class lifestyle, new political and ideological spaces will open up.

Because of globalization, the elites began to hoard their resources and insisted that they could no longer help pay for this new arrangement. The cost was shifted to the stagnating middle class, and they objected to this change. What the middle class failed to realize was that the elite retreat was not just from supporting the costs associated with racial justice; their retreat was a rejection of adequate support of all public structures and institutions. This shift has contributed to the assault on the middle class. Because non-whites are now trying to fit into a shrinking middle class, this assault is understood in racial terms instead of global terms. The current iteration of globalization, with its demands for no taxes and the distribution of fiscal responsibility downward, is contributing both to the decline of the middle class and the stalling of racial justice (Barlow 2003).

It is clear that we cannot properly address the problem of poverty and our failing urban infrastructures without using a racial language. If we do not use a racial language, we unreflectively move to the language of class. But this move presumes that we collectively have a functional handle on the concept of class, and we do not.[7] There is much to suggest that an adequate concept of class in the U.S. requires some understanding of race. Even acknowledging that these concepts are interrelated can mask the complex dynamic and lull one into reductionism. We can explain race by class and/ or we can explain class by race. But this error ignores the fact that, while interactive, there is not a one-to-one relationship. Consider the effort to explain racial segregation simply by class or poverty, which is often done. This attempted explanation fails to account for the difference between economic segregation and racial segregation. According to statistics from the Mumford Center, focused on New Orleans, the Dissimilarity Index between poor households and affluent households in New Orleans is 38.8.[8] This is to be expected, as affordability and level of income is a strong predictor of where people live. However, when we examine the Dissimilarity Index by race, we find that economic status plays a minor role. In all African American households in New Orleans (regardless of economic status), the Mumford Center found that the dissimilarity index between African American and whites is 67.7. If class had a one-to-one relationship with race, we would not see these types of differences. On average, the Mumford Center findings indicate that in most cities, neighborhoods are more segregated by race than class status. This makes it necessary to focus not only on class as it relates to race but also on race as a separate dynamic.

We are proposing structural racism as an alternative to thinking of race and class in individualistic ways (powell 2006). Structural racism differs from institutional racism in that institutional racism refers to practices and conditions in a single institution. While it is important to transform institutional behavior, that behavior cannot be thought of as located solely within the target institution. Just as individual strategies alone cannot adequately address institutional racism, focusing solely on single institutions cannot adequately address structural racism because the interaction of multiple institutions creates disparate effects.[9]

By using a structural analysis, we believe that race can be used as a transformative tool to collectively partake in the remaking and restructuring of society for the benefit not only of people of color, but for entire communities, regions, and the nation (Guinier and Torres 2002). When we are able to successfully transform these structural arrangements, we will be able to transform ourselves, including our group-based identities and the benefits they confer (The Center for Social Inclusion 2005). Using a structural racism lens will help us create a methodology for supporting conditions that lead to transformative changes. Our failure to develop an alternative to racialized space in residential areas, for example, is limiting both the life chances of individuals and the democratic potential of our country. However, if we begin to examine how transportation, educational systems, health care, and housing all interact to create racialized spaces, we can begin to create a space that is comprehensive and hopefully just in its applications. This will inch us closer towards creating a truly free democracy.

Analyzing society through a structural racism lens is predicated on the idea that the combined effects of institutional arrangements and structures have racialized outcomes even when individual structures appear to be race-neutral. A birdcage analogy, created by Marilyn Frye, illustrates this point (Frye 1983; Young 2001). Looking at each of the bars of a birdcage individually, it is hard to understand how they could restrict a bird. Yet, examining the birdcage in its entirety allows one to see how the bars link together to form a structure with a greater restrictive effect than each bar could have on its own. Only several bars, connected and arranged in a specific way, can form a cage. Like a birdcage, racism is a discrete arrangement of structures that limits potential and possibility. A structural racism lens, therefore, is needed to make sense of the complex interplay of factors that reproduce racial disparities and depress opportunities. A structural racism approach that directs our attention to racial considerations can implicate the design of institutional arrangements. And even more important than the design, structural racism helps us to focus on the actual work that institutional arrangements are doing in the production of racialized conditions and meaning.

Consider the appropriateness of connections between neighborhood and local schools. We cannot evaluate this appropriateness without knowing something about the neighborhood as well as the tax or funding structures. A local school district that draws students from the immediate area may be racially segregated if the housing market is segregated. Similarly, the funding base for the school district might be structurally inadequate if based in a low-wealth jurisdiction. In this example, taxation, zoning, housing, and wealth issues affect schools. These arrangements could easily produce low-income students who are physically segregated and dependent upon inadequate, segregated funding mechanisms. How we think about schools needs to be informed by the other institutions that impact education. A change outside of an educational institution can cause a decline in the economic yield that supports schools. This change could have a devastating impact on education without someone ever intending that result. Our efforts to integrate students are frequently frustrated by school boundaries issues and the way we have approached local control. As we think about the changing economy and our increasingly complex democracy, the way we think about and deliver education may need to be reconsidered. Education, like all institutions, exists in a web. Our goals can be frustrated or enhanced not only at the site of the educational institution, but also at the site of other institutions in alignment with our educational institutions. We must examine what work institutional arrangements *are* doing, not simply what they were designed to do. In a post-Jim Crow era, racial subordination will not be one of the stated goals, and there might be a number of legitimate reasons for the way we fund schools, draw school zones, and structure our housing market, but this does not mean that structural racism is not at play in the production of the racialized environments that are so prominent in our educational system. No single person may be responsible, but we are collectively responsible. If our goal is to create opportunity in order to effectively participate in the economy and our democracy, it behooves us to consider the factors that support and limit people in their participation in a just and equitable way.

This does not mean, however, that we cannot talk about individual responsibility. In fact, we must talk about it. At the same time, we need a new way of incorporating and discussing collective responsibility. As we think about responsibility, though, we must begin to move away from a liability model to a social connection model (Young 2003). It is no longer enough to blame individuals for social problems. Rather, we must recognize that individuals bear responsibility for injustice as far as their actions or inactions contribute to the larger processes and institutional arrangements that produce unjust outcomes.

Part of the difficulty in achieving this goal stems from the way people tend to separate the private and the public, the individual and the collective. The social structures that we create also recreate us. We must begin to talk about the interconnectedness between the public and the private, and examine how social structures distribute meaning and interest, as well as benefits and burdens. We often talk about "getting over racism" as if it is simply a false set of prejudices tacked onto already existing differences. This is not the case. Rather, our social and political structures create race as we know it based on a system of oppression and subjugation. In this way, race has been used to undermine the democratic process and ideals that we in this country share. Race as we understand it does not exist somewhere outside a system of racial disparities, just as whiteness does not exist outside of white supremacy (Roediger 1999).

Another part of the problem is that we often move to the institutional level without taking the next step outward to the structural level. That is, we have not begun to grapple with how racial subjugation can become inscribed into institutional structures. See, for example, the research that points towards racial and cultural bias in many U.S. standardized education tests and the relationship between test scores and access to further academic opportunities via tracking, scholarships, etc. (Rosner 2001a, 2001b). Yet a structural vantage point would move beyond this and start to consider how the complex interplay of factors as diverse as funding schools through property taxes, inadequate public transportation systems, intergenerational wealth transfer, racist acts by students or teachers, and the employment status of parents form a complex web that systematically denies educational opportunities to poor students of color.

While we propose the use of race as a transformative tool for change, we should acknowledge some of the challenges to this approach. A structural approach is not just about economic interest. Economic interest is important, but there are other considerations in using a structural analysis. For example, it has been found that whites have strong negative attitudes towards African Americans as well as toward the ideas of group and symbolic interest. Some studies have found that whites, while not exhibiting overtly racist attitudes towards African Americans, still hold less favorable feelings that in turn influence policy attitudes (Manza 2000). Furthermore, it has been found that in the presence of a large group of African Americans, whites will often become more sensitive to issues of race, presumably because of a perceived "threat" to their political, economic, and social status. Finally, in a society where segregation is present, racial and ethnic groups experience a sense of competition over a minimal amount of resources. As such, whites will generate stereotypes of non-whites to justify their dominance in the racially divided society.

But attitudes and interest themselves are not just givens. They are influenced by institutional arrangements, intragroup contact, and forms of leadership. These conditions are constantly changing and present both a challenge and an opportunity for transformative change.

One could use the changes in these conditions to soften or harden racial boundaries. This means, among other things, that what we do and how we do it matters. The point here is that we are in a newly changing environment that has present within it some fluidity.[10] A transformative approach to race requires that we open up the thinking of race to see how whites are both negatively and positively impacted by our institutional arrangements. We suggest that the negative impact is becoming more significant. But this does not mechanically result in multiracial coalitions or a convergence of interests. What options are on the table and how we think, act, and build institutions and practices matter. A transformative approach recognizes the interrelationship between race and class but does not reduce one to the other. This approach has much promise, but the promise it offers is not given. It requires that we better understand race, class, gender, and other phenomena. Race avoidance will not serve this transformative effort.

A New Lens, A New Vocabulary, A New Avenue for Change

Employing this lens provides a new vocabulary for talking about race and thinking about racial justice. No longer must we be caught up in issues of guilt and blame, in pointing fingers or decrying our innocence. Using this new lens allows us to understand how race continues to sort opportunity in this country, without having to find racists. This is not to say that this form of racial subjugation is somehow less harmful than previous, more overt forms. Structural racism can be just as deadly as a lynching, and just as effective at maintaining segregation as a "For Whites Only" sign. When blacks and Hispanics are systematically denied access to jobs, healthcare, and educational opportunities, and are living in unhealthy areas of concentrated poverty, frustration and anger are appropriate responses. However, the productive capability of the collective anguish felt after Katrina will be lost if it is directed at blaming individuals. Instead, we must channel it into a meaningful structural analysis that will allow us to avoid repeating the mistakes of the past, in part by imagining a new way of living together and creating an integrated and vibrant city. Realizing this vision requires the participation of everyone, black as well as white. The deleterious realities of structural racism in New Orleans did not start with Katrina; rather, Katrina showed us some of them in a striking way. These realities are not necessarily unique to this disaster. Time and time again, we have seen that disasters, whether "natural" or manmade, disproportionately affect the most marginalized members of society. In the severe heat wave that hit Chicago in 1995, for example, poor people, people of color, and the elderly were among those most likely to have died (Klinenberg 2002).

In New Orleans, the geography of race led directly to a disproportionate storm impact (Muro and Sohmer 2005). People of color were more likely to be living in areas of lower elevation, and therefore were at greater risk of being affected by flooding. Indeed, areas with less opportunity and high concentrations of poor people of color, such as the Ninth Ward, experienced the most damage (powell, Reece, and Gambhir 2005). Consequently, a purely class analysis is incapable of fully explaining what happened. The people who lived in these areas were poor, but they were also African-American, and like many other African-American urban dwellers, they had been concentrated in a depressed, low-opportunity area.

There is no doubt that the United States is facing a crisis of racialized poverty. Indeed, the way race plays out through our use of space and how that impacts access to opportunities for people of color is *the* civil rights struggle for the twenty-first century. Crises are tragic and horrible, but also offer tremendous opportunities for growth and change. Throughout the Gulf Coast, especially in New Orleans, we have an amazing opportunity to rebuild collectively. We can, if we choose to, rebuild the political and economic structures of that city, as well as the physical ones, with justice and equity in mind. We can, in fact, use a racially aware response to transform the region into a place where justice thrives, and New Orleans in particular into a metropolitan area that avoids many of the pitfalls that have caused other metropolitan areas to stagnate. An equitable metropolis is a thriving metropolis.

This process must be both coordinated and democratic. Without public participation, reconstruction will benefit those who already have a disproportionate voice in this country: primarily rich, wealthy, and white men. We must think about voting rights for displaced citizens to ensure that the most affected communities play a central role in reconstruction. A large part of this process will be developing a communications and technology infrastructure to allow the public access to information and the decision-making process.

First, we must eliminate concentrated poverty. Prior to Katrina, New Orleans had one of the highest rates of concentrated poverty in the country, second highest among the nation's 50 largest cities (Berube and Katz

2005). Most of these areas need to be rebuilt, but they must not be rebuilt as static replicas of what they were, nor can this opportunity be used as an excuse for displacing residents. There is tension here, to be sure, between the right of displaced residents to return and creating affordable housing that is not concentrated in a few sections of the city. This tension, however, can be mitigated in large part by involving those most affected by the storm in the planning process.

There are multiple proposals on the table for how this can be accomplished including: housing voucher programs, expanding the Low Income Housing Tax Credit, inclusionary zoning, and models based on previously successful programs such as the Gautreaux experiment in Chicago and HUD's Moving to Opportunity program (Polikoff 2006; Rosenbaum and DeLuca 2000). It is not within the scope of this chapter to critique the merits of each of these. However, it is clear that racial integration as well as economic integration needs to be a part of any effort to build mixed-income communities. The very scale of the rebuilding that needs to occur can be an advantage, as well as a challenge, because it offers an opportunity for a re-envisioning of what an integrated and livable city might look like.

Also, a racially and economically just framework has to focus on access to opportunity. It is clear that this needs to occur in New Orleans and the Gulf Coast area, but it also must include the thousands of displaced residents who may or may not return voluntarily. We run the risk of simply shifting the black urban poor from one city to another, and from one opportunity-deprived community to another. The planning process must include provisions for connecting the "Gulf Coast Diaspora" to affordable housing, job training, economic opportunities, quality education, transportation, and health care. We must treat the citizens of New Orleans as a democracy should—that is, with equal opportunity for all.

We must focus on providing access to opportunity explicitly, both during the reconstruction process as well as afterwards. The reconstruction of the Gulf Coast will be labor-intensive and require tens of thousands of people working in tandem in order to be successful. Current and former residents of the Gulf Coast should be hired first for these jobs, and local laborers should be paid a living wage. We must put job-training programs into place so that residents are able to take advantage of the opportunities available during the redevelopment. Citizens need to have meaningful oversight of the billions of dollars that will be brought in by private development corporations to guarantee that development occurs in a way that benefits their communities, and not simply the shareholders of these companies.

Transit problems were a principal reason that the violent impact of Katrina was so disproportionately shouldered by poor African Americans. We must not allow this to occur in the future, and state and local authorities should implement immediate plans for the evacuation of residents who lack access to personal transportation. Transit also remains a key factor in connecting people with parts of metropolitan areas where opportunity flourishes, job growth is occurring, and high-quality schools exist. The expansion of public transit has to be a priority going forward.

Access to educational opportunities significantly affects well-being later in life. Not only must the public schools of New Orleans be repaired, but planners must think proactively about the linkages between residential integration and school integration. In 2003–2004, for example, 46.9% of public schools in Orleans Parish were in the "Academically Unacceptable" category, while only 5.7% of schools across Louisiana were in this category (Greater New Orleans Community Data Center 2005b). Planners must begin to consider how residential segregation, which leads to school segregation, is affecting these test scores, causing all of our children to suffer now, which in turn shuts them out from opportunity for their futures.

Lastly, health and environmental concerns are going to remain a part of life in the Gulf Coast area for decades. Officials need to take all precautions to ensure the safety of workers involved in the cleanup and redevelopment process. They need to mandate uniform standards for cleanup so that some communities do not disproportionately shoulder the burden of exposure to toxins. Most importantly, there needs to be a long-term monitoring and a grievance system established to ensure the health and safety of Katrina survivors, one that provides affordable access to healthcare if health problems arise in the future. The scale of redevelopment that is needed offers an opportunity to construct the city and surrounding areas with the next hundred years in mind. There have been sizable advances in "green buildings" over the past two decades, as well as in more environmentally-friendly methods of construction and waste disposal. Redevelopment plans need to include environmental planning as an explicit part of the process.

Throughout this process we must be proactively attentive to the ways in which all of these aspects of opportunity—housing, education, job training, employment, health care and transportation—interact with one another structurally. Adopting a regional approach to planning, therefore, is essential. Segregation, fragmentation, and concentrated poverty create barriers to opportunity for people of color and undermine the vitality and competitiveness of the entire region. An approach to rebuild in a just way must look at regions as a whole unit and create ways to more equitably distribute resources and opportunity throughout the region. It is not a coincidence that some of the poorest parts of New Orleans are also the places where the African-American population is very high (Berube and Katz 2005; Bullard 2005). It is important to consider how segregated space interacts with race and poverty, economic health, and democratic norms.

The resource disparity between cities and suburbs hurts not only inner-city residents and those who live in areas that have become isolated, but also encourages a dysfunctional, fragmented system. This system encourages destructive competition such as sprawl, inefficient duplication, and divestment in infrastructure and people. The health of the city and older suburbs is linked to the health of the entire region.

Finally, we must keep the discourse of race and racism alive and inclusive, rather than subterranean and divisive. This will take some strategizing, given the current inadequacy of public discourse. We should support national and local media campaigns, community initiatives, grassroots organizations, interdenominational efforts, and political maneuvering to transform our understanding of race and class. We will need to pay particular attention not only to the needs of poor and middle class blacks and other non-whites, but to those of poor and middle-class whites as well. Globalization and devolution place the vulnerable on precarious footing that will require us to work together to recreate more equitable life opportunities in New Orleans and throughout the nation.

Conclusion

Given the hesitancy of the United States to confront or discuss race, even after a disaster like Hurricane Katrina brought race to our attention, it is time for a new way of speaking about race and racism. As we stumbled over words to describe the pictures that appeared in our newspapers and on our television sets, we discovered that we did not have an adequate frame for articulating what was going on, not only in New Orleans but also in this country every day. Katrina demonstrated that race and class are still salient in the United States, but discussing and understanding *how* they matter is an important part of envisioning a racially just and democratic society.

What we point towards in this chapter is an idea that racial disparities are recreated by the interactions between structures and institutions. Access to opportunity remains extremely limited for the urban poor who are disproportionately African-American because of the way we have structured our cities, taxation policies, and transportation systems. Space in this country is highly racialized—our central cities and inner-ring suburbs are declining rapidly while our outer-ring suburbs and exurbs grow at a tremendous pace. This, combined with the increasing fragmentation of our governance structures and the willingness of municipalities to wall themselves off from metropolitan areas, has had the effect of redirecting money and resources away from urban communities, which are stagnating economically because of a shrinking tax base, lack of jobs, and declining public schools, and which are being poisoned by antiquated factories, landfills, and other polluting industries.

As this book makes clear, there is no doubt that disasters of all types have large social costs, but how these costs are distributed is largely a function of our political and social structures. In the case of Katrina, those in impoverished, segregated, urban neighborhoods were uprooted from their homes as the waters rose but had no chance to escape because policymakers assumed they had the means to escape.

We all know that segregated, poor neighborhoods exist; yet we hesitate to talk about them, if we talk about them at all. We discuss the social problems that arise from having spaces cut off from opportunity, yet we refuse to include race in the discussion. Instead, we embrace any and all alternative explanations for this phenomenon. Too often, we revert to a colorblind stand, talking about poverty in the United States as if it can be divorced from race and is not one of the factors that *creates* racial disparities.

Historically, Americans have had multiple opportunities to eradicate white privilege and racial subjugation, from the Civil War to the Civil Rights Movement. In each instance, progressive forces believed that the moment of truth had arrived, that America had turned a corner and that there would be an effective restructuring of society capable of bringing about racial equality. Yet, it is obvious that racial disparities remain entrenched and are in some cases getting worse. To understand this phenomenon, we must understand that while we have begun to address the "southern" style of racism in this country—the specter of Bull Connor and the KKK—we have not yet begun to address to "northern" style of racism—that is inscribing racial disparities into our political and social structures without overtly focusing on race.

Incorporating a structural frame of analysis provides solutions. However, it requires a move away from the discourses of meritocracy and separation which dominate our discussions, to a framework that realizes that "we're all in this together." It also requires that we be willing to continually examine and reexamine the ways in which racial disparities are recreated, whether intentionally or not, because social structures often produce unintended, long-lasting outcomes. Lastly, it requires a new conceptualization of collective and shared responsibility for social problems. We must examine present inequities in light of the historical injustices that have allowed them to emerge, and come to hard terms with the extent that race remains a central part of how this country is organized (Young 2003).

As Guinier and Torres (2002) have argued, a reexamination of these social structures is important to us all in a democracy that wishes to thrive. By examining the "white space" that is currently created in the United States, we can begin to create a positive alternative to racialized space, one that includes all of us in an increasingly diverse society. To create this alternative, we must dismantle structures created using white privilege, but more importantly, we must expand social citizenship to benefit everyone as we look to create an equitable society.

It is important to remember that these "white spaces" founded upon privilege exclude not only non-whites, but increasingly trap whites. Divestment from our cities and public spaces is occurring across our urban landscape. This divestment and the resulting declining tax base leads to an eroding infrastructure and flight to the suburbs. Sprawling development is not only inefficient, but is highly subsidized through our public spending on new roads, highway maintenance, and sewer lines, etc. (Mazza and Fodor 2000).[11] As we spread the high-opportunity areas more thinly, this progress is followed closely by urban decay and decreasing opportunity for those in the central cities.

We must create structures in which new possibilities and new interests are free for all to participate in. Doing this will set us on the right course for creating a true democracy, one in which citizenship is a guarantee of access to opportunity, rather than an entrenched caste system.

Our brief sketch of key features of any equitable redevelopment plan for the Gulf Coast area is not meant as a blueprint for how this should occur, but rather as a template that forces us to expand the scope of many of the ongoing discussions about the process to include structural racism. We have no illusions about how daunting a task this is, yet we must face it if we are to address the hard questions of race and racism that Katrina brought to light. The hurricane was tragic, but it will be even more tragic if this opportunity for change, to literally rebuild a city from the ground up, is wasted.

A new New Orleans has an opportunity to be a model for the entire world. As a historically black city, it can now be at the forefront of addressing some of the patterns of metropolitan development that we argue are central to the way racism still functions in this country. We must evolve our thinking beyond the narrow view of individual acts and actions to a vision of race that accounts for the ways they interact with structures. By doing this, we can make race a useful tool capable of bolstering democracy and ushering in meaningful transformative change that benefits the nation as a whole.

References

Alesina, Alberto and Edward Glaeser. 2004. *Fighting Poverty in the US and Europe: A World of Difference*. Oxford: Oxford University Press.

Barlow, Andrew. 2003. *Between Fear and Hope: Globalization and Race in the United States*. New York: Rowman & Littlefield.

Berube, Alan and Bruce Katz. 2005. *Katrina's Window: Confronting Concentrated Poverty Across America* [online]. Washington, D.C., Brookings Institution [cited January 15, 2006]. http://www.brookings.edu/metro/pubs/20051012_Concentratedpoverty.pdf.

Blitzer, Wolf. 2005. Aftermath of Hurricane Katrina; New Orleans Mayor Pleads for Help; Race and Class Affecting the Crisis? [online]. CNN.com. September 1 [cited January 15, 2006]. http://transcripts.cnn.com/TRANSCRIPTS/0509/01/sitroom.02.html.

Bonilla-Silva, Eduardo. 2003. *Racism without Racists: Color-Blind Racism and the Persistence of Racial Inequality in the United States.* Lanham, MD: Rowman and Littlefield.

Bullard, Robert. 2005. Katrina and the Second Disaster: A Twenty-Point Plan to Destroy Black New Orleans [online]. Atlanta: Clark Atlanta University. December 23, 2005 [cited January 15, 2006]. http://www.ejrc.cau.edu/Katrinaupdate.html.

Bullard, Robert and Beverly Wright. 2005. *Legacy of Unfairness: Why Some Americans get Left Behind* [online]. Atlanta: Clark Atlanta University. September 29, 2005 [cited January 15, 2006]. http://www.ejrc.cau.edu/Exec%20Summary%20Legacy.html.

Clyne, Meghan. 2005. President Bush Is "Our Bull Connor," Harlem's Rep. Charles Rangel Claims [online]. *New York Sun.* September 23, 2005 [cited January 15, 2006]. http://www.nysun.com/article/20495.

Fagan, Amy. 2005. NAACP fights Bush Social Security Plan [online]. *The Washington Times.* April 11, 2005 [cited January 17, 2006]. http://washingtontimes.com/national/20050411-103458-1817r.htm.

Foner, Philip and David Roediger. 1989. *Our Own Time: A History of American Labor and the Working Day.* New York: Greenwood Press.

Ford, Richard. 1995. The Boundaries of Race: Political Geography in Legal Analysis. 107 *Harvard Law Review* 449, 451.

Frye, Marilyn. 1983. *The Politics of Reality: Essays in Feminist Theory.* Freedom, CA: The Crossing Press.

Greater New Orleans Community Data Center. 2005a. Lower Ninth Ward Neighborhood: People & Household Characteristics [online]. Greater New Orleans Community Data Center. March 23, 2005 [cited January 15, 2006]. http://www.gnocdc.org/orleans/8/22/people.html.

_____ 2005b. Orleans Parish: Schools and Testing [online]. July 12, 2005 [cited January 15, 2006]. http://www.gnocdc.org/orleans/education.html.

Guinier, Lani and Gerald Torres. 2002. *The Miner's Canary: Enlisting Race, Resisting Power, Transforming Democracy.* Cambridge, MA: Harvard University Press.

Katznelson, Ira. 2006. *When Affirmative Action Was White: An Untold History of Racial Inequality in Twentieth-Century America.* New York: W.W. Norton & Company.

Klinenberg, Eric. 2002. *Heat Wave: A Social Autopsy of Disaster.* Chicago: University of Chicago Press.

Laguerre, Michel. 1999. *Minoritized Space: An Inquiry Into the Spatial Order of Things.* Berkeley, CA: Institute of Governmental Studies Press.

Mahoney, Martha R. 2003. Class and Status in American Law: Race, Interest, and the Anti-Transformation Cases. *Southern California Law Review.* May.

Manza. Jeff. 2000. Race and the Underdevelopment of the American Welfare State. *Theory and Society* 29:819-832.

Massey, Douglas and Nancy Denton. 1993. *American Apartheid: Segregation and the Making of the Underclass.* Cambridge, MA: Harvard University Press.

Mazza, Patrick and Eden Fodor. 2000. Taking Its Toll: The Hidden Costs of Sprawl in Washington State [online]. Climate Solutions [cited February 8, 2006]. http://www.climatesolutions.org/pubs/pdfs/sprawl.pdf.

Muhammed, Dedrick, Attieno Davis, Meizhu Lui, and Betsy Leondar-Wright. 2004. The State of the Dream 2004: Enduring Disparities in Black and White [online]. United for a Fair Economy [cited February 8, 2006]. http://www.faireconomy.org/press/2004/StateoftheDream2004.pdf.

Muro, Mark and Rebecca Sohmer. 2005. New Orleans after the Storm: Lessons from the Past, a Plan for the Future [online]. Washington, D.C., Brookings Institution [cited January 15, 2006]. http://www.brookings.edu/metro/pubs/20051012_NewOrleans.pdf.

Orr, Larry, Judith D. Feins, Robin Jacob, Eric Beecroft, Lawrence F. Katz, Jeffrey B. Liebman, and Jeffrey R. Kling. 2003. Moving to Opportunity Interim Impacts Evaluation [online]. U.S. Department of Housing and Urban Development Office of Policy Development and Research [cited February 8, 2006]. http://www.huduser.org/Publications/pdf/MTOFullReport.pdf.

Polikoff, Alex. 2006. *Waiting for Gautreaux.* Chicago, IL: Northwestern University Press.

powell, john a. 2004. *Regional Equity, Race, and the Challenge to Long Island* [online]. The Kirwan Institute for the Study of Race and Ethnicity [cited February, 8 2004]. http://www.kirwaninstitute.org/multimedia/presentations/LongIslandERASEThursdayMay6.ppt.

_____ 2006. Rebuilding Communities and Addressing Structural Racism [tentative title]. *Clearinghouse Review.* May–June.

powell, john a, Reece, Jason and Gambhir, Samir. 2005. *New Orleans Opportunity Mapping – An Analytical Tool to Aid Redevelopment.* Columbus, OH: The Kirwan Institute for the Study of Race and Ethnicity.

Roediger, David. 1999. *The Wages of Whiteness: Race and the Making of the American Working Class.* New York, NY: Verso.

Rosenbaum, James and DeLuca, Stefanie. 2000. *Is Housing Mobility the Key to Welfare Reform? Lessons from Chicago's Gautreaux Program* [online]. Washington, D.C.: Brookings Institution [cited February 8, 2005]. http://www.brookings.edu/dybdocroot/es/urban/rosenbaum.pdf.

Rosner, Jay. 2001a. Expert report submitted on behalf of Intervening Defendants (Student Intervenors), *Grutter v. Bollinger,* 137 F. Supp. 2d 821. E.D. Mich. March 27, 2001. No. 97-75928.

Rosner, Jay, 2001b. Expert Reports on Behalf of Student Intervenors: Disparate Outcomes by Design: University Admissions Tests. 12 *La Raza Law Journal* 377, 377–386.

Rusk, David. 1999. *Inside Game/Outside Game: Winning Strategies for Saving Urban America.* Washington, D.C.: Brookings Institution.

Schill, Michael and Wachter, Susan. 1995. The Spatial Bias of Federal Housing Law and Policy: Concentrated Poverty in Urban America. 143 *University of Pennsylvania Law Review* 1285, 1286-90.

The Center for Social Inclusion. 2005. Thinking Change: Race, Framing and the Public Conversation on Diversity. What Social Science Tells Advocates About Winning Support for Racial Justice Policies [online]. New York [cited February 8, 2006]. http://www.kirwaninstitute.org/projects/DAP%20report%20ThinkingChange.pdf.

Yancey, George. 2003. *Who Is White? Latinos, Asians, and the New Black/Non-Black Divide.* Boulder, CO: Lynne Rienner Publishers.

Young, Iris Marion. 1990. *Justice and the Politics of Difference.* Princeton, NJ: Princeton University Press.

_____ 2001. Equality of Whom? Social Groups and Judgments of Injustice. *Journal of Political Philosophy,* Vol. 9, Issue 1, March: 1-18.

_____ 2003. Responsibility and Structural Injustice. Prepared for Princeton University political theory workshop. December 4.

Endnotes

1. Transcript from CNN's "The situation room": http://transcripts.cnn.com/TRANSCRIPTS/0509/01/sitroom.02.html.
2. This is in some ways reminiscent of when President Bush stated that the Social Security program should be changed because it discriminates against blacks. "African-American males die sooner than other males do, which means the system is inherently unfair to a certain group of people. And that needs to be fixed," Mr. Bush said at a Social Security event Jan. 11, 2005. His rationale was that African Americans do not live as long as white people in the U.S., so they receive fewer benefits. Yet, there was no inquiry into why this disparity in life expectancy exists and what might be done to address it.
3. Kanye West's comments, Sep. 2, 2005 – find full story at http://www.washingtonpost/com/wp-dyn/content/article/2005/09/03/AR2005090300165.html.
4. For more detailed statistics of New Orleans and the surrounding areas – see Robert Bullard's work on environmental racism - http://www.ejrc.cau.edu. Bullard is the director of the Environmental Justice Resource Center at Clark Atlanta University.
5. See Katznelson 2006, wherein political scientist/historian Ira Katznelson describes how New Deal policies and programs were weakened with the support of the South, which was concerned about blacks getting benefits equal to whites in the 1930s and 1940's. Foner and Roediger (1989) make a similar observation about the end of Reconstruction.
6. See http://www.nysun.com/article/20495 for article text.

7. Martha Mahoney (2003) argues that we use "class" in a very radical and unfamiliar way. She states that class is not only an economic formation, but also a cultural one. She posits that the way we construe class will affect how we conceptualize race as well as interest, which could harm not only people of color, but also can harm the class interests of white workers.

8. For detailed statistics from the Mumford Center, see "Segregation in Metro Areas – New Orleans, LA MSA" at http://mumford.albany.edu/census/segregation/SegIncNatPages/5560msaSegInc.htm. The Dissimilarity Index measures the degree of residential segregation in an area and shows the proportion of the minority population that would need to move to achieve complete racial integration. For instance, if an area had a white-black Dissimilarity Index of 75 (scores over 60 are generally considered high levels of segregation), then 75% of the white population would have to move to another neighborhood in order to make whites and blacks evenly distributed among neighborhoods and therefore desegregate housing in the area (powell 2004).

9. For a more thorough discussion of structural racism and its effects, see powell 2006,

10. George Yancey (2003) argues that we might be moving from a white/non-white society to a black/nonblack society. This could mean that blackness could extend beyond phenotype but could also come to mean a social position. Also, Iris Marion Young (1990) has noted that black men have moved from being exploited to being largely marginal. This is a dangerous position in society, one that could lead to eventual disposal of the black male. On the other hand, increasing numbers of whites are willing to support programs that better prepare blacks to compete both in school and in the workplace (Manza 2000).

11. This Washington study found that on average every new home produces about $33,000 in public-sector infrastructure costs. As such, the suburbs produce more cost (per capita) to the public sector for infrastructure.

CHAPTER 5

Abandoned Before the Storms

*The Glaring Disaster of Gender, Race,
and Class Disparities in the Gulf*

AVIS A. JONES-DEWEEVER AND HEIDI HARTMANN

As Hurricanes Katrina and Rita ravaged the Gulf Coast region, the impact of the storms made clear the lingering implications of America's persistent divides. For a time, at least, the outcome of race and class disadvantage in America became crystal clear and garnered long overdue attention. Yet glaring gender disparities throughout the affected areas remained largely unexamined. This chapter fills that void by exploring how the multiple disadvantages faced by the women of the Gulf both increased their vulnerability in a time of crisis and, unless proactively addressed, remain an impediment to their ability to rebuild their lives long after the storms.

Long before the devastation of the hurricanes, many women within the Gulf region were already living at the bottom. Women in the affected states were the poorest women in the nation, among the least likely to have access to health insurance, and, despite high work participation rates, the most likely to find themselves stuck in a cycle of low-wage work. Most disadvantaged were women of color, who often faced quite limited opportunities and outcomes, especially with respect to employment and earnings, educational attainment, and ultimately, the likelihood of living in poverty. To tease out the plight of the women in the region prior to the devastation that compounded their challenges and to catch a glimpse of the opportunities awaiting them in their relocated homes, we use employment and poverty data from federal government sources as well as indicators developed by the Institute for Women's Policy Research (IWPR) through our *Status of Women and the States* series to uncover the multiple disadvantages faced by women in the city of New Orleans, its broader Metropolitan Statistical Area (MSA), and the MSAs of Biloxi–Gulfport–Pascagoula, Mississippi, and Beaumont–Port Arthur, Texas.

Living at the Bottom

The images splashed across CNN in the wake of Katrina exposed to many the disastrous effects of poverty in America. Yet, poverty had long been a festering problem in the United States, growing for four years in a row and leaving the poor further and further behind. By the time Katrina made it to shore, more than 36 million people across the nation were poor and a large proportion (42.3%) lived in deep poverty, with incomes below 50% of the poverty threshold (U.S. Census Bureau 2005). Even for the "average" poor person, the struggle to make ends meet was intense by historical standards. By 2004, the average income of those living in poverty had dropped further below the poverty line than at any time since that statistic was first recorded back in 1975 (Center on Budget and Policy Priorities 2005). America's poor had truly hit bottom in the modern age.

For most Americans, imagining the struggles of the poor in this country is quite difficult, if not disturbing. Poverty is typically tucked away, either confined to an urban enclave avoided by those who aren't within its boundaries by accident of birth, or dispersed broadly, on a lonely country road far away from neighbors, jobs, and, in many respects, opportunity. In the lives of most Americans, one's only brush with poverty is the occasional discomfort felt due to the outstretched hand of a stranger on the street who claims to be homeless, or the annual newscasts from the local food bank come Thanksgiving or Christmas. In this land of opportunity, poverty is hidden from view, like a messy closet one hopes goes undiscovered by an important houseguest. Although we all know it's there—somewhere—for most, poverty goes unseen and unacknowledged, as does its implications for everyday life, and ultimately, survival—that is, unless you're the one who is poor.

For America's poor, poverty is the one reality that all too often cannot be escaped. Especially among the deeply entrenched urban poor, poverty doesn't go on vacation. It doesn't provide an occasional break. Instead, it remains disturbingly consistent and touches lives in every way imaginable. On any one day in 2004, anywhere between 614,000 to 854,000 households in America had at least one family member who went hungry because there was not enough money to ensure that everyone could eat (Nord,

Andrews, and Carlson 2005). Millions more lived amid overcrowded or substandard housing conditions, or couldn't rely on consistent housing at all as the escalating price of keeping a roof over one's head continued to far outpace the value of wages, as it had done for the past 40 years (National Low Income Housing Coalition 2004). For many, being poor meant being trapped in failing school districts, unable to assure a quality education and thus, a way out for their children. It meant being relegated to a place where no one else wants to live, isolated, and disjointed from the rest of society, and having a higher likelihood than others to being exposed to environmental dangers (U.S. Environmental Protection Agency 1993). In New Orleans, that meant being trapped on low ground. In the real lives of real people, poverty is having to decide at the end of the month which is most important—electricity, running water, gas, or any of the other pressing expenses that must be paid. Poverty demands frequent juggling because there is simply not enough to fulfill every need. That is the reality of poverty in America, a reality that has become increasingly difficult to escape. And in an era of restructuring, outsourcing, and low, stagnant wages, poverty, America's dirty little secret, not only lives on, but thrives.

As the prevalence and depth of poverty has grown over the years, the crumbling value of the minimum wage has made finding a way out next to impossible. After adjusting for inflation, the value of the minimum wage is at its second lowest point since 1955, ensuring that working, and working very hard, will not be enough to guarantee an above-poverty-level existence (Bernstein and Shapiro 2005). A single mother of two, for example, working 40 hours per week, 52 weeks a year, earns only $10,712 before taxes—a full $5,000 below the poverty threshold (Boushey 2005). Even with the Earned Income Tax Credit, which maxes out at roughly $4,000, her family income still falls below the poverty line. As a result, she falls squarely within the ranks of the working poor (Shulman 2003; Shipler 2004).

The above-cited example is not atypical. The face of the working poor in America is, more often than not, the face of a woman. It is women who make up the majority (60%) of America's minimum-wage workers and 90% of those who remain stuck in low-wage work throughout their prime earning years (Lovell 2004; Rose and Hartmann 2004). And ironically, those women who lived in the metropolitan areas impacted by Hurricanes Katrina and Rita were especially likely to encounter this fate. The women of the Gulf participated in the labor force at about the same rate as women in the nation overall, and, with the lone exception of those who resided in the Beaumont-Port Arthur, Texas area, women in this region were less likely than women nationwide to work part-time or for only part of the year. Yet, despite their strong attachment to the labor force, in each geographic area examined, their median annual earnings trailed those of women nationally, with the women in the city of New Orleans falling furthest behind (Jones-DeWeever et al. 2006).

Unemployment, too, was especially prevalent in the Gulf region. Prior to Katrina, the city of New Orleans was particularly hard hit, with unemployment rates over 50% higher than that of the nation as a whole. Still, for many, even the advantage of holding a job meant little in terms of ensuring a life free of poverty. In each affected area examined, more than two in five of those who were poor experienced poverty despite being employed, and within the affected Metropolitan Statistical Area (MSA) of Biloxi–Gulfport–Pascagoula in Mississippi, more than half of those who lived below the poverty line (52.7%) worked in 2004, far exceeding the national rate of 45.3%.[1]

Taken together, the evidence paints a picture of a hard-working people. Yet a strong work ethic failed to insulate them from the likelihood of being poor. Overall, poverty in the region was more commonplace than was the case nationwide. And, as is typical throughout this nation and around the world, women were considerably more likely to be poor than men, with women in New Orleans most at risk of poverty in the Gulf region. Fully one quarter (25.9%) of the women who made New Orleans their home lived in poverty, well outpacing the national poverty rate (14.5%) for women (Gault et al. 2005).

For those who faced life beyond their working years, poverty was all too common. Like younger women, older women were much more likely to face poverty in their golden years than their male counterparts. With the exception of Biloxi–Gulfport–Pascagoula, in every one of the four areas examined, the chance that women aged 65 years or older would live in poverty in this region exceeded the national rate and roughly doubled the rate of poverty experienced by elderly men. Also, like their younger counterparts, those who lived within the city of New Orleans were at greatest risk of poverty, as nearly a quarter (24.3%) of the Crescent City's older women lived below the poverty line (Gault et al. 2005).

Women in this region, then, both young and old, and particularly those who lived in New Orleans, faced a remarkably high likelihood of being poor. Most at risk were those who lived up to the responsibility of raising children on their own. In both the city of New Orleans and its broader Metropolitan Statistical Area, the percentage of female-headed families falling below the federal poverty line exceeded the national average, topping off at roughly 40% (Figure 5.1). And as Katrina loomed, it was these families who faced the impending crisis with the fewest resources at their disposal to make it out alive and to keep their families together as chaos emerged.

Even though poverty in the Katrina- and Rita-impacted areas was significant and clearly outpaced the nation as a whole, the high level of

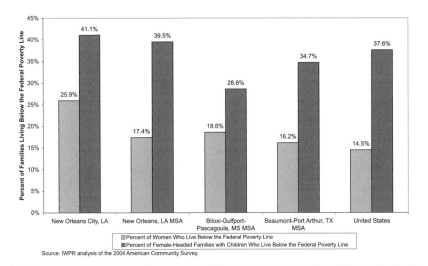

Source: IWPR analysis of the 2004 American Community Survey.

Figure 5.1

poverty experienced in the Gulf region is consistent with broader poverty proliferation throughout the South. As compiled and ranked by IWPR's *Status of Women in the States* (2004), all eight states in the South Central Region rank among the bottom third of all 50 states and the District of Columbia for the percent of women living above the poverty line. Mississippi ranks dead last, followed closely by Louisiana (ranked 47th) and Texas (ranked 44th). Kentucky (ranked 36th), the highest-ranked state in the region, still falls significantly below the mid-point for the nation as a whole (Werschkul and Williams 2004).

Not only are women in the Gulf region the most likely to be poor, they are also at high risk of being without health insurance. Texas ranked worst in the nation in terms of women's health insurance coverage, with Louisiana and Mississippi also falling near the bottom, ranking 49th and 43rd, respectively (Werschkul and Williams 2004).

So, while no state in the nation has escaped poverty's reach, and although most recently growth in poverty has been starkest in the Midwest (U.S. Census Bureau 2005), the South remains especially plagued by this problem. This southern legacy not only has a gendered dynamic, but a racial one as well.

Examining the Significance of Race

Lost on no one during the days immediately following the breach of the levees was the high concentration of African Americans left to fend for themselves in the middle of a ravaged city. But long before the storm, New

Table 5.1 Population 25 Years and Older with a College Degree or More by Sex and Race, 2004

City/MSAs	Women All	Women White	Women Black	Men All	Men White	Men Black
New Orleans City	28.6%	50.6%	18.9%	34.0%	61.8%	16.6%
Beaumont-Port Arthur MSA	16.4%	19.0%	12.7%	20.7%	23.7%	16.6%
Biloxi-Gulfport-Pascagoula MSA	18.2%	19.9%	9.7%	18.0%	19.9%	8.3%
New Orleans MSA	24.9%	30.2%	16.4%	28.3%	34.6%	15.6%
United States	25.6%	27.8%	17.5%	28.6%	31.7%	17.0%

Source: U.S. Census Bureau, American Community Survey, 2004. Compiled by the Institute for Women's Policy Research

Orleans, not unlike other urban areas across the nation, was in many ways a city sharply divided by race and class, as well as gender. The women of New Orleans and in the Gulf region generally lived very different lives across the racial divide. For example, despite being home to three Historically Black Universities (Dillard University, Southern University at New Orleans, and Xavier University of Louisiana), college degree attainment among African-American women in the city of New Orleans only slightly outpaced the national rate (18.9% vs. 17.5%). In the broader New Orleans MSA, degree attainment by African-American women fell slightly below the national norm (16.4% vs. 17.5%). White women in the city of New Orleans, however, like women in urban areas more generally, had very high college graduation rates. They greatly exceeded their counterparts nationally in college degree attainment (50.6% vs. 27.8%) and more than doubled the rate of degree attainment achieved by African-American women (50.6% vs. 18.9%). Only within the Beaumont–Port Arthur area, where degree attainment is relatively low for all groups, did the difference in degree attainment rates between African-American and white women drop below ten percentage points (Table 5.1).

The educational differences experienced by women across the racial divide most certainly carried over to the labor market. Within the managerial/professional fields, for example, white women's representation more than doubled that of African-American women in the city of New Orleans (65.7% of white women had managerial or professional jobs vs. only 27.2% of African-American women). White women also outpaced African-American women within the broader New Orleans metropolitan area, 45.9% vs. 28.6%, for a difference of more than 15 percentage points, significantly outpacing the national divide of 40% vs. 31%.[2]

Similarly, white women in the city of New Orleans earned a higher proportion of the white male salary (80.2%) than the national average (71.7%) and nearly doubled the proportion of white men's earnings achieved by

African-American women (80.2% vs. 43.9%). In fact, across each of the four hurricane-impacted areas examined that had available data, African-American women's earnings were less than half those of white men (43.9%) and well below the national ratio of African-American women's earnings to white men's earnings (62.7%). Although still lagging behind white men in each area examined, in no area did white women fail to exceed three-fifths of the earnings of white men (Table 5.2).

Looking statewide, women's earnings were especially low among those who lived in areas that bore the brunt of Hurricane Katrina. In fact, of the 43 states with sample sizes large enough to provide a reliable measure of African-American women's earnings, Louisiana ranked worst in the nation with full-time annual earnings of only $19,400. Mississippi followed closely, ranking next to last with median earnings of $19,900 for African-American women. White women also garnered comparatively low earnings in those states. Although exceeding African-American women's earnings, compared to white women in other states, white women's median earnings in Mississippi ($25,700) and Louisiana ($26,500) put them in the bottom third in the nation and well below the $30,900 median earnings for white women nationally. In contrast, for both groups, women's earnings in Texas well outpaced those of their counterparts in Louisiana and Mississippi and placed them within the top third of earnings nationally. Still, the earnings of African-American women in Texas failed to exceed the average earnings of African-American women nationwide, and the earnings of Hispanic women in Texas fell within the bottom third of all states (Werschkul and Williams 2004).

Labor force participation, too, varied greatly across race and gender and between geographic areas. In the city of New Orleans, for example, nearly three-fourths of white women (73.7%), as compared to approximately two-thirds of African-American women (66.5%), participated in the labor force in 2004. But in the New Orleans MSA, the two groups had nearly equal participation rates of 68.9% for African-American women and 67.8% for white women. The widest variation in labor force participation occurred in the Beaumont-Port Arthur area, where over four-fifths (81.2%) of African-American women participated in the labor force as compared with only 64.3% of white women.[3]

Also consistent with national trends, poverty in the Gulf region is highly correlated with race and gender. While overall women are consistently more likely to be poor than men, both throughout the affected areas as well as the nation as a whole, African-American women are especially vulnerable to poverty. Hardest hit were those who lived within the Biloxi–Gulfport–Pascagoula area and the city of New Orleans, where roughly a third lived below the federal poverty line (32.5% and 32.3%). As was the

Table 5.2 Women and Men's Median Annual Earnings for Full-Time, Year-Round Workers and Women's Earnings as a Percentage of White Men's, 2004

City/MSAs	All			White			Black			Hispanic		
	Women	Men	Wage Ratio to White Men	Women	Men	Wage Ratio to White Men	Women	Men	Wage Ratio to White Men	Women	Men	Wage Ratio to White Men
New Orleans City	$24,494	$30,014	53.9%	$36,445	$45,454	80.2%	$19,951	$25,216	43.9%	N/A	N/A	N/A
Beaumont-Port Arthur MSA	$28,164	$45,032	61.7%	$29,620	$45,675	64.8%	$21,552	$40,030	47.2%	N/A	N/A	N/A
Biloxi-Gulfport-Pascagoula MSA	$26,401	$36,729	71.9%	$27,004	$36,742	73.5%	N/A	N/A	N/A	N/A	N/A	N/A
New Orleans MSA	$25,978	$37,473	55.8%	$29,385	$46,530	63.2%	$20,798	$26,283	44.7%	$24,043	$29,385	51.7%
United States	$31,374	$41,194	68.8%	$32,678	$45,573	71.7%	$28,581	$32,686	62.7%	$24,030	$26,749	52.7%

Notes: N/A indicates insufficient sample sizes

Source: U.S. Census Bureau, American Community Survey, 2004. Compiled by the Institute for Women's Policy Research

case for African-American women, white women's poverty was most pronounced in the Biloxi–Gulfport–Pascagoula area, where 13.7% were poor; within New Orleans city and its broader MSA, however, white women's poverty was less than the national average of 10% (Table 5.3).

What a sad irony that one of the worst disasters in our nation's history occurred in an area populated by some of the nation's most disadvantaged citizens. Both African-American and white women in Mississippi and Louisiana had many fewer resources at their disposal than their counterparts nationwide. African-American women especially found themselves at the bottom. They were the lowest earners across both race and sex in Mississippi and Louisiana (Table 5.3) and, consequently, were the least likely to be equipped with the necessary resources to take themselves and their families out of harm's way. As a result, they largely stayed to face the storm on their own; and for those who survived, life will never be the same again.

Life After the Storms

One can only imagine the trauma of losing everything save the clothes on one's back, being separated from family, friends, and community, and suddenly forced to begin life anew in a random, unfamiliar place a long way— geographically, socially, and culturally—from home. This is the challenge facing many of those who have been displaced following the devastation brought by Katrina and Rita. But given the probability that those most likely to relocate were also the ones who faced the most severe challenges at home of poverty, limited educational background, and all the implications of a paycheck-to-paycheck existence, what might the relocated settlers now expect in the way of employment and other opportunities while awaiting the possibility of a newly rebuilt city? Unfortunately, our analysis of the data suggests very little in terms of improved economic opportunities. Table 5.4, which depicts information regarding a number of the cities and metropolitan statistical areas where evacuees were relocated, suggests that in their new homes, many evacuees will still be faced with high poverty rates, particularly among women and female-headed households, and, for African-American women, low median earnings for year-round, full-time work. In some areas, such as Jackson, Mississippi; Baton Rouge, Louisiana; Little Rock, Arkansas; Mobile, Alabama; and Atlanta, Georgia, poverty rates are even higher and/or earnings are even lower than in those environments left behind.

A few areas, though, suggest an environment that provides a more solid foundation for evacuees to rebuild their lives. Places like Charlotte, North Carolina; Richmond–Petersburg, Virginia; and Nashville, Tennessee boast comparatively lower poverty rates for women and female-headed families

Table 5.3 Percent of Men and Women Living Below the Poverty Line by Race and Ethnicity, 2004

	All		White		Black		Hispanic		Asian	
	Men	Women	Men	Women	Men	Women	Men	Women	Men	Women
New Orleans city	20.0%	25.9%	9.6%	9.2%	25.5%	32.3%	N/A	N/A	N/A	N/A
New Orleans MSA	12.1%	17.4%	5.1%	9.1%	23.6%	29.3%	7.2%	10.8%	6.9%	3.1%
Biloxi-Gulfport-Pascagoula MSA	13.6%	18.6%	11.3%	13.7%	20.9%	32.5%	N/A	N/A	N/A	N/A
Beaumont-Port Arthur MSA	12.1%	16.2%	8.6%	11.1%	14.9%	24.2%	30.4%	22.4%	N/A	N/A
United States	11.6%	14.5%	7.7%	10.0%	22.9%	28.0%	19.8%	24.3%	11.3%	12.1%

Notes: N/A indicates insufficient sample sizes

Source: U.S. Census Bureau, American Community Survey, 2004. Compiled by the Institute for Women's Policy Research

Table 5.4 A Comparison of Southern Cities and Metropolitan Statistical Areas (MSAs)

Geography	Poverty Rate for All Women	Poverty Rate for Female-Headed Families with Related Children Under Age 18	Median Earnings of African-American Women who Work Full-Time, Year-Round
Places			
Atlanta City, GA	29.2%	65.6%	$27,312
Charlotte City, NC	12.9%	34.7%	$27,823
Dallas City, TX	23.5%	43.1%	$28,176
Fort Worth City, TX	18.7%	39.6%	$24,217
Houston City, TX	21.0%	41.3%	$29,892
San Antonio City, TX	21.8%	48.4%	$30,929
New Orleans City, LA	25.9%	41.1%	$19,951
MSAs			
Atlanta, GA	13.7%	33.9%	$31,372
Baton Rouge, LA	18.0%	37.6%	$21,770
Charleston-North Charleston, SC	16.7%	39.6%	$20,766
Dallas-Fort Worth, TX	13.6%	32.7%	$29,925
Jackson, MS	21.7%	43.9%	$21,891
Lafayette, LA	22.1%	55.9%	$15,131
Lexington, KY	18.6%	49.6%	N/A
Little Rock-North Little Rock, AR	18.1%	44.8%	$26,110
Mobile, AL	17.1%	43.3%	$17,412
Nashville, TN	12.4%	36.8%	$31,152
Oklahoma City, OK	13.2%	34.3%	$27,448
Richmond-Petersburg, VA	7.9%	20.4%	$29,473
Savannah, GA	12.5%	28.7%	$22,025
Shreveport-Bossier City, LA	24.4%	55.4%	$20,897
Beaumont-Port Arthur, TX	16.2%	34.7%	$21,552
Biloxi-Gulfport-Pascagoula, MS	18.6%	28.6%	N/A
New Orleans, LA	17.4%	39.5%	$20,798

Notes: N/A indicates insufficient sample sizes.

Source: U.S. Census Bureau, American Community Survey, 2004. Compiled by the Institute for Women's Policy Research.

or have significantly higher earnings for African-American women. These positive conditions offer a glimmer of hope for improved opportunities to build a better and brighter future to those who have chosen to make their relocation permanent and to start the task of building a new life, livelihood, and home in new surroundings and without the social networks that had once defined a community.

Creating a Better Future for the Women of the Gulf

Life will never be the same for those who lost loved ones, material assets, family mementos, and the one place in the world they called home. The best that can be done for them is to ensure that for all, even the most disadvantaged, we use this crisis as a springboard to creating a future replete with opportunities for a better tomorrow. To fulfill that commitment we must ensure that the particular needs of women are not overlooked in the rebuilding process. Acknowledging and addressing the needs of women ultimately amounts to fulfilling the needs of children, families, and entire communities. The following would be a good start:

Invest in education and training to increase women's earning potential and foster opportunities to participate in the rebuilding process — Increased education and job-training efforts in the Gulf Coast region as well as those areas where many have relocated could provide the best foundation possible for many evacuees to be able to begin the long process of building a stable and secure future for themselves and their families. This investment could help break the cycle of living paycheck-to-paycheck and provide the first real opportunity many have had to acquire employment that moves them above the poverty line. Particularly key for women is access to nontraditional training, such as in the trades (e.g., carpentry, electrical, etc.). Training in the trades often requires apprenticeships that provide the opportunity to earn while learning and would ultimately expose women to a skill and a profession that would offer much greater income potential than that associated with most traditionally female work. Also, an expansion of the Workforce Investment Act, the legislation meant to provide training, could serve as a key avenue toward increasing women's representation in living-wage jobs (Gault et al. 2005).

Expand earning opportunities through better wages and fair hiring practices — Increasing the federal minimum wage is a long overdue necessity. Last raised in 1997, today's wage rate falls woefully short of providing adequate income for families struggling to keep up with the increasing costs associated with housing, transportation, childcare, and energy. To give workers a fair chance at escaping the cycle of poverty, they must first be paid fairly. Working for nearly a decade without receiving a wage increase while the cost of living continues to climb falls far short of a fair deal for American workers. And since women make up the bulk of those who work at and near minimum wage, it is their earning power that is disproportionately suppressed. To offer a real chance for workers to escape poverty, the minimum wage must be increased. But in addition to fair wages, fair hiring practices must be assured as well. Contractors should, whenever possible, be local or be required to hire local workers so that former residents of those areas most devastated have the opportunity to get back on their feet financially while rebuilding their lives and their communities. And finally, given the disproportionate race/class/gender dynamics of the post-Katrina impacts, now is the time to strengthen affirmative action requirements instead of dropping them entirely.

Stop the clock on TANF benefits for the victims of the storms — As early as January, 2002, 21,396 families in the state of Louisiana had reached the state or federal lifetime limit for TANF benefits. While the state did provide a number of extensions for a variety of reasons, including domestic violence, the lack of childcare or other support services, or recent job loss, over half (11,138) of those families had their TANF cases closed immediately (Bloom et al. 2002). Congress' post-Katrina action of providing extra assistance to states affected by Katrina or to states hosting evacuees does nothing to address the needs of those who had reached their limit prior to the storm or for legal immigrants affected by the storm. These oversights must be rectified. The clock must be stopped for those who have lost everything and must start over either in the affected areas or in an unfamiliar place, lacking the social networks that could help in rebuilding their lives.

Respect the needs of women and communities in the planning and rebuilding process, and engage the black middle class — Community is much more than physical structures. A community is, at its core, its people. In rebuilding New Orleans, the needs and concerns of its original inhabitants should be sought and acted upon. A careful balance must be achieved that respects pre-existing community culture and social networks while also seeking to create a better-served and better-maintained environment. Making sure that the voices of neighborhood leaders, including women's, civic, and religious group representatives, are sought, heard, and acted upon is a key component of living up to this responsibility. Also, making sure women are included in every phase of the rebuilding process helps ensure that their needs will not be overlooked and that they too will benefit from a rebuilding economy. From the urban and regional planners to the workers on the construction sites, the inclusion of women is key to making sure that the communities that are rebuilt and the workforce that is developed will be better and stronger than ever. Also key to the successful reemergence of New Orleans and its surrounding communities is the needed inclusion of the skills, talents, and cultural competency of the Black middle class. Home to three Historically Black Colleges or Universities, New Orleans has long been a city that has attracted and retained a strong African-American professional community. Drawing on this community now is key, not only for meeting the immediate and future skills needs of the region, but also as a means of doing so through a lens of cultural intelligence.

Make the provision of childcare a priority — Working families need access to affordable, quality childcare in order to be able to seek and maintain employment. This need is especially pronounced among those who are trying to rebuild their working lives in unfamiliar surroundings, as well as for those returning home and trying to start anew by helping to rebuild their damaged communities. Government subsidies could help by funding professional development and training for evacuees and returnees seeking childcare careers while simultaneously meeting the needs of those seeking quality, consistent care. Additionally, entrepreneurship support could be used to fund the establishment of centrally located, high-quality childcare centers and to enable some providers to initiate home-based childcare businesses. Childcare assistance for low-income families had fallen far short of the broader need well before Katrina came to shore. This tragedy most certainly has only increased that need. Now is the time to do a better job of supporting struggling families while fulfilling our unspoken commitment to the well-being of America's most helpless citizens, its infants and young children.

Fulfill the promise of attacking the poverty problem — When President Bush addressed the nation in September of 2005, he stated strongly that "we have a duty to confront this poverty with bold action" (Office of the Press Secretary 2005), yet the wheels of action have not only turned exceedingly slowly, one could argue that they have actually gone in reverse. Since that day, Congress has cut Medicaid services to poor children and the elderly in need of long-term care; it has expanded TANF work requirements without adequately funding the increased child care burden working families will undoubtedly face; and it has reduced child support enforcement dollars, which will ultimately negatively impact low-income single-parent families. All tolled, through his 2006 and 2007 budgets submitted to Congress, the President has proposed some $435 billion in cuts to programs meant to aid America's neediest citizens. Counter to his own call for bold action to confront the poverty problem, the President has instead moved boldly in the other direction, pushing forward with his plan to extend $648 billion in tax cuts to America's millionaires over the next 10 years, dwarfing the $150 billion currently committed to relief and reconstruction efforts in Katrina-impacted areas (Aron-Dine and Friedman 2006; Weinstein, Beeson, and Warnhoff 2006). What of the commitment to the poor? What of the commitment to the people of New Orleans?

The President was right when he called for bold action to confront poverty. Now he has the responsibility of living up to those words. To do so would mean a dramatic change in course from the current policy direction. A bold anti-poverty strategy would require, among other things, a commitment to affordable housing, expansion of the Earned Income Tax Credit, broad-scale investments in public education and adult education, and increased health care and childcare availability. At the core, these and other anti-poverty policy goals would require a shift in priorities on a national scale. Such a shift is possible. If we have learned nothing else, the Katrina tragedy has made painfully clear the very real human and fiscal costs associated with years of neglect and indifference. We simply cannot afford to go back to business as usual.

Conclusion

Ultimately, it is our responsibility to learn from the heartbreak of seeing mothers begging for milk for their dehydrated infants, from seeing children and the elderly stranded on rooftops pleading for help, and seeing the dead left without dignity and the dying suffering for days in their own waste. Lest we forget, these are the images of Katrina that should stay with us forever as a reminder of what can happen when we turn a blind eye to the implications of a society divided. We can and must do better. The women, children, and families of the Gulf deserve nothing less.

References

Aron-Dine, Aviva and Joel Friedman. 2006. The Skewed Benefits of the Tax Cuts, 2007-2016: If the Tax Cuts are Extended, Millionaires Will Receive More Than $600 Billion over the Next Decade. Washington, D.C.: Center on Budget and Policy Priorities.

Bernstein, Jared and Isaac Shapiro. 2005. Unhappy Anniversary: Federal Minimum Wage Remains Unchanged for Eighth Straight Year, Falls to 56-Year Low Relative to the Average Wage. Washington, D.C.: Center on Budget and Policy Priorities and the Economic Policy Institute.

Bloom, Dan, Mary Farrell, and Barbara Fink with Diana Adams-Ciardullo. 2002. Welfare Time Limits: State Policies, Implementation, and Effects on Families. New York: Manpower Demonstration Research Corporation.

Boushey, Heather. 2005. The Structure of Poverty in the U.S. Paper presented at the Congressional Black Caucus Foundation Summit Poverty, Race and Policy: Strategic Advancement of a Poverty Reduction Agenda.

Caiazza, Amy, April Shaw, and Misha Werschkul. 2004. Women's Economic Status in the States: Wide Disparities by Race, Ethnicity, and Region. Washington, D.C.: Institute for Women's Policy Research.

Center on Budget and Policy Priorities. 2005. Economic Recovery Failed to Benefit Much of the Population in 2004. Washington, D.C.: Center on Budget and Policy Priorities.

Gault, Barbara, Heidi Hartmann, Avis Jones-DeWeever, Misha Wershkul, and Erica Williams. 2005. The Women of New Orleans and the Gulf Coast: Multiple Disadvantages and Key Assets for Recovery, Part 1: Poverty, Race, Gender, and Class. Washington, D.C. Institute for Women's Policy Research.

Jones-DeWeever, Avis, Olga Sorokina, Erica Williams, Heidi Hartmann, and Barbara Gault. Forthcoming, 2006. The Women of New Orleans and the Gulf Coast: Multiple Disadvantages and Key Assets for Recovery, Part II: Employment and Earnings, Gender, Race, and Class. Washington, D.C. Institute for Women's Policy Research.

Lovell, Vicky. 2004. No Time to be Sick: Why Everyone Suffers When Workers Don't Have Paid Sick Leave. Washington, D.C.: Institute for Women's Policy Research.

National Low Income Housing Coalition. 2004. America's Neighbors: The Affordable Housing Crisis and the People it Affects. Washington, D.C.: National Low Income Housing Coalition.

Nord, Mark, Margaret Andrews, and Steven Carlson. 2005. Household Food Security in the United States, 2004. Washington, D.C.: USDA Economic Research Service. http://www.ers.usda.gov/Publications/err11/

Office of the Press Secretary, White House. 2005. President Discusses Hurricane Relief in Address to the Nation. http://www.whitehouse.gov/news/releases/2005/09/20050915-8.html

Rose, Stephen J. and Heidi Hartmann. 2004. Still A Man's Labor Market: The Long-Term Earnings Gap. Washington, D.C.: Institute for Women's Policy Research.

Shipler, David. 2004. The Working Poor: Invisible in America. New York: Knopf.

Shulman, Beth. 2003. The Betrayal of Work: How Low-Wage Jobs Fail 30 Million Americans. New York: New Press.

U.S. Census Bureau. 2005. Income, Poverty, and Health Insurance Coverage in the United States: 2004. Washington, D.C.: U. S. Government Printing Office.

U.S. Environmental Protection Agency. 1993. Environmental Equity: Reducing Risk for All Communities. Volume I: Workgroup Report to the Administrator. Washington, D.C. U.S. Environmental Protection Agency. http://www.epa.gov/compliance/resources/publications/ej/reducing_risk_com_vol1.pdf

Weinstein, Deborah, Jennifer Beeson, and Steve Wamhoff. 2006. Guide to the FY 2007 Federal Budget: What's at Stake for Human Needs. Washington, D.C.: Coalition on Human Needs.

Werschkul, Misha and Erica Williams. 2004. The Status of Women and the States. Washington, D.C.: Institute for Women's Policy Research.

Endnotes

1. IWPR analysis of the 2004 American Community Survey.
2. Ibid.
3. Ibid.

CHAPTER **6**

Katrina and the Politics of Later Life*

MARGARET MORGANROTH GULLETTE

The Scandal of the Unasked Questions

Amid all the devastations of Katrina, what group was *most* vulnerable? If you followed the news compassionately, you might say, "the poor," "African Americans," "women," "women of color." The best answer is actually "the old." Older New Orleanians were most at risk, by being also predominantly poor and female and African-American, and also (sometimes) weak, ill, or disabled. In New Orleans, 23% of the 484,000 citizens had disabilities. The figure was 50% for people over 65.[1] They couldn't crawl out on roofs or set off on the highways with their backpacks.

Age has been the most under-reported story of Katrina. The "vast majority" of the 1,322 people who died in New Orleans were old, Martin Smith reported on *Frontline*'s November 22, 2005 special on "The Storm"—but *Frontline* gave its shocking statistic only one sentence in an hour-long show. A September 14 *Washington Post* story began "Hurricane Katrina seemed to single out the elderly for particular punishment," but told the story of only one woman, Pearline Chambers, a widow of 86, who survived in her one-story house in the submerged Ninth Ward (Harden 2005: A24). To be sure, we were told repeatedly that dozens died in one nursing home, whose owners were charged with criminally negligent homicide.

* © 2006 Margaret Morganroth Gullette

A hospital is being investigated for euthanasia. But nursing-home deaths accounted for only 10% of the toll (O'Neil 2005:A1). The full story goes far broader and deeper than the cases of institutional abuse.

As of late November, 2005, 78% of the identified dead were over 51. 39% were over 75, and a quarter were between 61 and 75. 14% were only 51–60—perhaps the most startling figure, since most of us don't think of people in their fifties as aged.[2] Katrina was "one of the worst medical catastrophes for the aged in recent U.S. history," Roma Khanna concluded in the November 27 *Houston Chronicle*. "The elderly and critically ill plummeted to the bottom of priority lists as calamity engulfed New Orleans," said a September 19 *New York Times* article by David Rohde et al. Older people "had special needs neglected by disaster workers," Nancy Weaver Teichert reported in the September 13, 2005 *Sacramento Bee*. Even emergency workers may not know that dehydration, for example, occurs faster in elderly people and is harder to reverse. Others died of chronic illnesses "easily managed under normal conditions but that become lethal when access to medicine and treatment is cut off" (Fussell 2005) or when trauma is super-added.

I searched for attention paid to older people as a category, not only in the mainstream press but in the literature produced by aid organizations, even by nonprofits dedicated to women. The evidence that older people suffered was scattered everywhere; with rare exceptions, what was missing was a special focus on age. It was at the periphery of attention. From the news stories one could not tell even what age was being considered "old": over 80, over 65, over 50?

Ingrid Tischer of the San Francisco-based Equal Rights Advocates noticed that disabilty was also given only passing mention by the mainstream. "People with disabilities of all ages were shut out of shelters, denied transportation, communications, and left without medication and equipment necessary for survival. We will never know how many people with disabilities who lived in the community lost their lives" (Tischer 2005).

Another missing keyword was "women." Women live longer than men and thus tend to wind up alone, widowed, sicker, more disabled, or in nursing homes. Almost 25% of women over 65 in New Orleans were poor, more than double the national average, according to the Older Women's League (*Newsletter* 2005*)*. African Americans made up about 68% of the population of New Orleans, but were possibly as high as 80% of the survivors trapped inside the city (Seager 2005). Of those over 50 who remained behind, were more women? Were most of the older evacuees female? It is now possible to check the coverage under keywords like "elderly" and "women" via sources like Lexis-Nexis. Nobody is (yet) asking such questions, not even in the usual gender-wise resources. *Off Our Backs*, in an issue devoted both to Katrina and to "Women and Age," barely mentioned *older* women in its Katrina coverage, instead focusing on rape, the closing of abortion clinics, and the difficulties of taking care of "our children." "Women" meant, as it so often does in feminist writing, *younger* women.

Newspaper stories that included anything about old people, or people still missing, or bodies found belatedly, mostly referred to old women; and the accompanying photos are mostly of old women. One young woman told NPR, sobbing, that the family drove away, leaving both their mother and their grandmother in the path of the hurricane. The *Boston Globe* published a photo of evacuees in an airport, one a frail old woman left lying on a baggage conveyor. That was the image that struck my heart, stayed in my head, and led me to follow this story.

The mother and grandmother who were left behind might have remained because one or both believed it riskier to evacuate. Why didn't the media interview those who bravely stayed to care for dependents—for their adult children with disabilities, grandchildren, aged parents, other relatives?

By November it was generally known that "Most Katrina victims were elderly," the title of an October 24 *Washington Post* article by John Christofferson. What I expected in the "aftermath" thinkpieces and reporting were the stories behind the stories. First, I expected numerous local self-exams, like Peter Fimrite's piece about San Francisco, "Rights group warns disaster would imperil disabled, elderly" (2005:B5). I found few.

Mainly, I expected expanded coverage of age, now that it was clearly not the "special interest" of gerontologists and rights groups. But the neglect continued. Reporters had discovered African Americans and then moved on to analyze the situations of other categorizable injured groups they had overlooked—for instance, prisoners and the "unique" problem of teenage evacuees. But, what about the unique problems of "older evacuees," an obvious category? Scholarly surveys are already in the works.[3] Why didn't the media interview enough older people who escaped the drowned city, explicitly making recommendations for this group too?

Older people left homes they had lived in perhaps for decades, surrounded by friends, neighbors, and familiar geographies. Some were sent, alone, to noisy shelters in states far away, without social networks, medications, eyeglasses, walkers, or caretakers (Markley and Garza 2005). Many did not receive checks for employment, welfare, or Social Security for some time. Some were slow to register for help, because "older adults process the crisis at a different pace, may be less willing to ask for help ... [and] may have difficulty getting to or standing in line" (Wade 2005). Care providers wandered evacuation sites with lists of missing residents from group homes but lacked neighborhood lists of the vulnerable (Norris 2005:3). Are these evacuees also homesick, lonely, suffering in high percentages

from post-traumatic stress? As the news breaks about the disproportionate deaths and the disappearances and sufferings of so many older people,
what has been the psychological effect on people who know they are considered "old"?

Hurricanes do not "single out the elderly for particular punishment,"
despite what the *Washington Post* says. Human factors, not fate, make the
difference, given that so many New Orleanians survived. The specials the
New Yorker has done, on the "Cajun Navy" (volunteers with boats) and the
New Orleans Police Department, were appropriately focused on rescues
and failures of rescue. Why did people as young as 51 living outside of
institutions die and suffer in greater numbers than younger people? Did
younger rescuers fail to notice them or unconsciously shrink away? Were
there not enough relevant medical professionals, or were they inadequately
trained? Whether the deaths occurred at home, at the Convention Center,
on the road, in the shelters—what percentage was avoidable? These hard
questions weren't asked.

Think about the disconnects. Here in the real world, elderly people—
probably primarily women and poor women of color—were the neediest
among many grievously needy in a national emergency that took over the
news for months. These victims somehow fell to the bottom of "priority
lists." And there in the media was an unwillingness to linger on older people, an evasion of them as a group with special needs, an inability to distin-
guish among them by race, class, or gender. The press arguably did better
covering the deaths of elderly Parisians left abandoned in the European
heat wave of 2003. They saw that as a sociological phenomenon. When
there's no emergency, many journalists wail constantly about how many
old people there are in this country, and when there is a crisis that primarily concerns them, they fall silent.

Media silence has special consequences in an emergency. How many
organizations raised money to help elderly people who are impoverished
or returning to devastated nursing homes? How many fundraisers were
given for *them*? I went to one in Cambridge, enlivened by a gospel choir
made up of old men, the Silver Leafs, organized on behalf of the American
Association of Homes and Services for the Aging, AAHSA. My mother,
aged 91—who had evacuated in 2004 from her Florida home—danced and
clapped beside me, my husband, and our friends.

Many news sources in print, on radio, TV, and the Internet can be
given credit for bringing racism and classism to the fore in their Katrina
coverage. But this teachable moment should also have wrenched attention to age and ageism. Older people are diverse, like members of any
other demographic cohort; and people become more diverse as they age.
Age is therefore not always a salient category or a good predictor. But it

was in New Orleans. Age was shamefully forgotten. "Ageism" was the final keyword missing.

The inadequate coverage of Katrina teaches us that Americans of all ages need to focus on the elderly, women, and old age, with urgency and respect—and shock—so that *these* vulnerable are not forgotten again. "This is a wake-up call," said frantic geriatric social workers in Houston. But to wake up editors and writers about age, and through them all caring Americans, the alarm clock has to sound a lot louder than the tinkle of 2005.

An opportunity still exists for educating the public about the proliferating sources and profoundly alienating effects of ageism. It's high time to notice the politics of aging-past-youth in the United States and the world.

Age, Women, Poverty

A disaster like Katrina puts in high relief the situation that exists everywhere in this country every day. It should be obvious, but in our toxic ageist culture, replete with misinformation about the economic situation of people over 65, or even 45, it is worth repeating: Many are in desperate need in their later years, having been systemically disadvantaged throughout their life courses. Today "poor/near poor rates" for certain subgroups, like women or those over 75, far exceed the average 19% poor/near poor figure for all elderly.[4]

"Is Aging More Problematic for Women than Men?," Nancy R. Hooyman asks. Although many older minority men—especially Native Americans—are desperately poor and die prematurely, the answer is generally yes. As cohorts age into old age, "elders" are mainly women, who live longer than men and have earned less if they worked for pay. Women constitute more than 70% of the older poor (Hooyman 1997:126). The older a woman is, the likelier to be poor. The percent of black women below 125% of the poverty line rises from 18.3% at age 56 to 44.9% at age 80.[5] "Lifelong inequities for women [and for men] become exacerbated in old age" (Calasanti and Slevin 2001: 23).

After 65, a higher percentage of women than men hover around the "poverty line," mainly subsisting without pensions, because women tended not to obtain jobs that came with them. Many live on little but Social Security (women get considerably less than men if they get any) and are dependent on Medicaid, Meals on Wheels, and other social services. Many are unable to obtain Medicaid, doled out stingily by the states. Nor can lesbians and gays obtain spousal benefits, like widow benefits from Social Security. Never-married women have the highest incidence of poverty (Calasanti and Slevin 2001:101).

Such are the ones who eat cat food in order to pay for pharmaceuticals. Or they take only half their medication to be able to pay other bills.

The consequences of income inequality among people over 65 are the facts to concentrate on. New Orleanians with means either lived on higher, pricier ground or were able to leave, relying on social networks they had outside. Many older poor people living at home did not own cars, or couldn't find gas or drivers to get them out. Poverty constructs helplessness. Some had kin or friends watching their backs but the latter, too, have fewer resources. Poverty also generates ignorance, greater exposure to toxicity, anxiety, work stress, and related diseases, reduced access to medical and psychiatric care, dependency, and, in later life, worsening prejudice. Carroll Estes, one of the best of the critical gerontologists, pointed out decades ago that "the old" are divided by government programs into the "deserving" and the "undeserving," and often, given the topsy-turvy American ideal of self-reliance, it is the neediest who are considered the undeserving (Estes 1986:18–20).

Health in later life is also the result of earlier opportunities. Inequality in a country without national health care means, as political scientist Victor Wallis has written, "biologically [as it were] distinct communities, in which those with the necessary resources will attain formidable physical resistance and longevity, while the excluded sectors ... will sink to previously unimagined depths of misery" (Wallis 2000:505.) Many women and men fall to the bottom of this savage distribution as early as their fifties or sixties, struck by chronic illnesses decades younger than the middle classes. Rationing is implicit: Physicians make "clinical compromises" that result in "potentially beneficial treatments being withheld from their patients for financial reasons" (Kapp, quoted in Simms 2003:715).

The federal poverty line is actually set lower for those over 65. The rationale may be that their costs are lower, but that ignores money spent on health care. Older women in poor health spend more than half their income on health care. Women also have higher rates than men of institutional care (Calasanti and Slevin 2001:114, 34).

African-American women are worse off than white women. Fewer Black women receive Social Security. Older women of color spend a higher proportion of their income on medical treatment than whites (Calasanti and Slevin 2001:98, 114). And African Americans have the highest disability rates of any community (Tischer 2005).

Without stereotyping an age group or ignoring disabilities and prejudice at younger ages, I think it fair to note that people at older ages are likely to have special needs that are not well attended. Those over 65 suffer fewer acute illnesses than younger people but more chronic illnesses, which our public and private health care systems are not nearly as well organized to care for. Even the well-off on Medicare and private insurance suffer from ageism in medicine. Doctors prefer to treat "the worried well rather than the really sick" (Weil 2005:56). Anti-ageism training (certainly as important as geriatrics) is not required even in specialties where professionals will probably treat older people. The chronically ill may find doctors inattentive or inept. Pain management is not taught properly, so that when it counts, older people can be undermedicated as well as overmedicated. They need advocates. Aides to help them age-in-place, now considered a better solution than institutionalization, can be economically unavailable, deficient, or even abusive. The very old—those 85 and over, likely to need more help in the worst straits—are the fastest growing segment of the population.

Many older people are as resourceful as the silver fox driving a riding mower in David Lynch's film, *The Straight Story* (1999) or the women stranded together in the film *Strangers in Good Company* (1990). Indeed, the "rapid recovery and emotional balance" of Pearline Chambers after spending two days up to her neck in floodwater, suggests that (some) "healthy elderly people are often able to bounce back from adversity more quickly than younger people" (Harden 2005:A24).

The facts marshaled here should not make younger people despair that in later life they too might die disproportionately in an emergency. Trying to bring together data and stories about the victims of Katrina—and showing the difficulty of doing so—is my attempt to make the entire age class more visible, in an era when even the disasters of Katrina scarcely brought the issue out of oblivion. Society is responsible for acknowledging both aspects: that older people have equal rights, and that some have special needs. Yet they were invisible or unimportant when the city was told to evacuate, inside and outside the Superdome, or in the Convention Center, and now, to Congress, they still are. Why?

Was this ageism, combined with sexism, racism, ableism, and classism? Not hatred necessarily, but aversion, ignorance, or indifference, the spectrum of feelings of many haves for the have-nots? Before we blame everything on ageism in this limited, private sense, however, we should recognize the political, economic, and social distortions in the ordinary constructions of "older people" or, more exactly, *retirees*.

The Politics of Later Life: Misrepresenting Retirees, the Midlife, and Longevity

If readers do not already know the kinds of facts I just listed, and if pundits and politicians get to waltz away from them, it's because the right wing's long campaign to misrepresent retirees as primarily "greedy geezers" has been amazingly successful. That label appeared in March 1988 as the cover title of a *New Republic* story, charging that the budget was "cosseting the old," describing the lavish lifestyles of those featured in *Modern Maturity*, arguing that sympathy for "the aging" was "understandable if increasingly misdirected," given their power and money, and warning of a "revolt" of the younger against "a massive entitlements system" for the "unproductive" (Fairlie 1988:19, 20, 19). Such characterizations and prognostications have been endlessly repeated, adding new prejudices to younger people's feelings and threatening the generational contract on which federal old-age provision is primarily based. "Probably the most disturbing construction of aging [in the Reagan–Bush I years] is the contention that the nation's economic problems are caused by the elderly," Carroll Estes warned (1999:136).

Are there masses of "greedy geezers"? Some might apply the label instantly to current Senators and Representatives agitating for repeal of the Progressive-era estate tax. The rich lobby powerfully, whatever their age. (People over 65, by contrast, dilute any power they might have by not voting as an anti-ageist bloc.) Insofar as those with capital at any age can better afford gated mansions and sportive leisure, they can thank their Congress—for cuts in taxes for corporations, upper-income brackets, and capital gains.

It's true that older Americans are on average better educated than earlier cohorts, and with education comes higher income. More have better health and live to later ages without disease.[6] For many people—the scientists and doctors who reduce later-life mortality, positive-aging gurus, people whose products target "Boomers," and of course those who hope they will live long and well—this is good news. For the right-wing politics of individualism, austerity for the poor, and budget cuts for the rich, it is also good news, unfortunately. They write as if everyone about to retire or already retired were white, male, and comfortably middle-class, ignoring the middling as well as women, the poorest, oldest, and sickest, and—through the media they control—they cause us to forget the existence of the most vulnerable and their issues.

The "age-wage peak" is a useful index for measuring this misrepresentation. It is the age at which Americans earn most. For men and women, white and black, the age-wage peak is now 45 to 54. After that, on average, earnings decline. They're not high at the peak. In 2000, men of that age at the median (half of men earned less) took in only $41,000. The median peak dropped by 2004.[7] And women at their midlife peak may earn more than their mothers, but they still earn only 73% of what men earn. Since the mid-1980s, only about two-thirds of men aged 55–65 are even in the workforce, down from 90% in the early 1950s. Some were downsized. Most are disabled (CBO 2004:5).[8] Most of these people, of course, belong to the so-called "Baby Boomer generation."

The truth we never hear is that at midlife "Boomers" have the highest wage inequality of any recent generation. Younger "Boomers"—between 40 and 50, a time when they should be approximating their peak—have a 10% poverty rate, the highest level of poverty since the generation born before World War I (Hughes and O'Rand 2004). Among the hard facts "Boomers" face are the loss of pensions, midlife job loss and discrimination, the erosion of seniority systems in the professions and even unionized companies, the increasing number of hours they must work, outsourcing, and the weakening of anti-discrimination laws (Gullette 1997, 2004). It adds up to the loss of the American dream. And disadvantage in old age depends on systemic disadvantage in adulthood and especially midlife, of the kind that has been institutionalized over the past few decades.

When writers, realtors, the American Association of Retired Persons (AARP), and others treat "Baby Boomers" as a market niche—as consumers—they flatter them on their youth, health, fitness, sexiness, wealth, potential longevity, and their ability to create innovations that will serve their needs. *That's positive aging!* Without having the same political agenda as the right wing, the booster publications support the same image: that "Boomers"—aka those about to get Social Security—are too wealthy to need it. It's dangerous when two such misleading discourses overlap.

For over a decade, as well as being flattered as "Baby Boomers," this age class has simultaneously been given a bad character—as if 78,500,000 people could have a character. They are described not just as rich but as over-entitled, self-righteous, undeserving of their luck, envious oppressors of the young—and of course "aging" (Gullette 2004:Chap. 3). Now between 40 and 60, in responsible midlife, "aging Boomers" can be represented as "unproductive," "sick" future retirees, still unwilling to yield their supposedly vast power, who will gobble up more health care and retirement benefits than they deserve or than "we" can afford. Armageddon in the twenty-first century is supposedly going to be their fault.

In "alarmist demography"—as age critic Steve Katz calls it (1992:203)—their "aging" will deprive more meritorious "others"—younger others—of allegedly scarce resources. Former Colorado Governor Dick Lamm said, "My aging body can prevent your kids from going to college" (Kreck 2004: F2). This is nonsense: If Dick Lamm gets a hip replacement from Medicare, how would that affect whether the government cuts Pell Grants? Common talk like Lamm's pits useless, unhealthy elders and midlifers against the pitiful hard-working young. Playing his wicked game, I *could* say, "Should your kid be able to get new knees just because he recklessly plays football? And should that cost be billed to my mother, who enjoys life as much and might need a life-saving intervention?" Writer Abigail Trafford, rebutting generationalism, said, "I am sick of being blamed for bankrupting the country's future" (2005:F1).

The endless stream of articles about "aging America" or "graying Boomers" should make us wary. These catch-phrases have not emerged to celebrate longevity but to show how menacing it is. Since I started following the construction of "Baby Boomers" in 1991, hostility to those considered "aging" has gotten much worse. Now in the *New York Times* a recent lead snarls, "How to Save Medicare? Die Sooner" (Altman 2005). A *Washington Post* op-ed threatens that "workers may get fed up paying so much of their paychecks to support retirees, many of whom (they would notice) were living quite comfortably" (Samuelson 2005:A19). We know why "they" notice. Even kind-hearted Trafford, in her book *My Time*, talking positively about the "longevity boom," points to suicides among men over 65 with a dire warning, "If you can't find new purpose and pleasure in the bonus decades, you can get trapped in a biological [sic] purgatory. You feel too old to live, but too young to die" (2004:xxii). The *Atlantic Monthly*, with an article titled "The Coming Death Shortage. Why the Longevity Boom Will Make Us Sorry to be Alive" (Mann 2005), wins the Gross-Out Competition for Blatant Ageism award for 2005, which was quite a year for all the varieties.

Alarmist demography is mendacious about Social Security, the only safety net left in a risky market that does not provide enough good jobs for younger and midlife workers, let alone the old. Social Security is not in crisis. It is actually still sloshing with surpluses from midlife earners, which first attracted the thirsty attention of the financial markets and produced Alan Greenspan's chicken little rhetoric and Bush's four months of failed campaigning in 2005.

Alarmist demography callously ignores government's failures to provide health care and to maintain budget surpluses for future needs. *More* federal money on "the old," if spent on the illnesses associated with aging— like arthritis, cancer, and Alzheimer's—would promote medical innovations, new industries, and better health. A well-run national health system would provide more jobs in geriatrics and nursing, both of which are fields with shortages. Planning would *help* the economy as well as everyone who plans to get older.

Alarmist demography feeds America's growing age obsession. Obsession with decline is often taken to be an effect of advertising trying to sell us "anti-aging" products along with internalized self-disgust. The multibillion-dollar commerce in aging *does* exploit our insecurities. But to focus on Viagra or "hormone replacement" propaganda as the main cause of age anxiety is misleading. You can be no more than 40 and already be "too old" in our middle-ageist economy. Age anxiety is affecting people at ever-younger ages (Gullette 1997, 2004). Ageism may be an ancient prejudice, but middle ageism is our own local twenty-first-century toxin. People as young as 30 are made to feel "over the hill."

Age anxiety is being cleverly manipulated into a political tactic on behalf of a conservative agenda. The image of expensive codgers distracts attention from class warfare coming from the top—the Bush tax cuts for the rich, the budget surplus turned into a Frankenstein deficit, the cuts in social programs, the deadly quagmire in Iraq. All these cost much more than the modest changes Social Security needs to thrive beyond 2042, or than national health care. Once the alarms have been sounded, then come the "remedies"—weakening the very programs that are our nation's slender warrant of being a humane democracy.

A nation is not better off simply because it has an age pyramid bottom-heavy with youth: That is the demography of the most impoverished third-world countries, as Christine Overall notes in her remarkable book, *Aging, Death, and Human Longevity* (2003). Nor is a nation necessarily worse off because the ratio of workers to retirees has dropped: Economist Paul Krugman points out in a brilliant article in *The New York Review of Books* that a ratio of three workers per retiree has been the American situation for decades, and Social Security stayed in surplus (2005:6).

Morally as well as factually, it is wrong to draw a grim picture of the twenty-first-century sky falling because people live longer (Gee and Gutman 2000). Alarmist demography encourages younger people to give up on Social Security rather than fight for it. It makes those who are forced out of the workplace unconsciously ashamed to be cumbering the earth. How can anyone find "purpose and pleasure" in aging past youth when the culture is offering us lower wages and stereotyping at ever-younger ages? Will the retired in general start thinking at some point that we are "too old to live, but too young to die"?[9] Everyone hears constantly how expensive "heroic" end-of-life care is. Those of us in our middle years are being scolded into abandoning our claims on it. Philosophers debate whether there is a "duty to die" (Battin 1987; Overall 2003). Maybe "Boomers" should die before they get old. Maybe men should congratulate themselves on dying younger than women!

Alarmist demography makes those aging toward old age vulnerable to mean-spirited ideas about becoming "burdens." Vicious stereotypes can reduce their will to live (Levy, Ashman, and Dror 1999–2000). Their anxiety and depression may not get treated because of ageism. A report by the Alliance for Ageing Research found that "too many physicians and psychologists believe that late-stage depression and suicidal statements are normal and acceptable in older patients" (in December 2005). A writer in the *Washington Post* said, "Nor, *given the aging of the population*, is the topic of rational suicide likely to disappear" (Lerner 2004:HE01; my emphasis). Will "suicide" sound "rational" only when elderly people do it? Will we confront an American ideology of decline so harsh that suicide *becomes* rational for us in later life?

That there are debates about "the duty to die" is a shocking fact, or would be if age mattered. The slide toward demonizing the midlife and longevity demonstrates an escalation in the vexed process of being aged by culture, which endures from very close to birth until our last conscious breath. Here is a culture war we disregard at our peril.

Aftermaths

That woman crumpled on the baggage mover: If she got back home, will women carpenters and electricians be rebuilding, earning Davis-Bacon wages so *they* won't be poor when they get too old too work? What help will she get from federal sources? The American Association of Homes and Services for the Aging suggested that rental vouchers be distributed by a mobile unit "to reach special needs populations, including the elderly and disabled" (Norris 2005:2), but there is never enough Section 8 housing. If, as Chester Hartman (2005:4) learned, it will take $40,000–$100,000 per unit to repair houses and apartments—depending on how high the muddy, stinking water rose—where will she get it? Will psychotherapists come to her? Given that college professors can't understand Medicare Part D, will there be funding for people to guide her and people of younger ages through the labyrinth of regulations produced by multiple government agencies?

Although the experienced head of the AARP, an advocacy organization for people over 50, warned that recovery funds should not come "at the expense of other older and vulnerable people by chopping Medicare and Medicaid" (Novelli 2005:35), that seems to be precisely what is happening. Congress recently cut the Low Income Energy Assistance Program, a cut that disproportionately affects the hypothermia-prone in other parts of the country. The Republican budget cut Medicaid and the only federal programs for geriatric education (Levkoff 2006), even as exhausted and traumatized elders returned to New Orleans. Now Congress is cutting help for some states affected by Katrina, which are forced to cut their budgets as their revenues fall.

Here are some criteria for judging coverage of a disaster like Katrina, which raised so many other issues of human and governmental failures at local, state, and federal levels, for so many populations—but *not* the issue of age. We should be vigilant enough to press for answers. Will there be enough savvy reporting to change public opinion and create better laws, rules, or agencies responsible for knowing where the elderly and disabled women and men in a community live, and caring for both those in institutions and those at home in emergency situations? Are people of all ages wondering what their own city's or town's disaster-evacuation plans are like—worrying hard enough to call City Hall to find out? Will rescuers be better trained in the problems of the elderly and disabled?

Will there be enough ethical reflection to change private behavior, so that the next time younger people will hesitate to leave elderly relatives behind? Will you look around now and pick an older neighbor to help in an emergency, if you are not the oldest neighbor yourself? Will there be enough reporting to make people active on behalf of a collective anti-aging agenda? Is it even more crystal clear now that old people have as much right to survive as younger adults, or children?

Ageisms

Ageism at the level of feelings is a peculiar privilege, compelling but ominous. Ageism has this in common with racism or sexism: that it forbids thinking "we" can ever be *them*. For others, it is more like classism and ableism, which admit as a remote possibility that "I" might eventually lose ground, but quarantines those who have already lost. Knee-jerk disdain tosses older people like fashions: "They're history." All ageism is learned in a historical context. One clever study found that some form of behavioral aversion among children, not present at four or six, is acquired as early as age eight.[10] Other ageisms are dutifully acquired as new curricula emerge in one's culture or subculture: belief in imaginary cohorts like "Boomers" and "Xers," stereotypes of age classes, the purchase of talismans for hiding age signs, participation in generational war, discursive hostility, age segregation. Organized discrimination need not be malicious, only self-interested.[11]

Institutions that abet ageism and middle-ageism can do so because they are unopposed in fact, whatever regulations say. Business personnel policies discriminate against midlife workers despite the (enfeebled) Equal Employment Opportunity Commission (EEOC). In a harsh limitation of civil rights law, the Supreme Court said in *Kimel vs. Florida Board of Regents* (2000) that "States may discriminate on the basis of age." *Smith vs. City of Jackson* (2005), a Supreme Court ruling favorable to workers over 40, still found against the midlife defendants. We'll see how *Smith* gets applied. Even though midlife workers clamor for the jobs, high-tech immigrants are admitted by Congress; outsourcing continues uncontrolled; corporations and whole industries flee the country to avoid paying decent wages that rise up the age curve.

Ageism as a system is wrapped up in neoliberal state policy on behalf of postindustrial capital. Power, not the needs of the woman on the baggage mover or the 45-year-old on Workers' Comp, drives the ideology of decline. Our national state, like others, is "promoting and funding market solutions" in a "race to the bottom" to see "how much and how fast social expenditures may be reduced in order to transfer more national wealth to the corporate sector." The same is true of wages. The World Bank and the International Monetary Fund (IMF) are "at the forefront of attempts" to foster a political climate conducive to reducing state welfare for old age. This stance in turn has forced the International Labour Organization to make concessions that have expanded the role of privatized old-age benefits. They have also started to give in to the demand for countries in the Organization for Economic Cooperation and Development (OECD) to do what the United States has already done—raise the age of retirement.[12]

Ageism deals pain all around. Middle ageism hands it out earlier. Decline ideology puts the life course at risk globally.

Creating an Age Revolution

To fight the forces producing decline, Americans need to believe that an age revolution, in conjunction with other resistance movements, is urgent. It will take a major effort to convince them. Many people think the "Boomers" are so powerful that they can end ageism in America passively, merely by growing older. That is unlikely. Being sold billions in anti-aging products and being swept off the main stage of work life prematurely are not proofs of contravening power. And even if this large cohort could accomplish cultural changes—inspiring TV to show more than 1.5% of its characters as older—*systems* are not thus transformed. Half the American workforce will soon be over 40, but they would have to think of themselves not as "Boomer"-consumers but as *workers* in protest against the destruction of the midlife.

The revolution will have to be multifaceted. It's useful to attack ageism at the level of feelings. Those who repeat, "Remember you must get old" want us each to recognize early the continuity of our own life course, thus discovering in anti-ageism a good fight for our own old age. But much more is needed to transform behavior, language, and visual culture, interpersonal relations, the commerce in aging, employment practices, law, and public policy.

We know how to rescue the life course. It's the social justice agenda with anti-decline features. There would be less reason to lament becoming "gray" in America if the midlife were more green, the country more intent on raising wages, children and entry-level workers entitled to a golden head start, and everyone benefitting from health care. "Full Employment Plus"—job growth with particular attention to empowering the labor movement, explaining the value of seniority, and raising median wages at the age peak (Gullette 2004)—would mean less anxiety about aging out of the workforce. Social Security could be "bountiful"—as proposed by former Bush Treasury Secretary Paul O'Neill—based on an annuity ample enough to guarantee $50,000 a year (Alperovitz and Williamson 2006:16).

Simultaneously, we need a vast movement of consciousness-raising about age and being aged by culture. Age studies, the emerging multidisciplinary field that I have tried to represent in this chapter, is at its beginnings (Gullette 2004). Intellectually, emotionally, and ethically, we need a cultural criticism that is as smart about the category of age as many people have become in the last 40 years about race, gender, class, and ability—and as obdurate in objecting to bias. Anti-ageist curricula could start in kindergarten. Journalists, health practitioners, and the rest of us could try to raise our "Age-Consciousness I.Q." An intergenerational collective could pressure corporations, Congress, and even the Supreme Court and World Bank into relenting their attacks on the latter stages of the life course.

Conclusion

Katrina coverage of age was deplorable, perhaps the worst part of a bad year. 2005 was the year George Bush tried hardest to weaken Social Security; the year in which ageism in major media became so shrill; the year of the ambiguous Supreme Court decision in *Smith vs. City of Jackson.* America badly needs what Katrina could have provided: a vast anti-ageist conversation that will tune up the policy engines in order to target the forces of decline, and convince the most recalcitrant that later life needs to be spared the cruelties that are in the works.

Decline ideology is not just ageist, sexist, racist, or politically incorrect. It can be fatal—in this disaster and all the ones to come.

References

Allen, Scott. 2006. Harvard To Study Katrina's Long-term Psychological Toll. *Boston Globe*: A4. January 6.

Alperovitz, Gar and Thad Williamson. 2006. A "Top Ten" List of Bold Ideas. *The Nation*: 16–18. January 23.

Altman, Daniel. 2005. How to Save Medicare? Die Sooner. *New York Times*. Section 3: 1.

Battin, Margaret. 1987. Age Rationing and the Just Distribution of Health Care: Is There a Duty to Die? *Ethics* 97(2): 317–340. January.

Calasanti, Toni M. and Kathleen F. Slevin. 2001. *Gender, Social Inequalities, and Aging.* Walnut Creek, CA: Altamira Press.

Christofferson, John. 2005. Study: Most Katrina Victims were Elderly. *Washington Post*. October 24.

CBO (Congressional Budget Office). 2004. Disability and Retirement: The Early Exit of Baby Boomers from the Labor Force. November.

Dembner, Alice. 2005. Ageism Said To Erode Care Given To Elders. *Boston Globe*: A1, A4. March 7.

Estes, Carroll L. 1986. The Politics of Ageing in America. In *Dependency and Interdependency in Old Age: Theoretical Perspectives and Policy Alternatives*, edited by Chris Phillipson, Miriam Bernard, and Patricia Strang: 15–29. London: Croom Helm.

Estes, Carroll L. 1999. The Aging Enterprise Revisited. In *Critical Gerontology: Perspectives from Political and Moral Economy*, edited by Meredith Minkler and Carroll L. Estes: 135-146. Amityville: Baywood Publishing Company.

Fairlie, Henry. 1988. Talkin' 'Bout My Generation. *New Republic*, March 28: 19–22.

Fimrite, Peter. 2005. Rights Group Warns Disaster Would Imperil Disabled, Elderly. *San Francisco Chronicle*: B5. October 7.

Fussell, Elizabeth. 2005. Leaving New Orleans: Social Stratification, Networks, and Hurricane Evacuation. Social Science Research Council. September 26. http://www. understanding-Katrina.ssrc.org/Fussell.

Gee, Ellen M. and Gloria M. Gutman. 2000. *The Overselling of Population Aging*. Oxford: Oxford University Press.

Gullette, Margaret Morganroth. 1997. *Declining to Decline. Cultural Combat and the Politics of the Midlife*. Charlottesville: University Press of Virginia.

Gullette, Margaret Morganroth. 2004. *Aged by Culture*. Chicago: University of Chicago Press.

Harden, Blaine. 2005. With Age Comes Resilience, Storm's Aftermath Proves. *Washington Post*. September 14.

Hartman, Chester. 2005. Report from New Orleans. *Poverty and Race* 14(6): 3–5. November/December.

Healy, Patrick. 2004. Kerry Revives '92 Election Theme To Attack Bush. *Boston Globe*: A3. May 19.

Hooyman, Nancy R. 1997. Is Aging More Problematic for Women than Men? In *Controversial Issues in Aging*, edited by Andrew Scharlach and Leonard W. Kaye. Boston: Allyn and Bacon.

Hughes, Mary Elizabeth and Angela O'Rand. 2004. The Lives and Times of the Baby Boomers. Russell Sage Foundation and Population Reference Bureau. October. http://www.prb.org/AmericanPeople.

Isaacs, L. W. and D. J. Bearison. 1986. The Development of Children's Prejudice Against the Aged. *Journal of Aging and Human Development* 23: 175–195.

Katz, Steven. 1992. Alarmist Demography: Power, Knowledge and the Elderly Population. *Journal of Aging Studies* 6(3): 203–225.

Khanna, Roma. 2005. Katrina's Aftermath. *Houston Chronicle*. November 27.

Kimel vs. Florida Board of Regents. 2000. 120 S. Ct. 631.

Kreck, Dick. 2004. Lamm Book Sure To Stir Controversy. *Denver Post*: F2. February 9.

Krugman, Paul. 2005. America's Senior Moment. *The New York Review of Books*. March 10.

Lerner, Barron H. 2004. A Calculated Departure: For Someone in Good Health, Can Suicide Ever Be a Rational Choice? *Washington Post*. March 2.

Levkoff, Sue. 2006. Assault on the Elderly. *Boston Globe*: A19. January 13.

Levy, Rebecca, Oris Ashman, and Itiel Dror. 1999–2000. To Be or Not to Be: The Effects of Aging Stereotypes on the Will to Live. *Omega* 40(3): 409–420.

Louisiana Department of Health and Hospitals. http://www.dhh.dhh.louisiana.gov/offices/publications/pubs-145/DECEASED%20%victims%released_11-14-20005_publication.pdf.

Mann, Charles. 2005. The Coming Death Shortage. Why the Longevity Boom Will Make us Sorry to be Alive. *Atlantic Monthly*. May.

Markley, Melanie and Cynthia Leonor Garza. 2005. Katrina's Aftermath; Reaching out to Aid the Elderly, Frail. *Houston Chronicle*. September 10.

Norris, Michelle. 2005. Written Testimony of American Association of Homes and Services for the Aging. House Financial Services Committee. September 15. http://www.aahsa.org.

Novelli, William D. 2005. Katrina's Legacy. *AARP Bulletin*: 35. November.

Older Women's League. 2005. *Newsletter*. November 16.

O'Neil, Tim. 2005. Evacuee Finds Comfort in Arms of Family. *St. Louis Post-Dispatch*: A1. December 22.

Overall, Christine. 2003. *Aging, Death, and Human Longevity*. Berkeley: University of California Press.

Robinson, Barrie. 1994. Ageism. University of California, Berkeley: School of Social Welfare. http://www. ist-socrates.berkeley.edu/~aging/ModuleAgeism.html#anchor736321.

Rohde, David et al. 2005. Vulnerable and Doomed in the Storm. *New York Times*. September 19.

Samuelson, Robert J. 2005. Economic Death Spiral. *Washington Post*: A19.
Seager, Joni. 2005. Natural Disasters Expose Gender Divide. *Chicago Tribune*. September 14.
Simms, Mary. 2003. Opening the Black Box of Rationing Care in Later Life: The Case of "Community Care" in Britain. *Journal of Aging and Health* 15(4): 713–737. November.
Smith, Martin. 2005. The Storm. *Frontline*. November 22.
Smith vs. City of Jackson. 2005. No. 03-1160.
Teichert, Nancy Weaver. 2005. Katrina's Lasting Storm. Disaster Plans for Seniors Reviewed. *Sacramento Bee*. September 13.
Tischer, Ingrid. 2005. Private communication. December 16.
Trafford, Abigail. 2004. *My Time: Making the Most of the Rest of Your Life*. New York: Basic.
Trafford, Abigail. 2005. We Ain't Heavy . . . *Washington Post*: F1. February 15.
United States Census Bureau. 2005. *Current Population Survey*.
Wade, Leigh. 2005. Meeting Needs of Older Americans During Disasters. Senate Special Committee on Aging. October 5.
Wallis, Victor. 2000. Species Questions (*Gattungsfragen*): Humanity and Nature from Marx to Shiva. *Organization and Environment* 14(1): 500–507.
Weil, Andrew. 2005. *Healthy Aging: A Lifelong Guide to Your Physical and Spiritual Well-Being*. New York: Knopf.

Endnotes

1. The first figure, cited by Tischer 2005, comes from the National Council on Disability (www.Jfanow.org/jfanow/index.php?mode=A&id=2497). The second figure comes from Fussell 2005, based on 2000 Census data.
2. Louisiana Department of Health and Hospitals, as of November 28, 2005. www.dhh. louisiana.gov/offices/publications/pubs-145/DECEASED%20%victims%released_11-14-20005_publication.pdf. The numbers of dead were 88 from the 51–60 age group, 150 from the 61–75 age group, 268 from the over-75 group. Women and men died in almost equal numbers, although no gender breakdown by age is available. Many of the dead may never be identified.
3. A Harvard study, led by Ronald Kessler, professor of health care policy, will be evaluating whether recovery efforts are helping individuals affected by the disaster. A small survey by the Centers for Disease Control and Prevention in the fall of 2005 showed that more than 40% of survivors had signs of post-traumatic stress (Allen 2006:14).
4. Robinson 1994. "Near poverty" means 125% of the poverty level. Robinson believes "poor/near poor" is a better way to measure poverty rates of people over 65.
5. United States Census Bureau 2005. For white women, the rate rises from 9.8% at age 56 to 21.6% at age 80.
6. Overall writes that "the number of years of 'dependence-free life' in Canada is increasing, so that men are living 93% of their lives and women 88% of their lives in good health" (2003:8). In the United States, many factors—including inability to gain access to health care—may prevent equivalent compression of morbidity.
7. Data from 2004, from the Bureau of Labor Standards, http://www.bls.gov/opub/ted/2005/oct/wk5/art04.htm. My thanks to Robert Ross for help with the data.
8. Congressional Budget Office 2004. This was a study of people 50–61 not in the labor force. www.cbo.gov/showdoc.cfm?index=6018&sequence.
9. A man who had lost his salary and had huge health insurance payments told a Kerry rally in May 2004 that he was "too young to die and too old to rock and roll" (Healy 2004:A3).
10. Isaacs and Bearison (1986) measured if children sat farther away from adults if their grandparents' age than adults their parents' age, initiated eye contact less, spoke less.
11. For a new study from Dr. Robert Butler's International Longevity Center, detailing age discriminations, go to www.ILC.org.
12. All quotations in this paragraph come from Estes, Biggs, Phillipson, 2003: Chapter 7, 104, 109, 110.

---

* Section I was published, in an abbreviated version, on www.womensenews.org, December 14, 2005.

Where Is Home? Housing for Low-Income People After the 2005 Hurricanes

SHEILA CROWLEY

The Gulf Coast hurricanes of 2005, especially Hurricane Katrina that made landfall on August 29, precipitated a housing crisis of historic proportions. Hundreds of thousands of people were displaced from their homes. Tens of thousands of homes were destroyed or severely damaged by the winds and storm surge of the hurricane itself or were ruined by the floods that breached the levees guarding the low-lying areas of New Orleans.

The trauma caused directly by the storms and floods was compounded first by the dismal disaster response and the belated evacuation of at least 100,000 people. The trauma has been exacerbated and extended by a temporary housing program that could not have been more poorly designed and executed if it had been purposely intended to fail. Many thousands of displaced people remain in a transitional state, not knowing when or if they can return to their homes or even to their communities. The people with the fewest resources are experiencing the greatest level of uncertainty. Despite the kindness of many ordinary citizens and governments in aiding evacuees from the Gulf Coast, this disaster is a monumental failure by the federal government to protect and care for its people.

At a time when there are at least 4.5 million more extremely low-income households in the United States than there are affordable rental housing units (Pelletiere 2006), the loss of a sizable portion of the supply of homes affordable to low-income people accentuates the catastrophe. With people from the Gulf Coast evacuated to every state, the District of Columbia, Puerto Rico, and the Virgin Islands, the demands on the housing market nationwide have escalated as communities try to make room for the displaced.

The housing story of the disaster in the Gulf Coast has multiple and interlocking dimensions that remain in flux several months after the storm. New data and issues emerge almost daily. However frustrated researchers, analysts, advocates, and policymakers may be with the instability of information, it cannot compare to that of people who have lost their homes and are directly and adversely affected by the lingering uncertainty. This analysis begins with a review of data about the pre-Katrina population and housing stock in the affected area. Next, information about how many people were displaced and some of their characteristics, as well as the extent of damage to the housing stock, are offered, however tentatively. From the onset of the disaster, accurate accountings of its impact on people and homes have been hard to come by. Of the many failures of the disaster response, the failure to have in place a system of data collection and to carry out an analysis to inform the response and recovery ranks among the highest.

This review then turns to the federal government's response to the housing disaster. The temporary housing programs that are run by the Federal Emergency Management Agency (FEMA) to assist displaced people until they can return to their homes or are permanently rehoused elsewhere are explored in detail, even as the programs keep changing. The housing elements of the recovery and rebuilding plans also are covered to the extent that they are known, with a focus on the federal role. The chapter closes with reflections on the meaning of the housing response to the Gulf Coast disaster for the American community.

The Numbers

The television images that circled the globe in the long days after the storm showed that the victims of the storm most in harm's way and most neglected by the government's response were largely poor and Black, many of whom were elderly or disabled. In any disaster, it is the lowest-income people who suffer the most and have the most difficulty recovering. But the paucity of data ten months after the storm about precisely who was displaced and what their current circumstances are is scandalous. What follows are some of the major quantitative data sources that offer a glimpse into the extent of displacement and housing damage. When possible, data included here cover Alabama, Louisiana, Mississippi, and Texas, the states that sustained damage from both Hurricanes Katrina and Rita, which made landfall on September 24, 2005. In some cases, the data are only applicable to areas affected by Hurricane Katrina, which are in Alabama, Louisiana, and Mississippi. In still other cases, the data also cover Hurricane Wilma, which hit Florida on October 24, 2005.

How Many People Were Affected?

FEMA reports receiving over 2.6 million applications for individual disaster assistance from residents of Louisiana, Mississippi, Alabama, and Texas as of March 14, 2006 (DHS FEMA 2006e). Two-thirds (66%) are seeking disaster aid due to Hurricane Katrina and, therefore, are from Louisiana, Mississippi, and Alabama only (DHS FEMA 2006h). The remaining one-third are for Hurricane Rita relief, which affected Louisiana and Texas.

The applications for FEMA assistance were made on behalf of households who may or may not have evacuated and who may or may not have been displaced. Thus, 2.6 million applications for assistance is not a proxy for people or households displaced.

Although applicants were located in every state at the time of application, 92% were from the four states that were directly hit: Louisiana has 42% of the applicants, Texas has 25%, Mississippi has 20%, and Alabama has just 5%. Another 4% were in four neighboring states of Arkansas, Tennessee, Georgia, and Florida, 1% were in California, and 3% were scattered throughout the rest of the country (DHS FEMA 2006f).

The Congressional Research Service (Gabe, Falk, and McCarthy 2005) estimated in November 2005 that 711,698 people were "acutely impacted" by Hurricane Katrina, meaning they lived in neighborhoods that experienced flooding or significant structural damage. The vast majority (90.6%) of acutely impacted people lived in Louisiana, with 9.3% in Mississippi, and only 0.1% in Alabama.

Using 2000 Census data, CRS estimates that 44% of the acutely impacted population was Black. For New Orleans alone, 73% of the people in this category were Black. Those 65 years of age or older accounted for 12% of the acutely impacted group, and children under 18 years of age were another 25% (Gabe, Falk, and McCarthy 2005).

The income analysis by CRS is also based on 2000 Census data, which reports the number of people by federal poverty status in 1999. 21% of the acutely impacted had incomes at or below the federal poverty level, and another 20% had incomes between 100% and 199% of the federal poverty level. The poverty threshold in 2004 was $19,307 annually for a family of four and $9,645 for one person living alone (Gabe, Falk, and McCarthy 2005).

Area median income (AMI), the income measure used in federal housing programs, can only be roughly compared with the federal poverty measure, but offers a transition to understanding the implications of the cost of housing lost in the disaster. A low-income household, using the federal definition, has an annual income at or less than 80% of AMI; extremely low income is 30% or less than AMI. Low income in 2005 before Katrina ranged from $35,120 to $44,040 annually in the fourteen jurisdictions cited in the CRS analysis. Extremely low income ranged from $13,170 to $16,515. In the six parishes in the New Orleans Metropolitan Statistical Area, low income was $40,800 and extremely low income was $15,300 in 2005 (Wardrip, Pelletiere, and Crowley 2005).

How Many Homes Were Lost?

A September 2005 analysis by the National Low Income Housing Coalition (NLIHC) showed 302,405 housing units seriously damaged or destroyed by Hurricane Katrina, based on an overlay of National Geospatial Intelligence Agency pre- and post-Katrina maps on census blocks and using 2000 Census data (NLIHC 2005c). The jurisdictions included in the NLIHC report are the same counties or parishes in Alabama, Louisiana, and Mississippi that are in the CRS report. The total number of housing units in these jurisdictions, according to the 2000 Census, was 412,844 (U.S. Census Bureau 2000). Thus, 73% of all homes in the most affected areas were damaged or destroyed.

Of the damaged or destroyed units, 53% were owner-occupied, and 47% were rental units. NLIHC estimates that 71% of all the affected units were affordable to low-income households, including 57% of the ownership units and 88% of the rental units. The analysis shows that 47% of the lost or damaged units were in New Orleans, a majority (55%) of which were rental units. Of all the housing stock lost in New Orleans, 79% was affordable to low-income households. Of all the lost units in New Orleans affordable to low-income households, 65% were ownership units and 89% rental housing (NLIHC 2005c).

After several months of no official estimates of damage, data compiled by FEMA and analyzed by HUD's Office of Policy Development and Research (PDR) were made available in March 2006. These data are considered preliminary, but provide the first official snapshot of the impact of Katrina, Rita, and Wilma on the Gulf Coast housing stock. HUD estimates that 932,944 homes were damaged in Alabama, Louisiana, Mississippi, Texas, and Florida. Of these, 30% sustained severe or major damage. Owner-occupied homes comprised 62% of the most damaged housing (HUD PDR 2006).

Louisiana sustained the most damage to its housing, both in absolute numbers and in percentage of damaged housing of total housing stock. Of the 1,656,053 total homes in Louisiana prior to the hurricanes, 31% were damaged and 12% had severe or major damage. Of Mississippi's 1,046,434 homes, 21% were damaged, 6% with severe or major damage. In contrast, only 0.2% of housing in Alabama, 0.2% in Texas, and 0.003% in Florida had severe or major damage (HUD PDR 2006).

HUD reported that there were a total of 103,010 occupied public or assisted units, including privately-owned units rented by Section 8 voucher holders, in the Katrina-affected areas of Louisiana, Mississippi, and Alabama prior to the disaster. The number of units damaged was 41,161, with 15,199 sustaining damage severe enough to render them uninhabitable (Jackson 2006). According to a March 2006 HUD report, 27 Public Housing Agencies (PHAs) in Alabama, Louisiana, Mississippi, and Texas have units that sustained catastrophic (defined as uninhabitable) or major damage. Of the total of 21,682 units operated by these PHAs, at least 63% are included in the catastrophic or major damage category, with the number of units damaged for ten PHAs not yet reported. The HUD report indicates that the Housing Authority of New Orleans (HANO) owns 8,421, or 39%, of the public housing units in the affected area, 7,125 of which incurred catastrophic or major damage. The next largest PHA to sustain heavy damage to its stock is the Mobile, AL PHA, where all 4,068 units sustained major damage (HUD 2006d).

According to another HUD report, there were 82,404 units of privately owned, HUD-assisted housing in the affected areas in Alabama, Louisiana, and Mississippi. Over three-quarters (76%) of the stock with project-based assistance[i] is Section 8 project-based housing. Another 22% is Section 202 housing for the elderly, and the remaining 2% is Section 811 housing for people with disabilities. Damage reports were only available for Louisiana and Mississippi and were not broken down by type of housing assistance. Of the 66,967 HUD-assisted units in these two states, 28% sustained damage, with 19% sustaining "severe" damage (HUD 2006e).

While it is difficult to draw specific conclusions from these self-described preliminary data, the following is clear:

- At least 700,000 people lost their homes, and some 300,000 of them were low-income, if not poor, by federal poverty standards.
- The extent of damage to housing is unprecedented in the area and in the nation.
- Louisiana experienced the greatest amount of and the most severe damage to its housing stock, with New Orleans sustaining the greatest loss.
- Homeowners and renters alike lost their homes.
- Housing that was affordable to low-income people comprised the majority of what was lost.

The Federal Government Response: Temporary Housing

The post-hurricane housing circumstances of many of the displaced people constitute a second disaster. The federal government has been roundly criticized for its failure to assure decent emergency shelter to carry out federal law[2] requiring that all people in the United States who are displaced by natural disaster be assured safe and affordable temporary housing and assistance to regain long-term housing stability (Collins and Lieberman 2006; Fischer and Sard 2006; Frank and Waters 2005; Hsu and Connelly 2005; Lipton 2005c; NLIHC 2005i; Powell 2005; Sarbanes 2005; Steinhauer and Lipton 2006; Torpy 2005; Weisman 2005). This failure has compounded the hardship, confusion, and trauma of the people most in need of assistance.

Diversion of Existing Low-Income Housing Resources

In the scramble to find shelter for displaced people as they were dispersed to cities across the country, housing providers were called upon to assist. HUD encouraged local PHAs to prioritize evacuees for public housing units and Housing Choice Vouchers (Bernardi 2005; HUD 2006a). Low-income housing advocates and people on waiting lists for housing assistance quickly raised concern that scarce existing housing aid intended for local people was going to evacuees, pitting one needy group against another (Bromage 2005; "Las Vegas Homeless Advocates" 2005; Rodriguez 2005; Stewart 2005; Young 2005). In an email to the author on September 8, 2005, a homeless shelter operator in a small city in the Northeast wrote:

> I have been sitting through meetings [and] press conferences regarding the devastating disaster in the Gulf region and how we can help. The ... Housing Authority is setting units aside for evacuees while all our shelters are full...I sat with one family of the 35 families and 90 kids in our shelter today who had a story that is devastating, if anyone cared to listen. 100 families are in shelter in our city tonight. Everyone in the political and human service community seems to be running around in a frenzy in the wake of the tragedy. But what happens when that goes away and they have done their hero moment and all of these families with huge needs remain our day-to-day responsibility and the compassion dies down? Is there a way ... to be real and say this is the time to put more money into Section 8? I cannot stand to see resources that are so minimal strained beyond their limits.

(Personal communication, September 8, 2005)

Although HUD had assured Congress that it was no longer recommending that PHAs give preference to evacuees, its website told a different story. In an October 18, 2005 letter to HUD Secretary Alphonso Jackson, Representative Barney Frank (D-MA), Ranking Member of the House Financial Services Committee, the committee with jurisdiction over HUD programs, complained that documents on the HUD website continued to encourage PHAs to use their existing resources for evacuees (Frank 2005).

A particularly egregious diversion of low-income housing resources occurred in Texas, where 7,000 vacant low-income housing tax credit (LIHTC) rental units[3] were made available to Katrina evacuees (TDHCDA 2005). On September 2, 2005, U.S. Treasury Secretary John Snow announced suspension of income restrictions for LIHTC properties, making the housing available to evacuated families regardless of income (U.S. Department of Treasury 2005), a move supported by the apartment industry (NMHC 2005) and condemned by low-income housing advocates (TXLIHIS 2005). The thousands of poor families on housing assistance waiting lists in Texas prior to the storms had been unable to rent any of these vacant homes, because the rent was more than they could afford and there were no housing vouchers to help them bridge the gap between what the housing cost and what they could afford.

Fair Housing Violations

The racial dimensions of the housing crisis created by the 2005 hurricanes are undeniable. The public face of the Katrina evacuee is Black. In the immediate aftermath of the disaster, many speculated, indeed hoped, that the poverty among Black Americans exposed by the storms and floods would inspire a renewed commitment to racial and economic justice in the United States. The public response was abundant, with monetary and in-kind donations. Also, remarkably, thousands of people opened their own homes as temporary shelters. But even in this generous outpouring, illegal discrimination reared its ugly head.

Hundreds of homes were offered to evacuees via Internet sites. An investigation by the Greater New Orleans Fair Housing Action Center revealed at least five websites (including one sponsored by FEMA) offering aid to evacuees that published illegally discriminatory ads. Examples of the innumerable offending ads are: "We prefer a white couple;" "I would love to house a single mom with one child, not racist, but white only;" "We would prefer a white Christian couple;" "Prefer white or Hispanic background;" and "Room and board available for white, Spanish, or Indian single female" (Perry, James 2006).

The Greater New Orleans Fair Housing Action Center filed administrative complaints with HUD against the five websites on December 23, 2005. However, some of the website sponsors assert they are not subject to the publishing provisions of the federal Fair Housing Act, claiming defense under the Communications Decency Act (CDA) that limits their liability for certain kinds of speech. Fair housing advocates are urging Congress to amend the CDA to explicitly forbid discriminatory advertising on the Internet (Perry, James 2006).

Evacuees have experienced considerable illegal discrimination in their search for housing to rent in communities to which they have been evacuated. Because such a large number of people of color were thrust into the rental housing market at one time, the National Fair Housing Alliance (NFHA) initiated a testing program[4] in Florida, Alabama, Georgia, Texas, and Tennessee. In 65 cases of testing landlords in these states, Black people were discriminated against in two-thirds of the cases. Administrative complaints have been filed with HUD against five apartment complexes based on these results (Smith, Shanna 2006a).

As the agency with responsibility for enforcing the federal fair housing law, HUD reports that it has taken action in response to the discrimination against evacuees in the rental housing market (HUD 2006a). On October 25, 2005, newly confirmed Assistant Secretary for Fair Housing and Equal Opportunity Kim Kendrick sent an open letter to the housing industry reminding them of their fair housing obligations in dealing with evacuees and providing a toll-free number for people who think they have been illegally denied access to housing (Kendrick 2005). In January 2006, HUD announced an advertising campaign to inform evacuees of their rights under federal fair housing laws. The Ad Council produced public service announcements for all major media. However, they are only aired on or printed in donated media space (HUD 2006b).

In a meeting with civil rights and low-income housing advocates on January 31, 2006, HUD Secretary Alphonso Jackson indicated he would not tolerate fair housing violations against hurricane evacuees, and that he was authorizing Secretary-initiated complaints against the worst offenders (personal communication, January 31, 2006). Secretary-initiated complaints, which may be made even in the absence of individual complainants, are relatively infrequent and their use under these circumstances indicates some degree of seriousness of HUD's intent.

However, the Secretary's words belie a lack of commitment to funding fair housing programs. The President's fiscal year 2007 proposed federal budget, sent to Congress on February 6, 2006, cut fair housing programs (NLIHC 2006b), curtailing funding for the very organizations that root out and expose fair housing violations. Moreover, HUD's delays in the repair and repopulating of public and assisted housing in the affected areas, and New Orleans in particular (Filosa 2006c; Walsh 2006a), indicate that

HUD's desire to "affirmatively further fair housing" in all HUD programs is less than whole-hearted.

FEMA: The Disaster of a Disaster Response

The Stafford Act authorizes FEMA to expend federal funds to provide assistance to states and local communities once the President has issued a disaster declaration. Among the numerous duties it has for disaster relief, FEMA is supposed to help displaced people obtain temporary housing. This assistance takes two forms. Section 403 is the Public Assistance (PA) Program that makes funds for emergency shelter available to state and local governments, as well as social service agencies. Section 408 is the Individual and Households Program (IHP) that makes longer-term, but still temporary, housing assistance available directly to displaced people who meet certain criteria. Under Section 408, a displaced household is entitled to up to $26,200 for rent, home repairs, and other personal costs. Rent assistance can be provided for up to 18 months or until the $26,200 limit is reached, whichever comes first (Sard and Rice 2005). It was under Section 408 that FEMA issued $2,000 to every person registered for FEMA assistance in the days immediately after the disaster, which will be applied to each household's $26,200 limit.

Trailers — FEMA's initial response after the disaster was its standard disaster response: to order trailers. Providing a displaced household with a rent-free trailer for up to 18 months as an alternative to rent assistance is authorized under Section 408. Early reports were that FEMA had ordered 300,000 travel trailers and mobile homes (Lipton 2005a). The prospect of several hundred poor families segregated together in trailer camps removed from transportation, jobs, schools, health care, and shopping provoked a widespread outcry across the political spectrum (Cohn 2005; Olson and Weicher 2005; Rehm 2005).[5] Although trailers had to be part of the solution in areas with acute housing shortages, FEMA soon backed off of its reliance on trailers as the preferred temporary housing choice. According to FEMA, the total number of trailers occupied by the Katrina and Rita evacuees was 87,824 as of March 6 (personal communication, March 7, 2006). These include both trailers that were grouped together in camps, as well as trailers placed on the property of individuals to provide shelter while homeowners repair their houses.

The trailer program has been plagued by controversy. FEMA has been unable to meet the demand for trailers, only able to install 500 a day, with a waiting list of over 40,000 in Louisiana alone (Collins and Lieberman 2006). News images of thousands of manufactured homes sinking into the mud in a field near Hope, Arkansas became a symbol of FEMA's incompetence (Brand 2005; Neuman 2006). Siting of trailers has been met with NIMBY resistance by some parish governments in Louisiana and by neighbors in New Orleans (Hustmyre 2005; Jensen 2005; Tizon 2005; Trailer Troubles 2006). The HUD Secretary has initiated his own fair housing complaints against some parish governments for refusing to site trailers, claiming their refusal may be racially motivated (Kendrick 2006). Moreover, the trailers come with another fair housing problem: They are not accessible to some people with physical disabilities, a situation that has provoked other complaints and a lawsuit (Advocacy Center 2006).

Perhaps the most bizarre problem with the trailers is they are structurally unsuitable for hurricane-prone areas. As Mississippi Governor Haley Barbour (2006) put it, the trailers "do not even provide the most basic protection from high winds or severe thunderstorms." As the new hurricane season is upon us, people who now reside in the trailers and local advocates are increasingly concerned about what will happen when the next big storm hits (Factoring the Forecast 2006; Lipton 2006; personal communications, April 6, 2006). The unstable nature of the trailers is part of the impetus for the push for "Katrina Cottages," modular units built on foundations that can become permanent homes and that reportedly can be produced for less than the cost of trailers (Barbour 2006; Radelat 2006; Waller 2006). However, limited as the trailers are, as one evacuee living in a trailer told the author, "It is better than living in a tent" (personal communication, April 6, 2006). Tents were the only shelter for many people in the immediate weeks after the storm, especially in Mississippi, and some people were still in tents as of mid-May 2006.

Hotels and Motels — Yet another expensive and contentious form of temporary housing was hotel/motel rooms. Initially, as part of the national disaster response plan, the American Red Cross placed displaced people in hotels and motels, to be paid for by FEMA 403 funds. But responsibility for administering the hotel program was transferred to FEMA when the need to support people in hotels extended past the time that the Red Cross defined as its mission. At the peak of hotel usage, FEMA reports it was paying for 85,000 rooms a night (DHS FEMA 2006b). FEMA's repeated attempts to end the hotel program and compel evacuees to move elsewhere resulted in a lawsuit (*McWaters v. FEMA* 2005) and a widespread public outcry against FEMA (Adcox 2005; Blumenthal and Lipton 2005; Driver 2005; FEMA's Latest Fumble 2005; Lipton 2005c; Newsom Slams 2005; NLIHC 2005h; Thompson 2005; What Next 2005; With Holidays Coming 2005). In December 2005, a Louisiana-based U.S. District Court Judge, Stanwood R. Duval, Jr. issued a temporary restraining order enjoining FEMA from proceeding with its December 15, 2005 hotel assistance deadline. In his ruling, Judge Duval called FEMA's actions "numbingly insensitive" and "unduly callous" (*McWaters v. FEMA* 2005). Creating confusion and worry among the hotel dwellers, FEMA announced numerous deadlines for hotel aid, only to be forced to extend peoples' stays when it was apparent they had nowhere to go, but each time causing the hotel population to dwindle (Graczyk 2005; Some Katrina Evacuees 2006). According to FEMA, there were just 1,747 hotel rooms still occupied by evacuees and being paid for by FEMA as of April 5, 2006 (personal communication, April 10, 2006).

Rent Assistance Under Section 403: States and Cities — Many people who were evacuated out of the immediate disaster area were provided homes in apartments rented by states, local governments, and social service agencies that agreed to pay landlords directly in anticipation of reimbursement from FEMA through Section 403. FEMA reports that 60,000 units have been rented under this program (DHS FEMA 2006d). This was an unusual move on FEMA's part in response to the huge numbers of evacuees pouring into other communities from the affected areas, which promised to quickly overwhelm the ability of governments and nonprofit organizations to provide traditional mass shelters. Because of the scale of the evacuation to most other states, it was necessary to declare receiving states as disaster areas as well so that Section 403 funds could be spent there. Providing short-term housing in this manner was supposed to give FEMA time to figure out how to deploy its Section 408 resources. The Inspector General (IG) for the Department of Homeland Security (DHS)[6] called it "resourceful and innovative" (DHS OIG 2006:108) under the circumstances. However, the IG was critical of FEMA for agreeing to let the cities and states enter into contracts for one-year leases, as well as for not requiring people who were to be assisted to be registered with FEMA. These ad hoc decisions have contributed to the chaos that ensued for people housed under this program (DHS OIG 2006).

This program has been fraught with conflict, as FEMA has tried to end payments to governments under Section 403 and shift people to the IHP (Section 408), if they are eligible (Batsell 2006; Saugier 2006; Smith, Cheryl 2006b). Landlords who have leases with the state or local government are uncertain if the leases will be honored. These households were to have moved into FEMA's Transitional Housing Program by March 1, 2006, only to have the date extended again to May 31, 2006 (DHS FEMA 2006g). News accounts began to surface in early April 2006 of low-income people living in apartments paid for under Section 403 who FEMA deemed ineligible for IHP rent assistance and whose rent aid will thus end (Davis, Andy 2006; Snyder 2006b; Some Refugees in Alabama 2006). Some 18,000 of the 55,000 households remaining in these rental units at the end of April were determined ineligible for continued aid according to FEMA (Dewan 2006b).

The Governor of Tennessee announced he was reopening mass shelters in anticipation of people becoming homeless again. In response to protests from the Mayor of Houston, FEMA extended the deadline to June 30, 2006 for some evacuees in Houston (End of Rental Program 2006). Newspaper editorials characterized the latest actions as "Still Battering the Katrina Homeless" (2006) and "Another FEMA Housing Mess" (2006). Another lawsuit against FEMA on behalf of this class of evacuees was filed in U.S. District Court in Houston on May 19, 2006 (Snyder 2006d). The judge declined to issue a Temporary Restraining Order, blocking FEMA from cutting off the 403 aid, when FEMA granted extensions to June 30 in other Texas cities (Snyder 2006e).

Rent Assistance Under Section 408: Transitional Housing Program — On September 23, 2005, Homeland Security Secretary Michael Chertoff and HUD Secretary Alphonso Jackson announced the establishment of a two-part Transitional Housing Program that would provide financial assistance under the Section 408 IHP for evacuees to rent housing in the private market. The first part, operated by FEMA, would provide rent assistance directly to eligible evacuees. The second part, operated by HUD on a "mission assignment" with funds from FEMA, would provide voucher-like aid to displaced households that were receiving some form of HUD assistance prior to the hurricane (DHS 2005a).

Notably, the program announced by the two members of the Bush Cabinet did not involve the use of the Housing Choice Voucher program, the existing rent assistance program run by 2,600 PHAs across the country that had been used successfully to rehouse people displaced by the Northridge Earthquake in 1994 near Los Angeles (PRRAC 2005; Rehm 2005). This is despite the fact that the Senate had passed legislation on September 14 to appropriate $3.5 billion to fund 350,000 housing vouchers for Katrina evacuees (NLIHC 2005d). However, the momentum developing for the Housing Choice Voucher solution may have been the impetus for the Bush Administration to announce its own approach. The Housing Choice Voucher program has been under attack by the Bush Administration for several years,[7] so relying on the program for the disaster response would have been counter to the Bush housing agenda (DeParle 2005; Krugman 2005b; Stonewalling the Katrina Victims 2005).

The FEMA part of the program provided $2,358 to each eligible household to cover three months of rent. The specific amount of $2,358 represented the national Fair Market Rent for a two-bedroom unit.[8] The assistance was provided directly to the displaced household in the form of a check or direct deposit to a bank account. Eligible households were those who owned or rented a home that FEMA could verify as uninhabitable. Each household had to register with FEMA to be eligible for assistance (DHS 2005a; Sard and Rice 2005).

The process of distributing these funds has been an exercise in mishaps and confusion that would be comical if the consequences were not so dire. Although FEMA reported that some addresses were considered to be homes that were uninhabitable by virtue of where they were located, thereby precluding the need for an inspection (DHS FEMA 2006a), there seemed to be no rhyme or reason to when or if a household was deemed eligible. Fears that housing aid expedited by bypassing the need for on-site inspections would be approved in error emerged after the program was underway, causing delays and inconsistent information to waiting applicants (DHS OIG 2006). People who did receive the initial amount of $2,358 often did not know it was to be used strictly for housing. The checks or direct deposits were issued by the U.S. Department of Treasury, but the instructions for use of the funds were mailed by FEMA, arriving days or weeks after the funds had already been spent. Initially, FEMA announced that if a family could not verify with receipts that the $2,358 was used for housing, they would not be eligible for additional rent assistance (Lipton 2005b). FEMA was forced to rescind that decision as well (*McWaters v. FEMA* 2005).

A family that received the initial $2,358 in rent assistance for three months has to go back to FEMA to be recertified for additional assistance. Despite being directed by Congress to issue guidance on eligibility and application procedures for ongoing assistance by January 13, 2006 (Rice and Sard 2006), FEMA has yet to do so as of this writing (mid-May 2006). Decisions continue to be made on a case-by-case basis.

Some evacuees have been denied continued assistance, either through the conversion from Section 403 to Section 408 or via recertification for Section 408, because FEMA reports that their homes in Louisiana or Mississippi were ready for them to reoccupy. Incredulous, Houston Mayor Bill White sent his own team of housing inspectors to New Orleans to assess some of the homes of Houston-based evacuees whom FEMA wanted to send home. They discovered that many of the homes were still heavily damaged and not habitable (Snyder 2006c). In other cases, evacuees have been told they no longer need assistance because they can go home, even though their former landlords may have raised rents or even rented out the properties to other people. Even if someone's former home may be livable, there is no assurance that family members will have jobs or schools in their home community.

KDHAP — The second part of the Transitional Housing Program announced on September 23, 2005 and operated by HUD with a mission assignment[9] from FEMA, was the Katrina Disaster Housing Assistance Program (KDHAP). Responsibility for displaced households who were previously receiving HUD assistance, including public housing, Section 8 project-based aid, Housing Choice Vouchers, Section 202, Section 811,[10] and others, was retained by HUD. After some debate and challenge by advocates to the decision to move displaced households with Housing Choice Vouchers into KDHAP, instead of letting them transfer their vouchers to the community to which they relocated, HUD relented and allowed voucher holders to choose between continuing under their non-emergency assistance or enrolling in KDHAP (Sard and Rice 2005).

Also eligible for KDHAP were people who were homeless prior to the disaster *and* who were participating in HUD-funded homeless service programs. Notably excluded were homeless people who were not in HUD programs. The National Alliance to End Homelessness (2005a) estimated that 6,000 to 10,000 people in the affected areas who were homeless prior to the storm were not eligible for any disaster aid.

KDHAP assistance was administered by local PHAs and provided in the form of direct payment to landlords. The amount of assistance was based on the Fair Market Rent for the jurisdiction where the household is located, in contrast to the FEMA program in which assistance is based on the national Fair Market Rent (Sard and Rice 2005).

There were at least three serious barriers to an eligible family receiving KDHAP assistance. First, housing authorities were not required to participate in KDHAP. So if an evacuee was in a jurisdiction with a nonparticipating PHA or a jurisdiction without a PHA, he or she had to relocate or do without assistance. PHAs were reluctant to become involved because there was no guarantee of assistance past the first few months and because the fee provided would not cover the cost of security and utility deposits, nor the search assistance needed to place a family in a new home. According to HUD, only 355 PHAs out of 2,600 nationwide that administer vouchers had agreed to administer KDHAP as of December 1, 2005 (HUD PIH 2005).

Another onerous barrier was the process of signing up for KDHAP. The first step was for the family to register with FEMA, but FEMA registration did not mean one had also applied for KDHAP. A family had to know to apply for KDHAP and affirmatively do so. FEMA may have determined that a household was not eligible for FEMA assistance because it previously received HUD assistance, but there was no assurance that FEMA would tell the family how to apply for KDHAP or even if it was eligible for HUD assistance.

Finally, the reluctance by PHAs to work with displaced people who were homeless, previously homeless, or who were housed through the HUD Housing for Persons with AIDS (HOPWA) program forced HUD to create yet another program called KDHAP-SN (for special needs). Guidance for this program was not issued until six months after the storms. Under this program, HUD designated one local homeless service provider in each community to be the KDHAP-SN Administering Agency (KAA), with the responsibility to assist pre-Katrina homeless people and others with special needs in accessing housing assistance through the PHA and in finding housing to rent in the community (HUD PIH 2006b). HUD did not indicate how a KDHAP-SN-eligible person was to know that he or she was eligible or how to find the KAA that he or she was supposed to contact. KDHAP-SN set up yet another level of service barriers for some of the most vulnerable of displaced people. There was one positive improvement, however, when KDHAP-SN was established: Pre-Katrina homeless people who were not receiving services from a HUD-funded program were now eligible (HUD CPD 2000).

Flawed Design — A fundamental flaw in the bifurcation of longer-term assistance between FEMA and HUD was that some displaced people were not eligible for either form of aid. The criteria for eligibility did not cover people who were neither home owners nor renters. A common housing practice among low-income people is "doubling-up," where more than one household resides at the same place because one or both households cannot afford their own homes. Under the FEMA program, only one household was eligible, so if two households registered with FEMA and gave the same previous address, one household was disqualified. This is referred to as the "shared household" rule. While FEMA officials indicated on more than one occasion that there might be exceptions to the rule, no guidance on what would constitute an exception has been issued. People denied assistance under the shared household rule are encouraged to appeal the denial (Sergeant Shriver Center 2006; Smith, Cheryl 2006a).

Another flaw is that even if a household is approved for assistance and actually received it, it is still not assured it will be able to afford to rent a home. In most urban housing markets, the actual rents far exceed the national Fair Market Rent, the standard used for the FEMA assistance (Torpy 2005). How a household could have its assistance adjusted to reflect local market conditions was never made clear. Also, FEMA regulations precluded use of the funds for security deposits or utilities, which can be quite costly, further burdening poor households with the need to find these resources elsewhere in order to use what aid FEMA did provide (Sard and Rice 2005). Moreover, even if the amount of rent assistance were enough to pay the monthly rent, the fact that FEMA only provided assistance in three-month increments was a serious deterrent to landlords agreeing to rent to evacuees who depend on the FEMA rent assistance program (Sard and Rice 2005).

Finally, FEMA's Transitional Housing Program and HUD's KDHAP could only work in markets where there are vacant units with willing landlords. In most places closest to the affected area, there are few or no vacancies at all and the cost of rental housing has skyrocketed. One displaced person who was still living in a hotel in Baton Rouge despite having received the $2,358 check from FEMA provided the following testimony at a congressional hearing:

> I got a check from FEMA for $2,358. This money is supposed to be for three months of rent. My daughter and I started looking at homes and apartments. Everything we saw was over $1,000, here in Baton Rouge. We couldn't find anything we could afford, so I called FEMA. FEMA gave us a housing referral number, an 800 number that I should call and get apartment referrals. We utilized that number, and the FEMA people gave us referrals to 5 apartments in Baton Rouge.
>
> These apartment owners, the landlords, wanted me to prove that my monthly income is three and a half to four times my monthly rent costs. But I have no income because I'm currently unemployed! Unemployed people cannot rent apartments. This may work after hurricanes in Florida, to give people money to rent apartments, but it doesn't work here. People in Florida lost only their homes; they didn't lose their jobs, too. They didn't have their entire city floating under water.
>
> Then it occurred to me: Why is FEMA referring me to apartments I cannot qualify for? 99% of the applicants who need these apartments aren't qualified. They are on unemployment, because they lost not only their homes, they lost their jobs. Why is FEMA sending us to apartments we can't rent? Nobody has answered that question for me.
>
> (Stewart 2006)

In February 2006, HUD adjusted the Fair Market Rents upward in Baton Rouge and New Orleans, bringing the level of HUD assistance closer to actual rents in these areas (NLIHC 2006e).

An unknown number of people have been left with no housing assistance. These are people who were displaced and who were then taken in by family or friends in the surrounding areas. If they are still residing in these temporary arrangements, they are ineligible for rent assistance because they have not yet rented another place. But if they are in areas where there is no rental housing to move to, they are essentially stranded, caught in a FEMA Catch-22.

In December 2005, Congress reallocated $390 million of previously appropriated FEMA disaster relief funds to HUD to move people from KDHAP and to help previously HUD-assisted people displaced by Hurricane Rita into the now-named Disaster Voucher Program (DVP), for which HUD issued guidance on February 3, 2006. KDHAP expired on January 31, 2006. A family's KDHAP voucher is to be converted to DVP by amending its existing KDHAP rent subsidy contract and lease. Although DVP is intended to operate more like the standard Housing Choice Vouchers, there are some important differences: There are no income eligibility or tenant contribution requirements for DVP rental vouchers, and they can last only until September 30, 2007 (HUD PIH 2006a).

Outcomes to Date — FEMA reports that as of May 3, 2006, 723,262 households had received the first three months of rent assistance through its Transitional Housing Program. Just 246,786 households had requested recertification for continued assistance, and only 180,636 have been approved. The vast majority of the households (83%) who received the first installment of rent are in Louisiana, Mississippi, and Texas; another 10% are in Alabama, Arkansas, Florida, Georgia, and Tennessee; and 1% are in California. The remaining 5% are in other states and territories. Three-quarters (74%) of those who have been recertified are in the three states with the most evacuees (DHS FEMA 2006j).

HUD now estimates that up to 32,000 households are eligible for the Disaster Voucher Program, based on the assessment of damage to their pre-Katrina homes. As of March 18, 2006, approximately 20,600 households had applied for KDHAP/DVP and around 12,350 had used the assistance to lease new homes (Jackson 2006). Enrollment in both the FEMA and HUD programs is expected to increase as families in the 403 apartment rent assistance program move into IHP or DVP.

Temporary Housing, Failure of Government — The numbers that FEMA and HUD report about the transitional housing programs tell one of two possible stories. One story could be that people have found their own way and do not need additional assistance. The other story is that the program is so badly designed and implemented that people are unable to use it or have so much trouble accessing it that they give up. The stories of people trying to get through to and get a straight answer out of FEMA are now legendary. The prospect of growing numbers of people made homeless a second time is quite real (Snyder 2006a).

A story from Colorado illustrates the absurdity of the temporary housing response to the Gulf Coast disaster. Catholic Charities of Denver rented homes for 900 evacuated families under contract with the State of Colorado, which expects reimbursement from FEMA under Section 408. All of these families will have their 403 aid end. Some have been transferred to Section 408 IHP. About 120 families lived in HUD-assisted housing in Louisiana and Mississippi, making them ineligible for Section 408, but eligible for DVP. But the Denver PHA was not participating in DVP, so these families were left with no aid. Only an intervention by senior HUD officials provoked by a national housing advocacy organization convinced the Denver PHA to sign up to distribute the Disaster Vouchers. This situation was resolved, but no systemic change took place (personal communication, May 2, 2006).

In its own assessment of "lessons learned" from the Katrina disaster issued on February 23, 2006, the White House recommends that HUD, not FEMA, be the lead agency for providing housing for people displaced by future disasters (Office of the President 2006). Low-income housing advocates are calling for all the rent assistance that current evacuees continue to need to be transferred to the Disaster Voucher Program at HUD (Fischer and Sard 2006; NLIHC 2006h).

Fed up with FEMA's incompetence, Representatives Richard Baker (R-LA) and Barney Frank (D-MA) introduced legislation that will transfer all long-term (30 days or more) disaster housing assistance from FEMA to HUD (H.R. 5393 2006). The bill was approved in the House Financial Services Committee on June 14, 2006, but has tougher hurdles to overcome in the committees with oversight over FEMA (NLIHC 2006k). An identical bill, S. 2983, was introduced in the Senate by Senator Mary Landrieu (D-LA). Expressing the sentiments of large numbers of displaced people and the people in communities across the nation who are trying to help them, Senators Susan Collins (R-ME) and Joseph Lieberman (D-CT), Chair and Ranking Member respectively of the U.S. Senate Committee on Homeland Security and Governmental Affairs, wrote to Homeland Security Michael Chertoff on March 14, 2006. The Senators said:

> We are writing to urge you to take immediate steps to address the critical shortfalls in FEMA's effort to provide transitional housing for victims of Hurricane Katrina ….
>
> Almost six months after Hurricane Katrina ravaged the Gulf Coast, housing remains among the most pressing challenges facing thousands of residents in the region. Significant problems remain with transitional housing, including FEMA's hotel/motel program, which has imposed deadlines that are leaving many Katrina survivors struggling to find shelter. FEMA's manufactured housing program, which should be an alternative, has been hampered by confusion and

inefficiency. The lack of a unified and coordinated federal disaster strategy is encumbering the delivery of federal housing assistance to storm victims and is sure to be an issue in future disasters. Our government's inability to help thousands of Americans who were forced from their homes find adequate housing is unacceptable.

(Collins and Lieberman 2006)

Nonetheless, when given the opportunity to reduce FEMA's role in the transitional housing response to Katrina and move temporary housing aid to HUD, Congress has been unwilling to do so to date despite its own high level of frustration with FEMA. In June 2006 Congress appropriated $6 billion more to FEMA, which includes ongoing housing assistance. Even while agreeing to give FEMA more emergency funding, Congress chastised FEMA for the "lack of a housing policy in the Gulf Coast" (H.R. 4939 2006). Congress instructed the Department of Homeland Security to submit a proposal and expenditure plan for meeting evacuees' housing needs to the Senate and House Committees on Appropriations by the end of July 2006 (NLIHC 2006j).

The Bush Administration's choices in how to respond to the housing and other basic needs of the people displaced by the hurricanes of 2005 are not surprising, however distressing they may be. They are rooted in a fundamental resistance to the notion of government as the solver of problems. Both in his failure to appoint competent people to run critical agencies and in his failure to use existing government programs that work to help people in great need, President Bush demonstrated his disregard for the role and responsibility of the federal government to assure the basic well-being of its citizens (Gosselin and Alonso-Zaldivar 2005; Krugman 2005a).

How people who are supposed to be served by a social program actually access that service reveals much about the intent of the program's designers. If access is understandable, reasonably fast, and respectful, then the program will maximize utilization by the intended beneficiaries. If access is confused, delayed, and dehumanizing, the effect is to limit utilization. Given what is known about the federal government's "program" to provide temporary housing for Gulf Coast evacuees many months into its implementation, an unavoidable conclusion is that it was intended to help as few people as possible.

The Federal Government Response: Rebuilding

Gulf Coast recovery czar Donald Powell says that his first priority for Gulf Coast recovery is "levees, levees, levees," and his second priority is "housing, housing, housing" (Brookings 2006). The "levee" priority, of course, is about repair and strengthening of the levee system in New Orleans that breached, causing the floods that damaged so much of the city's housing. For New Orleans, the future of the levees and the future of the city are one and the same. Many people will not return until they feel assured that the levees will hold against future storms (Fetterman 2006). The estimated price tag for the levees has fluctuated considerably in the months since the hurricane, settling at $6 billion as of this writing (mid-May 2006), most of which will come from the federal government (Whoriskey and Hsu 2006).

Solving the levee problem may pale in comparison to solving the housing problem. It is impossible to disentangle the housing problems in the Gulf Coast from its other major institutional crises. The challenge for public officials and private enterprise is to restore housing, health care, schools, jobs, and commercial establishments in concert with one another. Most people cannot return in the absence of any one of these elements of community life (Rivlin 2006; Sayre 2006). Moreover, rebuilding has stalled because there is not enough housing for the workforce needed for the task (Carr 2005a). In New Orleans, until FEMA announced the new elevations required for new or repaired buildings on April 12, 2006, many individual property owners were unable to decide if they would repair or sell their property (Nossiter and Schwartz 2006; Whoriskey and Hsu 2006).

Decision-making about rebuilding resides at every level of government. In the days immediately after the magnitude of the disaster became apparent, including its multistate nature, some Members of Congress (including Republicans in the Senate) and advocates called for creation of a federal authority with the power and resources to act quickly and decisively, and headed by someone who reported directly to President George W. Bush (Hogue 2005; Crowley 2005). A "Marshall Plan" was the answer, equating the destruction in the Gulf Coast with that of Europe after World War II (Sandalow 2005; Bumiller and Stevenson 2005).

But there was no appetite for such an approach in the Bush Administration (Hogue 2005). In his address to the nation on September 15, 2006 from Jackson Square in New Orleans, President Bush said the "federal government will be fully engaged in the mission, but …state and local leaders will have the primary role in planning for their own future" (Bush 2005). The Administration and the Congress adopted the posture that state and local officials would have to decide what was needed, what they wanted, and request the federal government's help.

However, on November 1, 2005, the President issued an Executive Order that directed the Secretary of Homeland Security to establish a position of Federal Coordinator for Gulf Coast Recovery and Rebuilding, with the person filling the position to be selected by the President and appointed by the Secretary of DHS. The Congressional Research Service called this arrangement "unusual," citing potential conflict with Congressional appointment and oversight responsibilities (Hogue 2005). The lines of authority were somewhat ambiguous: Does the Federal Coordinator report to the President or the Secretary of Homeland Security?

President Bush tapped Donald E. Powell, Chairman of the Federal Deposit Insurance Corporation, to be the federal coordinator. Powell was tasked with supporting "state and local community rebuilding efforts," "focus[ing] on the mid-term to long-term issues surrounding Gulf Coast recovery" (DHS 2005b). While his power and authority are limited (Brookings 2006), Powell appears to be committed to getting federal resources dedicated to the rebuilding. A newspaper profile describes his "epiphany" about the federal responsibility for the devastation of New Orleans. He toured the city on foot by himself and talked to ordinary people one-on-one and "realized that while Mississippi was an act of God, Louisiana was an act of God and man. There were some flaws. The levees breached" (Dewan 2006a).

The development of housing rebuilding plans by the affected cities and states has been chaotic. The multitude of issues contributing to the complexity and difficulty of making good decisions about housing can only be touched on here, as an in-depth examination is beyond the scope of this chapter. However, at the core of the rebuilding dilemma is the lingering legacy of American racism. Just as the failed emergency response to Katrina exposed the intersection of race and poverty the United States for all the world to see, the process of simply planning for rebuilding is laying bare the deeply embedded race and class divisions in these most southern of states.

Fundamental to the future of housing in the Gulf Coast is the question of who has the right to return. Is each displaced person who wants to come home going to be welcome, as evidenced by housing plans that make room for everyone? In New Orleans, in particular, the issue of the city's "footprint" loomed large. Should those areas of the city that were most in harm's way of flooding be rebuilt or should they be turned into green space? Some of the most historic Black neighborhoods in New Orleans were on the lowest ground and sustained some of the most severe damage. Shrinking the footprint is equated with reducing the Black population of New Orleans, presaged by HUD Secretary Alphonso Jackson, as reported by the *Houston Chronicle*: "Whether we like it or not, New Orleans is not going to be 500,000 people for a long time.... New Orleans is not going to be as black as it was for a long time, if ever again" (Rodriguez and Minaya 2005).

Low-income housing advocates are faced with the perennial conundrum of how to simultaneously maximize racial and economic residential integration and preserve affordable housing for the lowest-income people.

On one hand, the damage to the housing stock offers an opportunity to break up long-standing patterns of residential segregation, especially in public and assisted housing. On the other hand, many low-income people will not be able to return unless the housing in these neighborhoods is restored. Mixed-income housing and neighborhoods are recommended in the plethora of experts' papers and plans that have come in Katrina's wake. But the probability is almost zero that enough new housing affordable to the lowest-income people will be built to replace the numbers of affordable units they could afford that were lost. Even if funds were made available to do so, NIMBY fights will prevent the siting of affordable housing for the very poor in many neighborhoods. In the absence of leadership committed to both the right to return and inclusive communities, the people with the fewest resources will have the fewest housing opportunities in the rebuilt Gulf Coast.

Federal Legislation

Nearly a dozen bills that address rebuilding in the Gulf Coast have been introduced in Congress since the hurricanes hit, generated primarily by legislators from the affected states. Yet no coherent legislative strategy has emerged. The local press has noted the small number of members of Congress who have taken time to visit the Gulf Coast (Alpert 2006). Only the Housing and Community Opportunity Subcommittee of the House Financial Services Committee held housing-specific hearings in 2005. To his credit, Housing Subcommittee Chairman Robert Ney (R-OH) convened field hearings in New Orleans and Gulfport, Mississippi on January 13 and 14, 2006, with a broad range of witnesses including evacuees (U.S. House of Representatives 2006). The Senate Banking, Housing, and Urban Affairs Committee did not hold a single hearing on housing in the aftermath of the hurricanes in 2005, but spent considerable time on the problems in the National Flood Insurance Program. Despite representing a Katrina-battered state, Senate Banking Committee Chairman Richard Shelby (R-AL) has called only one hearing to date on housing in the aftermath of the disaster. Held on February 15, 2006, the only witnesses were federal officials (U.S. Senate 2006).

Homesteading — The Bush Administration has brought forward only one housing proposal of its own, a homesteading bill that was introduced on December 13, 2005 in the Senate (S. 2088) with a companion House bill (H.R. 4515). The bill would create a homesteading program at HUD through which low-income people who have been displaced from a federally-designated disaster area could obtain federally-owned vacant land or single-family or small multifamily properties. They would be required to meet certain threshold conditions, such as a term of occupancy and repair of existing property, or building a new home in the case of vacant land, in order to obtain title to the property without cost after a set period of time (S. 2088 2005). Although there was little disagreement that homesteading was a good idea, its limited scope evoked criticism as an inadequate response to a disaster of this magnitude (Calmes 2005; Fischer and Sard 2005). Neither bill shows any signs of moving.

The "Baker Bill" — H.R. 4100, the Louisiana Recovery Corporation Act, was introduced in October 2005 by Representative Richard Baker (R-LA), who represents the Baton Rouge area. The "Baker Bill" would have created a federal authority to buy properties from individual landowners at 60% of their pre-hurricane equity and pay off mortgage holders at 60% of the remaining debt. The authority would be able to assemble large tracts of land to sell for redevelopment. Previous owners would have the right of first refusal to purchase properties subsequently sold by the Corporation. Funding would come from the sale of bonds to be paid with the resale of the land.

For several weeks, the idea of the Louisiana Recovery Corporation was widely embraced (except by staunch conservatives) in Louisiana and Washington (Nossiter 2006). The bill was reported out of the House Financial Services Committee on December 15, 2005 by a 50-5 vote, amended to include several housing provisions from H.R. 4197 (the Hurricane Katrina Recovery, Reclamation, Restoration, Reconstruction, and Reunion Act of 2005. H.R. 4197 is a comprehensive hurricane recovery bill introduced earlier by the members of the Congressional Black Caucus). The amended bill authorized funds for several HUD programs, including $13 billion for CDBG,[11] $1.5 billion for the HOME program, $100 million for HOPE VI, $100 million for public housing capital repair, and $2.5 billion for emergency voucher assistance, with the funds coming from previously appropriated disaster funds. The bill also authorized the Louisiana Recovery Corporation to operate an urban homesteading program. However, the conservatives won out and the White House opposed the Baker plan. Gulf Coast Recovery Federal Coordinator Powell delivered the message in a February 2, 2006 *Washington Post* op-ed in which he criticized the Baker plan as creating a federal bureaucracy that would bypass local decision-making and interfere in the free operation of the market (Powell 2006).

Affordable Housing Fund — In May 2005, the House Financial Services Committee had approved H.R. 1461, the Federal Housing Finance Reform Act of 2005, also introduced by Congressman Baker. The primary purpose of H.R 1461 was to strengthen federal regulation of Fannie Mae and Freddie Mac, the two giant Government Sponsored Enterprises (GSEs) that support the American housing mortgage system.[12] Low-income housing advocates used the opportunity presented by GSE reform to expand the GSEs' role in affordable housing. The Fund would be capitalized with 5% of Fannie and Freddie's after-tax profits, estimated to be up to $1 billion a year. Despite vociferous objections from the ultra-conservative members of the Committee, the bill was voted out 65-5 (NLIHC 2005a).

However, the House Republican leadership refused to let the bill come to the floor for several months. Although the bill was eventually approved by the House, with the Affordable Housing Fund directed to the Gulf, it also contained draconian anti-voting language insisted on by the ultra-conservatives as a condition to letting the bill come up for a vote (NLIHC 2005f).[13] S. 190, the GSE reform bill, is stalled in the Senate as of this writing (mid-May 2006). The bill will die if not passed by the close of 109th Congress at the end of 2006. The Affordable Housing Fund in H.R. 1461 remains the only federal legislation to date that would specifically target housing production and repair funds to the lowest-income households affected by the Gulf Coast disaster.

Tax Credits — One piece of hurricane legislation that was enacted was H.R. 4440, the Gulf Opportunity Zone Act of 2005, introduced by Representatives William Jefferson (D-LA) and Jim McCrery (R-LA) and signed into law on December 22, 2005. The "GO Zone" was first proposed by President Bush in his September 15, 2005 speech from New Orleans and included a myriad of tax breaks for businesses (Bush 2005). The tax code route for hurricane recovery was a primary recommendation in a September 2005 Heritage Foundation paper, including the designation of devastated areas as "opportunity zones" (Meese, Butler, and Holmes 2005).

H.R. 4440 also included an unprecedented increase in Low Income Housing Tax Credits for the three states hit by Katrina, to be used to build homes only in the hurricane-affected areas (H.R 4440 2005). Importantly, LIHTC income-targeting requirements were not waived in the bill, but the need for vouchers or other form of operating subsidy remains if any of the new units will be affordable to the lowest-income families. The increased credits will be able to support production of an estimated 54,000 rental units (Fischer and Sard 2006). The bill does contain a "use it or lose it" provision, meaning that unused credits will be rescinded at the end of each year. Low-income housing advocates are concerned about the capacity of the states to expend such an exponential increase in tax credits in the first year. In 2004, Louisiana produced 1,000 LIHTC units; in Mississippi, there were just 743 new units (Corkery 2005).

First Rebuilding Supplemental Appropriation — On October 28, 2005, President Bush asked Congress to reallocate $17.1 billion of previously appropriated disaster relief funds to other federal agencies for hurricane rebuilding efforts (Office of the President 2005). Included in his proposed reallocation was $2.2 billion to HUD for housing programs: HOME—$70 million, CDBG—$1.5 billion, Urban Homesteading—$250 million, and the previously discussed $390 million for the Disaster Voucher Program (DVP). Senator Thad Cochran (R-MS), Chairman of the Senate Appropriations Committee, pushed for considerably more HUD funding, and the final bill contained $11.5 billion in CDBG funds and $390 million for DVP. The total of $29 billion in supplemental and reallocated appropriations for hurricane recovery was attached to the Department of Defense Appropriations Act of 2005 that was enacted on December 30, 2005 (NLIHC 2005k).

The bill directed HUD to develop a formula based on need for distribution of the CDBG funds to the five hurricane damaged states: Louisiana, Mississippi, Alabama, Texas, and Florida. The bill specifically limited any state from getting more than 54% of the allocation, a move by Senator Cochran to assure that a sizable portion of the funds went to Mississippi, even though almost three-quarters of the damage occurred in Louisiana. The bill also reduced the income-targeting for use of CDBG funds to 50% to benefit low- and moderate-income households, instead of 70%. The HUD Secretary was also given the authority to waive even the 50% requirement if the state could demonstrate a "compelling need" (NLIHC 2005k).

The formula that HUD created distributed the $11.5 billion in CDBG funds as follows: Louisiana—$6.210 billion, Mississippi—$5.058 billion, Florida—$83 million, Texas—$75 million, and Alabama—$74 million (HUD 2006c). The distribution plan was not received well in Texas, whose Governor, Rick Perry (R), was quite critical of Washington's treatment of his state when he was called to testify on Capitol Hill in March 2006. He requested an additional $2 billion in CDBG funds for Texas alone (Perry, Rick 2006), a plea so far ignored.

Second Rebuilding Supplemental Appropriation — That Louisiana had been shortchanged in the first CDBG allotment was abundantly clear (Blanco 2006; Dao 2006). Federal Coordinator Donald Powell is credited with convincing the White House to request $4.2 billion in additional CDBG funds specifically for housing in Louisiana (Dewan 2006a). The President sent another Supplemental Appropriations proposal for $92 billion to the Hill on February 16, 2006, with $19.8 billion for hurricane recovery and the rest for the war in Iraq (NLIHC 2006c). The supplemental appropriations were finally signed into law on June 16, 2006. Louisiana will get its full $4.2 billion in CDBG funds as the President requested. Another $1 billion in CDBG funds was added to go the four other affected states. Of the total $5.2 billion, not less than $1 billion must be used to repair or replace lost affordable rental housing stock, including public and assisted housing. The same weakening of CDBG income targeting rules that were added to the first supplemental appropriation were included again (NLIHC 2006j).

Flood Insurance — The compensation that insurance will provide property owners for damage to their homes is a crucial element in the calculation of the cost for repair and reconstruction of housing in the Gulf Coast. The amount of property insurance payments, and the nature and sufficiency of insurance held by property owners, will be part of equation for the amount of direct aid given to home owners through the CDBG program.

Historically, private insurance companies have not been willing to insure against floods; the risks are high and the cost unpredictable. The federal government has had to fill the void with disaster assistance. As an alternative to after-the-fact disaster aid, Congress established the National Flood Insurance Program (NFIP) in 1968, a federal program run by FEMA and carried out in cooperation with local governments, mortgage-lenders, and the insurance industry. Property owners with homes in areas at risk of flood, known as 100-year flood plains, and with mortgages from federally-regulated lenders, are required to buy flood insurance. Not required to have flood insurance under the NFIP are property owners without mortgages, with mortgages from unregulated lenders, and/or with property outside 100-year flood plains (Walker 2006).

Of the 836,637 owner-occupied housing units that sustained any damage from Katrina, Rita, and Wilma, 150,251 (18%) had flood damage (the rest had wind damage). Of these, 102,254 homes were within the 100-year flood plain, and 68% had flood insurance. Of the 46,997 units with flood damage outside the 100-year flood plain, just 34% were insured against floods. Three-quarters of the owner-occupied homes that incurred flood damage are in Louisiana and 36% are in New Orleans. Two-thirds (64%) of the flood-damaged owner-occupied units in Louisiana and in New Orleans had flood insurance (HUD PDR 2006). The maximum amount of insurance available for a single-family home is $250,000 (DHS FEMA 2006i).

The insurance pay-outs from Hurricanes Katrina, Rita, and Wilma, predicted to be $23 billion, will be greater than the sum of all claims ever paid by NFIP. In November 2005, Congress increased FEMA's borrowing authority from the U.S. Treasury from $1.5 billion to $18.5 billion through fiscal year 2008. The program was not considered actuarially sound, even prior to these astronomical claims. Premiums paid represent only a small fraction of the risk, and management by FEMA has been poor. FEMA is highly unlikely to be able to pay back funds borrowed to meet these claims. Thus, the cost of the NFIP bail-out will be added to the federal government's costs for hurricane recovery (Walker 2006). Legislative proposals to reform NFIP in the aftermath of Katrina are drawing the ire of the homebuilding and real estate industries for fear that more accurately drawn flood maps and premiums that reflect true risk will restrain new development (Drew and Treaster 2006).

Other Federal Aid

The role of the federal government in the rebuilding process also includes Administration actions not dependent on legislative approval. Other federal programs provide funds to home owners to help repair their homes or to prevent foreclosure: the Small Business Administration, FEMA's Individual and Households Program, the USDA Rural Housing Service, and HUD's Mortgage Assistance Program.

Small Business Administration Disaster Loans and FEMA IHP — Home owners may also be eligible for low-interest disaster loans from the Small Business Administration for repairs to their homes not covered by insurance, but only if they can demonstrate they are creditworthy by SBA standards. Home owners can borrow up to $200,000 for 30 years at interest rates determined by their ability to borrow elsewhere (SBA n.d.a). The SBA will also refinance existing mortgages to include repair funds on top of the existing mortgage for those who may not qualify for an SBA loan. Funds may only be used to repair damage, not make improvements, with the exception of structural changes, such as increasing elevation, to reduce risk of damage in another disaster (SBA n.d.b).

The Small Business Administration has been the subject of nearly as much criticism in its handling of the Katrina disaster as FEMA has been. Its slow rate of processing loan applications has been blamed for many business failures in the Gulf area (Olson 2005). But the attacks have been most scathing for SBA's handling of home repair loans, with most applications being denied (Eaton and Nixon 2005; The Poor Need Not Apply 2005). The agency says it has approved 40% of loans, but congressional investigators put the approval rate at 30% (Nixon and Eaton 2006).

Rural Housing Service — Among the many disaster response responsibilities of the USDA is assistance to low-income home owners with loans from the Rural Housing Service. RHS borrowers in the disaster areas received a six-month moratorium on mortgage payments, and RHS-guaranteed lenders were instructed to grant forbearance to home mortgage-holders affected by Katrina. RHS also is providing low-cost repair loans to homeowners with hurricane damage. RHS estimated that there were

80,000 homeowners with USDA direct or guaranteed loans in the affected area (USDA 2005).

FHA Mortgage Assistance — As part of its hurricane recovery program, HUD announced a Mortgage Assistance Initiative on December 12, 2005. HUD will provide mortgage assistance for up to 20,000 displaced households with Federal Housing Administration (FHA)-insured mortgages. Eligible households are those whose homes are repairable and who are committed to return to their homes. They must be able to verify loss of income or other reasons why they cannot make mortgage payments and have missed at least four, but not more than twelve, payments. HUD will make their mortgage payments for up to twelve months (HUD 2005). HUD reports that just 2,000 home owners have been assisted through this program in the first four months. The lower than expected participation rate is attributed to the continuing uncertainty that many home owners have about when or if they will be able to return to their homes and what other kinds of aid may be available to them (personal communication, April 27, 2006).

Although not part of rebuilding per se, a new HUD initiative announced on April 24, 2006 will make 20,000 HUD-owned single-family homes available for purchase by people displaced by the Gulf Coast disaster. These homes will be discounted by 10%, have FHA-insured mortgages, and some will qualify for home rehab loans for up to 15% of the purchase price (HUD 2006g). HUD-owned properties are generally FHA-insured homes whose previous owners have defaulted on their mortgages. They are located all over the country, and the condition of these houses varies considerably, with none expected to be pristine. Still, for some displaced families, this program may offer an opportunity for home ownership that otherwise would have eluded them.

The State Plans

This analysis now turns to the state plans for rebuilding their housing stock. Each of the affected states has approached their recovery processes differently, with the most extensive work required for the states with the most damage, Mississippi and Louisiana. Because the federal government is providing the bulk of resources needed for rebuilding, ultimately all the plans must be boiled down to "action plans for disaster recovery" submitted to HUD as a condition of receipt of the emergency CDBG appropriations detailed above.

The action plans are to emphasize how the state will prevent future damage of similar magnitude with new land use and construction standards, as well how the state will monitor and account for how the funds are used.

The plan also must describe how the state will address the housing needs of all income groups, including plans to prevent and address homelessness among extremely low-income families and people with special needs. HUD also allowed for submission of initial partial plans as well, amending the plan until all allocated funds have been used (*Federal Register* 2006c). Only the Mississippi and Louisiana plans will be covered here.

Mississippi: Building Back Better Than Ever — In the days following Hurricane Katrina's destruction of the Mississippi Gulf Coast, Governor Haley Barbour appointed a 50+-member commission to make recommendations on how to proceed with the recovery. The Governor's Commission on the Recovery, Rebuilding, and Renewal was chaired and partially funded by James L. Barksdale, former CEO of Netscape, Republican fundraiser, and Mississippi philanthropist (Corcoran 2006). Vice Chairmen included Derrick Johnson, State Director for the Mississippi NAACP. Over 500 citizens served on multiple task forces. Numerous town meetings and charrettes were held in the affected counties throughout the fall. New Urbanism proponents were brought in to envision the future of Gulf Coast communities based on the mixed-income, mixed-used, neo-traditional design principles espoused by many HOPE VI developers (Governor's Commission 2005).

The Affordable Housing section of the Commission's report stresses how many people who were displaced had low incomes from low-wage jobs. Although the housing recommendations are thorough and specific, they emphasize home ownership and asset-building. The role of rental housing is acknowledged, but underdeveloped (Governor's Commission 2005). A memo to Governor Barbour, co-authored by Commission Vice Chairman Johnson, critiques and expands on the Commission's recommendations to focus more purposefully on the needs of the lowest-income people, including elderly and disabled people, and the importance of rental housing. The memo calls for specific uses of the new CDBG funds to achieve some of these objectives (Johnson, Bey, and Rich 2006).

Nonetheless, the Mississippi plan for its use of CDBG funds approved by HUD Secretary Alphonso Jackson on April 4, 2006 deals with homeowners exclusively. It is a partial plan that accounts for just $3.4 billion of the state's $5 billion initial CDBG allocation. Homeowners whose homes suffered flood damage will receive grants up to $150,000 in exchange for permanent covenants on the property regarding requirements on building codes, flood insurance, and elevation intended to minimize future flood damage and potential public expense. The grant amount per house is based on the assessed value of the home before the storm, multiplied by the percent of the home that was damaged, minus proceeds from home owner insurance, SBA disaster loans, and FEMA grants. Eligibility is limited to home owners who maintained their primary residence in the four most-affected counties on the day of the hurricane, who had home owner's insurance, and whose homes were outside of 100-year flood plains (Mississippi Development Authority 2006). The rationale behind the eligibility requirements is that these are home owners who relied on FEMA's assessment that they did not need flood insurance because of where their property was located, and therefore should not be penalized for failing to have insured their homes against flooding.

There are no income tests for the grants under the Mississippi plan, despite the federal requirement that at least 50% of the funds benefit people at 80% or less of the area median income. Indeed, people excluded from the grant program are likely to be some of the lower-income residents in the affected counties, as they are less likely to have flood or property insurance. This is especially true of property owned by heirs to the original owners on which no mortgage exists.

On June 14, 2006, HUD officially waived Mississippi's obligation to use at least half of its CDBG funds for the benefit of low- and moderate-income people. In the waiver notice, HUD allows Mississippi to compensate people for housing loss in an "income-blind manner because the disaster affected households without regard to income." The notice goes on to say that Mississippi will "examine other housing needs and pursue other sources of funding to assistance for other compelling housing needs, such as for homeless and special needs populations, for low income renters, and for uninsured low-income homeowners" (*Federal Register* 2006c p. 34459).

Mississippi has agreed to set aside $100 million of its CDBG allocation to restore public housing in the state. However, the current plan sets income targeting for CDBG funds for public housing at 60% of the area median or less, which corresponds to the income targeting of LIHTC units, setting the stage for the restored public housing in Mississippi to no longer be affordable for the people who lived there before the disaster (Bishop 2006).

Louisiana: The Road Home — The devastation in Louisiana made planning for recovery more complicated than it was in Mississippi (Fetterman 2006). The politics in and between the two states also disadvantaged Louisiana. With a Governor who is a prominent national Republican with close ties to the White House and two Republican Senators with considerable seniority, Mississippi did not want for federal resources. Louisiana has a Democratic Governor whose relationship with the White House was bitterly strained at the height of the disaster and two Senators with no seniority, only one of whom is a member of the majority party in Washington.

Uncertainty about the federal commitment to levee repair and housing rebuilding has hampered Louisiana's progress.

New Orleans — Another difference between recovery in Mississippi and Louisiana is the city of New Orleans, with a controversial mayor and its own ideas about how to rebuild. Although New Orleans has provided much of the visual and cultural backdrop for how the nation understands the Gulf Coast disaster, Baton Rouge is the capital of the state, and under the aid structure set up by Congress and the President, it is where the decisions will be made. Whatever plans New Orleans developed, they will be subordinate to what the state decides to do.

New Orleans Mayor Ray Nagin appointed the 17-member Bring Back New Orleans Commission in late September 2005, and it submitted its final report in March 2006 (New Orleans Commission 2006; Rivlin 2005). Along the way, tensions erupted over which neighborhoods would or would not be allowed to rebuild. A report by the Urban Land Institute recommended the notorious shrinking of the footprint with a buy-out of property owners in lower-lying areas (Carr 2005b). With protests by neighborhood activists and civic leaders mounting, Mayor Nagin distanced himself from the ULI report (ACORN 2005; Davis, Mike 2006). In January 2006, a proposal emerged from the Commission to allow rebuilding in neighborhoods that could demonstrate their viability within four months, only to provoke a new wave of protests (Donze and Russell 2006). The final report will allow people to rebuild in any neighborhood, but at their own risk if located in areas that are prone to flood (New Orleans Commission 2006).

The ability of most property owners to even decide about rebuilding in New Orleans was delayed until mid-April when FEMA finally released its new flood maps and construction guidelines for the city (Fetterman 2006). Coupled with pledges for levee repair, this new information allowed residents to know what would be required for rebuilding in order to be eligible for flood insurance from NFIP. Any house that was destroyed or incurred more than 50% damage will have to be elevated by three feet to meet new standards. Anticipating that the standards would be much more stringent, many home owners and officials were relieved by FEMA's announcement. The relative leniency of the new requirements bodes well for the return of New Orleanians, but some experts have criticized them as setting the stage for significant loss in future hurricanes (Nossiter and Schwartz 2006; Whoriskey and Hsu 2006).

The Louisiana Recovery Authority (LRA) — The LRA was created by Governor Kathleen Babineaux Blanco's October 15, 2005 executive order. The order provided for a Board of Directors appointed by the Governor and establishment of an LRA office within the state government. The LRA chair is Dr. Norman Francis, the President of Xavier University, a historic Black college in New Orleans that was heavily damaged in the disaster. The vice chair is Walter Isaacson, CEO of the Aspen Institute in Colorado and former CEO of CNN and managing editor of *Time Magazine*. The LRA board has 33 members and hundreds of other people serving on task forces. Its principal product to date has been *The Road Home*, the housing recovery plan for the state, approved by the board on April 26, 2006 and by the Louisiana Legislature on May 10, 2006 (LRA 2006a; Maggi 2006). The Louisiana Plan was approved by HUD on May 30, 2006 (HUD 2006j).

With the additional $4.2 billion in CDBG funds now approved, Louisiana has a total of $10.4 billion. The state plans to spend $8.08 billion on housing, with $6.35 billion to assist home owners, $1.54 for affordable rental housing, and $26 million for housing for homeless people (LRA 2006b).

The homeowner recovery plan in Louisiana differs from that in Mississippi in that all homeowners who sustained damage are eligible for up to $150,000 per household if the homeowner can demonstrate that the home was owned and occupied by his or her family on the day the hurricane hit. Only single-family homes and duplexes are eligible. The household must have registered with FEMA. The house needs to have been destroyed or sustained major damage using FEMA criteria. For homeowners who did not carry the proper insurance, including flood insurance in 100-year flood plains, there will be a 30% reduction in the size of their grants. The amount of each grant will be based on the pre-storm value of the home times the percent of damage, less insurance payments, FEMA grants, and other aid. Homeowners who agree to stay and repair their homes will receive grants based on the full value of their property, but those who sell their homes will only be allowed to apply 60% of pre-Katrina value to their grant calculations, thereby incentivizing homeowners to stay and rebuild. The Mississippi plan has no such incentives, but, like the Mississippi plan, Louisiana grant recipients must agree to legally binding commitments to repair and improve their homes to mitigate future danger and maintain all required insurance (LRA 2006b).

Unlike Mississippi, Louisiana is attempting to address rental housing needs in *The Road Home*. Governor Blanco and LRA officials acknowledge the importance of affordable rental units to the return of the workforce needed to jump-start the state's economy (Blanco Says 2006). The major rental housing resource proposed in the LRA plan is the Low Income Housing Tax Credit "PiggyBack" program, which will cost $552 million. Essentially, CDBG funds would be used to capitalize a reserve fund to provide operating subsidies for a portion of the new LIHTC units to make them affordable to families at the lowest income levels. The plan projects up to 18,000 new LIHTC units to families with incomes at or less than 60% of the area median—a grand total of 9,000 units (LRA 2006b). Again, the scope relative to the need is wholly inadequate. Moreover, providing operating subsidies with CDBG funds is considered an inefficient use of these dollars; Section 8 project-based vouchers would be a far better approach (NLIHC 2006g).

The Louisiana plan falls short of meeting its obligations under CDBG. HUD issued certain waivers of CDBG regulations for the Louisiana plan on June 14, 2006, but did not waive the 50% requirement as it did for Mississippi (*Federal Register* 2006b). An administrative complaint was filed with HUD on June 20, 2006, charging that the Louisiana plan failed to assure that at least 50% of its CDBG funds would serve low- and moderate-income people and that the plan failed to affirmatively further fair housing (Quigley 2006).

Public Housing

Public housing in New Orleans has long had the reputation as badly run, corrupt, and home to all the stereotypical ills of public housing—crime, drugs, unemployment, teen pregnancy, school failure, and welfare dependence. Mismanagement led to physical deterioration and poor living conditions for residents. The administration of the Housing Authority of New Orleans (HANO) had become so dysfunctional that HUD forced it into receivership in 2002 (HUD 2006h). Under the HUD receiver, several public housing projects had been or were being redeveloped under HOPE VI when Katrina hit, with all the controversy that HOPE VI brings.[14] All public housing was closed when the residents were evacuated. Most of the public housing in New Orleans remains closed months after the storm, even those developments that sustained minor damage, despite the severe housing shortage and the sizable percentage of the city's rental housing stock that public housing represents. The public housing residents of New Orleans are nearly 100% Black.

The uncertain future of public housing in New Orleans was heralded a few days after the storm when it was reported that Representative Richard Baker (R-LA) was heard to say, "We finally cleaned up public housing in New Orleans. We couldn't do it, but God did it" (Babington 2005). While Mr. Baker disavowed that he meant anything but concern for the well-being of the residents (Shields 2005), his assertion has come to symbolize the low regard officialdom has for public housing in New Orleans.

Low regard for at least some of the tenants was expressed in February 2006 when the President of the New Orleans City Council, Oliver Thomas, announced his position that the only public housing residents who should be allowed to return are those who are employed. "We don't need soap opera watchers right now. We are going to target those who are going to work," said Thomas at a public meeting (Varney 2006a). Thomas later qualified his position to say he did not mean to exclude elderly and disabled people who are unable to work, but asserted that he had received overwhelming support for his position from New Orleans citizens and from the HUD receiver in charge of HANO (Varney 2006b). He was rebuked, however, on the editorial page of the *Houston Chronicle*: "Thomas' statements make one wonder how he ... would have treated poor Houstonians had the municipal roles been reversed and 100,000 Texans fled to New Orleans...Everyone who fled...deserves the same warm welcome back that they received upon arriving in Houston" (No Welcome Home 2006). Echoing Thomas, HUD Secretary Alphonso Jackson told reporters in April that he thinks only the "best residents" should be allowed to come back to their homes in New Orleans public housing (Walsh 2006b).

Meanwhile, public housing residents and their advocates are protesting HANO's stalled repair and reopening of complexes that were occupied before the storm (Arena 2006; Fausset 2006b; Filosa 2006b; Filosa 2006d; Sabludowsky 2006; Walsh 2006b). The doors and windows in several complexes have been sealed shut with metal plates that cover the entire opening. In places where residents have been able to get in, they found that their belongings had been pillaged and discovered rapidly spreading mold, evidence of neglect by HANO in the residents' absence (Filosa 2006a; Flaherty and Vitry 2006). Iberville, the development closest to the undamaged French Quarter, is open to a small fraction of its former residents, but seems to have little repair activity underway and a good number of squatters. It has long been in the crosshairs of major developers because of the high value of the land and its proximity to the tourist district (Fausset 2006b). Lafitte, of the same vintage and a few blocks away from Iberville, remains closed despite receiving minimal damage (Little 2006). Both are brick, three-story structures with traditional New Orleans ironwork.

HUD Secretary Alphonso Jackson announced on May 30, 2006 that he was directing $154 million to rebuild New Orleans public housing (HUD 2006j). These are previously allocated funds to HANO that HUD is not using because the residents are not in residence. HANO has also submitted no fewer than seven applications for GO-ZONE Low Income Housing Tax Credits, foreshadowing the redevelopment of public housing for higher income people than those who were displaced. New Orleans public housing residents have taken to the streets to demand the right to reclaim their homes. Some have defied the fences and no trespassing signs to reclaim their homes (Roberts 2006). Others have set up tent cities outside the grounds of their complexes vowing to stay until they move back into their homes (Filosa 2006e).

With promises that eventually all displaced public housing residents who want to return to New Orleans will be welcomed back, HUD announced its plans for the redevelopment of the public housing stock on June 14, 2006. HUD intends to reopen 2,000 public housing units by the end of summer, but also intends to demolish several thousand units in major complexes throughout the city to make way for new development (HUD 2006k). In a city with a woeful shortage of affordable rental housing today, this plan was met with considerable criticism as another example of the failed federal response to Katrina (Elie 2006).

For those who believe that public housing is a failed program that fosters dependency, crime, and racial segregation, Hurricane Katrina offers the opportunity to replace and possibly reduce assisted housing in New Orleans. For those who call Lafitte or Calliope or Magnolia home, despite any shortcomings, and who long to return, they have been displaced by both Hurricane Katrina and government inaction and indifference. For those who perceive the continued dislocation of New Orleans residents as willful, the state of public housing today represents the ethnic cleansing of New Orleans.

Conclusion

Hurricane Katrina will be remembered as a seminal event in American history. The emptying of whole communities happened overnight. The dimensions of the diaspora are unprecedented in modern America. The destruction is so vast that it is only possible to comprehend by going to the Gulf Coast and seeing for oneself. Katrina is about wrenching hundreds of thousands of people from homes to which most will never return. Katrina is about the sudden and complete loss of all that home means—safety, respite, privacy, comfort, and security.

Katrina is also about the generosity of ordinary people. One of the ways Katrina will be remembered is by the common decency of many people who traveled to the Gulf to volunteer to put a new roof on for a stranger or to strip moldy sheetrock out of houses still standing. Would that the considerable charitable instincts of the American people were sufficient in the face of a disaster of this scope.

But they are not. Human beings organize governments to do what individuals cannot do for themselves, with protection and recovery from wholesale catastrophe at the top of the list. Unless policy and practice take a different turn from where they appear to be heading at this time, Katrina will be remembered as a massive public failure—a failure of political will to "do what it takes," as President Bush promised he would in his speech to the nation on September 15, 2006 from New Orleans (Bush 2005; Hsu 2006).

The future of public housing in New Orleans is just one skirmish in the larger battle of who wants to return, who has the right to return, who will be able to return, who will be welcome to return, and who decides. Polling data suggest that somewhat less than half of evacuees want to come home (Dangerfield 2006; *Washington Post* 2005; Zogby et al. 2006). Indeed, Katrina has given some people a chance for a better life. Katherine Boo's (2005) poignant portrait of 13-year old Jasmine, who escaped from her abusive, addicted mother in New Orleans to her long-lost, welcoming father in Minnesota through the emergency shelter in Houma, Louisiana, is a case in point. Jason DeParle (2006) captured the hopefulness of a New Orleans family reveling in the opportunities that Atlanta offers them. Yet there are others for whom home is home, and nothing else will do. The author met a man who had just returned to his home in public housing in New Orleans. He had been in Arkansas, where the streets were clean, the people were gracious, and the mountain vista was beautiful. But it was not where he belonged, and he ached to return (personal communication, May 9, 2006). For many people, the reality is that they just do not know what to do. They are coping with being dislocated again by FEMA. They are paralyzed by depression and cannot make good decisions. Or they cannot make personal decisions until official decisions are made, which have been slow in coming (Edney and Prince 2006).

While policymakers have been dithering, the modern-day carpetbaggers have moved in. Speculators are buying up property at bargain prices, and multinational corporations are getting richer off of FEMA contracts. The forces against inclusive redevelopment are mighty (Davis, Mike 2006). The political dynamics of weakening the Democratic voter base by keeping low-income Black people from coming home are not to be underestimated.

Massive dislocation and loss have already happened and cannot be undone. But how Americans decide to ameliorate the suffering that the dislocation caused is a choice we still can make. A commitment to a national housing agenda that assures a sufficient supply of affordable housing for everyone in neighborhoods and communities of their choosing, including those of limited means, is a good place to start.

The prospect of families — especially poor, Black families who are already burdened by the legacy of American racism — never having the chance to go home after Katrina should weigh heavily on the hearts of all Americans. The pain of their forced exile will be embedded in the narratives of their families and shape their sense of themselves as Americans for generations to come. Unless everyone who was displaced by Katrina experiences genuine choice about where he or she will settle at the end of the day, Katrina will leave an indelible stain on the American soul.

References

ACORN. 2005. Katrina Survivors Denounce New Orleans Rebuild Plan as Unfairly Prioritizing Wealthy, White Neighborhoods. *Hurricane Katrina News and Information*. November.

Adcox, Seanna. 2005. S.C. Cares Commits to Continue Housing Evacuees After Dec. 1. *Associated Press*. November 17.

Advocacy Center. 2006. People with Disabilities Sue FEMA. Press Release, February 21. Retrieved from http://www.femaanswers.org/images/6/66/Brou_v_FEMA_press_-2.pdf.

Alpert, Bruce. 2006. In Congress, Vast Majority Yet to See Ruins. *New Orleans Times-Picayune*. January 11.

Another FEMA Housing Mess. 2006. *Baton Rouge Advocate*. Editorial. May 3.

Arena, Jay. 2006. We're Back! Reopen Our Homes Now. *ZNet*. February 26. Retrieved from http://www.zmag.org.

Babington, Charles. 2005. Some GOP Legislators Hit Jarring Notes in Addressing Katrina. *Washington Post*. September 10.

Barbour, Governor Haley. 2006. Testimony before Committee on Appropriations, U.S. Senate. March 6. Retrieved from http://www.appropriations.senate.gov/hearmarkups/gov'stestimony-fullapprops-march06.htm.

Batsell, Jake. 2006. Deadline Doesn't End Plano's Katrina Role. *Dallas Morning News*. March 31.

Bernardi, Deputy Secretary Roy. 2005. Hurricane Katrina Response, Recovery, and Relief Efforts at HUD. Testimony before Appropriations Subcommittee on Transportation, Treasury, and Housing and Urban Development, the Judiciary, District of Columbia and Related Agencies, U.S. House of Representatives. September 27. Retrieved from http://www.hud.gov/offices/cir/test092705.cfm.

Bishop, Cathy. 2006. Comments on the Public Housing Program CDBG Disaster Recovery Action Plan. Unpublished document. June.

Blanco, Governor Kathleen Babineaux. 2006. Testimony before Committee on Appropriations, U.S. Senate. March 7. Retrieved from http://www.appropriations.senate.gov/hearmarkups/3-5BBTtestimonyFinal.htm

Blanco Says Affordable Housing Crucial to Getting Families Back. 2006. *Baton Rouge Advocate*. March 15.

Blumenthal, Ralph and Eric Lipton. 2005. FEMA Broke Its Promise on Housing, Houston Mayor Says. *New York Times*. November 17.

Boo, Katherine. 2005. Shelter and the Storm. *The New Yorker*. November 28.

Brand, Aaron. 2005. Rep. Mike Ross Critical of FEMA Mobile Home Delay. *Texarkana Gazette*. December 15.

Bromage, Andy. 2005. Some Worry Aid Will Be At Expense of City's Poor. *New Haven Register*. September 9.

Brookings Institution. 2006. Rebuilding After Katrina: Forming the Federal-State-Local Partnership for Southern Louisiana. Brookings Metropolitan Policy Forum, Washington, DC. February 21. Retrieved from http://www.knowledgeplex.org/news/147730.html.

Bumiller, Elisabeth and Richard W. Stevenson. 2005. Speech is Expected to Focus on Vision for Reconstruction. *New York Times*. September 15.

Bush, President George W. 2005. Address to the Nation from Jackson Square on Hurricane Relief. September 15. Transcript retrieved from http://www.whitehouse.gov/news/releases/2005/09/print/20050915.8.html.

Calmes, Jackie. 2005. Bush Presents Post-Katrina Housing Plan. *Wall Street Journal*. September 19.

Carr, Martha. 2005a. Housing Shortage Hinders Rebound. *New Orleans Times-Picayune*. October 16.

_____ 2005b. Rebuilding Should Begin on High Ground. *New Orleans Times-Picayune*. November 19.

Cohn, Jonathan. 2005. Trailer Trash: Katrina Victims Need Real Housing. *The New Republic*. September 26.

Collins, Senator Susan and Senator Joseph Lieberman. 2006. Letter to Secretary of U.S. Department of Homeland Security Michael Chertoff. March 14. Retrieved from http://www.nlihc.org/news/031406collinsletter.pdf.

Corcoran, Elizabeth. 2006. From Microsoft to Katrina: Jim Barksdale. *Forbes*. January 30.

Corkery, Michael. 2005. Housing Tax Credit May Be New Orleans's Answer. *Wall Street Journal.* October 12.

Crowley, Sheila. 2005. Letter to President George W. Bush on behalf of National Low Income Housing Coalition. September 13. Retrieved from http://www.nlihc.org/news/091306presletter.pdf.

Dangerfield, Peter. 2006. *Citizen Participation: Informing Public Policy For Rebuilding New Orleans.* Total Community Action, Inc. & Associates, New Orleans, LA. January. Retrieved from http://www.tca-nola.com/publications/citizen-participation.pdf.

Dao, James. 2006. U.S. Plans $18 Billion More for Gulf, but Local Officials Are Skeptical. *New York Times.* February 3.

Davis, Andy. 2006. Some Storm Refugees Losing Housing Help. *Arkansas Democrat Gazette.* April 9.

Davis, Mike. 2006. Who Is Killing New Orleans? *The Nation.* April 10.

DeParle, Jason. 2005. Storm and Crisis: Housing; Lack of Section 8 Vouchers for Storm Evacuees Highlights Rift Over Housing Program. *New York Times.* November 8.

_____. 2006. Katrina's Tide Carries Many to Hopeful Shores. *New York Times.* April 23.

Dewan, Shaila. 2006a. Behind Louisiana Aid Package, A Change of Heart by One Man. *New York Times.* March 20.

Dewan, Shaila. 2006b. Evacuees Will Find Housing Grants End Soon. *New York Times.* April 27.

Donze, Frank and Gordon Russell. 2006. 4 Months to Decide. *New Orleans Times-Picayune.* January 11.

Drew, Christopher and Joseph B. Treaster. 2006. Politics Stalls Plan to Bolster Flood Insurance. *New York Times.* May 15.

Driver, Anna. 2005. Some Katrina Victims Face NY Homeless Shelters. *Reuters.* November 18.

Eaton, Leslie and Ron Nixon. 2005. Loans to Homeowners Along Gulf Coast Lag. *New York Times.* December 15.

Edney, Hazel Trice and Zenitha Prince. 2006. New Orleans Residents Ponder Their Future. *Afro-American Newspapers.* March 29. Retrieved from http://www.afro.com.

Elie, Lois. (2006, June 16). "Katrina Builds Hall of Shame." *New Orleans Times-Picayune.*

End of Rental Program Might Force Katrina Shelters to Reopen. 2006. *Associated Press.* April 30.

Factoring the Forecast. 2006. Editorial. *New Orleans Times Picayune.* April 6.

Fausset, Richard. 2006b. Few Have Returned to Iberville Projects, and Six Others Remain Closed. *Los Angeles Times.* April 21.

Federal Register. 2006a. Department of Housing and Urban Development: Allocations and Common Application and Reporting Waivers Granted to and Alternative Requirements for CDBG Disaster Recovery Grantees Under the Department of Defense Appropriations Act, 2005. 71(29): 7666–7672. February 13.

_____. 2006b. Department of Housing and Urban Development. Waivers Granted To and Alternative Requirements for the State of Louisiana's CDBG Disaster Recovery Grant Under the Department of Defense Emergency Supplemental Appropriations to Address Hurricanes in the Gulf of Mexico and Pandemic Influenza Act, 2006. 71(114): 34451-34457. June 14.

_____. 2006c. Department of Housing and Urban Development. Waivers Granted To and Alternative Requirements for the State of Mississippi's CDBG Disaster Recovery Grant Under the Department of Defense Emergency Supplemental Appropriations to Address Hurricanes in the Gulf of Mexico and Pandemic Influenza Act, 2006. 71(114): 34457-34461. June 14.

FEMA's Latest Fumble. 2005. *Northeast Mississippi Daily Journal.* Editorial. November 18.

Fetterman, Mindy. 2006. Replacing Housing Off to a Slow Start. *USA Today.* April 17.

Filosa, Gwen. 2006a. HANO Urged to Reopen Complexes. *New Orleans Times Picayune.* February 15.

_____. 2006b. HANO Protest Becomes Scuffle. *New Orleans Times Picayune.* April 5.

_____. 2006c. Public Housing Still Empty. *New Orleans Times Picayune.* April 9.

_____. 2006d. Public Housing Residents Demand to Reoccupy Units. *New Orleans Times Picayune.* May 4.

_____. 2006e. Displaced Residents Demand Access to Public Housing. *New Orleans Times-Picayune.* June 3.

Fischer, Will and Barbara Sard. 2005. *Bringing Katrina's Poorest Victims Home: Targeted Federal Assistance Will Be Needed to Give Neediest Evacuees Option to Return to Their Hometowns.* Center on Budget and Policy Priorities, Washington, DC. November 3.

_____ 2006. *Housing Needs of Many Low-Income Hurricane Evacuees Are Not Being Adequately Addressed.* Center on Budget and Policy Priorities, Washington, DC. February 27.

Flaherty, Jordan and Jennifer Vitry. 2006. (More) Loss and Displacement in New Orleans. *AlterNet.* January 12. Retrieved from http://www.alternet.org.

Frank, Representative Barney. 2005. Letter to Secretary of U.S. Department of Housing and Urban Development Alphonso Jackson. October 18. Retrieved from http://www.house.gov/banking_democrats/HUDJacksonKatrinaletter180c505.pdf.

Frank, Representative Barney and Representative Maxine Waters. 2005. Reps. Frank and Waters: Where's the Katrina Housing Plan? Press Release. November 8. Retrieved from http://www.house.gov/banking_democrats/pr11082005a.html.

Gabe, Thomas, Gene Falk, and Maggie McCarthy. 2005. *Hurricane Katrina: Social-Demographic Characteristics of Impacted Areas.* Congressional Research Service, Washington, DC.

Gosselin, Peter G. and Ricardo Alonso-Zaldivar. 2005. Limiting Government's Role. *Los Angeles Times.* September 23.

Governor's Commission on Recovery, Rebuilding, and Renewal. 2005. *After Katrina: Building Back Better Than Ever. A Report to the Honorable Haley Barbour, Governor of State of Mississippi.* December 31. Retrieved from http://www.governorscommission.com/final.

Graczyk, Michael. 2005. FEMA Says It Will Work Out Refugee Housing, FEMA Tries to Ease Fears. *Associated Press.* November 17.

H.R. 4100. 2005. Louisiana Recovery Corporation Act, 109th Cong.

H.R. 4197. 2005. Hurricane Katrina Recovery, Reclaimation, Restoration, Reconstruction, and Reunion Act of 2005, 109th Cong.

H.R. 4939. 2006. Emergency Supplemental Appropriations Act for Defense, the Global War on Terror and Hurricane Recovery of 2006 (Reported out of Senate). 109th Cong.

H.R. 4440. 2006. Gulf Opportunity Zone Act of 2005, 109th Cong.

H.R. 5393. 2006. Natural Disaster Housing Reform Act of 2006, 109th Cong.

Hogue, Henry. 2005. *Federal Hurricane Recovery Coordinator: Appointment and Oversight Issues.* Congressional Research Service, Washington, DC.

Hsu, Spencer. 2006. Post-Katrina Promises Unfilled. *Washington Post.* January 6.

Hsu, Spencer and Ceci Connelly. 2005. Housing the Displaced is Rife with Delays. *Washington Post.* September 23.

Hustmyre, Chuck. 2005. Residents, Evacuees Jam Meeting. *Baton Rouge Advocate.* November 9.

Jackson, Secretary Alphonso. 2006. Testimony before Committee on Banking, Housing, and Urban Affairs, U.S. Senate, Answers to follow up questions submitted in writing. Unpublished document. February 15. Retrieved from http://www.nlihc.org/news/042706.pdf.

Jensen, Lynne. 2005. FEMA Trailer Plans Hits Stoplight in New Orleans. *New Orleans Times Picayune.* December 1.

Johnson, Derrick, Deborah Bey, and John Rich. 2006. Memo to Governor Haley Barbour and Mississippi Development Authority Re CDBG Programs for Renters, Moderate and Low Income Households, Senior Citizens, and People with Disabilities. Unpublished Document. February 10.

Kendrick, Assistant Secretary Kim. 2005. Open letter on fair housing and evacuees. October 25. Retrieved from http://www.hud.gov/fairhousing.

_____ 2006. Testimony before Subcommittee on Housing and Community Opportunity, U.S. House of Representatives. February 28. Retrieved from http://financialservices.house.gov/media/pdf/12140HUD.pdf.

Krugman, Paul. 2005a. Tragedy in Black and White. *New York Times.* September 19.

_____ 2005b. Miserable by Design. *New York Times.* October 3.

Las Vegas Homeless Advocates Complain of Plans to House Evacuees. 2005. *Las Vegas Sun.* September 8.

Little, Robert. 2006. Barred from Coming Home: New Orleans Poor Are Shut Out of Public Housing. *Baltimore Sun.* February 19.

Lipton, Eric. 2005a. A Rush to Set Up U.S. Housing for Storm Survivors. *New York Times.* September 13.

_____ 2005b. Hurricane Evacuees Face Eviction Threats at Both Their Old Homes and New. *New York Times.* November 4.

_____ 2005c. FEMA Is Set to Stop Paying Hotel Cost for Storm Victims. *New York Times.* November 16.

_____ 2006. Trailers, Vital After Hurricane, Now Pose Own Risks on Gulf. *New York Times.* March 16.

Louisiana Recovery Authority. 2006a. Update: About Us. Retrieved from http://www.lra.louisiana.gov.

Louisiana Recovery Authority. 2006b. The Road Home Housing Programs: Action Plan Amendment for Disaster Recovery Funds. May 3. Retrieved from http://www.lra.louisiana.gov/assets/roadhomehousingactionplan050306.pdf.

Maggi, Laura. 2006. Housing Grants Now Need Action in Congress. *New Orleans Times Picayune.* May 11.

McWaters v. FEMA, Case 2:05-cv-05488-SRD-DEK, Document 38. 2005. E.D. La. 2005. December 12.

Meese, Edwin, Stuart Butler, and Kim Holmes. 2005. *From Tragedy to Triumph: Principled Solutions for Rebuilding Lives and Communities.* Special Report #05. Heritage Foundation, Washington, DC.

Mississippi Development Authority. 2006. Homeowner Assistance Program Partial Action Plan. March 31. Retrieved from http://www.hud.gov/content/releases/pr06-036ms.pdf.

National Alliance to End Homelessness. 2005a. *HUD Program May Strand Many Previously Homeless Katrina Victims.* Retrieved from http://www.endhomelessness.org/do/uncoveredhomelesskdhap.pdf.

National Low Income Housing Coalition. 2005a. House Committee Approves New Affordable Housing Fund. *Memo to Members* 10 (21).

_____ 2005c. *Hurricane Katrina's Impact on Low Income Housing Units Estimated 302,000 Units Lost or Damaged, 71% Low Income.* Research Note #05-02. NLIHC, Washington, DC. September 22.

_____ 2005d. Emergency Vouchers Win in Senate. *Memo to Members* 10 (36).

_____ 2005f. Affordable Housing Fund Passes House with Restrictions, But Not Without a Fight. *Memo to Members* 10 (42).

_____ 2005g. Funding for Emergency Vouchers Not Included in Conference Report. *Memo to Members* 10 (43).

_____ 2005h. NLIHC Comments on FEMA Plan to Give Displaced Evacuees Two Weeks Notice. Press Release. November 16. Retrieved from http://www.nlihc.org/press/111705pr.html.

_____ 2005i. National Housing Advocates Call on Administration and Congress for Action on Housing Hurricane Victims. Press Release. November 30. Retrieved from http://www.nlihc.org/press/113005pr.html.

_____ 2005k. 1% Across the Board Cuts, Katrina Reallocation Bill Included in Final Department of Defense Appropriations Bill. *Memo to Members* 10 (49).

_____ 2006b. FY07 Budget Chart for Selected Programs. February 15. Retrieved from http://www.nlihc.org/news/021506chart.pdf.

_____ 2006c. President Sends $19.8 Billion Disaster Supplemental Budget Request to Congress. *Memo to Members* 11 (7).

_____ 2006d. *2006 Advocates' Guide to Housing and Community Development Policy.* NLIHC, Washington, DC.

_____ 2006e. HUD Increases Fair Market Rents in New Orleans, Baton Rouge, Others. *Memo to Members* 11 (9).

_____ 2006g. Comments to Louisiana Recovery Authority The Road Home Housing Programs Action Plan Amendment for Disaster Recovery Funds. April 17. Retrieved from http://www.nlihc.org/news/.

_____ 2006h. Advocates Seek Improvements to Senate Hurricane Recovery Supplemental Spending Bill. *Memo to Members* 11 (16).

_____ 2006j. "Conferees Agree on Final Housing Spending Plan." *Memo to Members,* 11(23).

_____ 2006k. "Disaster Housing Bill Progresses." *Memo to Members,* 11(24).

National Multi Housing Council. 2005. Apartment Sector Requests Temporary Waiver of Federal Housing Regulations. Press Release. September 7. Retrieved from http://www.nmhc.org/Content/ServeContent.cfm?ContentItemID=3557&IssueID=164.

Neuman, Johanna. 2006. The Land of 10,770 Empty FEMA Trailers. *Los Angeles Times.* February 10.

New Orleans Commission Issues Final Report. 2006. *Associated Press.* March 20.

Newsom Slams Bush Decision to Cut Off Hotel Vouchers for Katrina Victims at Beginning of Holidays. 2005. *San Francisco Sentinel.* November 17.

Nixon, Ron and Leslie Eaton. 2006. For Hurricane Victims, A Flawed System. *New York Times.* April 21.

No Welcome Home. 2006. *Houston Chronicle.* Editorial. February 24.

Nossiter, Adam. 2006. A Big Government Fix-It Plan for New Orleans. *New York Times.* January 5.

Nossiter, Adam and John Schwartz. 2006. Lenient Rule Set for Rebuilding in New Orleans. *New York Times.* April 13.

Office of the President of the United States. 2005. Fact Sheet: President Bush Requests Rescission and Reallocation Packages. October 28. Retrieved from http://www.whitehouse.gov/news/releasee/2005/10/print/20051028-6.html.

_____ 2006. *The Federal Response to Hurricane Katrina: Lessons Learned.* Retrieved from http://www.whitehouse.gov/reports/katrina-lessons-learned.pdf.

Olson, Elizabeth. 2005. Up and Running; In New Orleans, the Wait for Federal Loans Drags On. *New York Times.* November 16.

Olson, Edgar O. and John C. Weicher. 2005. Housing the Poorest Hurricane Victims–Now. Manuscript sent to Sheila Crowley on September 23, 2005.

Pelletiere, Danilo. 2006. *The Rental Housing Affordability Gap: Comparison of 2001 and 2003 American Housing Surveys.* National Low Income Housing Coalition, Washington, DC.

Perry, James. 2006. Testimony before Subcommittee on Housing and Community Opportunity, U.S. House of Representatives. February 28. Retrieved from http://financialservices.house.gov/media/pdf/022806jp.pdf.

Perry, Governor Rick. 2006. Testimony Before Appropriations Committee, U.S. Senate. March 7. Retrieved from http://appropriations.senate.gov/hearmarkups/hurricanefundingtestimonyfinaleformittedfor.

Poverty and Race Research Action Council. 2005. Hurricane Katrina: Lessons for HUD from the 1994 Los Angeles Earthquake. September 12. PRRAC, Washington, DC.

Powell, Donald E. 2006. Rebuilding Wisely. *Washington Post.* February 2.

Powell, Michael. 2005. In Mississippi, Time Now Stands Still: Recovery is Stagnant in Post-Katrina Towns. *Washington Post.* November 25.

Quigley, Bill. 2006. Administrative Complaint Challenging the Misuse of Federal Community Development Block Grants By the State of Louisiana in "Road Home" Expenditures of Federal Funds Because There is No Guarantee of A "Fair Share" for Low and Moderate Income Renters and Homeowners. June 20. Retrieved from http://www.nlihc.org/neww/062206.pdf.

Radelat, Ana. 2006. Senate May OK Money for Katrina Cottages. *USA Today.* April 3.

Rehm, Diane. 2005. Transcript of Diane Rehm Show. WAMU-National Public Radio, Washington, DC. October 5. Retrieved from www.nlihc.org/news/rehmtranscript10-5-05.pdf.

Rice, Douglas and Barbara Sard. 2006. *FEMA Misses Congressional Deadline to Issue Guidance on Continued Housing Assistance For Hurricane Katrina Victims.* Center on Budget and Policy Priorities, Washington, DC.

Rivlin, Gary. 2005. New Orleans Enlists VIPs for Rebuilding. *New York Times.* October 1.

_____ 2006. Patchy Recovery in New Orleans. *New York Times.* April 5.

Roberts, Michelle. 2006. "Residents, Volunteers Clean Public Housing Units." *Associated Press.* June 10.

Rodriguez, Lori. 2005. Evacuees Are First Priority for Public Housing Houston Official Says Reacting to Crisis Situation. *Houston Chronicle.* September 8.

Rodriguez, Lori and Zeke Minaya. 2005. 'Population Shift, New Orleans' Racial Make-up Up in the Air. *Houston Chronicle.* September 28.

S. 2088. 2005. Hurricane Katrina Recovery Homesteading Act of 2005, 109th Cong.

Sabludowsky, Steve. 2006. New Orleans Post Katrina Housing Needs New Vision. *Bayou Buzz.* April 5.

Sandalow, Mark. 2005. Hurricane Katrina: Congressional Reaction. *San Francisco Chronicle.* September 15.

Sarbanes, Senator Paul. 2005. Letter to Senators Thad Cochran and Robert Byrd. December 8. Retrieved from http://www.nlihc.org/news/120905sarbanes.pdf.

Sard, Barbara and Douglas Rice. 2005. *Changes Needed in Katrina Transitional Housing Plan to Meet Families' Needs.* Center on Budget and Policy Priorities, Washington, DC.

Sargeant Shriver National Center on Poverty Law. 2006. FEMA Answers. Retrieved from http://www.femaanswers.org/index.php/FEMA_Answers.

Saugier, Mari. 2006. Some Evacuees Frustrated Over Housing, Disorganized Plan Left Many Confused. *Corpus Christi Caller-Times.* March 2.

Sayre, Alan. 2006. Post-storm New Orleans Economy a Huge Question Mark: Housing Shortages Are on the Minds of Everyone. *Associated Press.* March 28.

Shields, Gerard. 2005. Baker Claims Misquote on N.O. Housing Loss. *Baton Rouge Advocate.* September 10.

Smith, Cheryl. 2006a. One Stroke Forward, Two Strokes Back – Hurricane Victims Tread Rising Bureaucratic Waters. *Austin Chronicle.* February 24.

_____ 2006b. Evacuee Limbo, Eviction Trickle. *Austin Chronicle.* March 24.

Smith, Shanna. 2006a. Testimony before Subcommittee on Housing and Community Opportunity, U.S. House of Representatives. February 28. Retrieved from http://financialservices.house.gov/media/pdf/022806ss.pdf.

Snyder, Mike. 2006a. Housing Shortage Could Leave Evacuees Homeless. *Houston Chronicle.* March 29.

_____ 2006b. Evacuees May Be Denied Aid. *Houston Chronicle.* April 13.

_____ 2006c. FEMA Deemed These Homes Habitable. *Houston Chronicle.* April 13.

_____ 2006d. Cut Off Families Sue FEMA. *Houston Chronicle.* May 19.

Some Katrina Evacuees Get FEMA Extension. 2006a. *Associated Press.* February 23.

Some Refugees in Arkansas to Lose FEMA Housing Aid. 2006. *Pine Bluff (Arkansas) Commercial.* April 9.

Steinhauer, Jennifer and Eric Lipton. 2006. Storm Victims Face Big Delay to Get Trailers. *New York Times.* February 9.

Stewart, Jocelyn Y. 2005. Katrina's Aftermath: Hurricane Victims Go to Top of Some Public Housing Lists. *Los Angeles Times.* September 9.

Stewart, Patricia. 2006. Testimony before House Subcommittee on Housing and Community Opportunity, U.S. House of Representatives. Unpublished document. January 13.

Still Battering the Katrina Homeless. 2006. *New York Times.* Editorial. April 29.

Stonewalling the Katrina Victims. 2005. *New York Times.* Editorial. November 14.

Snyder, Mike. (2006x, May 31). "Judge Denies Extension for 'Ineligible' Evacuees." *Houston Chronicle.*

Texas Department of Housing and Community Development Affairs. 2005. IRS Approves Waiver, Frees Up Vacant TDHCA Tax Credit Units for Katrina Evacuees. Press Release. September 2. Retrieved from http://www.tdhca.state.tx.us/ppa/docs/press_releases/050902-IRS_waiver-050902.pdf.

Texas Low Income Housing Information Service. 2005. Findings of the Katrina Housing Forum. *Housing Matters: Meeting the Long Term Needs of Hurricane Evacuees in Texas.* 2-10.

The Poor Need Not Apply. 2005. *New York Times.* Editorial. December 21.

Thompson, Representative Bernie. 2005. Letter to FEMA Acting Director R. David Paulison. November 18. Retrieved from http://www.hsc-democrats.house.gov/NR/rdonlyres/CD8B36EC-4785-4580-BE18-859DB21A1721/0/FEMAContinueHousing.letter.pdf.

Tizon, Tomas Alex. 2005. La. Trailer Villages Bring Hope, Some Fear. *Los Angeles Times.* December 15.

Torpy, Bill. 2005. $11 Million Per Night to House Evacuees. *Atlantic Journal-Constitution.* October 15.

Trailer Trouble Chills New Orleans – FEMA Relations. 2006. *Reuters.* April 3.

U.S. Census Bureau. 2000. American FactFinder–Census 2000 Summary File 3(SF3). Retrieved from http://factfinder.census.gov/home/saff/main.html?_lang=en/.

U.S. Department of Agriculture, Rural Development. 2005. Hurricane Katrina Recovery Resources from Rural Development. Retrieved from http://www.rurdev.usda.gov/rd/disasters/katrina.html.

U.S. Department of Homeland Security. 2005a. U.S. Government Announces a Comprehensive Transitional Housing Assistance Program for Katrina Evacuees. Press Release. September 23. Retrieved from http://www.dhs.gov/dhspublic/display?theme=43&content=4848.

———— 2005b. Coordinator Named to Lead Federal Recovery and Rebuilding Activities. Press Release. November 1. Retrieved from http://www.dhs.gov/dhspublic/display?content=4917.

U.S. Department of Homeland Security, Federal Emergency Management Agency. 2005. *Help After a Disaster: Applicant's Guide to the Individual and Households Program*. Retrieved from http://www.fema.gov/pdf/assistance/process/help_after_disaster_english.pdf.

———— 2006a. Disaster Assistance Frequently Asked Questions. Retrieved from http://www.fema.gov/assistance/dafaq.shtm.

———— 2006b. FEMA Concludes Short-Term Lodging Program; Longer Term Housing Efforts Continue. Press Release Number HQ-06-020. February 1. Retrieved from http://www.fema.gov/news/newsrelease.fema?id=23158.

———— 2006d. FEMA News: Frequently Asked Questions. Press Release Number FNF-06-03. February 27. Retrieved from http://www.fema.gov/news/newsrelease.fema?id=23881.

———— 2006e. Katrina and Rita Applications Registration Deadline Extended to April 10. Press Release Number HQ-06-040. March 10. Retrieved from http://www.fema.gov/news/newsrelease.fema?id=24221.

———— 2006f. IA Applicant Location by State: Katrina and Rita Only, as of 3/17/2006. Retrieved from www.fema.gov/pdf/press/katrina_afer/locations_applications_combined_maps.pdf.

———— 2006g. Conversion of Assistance – 403-408. March 26. Retrieved from http://www.femaanswers.org/images/f/f1/DSG_-_Conversion_of_Assistance_403-408_-_Signed.pdf.

———— 2006h. Hurricane Katrina Information. Retrieved from http://www.fema.gov/press/2005/resources_katrina.shtm.

———— 2006i. How the NFIP Works. April 5. Retrieved from http://www.fema.gov/business/nfip/how.shtm.

———— 2006j. Hurricane Katrina and Rita Rental Assistance and Recertification. Unpublished document. May 3.

U.S. Department of Homeland Security, Office of Inspector General. 2006. A Performance Review of FEMA's Disaster Management Activities in Response to Hurricane Katrina. Office of Inspections and Special Reviews. OIG-06-32. March.

U.S. Department of Housing and Urban Development. 2005. HUD Announces Mortgage Assistance for Disaster Victims. Press Release HUD No. 05-164. December 5. Retrieved from http://www.hud.gov/news/release.cfm?content=pr05-164.cfm.

U.S. Department of Housing and Urban Development. 2006a. HUD's Response To Hurricanes in the Gulf of Mexico. Retrieved from http://www.hud.gov/news/katrina05response/cfm.

———— 2006b. HUD and Ad Council Launch Campaign to Fight Evacuee Housing Discrimination. Press Release HUD No. 06-006. January 19. Retrieved from http://www.hud.gov/news.

———— 2006c. Jackson Announces Distribution of $11.5 Billion in Disaster Assistance to Five Gulf Coast States Impacted by Hurricanes. Press Release. January 25. Retrieved from http://www.hud.gov/news/release.cfm?content=pr06-011.cfm.

———— 2006d. Katrina $ Damage by PHA. Unpublished document. March 15.

———— 2006e. Units in Affected Areas (AL, LA, and MS). Unpublished document. March 20.

———— 2006g. HUD To Sell Homes at Discount to Disaster Victims. Press Release HUD No. 06-046. April 26. Retrieved from http://www.hud.gov/news.

———— 2006h. HUD Names New Recovery Advisor and Receiver to Advance Current HANO Hurricane Recovery Efforts. Press Release HUD No. 06-043. April 14. Retrieved from http://www.hud.gov/news.

———— 2006i. "Jackson Approves Louisiana's $4.6 Billion 'Road Home Program.'" Press Release No. 06-058. Retrieved from http://www.hud.gov/news/release.cfm?content=pr06-058.cfm. May 30

———— 2006j. "HUD Outlines Aggressive Plan to Bring Families Back to New Orleans' Public Housing." Press Release No. 06-066. Retrieved from http://www.hud.gov/news/release.cfm?content=pr06-066.cfm. June 14.

U.S. Department of Housing and Urban Development, Office of Community Development and Planning. 2000. General definition of homeless individual. Retrieved from http://www.hud.gov/offices/cpd/homeless/rulesandregs/laws/title1/sec11302.cfm.

U.S. Department of Housing and Urban Development, Office of Policy Development and Research. 2006. Current Housing Unit Damage Estimates: Hurricanes Katrina, Rita, and Wilma, February 12, 2006. Unpublished document.

U.S. Department of Housing and Urban Development, Office of Public and Indian Housing. 2005. KDHAP Participating Public Housing Authorities. December 1. Retrieved from http://www.nlihc.org/news/120905kdhapsn6.xls.

_____ 2006a. Notice PIH 2006-12, Subject: Disaster Voucher Program (DVP) Operating Requirements. February 3. Retrieved from http://www.hud.gov/offices/pih/publications/notices/06/pih2006-12.pdf.

_____ 2006b. Disaster Voucher Program (DVP) Supplemental Guidance: Rental Assistance for Special Needs Families Displaced by Hurricanes Katrina and Rita. February. Retrieved from http://www.hud.gov/offices/pih/publications/dvpsnguidance.pdf.

U.S. Department of Treasury. 2005. Treasury and IRS Expand Availability of Housing for Hurricane Victims. Press Release JS-2698. September 2. Retrieved from http://www.treasury.gov/press/releases/js2698.htm.

U.S. House of Representatives, Financial Services Committee, Subcommittee on Housing and Community Opportunity. 2006. Housing Options in the Aftermath of Hurricanes Katrina and Rita. Field hearings. January 13–14. Retrieved at http://www.financialservices.house.gov/hearings.asp?formmode=detail&hearing=436 and 437.

U.S. Senate, Committee on Banking, Housing, and Urban Affairs. 2006. Rebuilding Needs in Katrina-Impacted Areas. Hearing. February 15. Retrieved at http://www.banking.senate.gov/index.cfm?fuseaction=hearings.details&hearingID=191.

U.S. Small Business Administration. n.d.a. Disaster Loans – Fact Sheet. Retrieved from http://www.sba.gov/disaster_recov/fact_sheet_Louisiana_Hurricane_Katrina.pdf.

_____ n.d.b. Hurricane Disaster Assistance. Retrieved from http://www.sba.gov/disaster_recov/Disasterrecovery.pdf.

Varney, James. 2006a. HANO Wants Only Working Tenants. *New Orleans Times Picayune*. February 21.

_____ 2006b. Thomas Stands by Rules for Re-entry. *New Orleans Times Picayune*. February 25.

Walker, David M. 2006. Federal Emergency Management Agency: Challenges for the National Flood Insurance Program. GAO-06-35T. Testimony before Committee on Banking, Housing, and Urban Affairs, U.S. Senate. January 26. Retrieved from http://www.banking.senate.gov/_files.ACF7BAE.pdf.

Waller, Scott. 2006. 'Katrina Cottage' Could Meet Housing Need. *The Clarion-Ledger* (Mississippi). January 15.

Walsh, Bill. 2006a. As HUD, Local Officials Debate, New Orleans Public Housing Remains in Limbo. *Newhouse News Service*. March 30.

_____ 2006b. Official Blunt on Public Housing. *Newhouse News Service*. April 25.

Wardrip, Keith, Danilo Pelletiere, and Sheila Crowley. 2005. *Out of Reach 2005*. National Low Income Housing Coalition, Washington, DC.

Washington Post/Henry J. Kaiser Family Foundation/Harvard School of Public Health. 2005. *Survey of Hurricane Katrina Evacuees*. September. Retrieved from http://www.washingtonpost.com/wp-srv/politics/polls/katrina-poll91605.pdf.

Weisman, Jonathan. 2005. Critics Fear Trailer "Ghettos" – Right, Left Target FEMA Initiative. *Washington Post*. September 16.

"What Next" for Victims of Katrina? 2005. *Hattiesburg (MS) American*. November 18.

Whoriskey, Peter and Spencer Hsu. 2006. Wait Ends on Rules for Katrina Rebuilding. *Washington Post*. April 13.

With Holidays Coming, Evacuees Will Be Sent Packing. 2005. *Austin-American Statesman*. Editorial. November 22.

Young, Earni. 2005. Victims Would Get PHA Priority. *Philadelphia Daily News*. September 3.

Zogby, John, John Bruce, Rebecca Wittman, and Karen Scott. 2006. *A Second Survey of Hurricane Evacuees Living in Houston*. Zogby International for the City of Houston. March.

Endnotes

1. Project-based assistance means that HUD provides monthly subsidies to owners to bridge the gap between the contract rent and 30% of the tenant's income, the affordability standard applied to public and assisted housing. These are among the most affordable homes to the lowest-income people.

2. Robert T. Stafford Disaster Relief and Emergency Assistance Act, as amended by Public Law 106-390, October 30, 2000. See http://www.fema.gov/library/stafact/shtm#4.

3. LIHTC is a federal program that distributes tax credits on a per capita basis to states, which in turn distribute them on a competitive basis to developers who use the tax credits to amass equity from investors. LIHTC properties must be affordable to households with incomes at 50–60% of AMI. They are only affordable to lower-income people if coupled with some kind of rent subsidy such as housing vouchers.

4. Testing in fair housing involves sending two testers, one White and one Black or other racial minority, who are otherwise equivalent in income and qualifications, to the same housing gate-keeper (landlord, rental agent, realtor, seller), and determining if there is differential treatment based on race.

5. For example, a National Public Radio broadcast on October 5, 2005 featured Ronald Utt of the conservative think tank the Heritage Foundation and Bruce Katz, a former Clinton Administration HUD official, now with the Brookings Institution. Both spoke against the extensive use of trailers in trailer parks and who advocated for housing assistance in the form of housing vouchers (Rehm 2005).

6. FEMA became an agency in the Department of Homeland Security when the Department was created in 2002, after being a stand-alone Cabinet-level agency during the Clinton Administration.

7. HUD Secretary Jackson has repeatedly asserted that the cost of the voucher program is straining the HUD budget and that income-targeting in the voucher program is too low, preventing more deserving people from getting assistance. The Bush Administration has tried to block grant the voucher program and to cut its funding, without success in the Congress. For a complete review of the voucher program, go to www.nlihc.org/news/index.htm and read sections on State and Local Flexibility Act and Vouchers.

8. The Fair Market Rent is a figure developed by HUD each year that represents what it costs to rent a modest rental unit in a locality. For a detailed explanation of the Fair Market Rent, see Wardrip, Pelletiere, and Crowley 2005, Appendix B.

9. The Stafford Act authorizes FEMA to task other federal agencies with some disaster relief responsibilities and to reimburse the other agencies for costs incurred.

10. For a complete description of all HUD programs, see National Low Income Housing Coalition 2006d.

11. The Community Development Block Grant (CDBG) was established in 1974 when a collection of categorical urban redevelopment programs was collapsed into one block grant. CDBG has been a mainstay of city budgets ever since. State and local politicians like its flexibility in eligible uses and relatively broad income-targeting requirements. States and localities are required to spend 70% of their CDBG funds to benefit low- and moderate-income people (in CDBG terms, these are households with incomes at or below 80% of the area median). CDBG funds, like all federal housing funds, are also required to be used in a manner that "affirmatively furthers fair housing." For a complete description of all HUD programs, see National Low Income Housing Coalition 2006d.

12. The GSEs are private corporations chartered by Congress that are the major purchasers of mortgages in the secondary market and which provide liquidity to the overall mortgage market. Both Fannie Mae and Freddie Mac have been rocked with accounting scandals and leadership shake-ups in recent years, fueling calls for greater regulation.

13. As a condition of eligibility to apply for and receive grants from the Affordable Housing Funds (AHF), nonprofit organizations are prohibited from engaging in otherwise legal nonpartisan voter activity, including voter registration, education, and get-out-the-vote activities. The prohibitions apply not just to their use of AHF grants, but to all of the organization's funds. For-profit companies are not subjected to the same restriction.

14. HOPE VI is a HUD program used to redevelop "severely distressed" public housing, with goals of reducing density and creating mixed-income housing. Most HOPE VI projects have resulted in a net loss of affordable housing units in the communities where they exist and in substantial displacement of some of the lowest-income people who resided in the public housing that was demolished.

CHAPTER 8

Reclaiming New Orleans' Working-Class Communities

ROBERT O. ZDENEK, RALPH SCOTT, JANE MALONE, AND BRIAN GUMM

A powerful editorial in the December 11, 2005 *New York Times*, "Death of an American City," raised the specter that without national political will and leadership, New Orleans would be left to rot from the ravages of hurricane damage. Part of raising New Orleans from its "political deathbed" involves demonstrating that homes and other key structures in working-class neighborhoods can be restored and reoccupied in a timely—yet safe and healthy—manner, at a far lower cost than razing and rebuilding the city.

One critical trend that has helped jump-start the city's recovery is residents' reoccupancy of thousands of structurally sound New Orleans homes. Hurricanes Katrina and Rita did not affect all New Orleans area neighborhoods equally. By October 2005, some flood-affected, predominantly well-to-do communities were already beginning to repopulate, and homes were being saved and restored. As of January 2006, other, usually poorer, working-class neighborhoods affected by flooding and reflooding were still almost vacant, and housing restoration was sparse. Most of the displaced residents of these communities are African Americans and other people of color.

Throughout the five months after Katrina hit, authorities continued to discourage former residents from returning to some low-income communities, citing all-too-real health and safety risks. Indeed, flood-damaged homes pose a range of health and safety hazards, including mold, deteriorated lead-based paint, carbon monoxide hazards, contamination with toxic chemicals and materials, pest infestations, structural damage, and injury hazards. Contrary to some earlier reports, however, by the end of 2005 it was clear that many older homes in lower-income and working-class neighborhoods of color could be saved and rebuilt. Many homes in affected neighborhoods such as the Ninth Ward and parts of Gentilly, Hollygrove, and Upper Carrollton were built with board sheathing and plaster that are quite resistant to mold and better able to survive sustained water submersion and intrusion than newer homes made with more porous materials that are highly susceptible to mold and water damage.

Homes determined to be structurally sound must be assessed for health hazards. The results of home investigations should be communicated quickly and thoroughly to residents—both owner-occupants and renters—so they can make informed decisions about whether to reoccupy their homes and avoid exacerbating hazards through unsafe cleanup and repair methods.

There is a growing body of practice, tools, and knowledge developed by the Alliance for Healthy Homes, a national nonprofit organization, and others that can minimize health and environmental barriers in order to spur the reoccupancy and revitalization of housing in vibrant, affordable working-class neighborhoods, neighborhoods that have been a hallmark of New Orleans for over a century. Without the practical environmental remediation of these houses, major sections of New Orleans will continue to be virtual "ghost towns," with nothing but passing memories and abandoned dwellings.

Many organizations, ranging from The Sierra Club to the American Planning Association to the U.S. Green Buildings Council, issued statements of overarching principles for rebuilding after Katrina and Rita that call for displaced residents to have the right and the ability to return, and for respecting and including displaced residents in decision-making. However, none of these important statements will bear fruit unless salvageable homes can be saved and rebuilt to form a core from which communities can repopulate and redevelop.

This chapter focuses on major factors affecting the environmental restoration of houses; short-term and long-standing environmental conditions in New Orleans; an action strategy for saving and restoring homes and other dwellings; the training, technical support, and equipment needed for safely reclaiming homes in New Orleans; and the resources and supports that residents, do-it-yourself providers, contractors, elected officials, and community-based organizations can utilize. The premise of this chapter is that displaced residents who want to return must be able to do so—but they should not come back to an unhealthy environment without first taking appropriate precautions, and they should understand the major health and environmental issues affecting their homes.

Environmental Conditions

Existing Conditions before Hurricanes Katrina and Rita

Ambient Health Hazards: The area along the Mississippi River between Baton Rouge and New Orleans contains hundreds of hazardous waste sites from mines, factories, and chemical plants, many of which were located there to facilitate shipping. The area, one of the most impoverished in the country, has been labeled "Cancer Alley" due to extremely high levels of toxic emissions associated with various ailments, including cancers, birth defects, asthma, and bronchitis (Physicians for Social Responsibility 2004). In 2003, Louisiana ranked second highest overall in cancer mortality rates among all states and Washington, D.C. The annual age-adjusted mortality rate for cancer deaths per 100,000 people is 230.4 in Louisiana, compared to a national average of 199.8 (Centers for Disease Control and Prevention 2004). In Louisiana, the data indicate that blacks are at higher risk than whites for death from heart disease, cancer, and stroke, according to the 2003 Louisiana Health Report Card (Louisiana Department of Health and Hospitals 2003). Blacks also show higher death rates than whites for lung, colorectal, breast, and prostate cancers. The possible links to environmental exposures, such as poor air quality and hazardous waste contamination, are palpable.

Indoor Health Hazards: Beginning two years before Hurricanes Katrina and Rita struck the Gulf Coast, Louisiana ACORN participated in the Community Environmental Health Resource Center, a project of the Alliance for Healthy Homes designed to support community-based organizations' use of environmental sampling to identify health hazards in low-income homes and advance policy solutions. Louisiana ACORN's trained hazard assessment investigators visited 258 homes in the Lower Ninth Ward in 2003. Slightly more than half of the homes were owner-occupied, most were multifamily, and 96% of the households were African-American. The assessment of conditions in these New Orleans homes revealed:

- 33% of homes had excessive moisture problems.
- 56% of the homes appeared to have at least one hazard (e.g., excessive moisture or pest infestation) that can trigger asthma or other respiratory-related problems.

In addition to the problems specific to the Lower Ninth Ward, three other issues were discovered through Louisiana ACORN's sampling:

- 62% of the homes had lead dust hazards on floors, windowsills, or both.
- The highest levels of lead among ten U.S. sites for each type of lead hazard (floor dust, sill dust, and play area soil samples) were found in New Orleans.
- Using data from the same survey and aggregating the results of sampling floor dust, sill dust, and loose paint chips for interior lead hazards, on average 38% of U.S. homes had a lead hazard and 64% of New Orleans homes had a hazard (Alliance for Healthy Homes 2005).

Conditions after Hurricanes Katrina and Rita

Throughout the fall and early winter of 2005, messages in the news media about New Orleans' health and housing conditions fluctuated from reassurances that it was perfectly safe to return to dire warnings that the houses and yards were all filled with poisons.

One study team led by the Natural Resources Defense Council (NRDC 2005) reported in mid-November that ambient airborne mold levels posed a serious health risk that "could trigger serious allergic or asthmatic reactions in sensitive people." The team found that indoor air quality was even worse, rendering the homes they tested "dangerously uninhabitable by any definition." While the American Academy of Allergy and Immunology considers outdoor mold levels of 50,000 spores per cubic meter "very high," the spore counts in six New Orleans neighborhoods, including the Lower Ninth Ward, exceeded 77,000. Local advocates and NRDC called for federal agencies to provide clear information about precautions and offer personal protective equipment (gloves, respirator, safety glasses, and a Tyvek coverall).

Another NRDC-led study identified dangerously high levels of arsenic, DDT and two other pesticides, petroleum products (diesel fuel and polyaromatic hydrocarbons), lead, and other chemicals and heavy metals in soil samples of the sediment covering New Orleans after the flooding from the hurricanes. Arsenic causes cancer of the bladder, skin, and lungs, and damages the liver and kidneys. Residue of the pesticides, which are linked to neurological problems and hormonal system disruption, were found near an abandoned pesticide factory. NRDC's Dr. Gina Solomon stated in a December 1, 2005 press release that "residents face a health risk because they can easily inhale contaminated sediment or get it on their skin when they are trying to clean it up" (NRDC 2005).

Soil sampled by a research team from Texas Tech University found elevated levels of lead, arsenic, iron, and pesticides. The researchers believed that lead (primarily from past use of leaded gasoline) had been buried under vegetation and soil during the past century and was suspended by the floodwaters, then redeposited elsewhere. The same team found high levels of pathogenic bacteria in water samples (David Brown 2005).

The U.S. Environmental Protection Agency asserted that the levels of organic compounds, hydrocarbons, pesticides, and heavy metals found in the soil are "similar to the historical levels found in these parishes before Katrina and to other urban areas throughout the nation" (Knickerbocker 2005). A Louisiana state health officer echoed the view that problems were no worse than before the recent flooding, except for sites in New Orleans' Gentilly and the Lower Ninth Ward communities contaminated with arsenic and petroleum (Matthew Brown 2005).

Regardless of which view of current environmental conditions best reflects reality, caution is in order. Even if hazards are severe, it is possible to manage these hazards as people return to their homes and communities. Demonstration projects in fall and winter 2005 by the National Center for Healthy Housing, NRDC, and others proved that trained workers using personal protective equipment can accomplish the removal of wet, mold-covered building materials and belongings as well as pave the way for the repair of structurally sound housing, including housing with wooden frames and cladding. Resources and political will are needed to empower residents to both overcome a lack of knowledge regarding health hazards and make informed choices about their future. Health threats from environmental issues that can be solved must not be used as an excuse to abandon or demolish structurally sound buildings or write off playgrounds and yards—or even entire communities.

Challenges and Barriers

A healthy housing restoration and rebuilding strategy for New Orleans faces several major environmental, political, and economic hurdles. Some predate the 2005 hurricanes, while others were exacerbated by Katrina's and Rita's devastating floods.

- *Erosion of protective Gulf Coast wetlands:* Rapid erosion of barrier islands and other coastal wetlands in the Mississippi Delta and Gulf of Mexico has been occurring for over a century. Storm surges from hurricanes press closer each year to populated areas that are less and less protected from direct water damage. Slowing erosion and re-establishing barrier islands as well as large tracts of wetlands are critical to minimizing the impacts of storm surges from future hurricanes.

- *Climate that fosters mold and moisture problems*: New Orleans has a very humid climate that is ideal for the growth of mold. Indoor mold levels were made much worse by flooding, water damage, and the lack of air conditioning and other mechanical ventilation during and following the hurricane strikes. Many of the flood-ravaged, abandoned, and salvageable dwelling units had dangerously high levels of mold at the end of 2005, which must be resolved in the initial stages of home restoration before the dwellings can be reoccupied. Training in health, safety, and personal protective equipment (PPE) are prerequisites for clearing out moldy furnishings and other possessions, removing moldy and damaged building components, and cleaning and drying out homes. Use of mold-resistant building materials and techniques appropriate to the area's climate in reconstruction can help minimize future mold problems.
- *Duration of flooding*: Many houses and neighborhoods were under water for an extended period of time, or were flooded a second time after Hurricane Rita, resulting in the spread of mold, chemicals, sewage, and other environmental hazards. These substances can be mediated, but it is critical to provide PPE and appropriate tools to help eliminate these toxins.
- *Lack of coordinated and targeted strategy*: Four separate governmental jurisdictions were attempting to respond to New Orleans' hurricane damage and evacuees by the end of 2005—FEMA and other federal agencies; the New Orleans Mayor's Office; the New Orleans City Council; and the State of Louisiana. The print and television media showed the lack of coordination in rebuilding efforts. There is either a lack of political will or a failure to understand where to focus the rebuilding efforts in neighborhoods that were severely impacted and depopulated. It is important to begin in several locations with a critical mass of returning residents along with community and economic institutions that can spur cleanup in order to demonstrate the viability of reclaiming salvageable homes for other residents who want to return. As of May 2006, there was no genuine governmental public health strategy that had emerged to expedite the systematic cleanup of structurally sound housing that was flooded.
- *Housing reoccupancy has been overlooked*: Throughout the fall of 2005, there were few messages of encouragement from elected officials and the media that indicated that many houses could indeed be saved, cleaned, and reoccupied. For New Orleans to be re-populated in a significant manner, the restoration of existing housing

will be necessary. New Orleans has traditionally had one of the most affordable housing stocks in the U.S., occupied by multiple generations of residents with limited incomes. The restoration of these units, where possible, is a prerequisite for thousands of former residents to return to New Orleans.

- *It takes time to build new housing*: Developing new housing is time consuming and requires significant capacity and resources. Prior to the hurricanes, the nonprofit housing sector in New Orleans was weak compared to other major metropolitan areas. Leaders of these institutions were dispersed as a result of the flooding from the hurricanes, and many are grappling with the recovery of their own properties. No matter how many efforts are made on the state and federal level to appropriate recovery and rebuilding funds, there needs to be a delivery system and dedicated funding stream put in place, all of which takes time.

- *Larger system issues*: As of May 2006, residents in numerous sections of New Orleans were without electricity and gas, surviving off generators and other temporary forms of power. Although the President pledged in December 2005 to increase federal funding by $1.6 billion for rebuilding levees to provide protection from a Category 3 hurricane, little action has yet been taken to actually repair the levees in order to prevent another catastrophic flood. Funding to strengthen levees to withstand storms more severe than Category 3 remained uncertain, and land restoration was projected to take many years. Without a broad and committed vision focusing on larger systems and momentum, pushed by citizens who want to reclaim their homes and former neighborhoods, it will be extremely difficult to rebuild New Orleans.

- *Insurance*: By May 2006, confusion was still rampant among the general public about what insurance will cover and what replacement and repair work it will not pay for. There remained a need for FEMA, private underwriters, and others to clarify what is covered and what will be covered in the future, for both homeowners' insurance and flood insurance. Both the insurance industry and government have misled numerous home owners, and it is government's responsibility to clarify and correct those situations.

Means of overcoming the barriers to reoccupancy

The challenges and barriers that must be overcome to recover New Orleans and the Gulf Coast region are fairly imposing, but they are not insurmountable. Some of the key steps for building momentum towards reoccupancy follow:

- *Work with local leadership and organizations*: Outside technical assistance organizations will have limited impact unless they are connected to local leadership and efforts that are best suited to identifying the priorities, capacities, and strengths of residents and others. Louisiana ACORN, with 9,000 members in pre-Katrina New Orleans, has emerged as the leading advocacy organization working to ensure that working-class residents, who are predominantly African-American, are provided the opportunity to reclaim their homes as long as dwellings and neighborhoods are safe and free from environmental contaminants. ACORN has basic knowledge of environmental cleanup and how to train residents in assessing and mitigating mold, lead-based paint, and other contaminants.

- *Invest time in learning about local conditions and in building relationships with local institutions*: New Orleans had a history of environmental pollution, both outdoor and indoor, that was severely exacerbated by the extent and duration of hurricane-related flooding. Equipment, protocols, training, and resources need to be tailored to local conditions in New Orleans and other Gulf Coast communities. Experts outside the region can help train do-it-yourselfers, contractors, community-based organizations, and others in safe techniques needed for reclaiming structurally sound dwellings. The skills, resources, and supports of these organizations can be coordinated to achieve expertise and scale. This is critical, since the reclamation of the Gulf Coast cannot occur just one house at a time. Rather, groups of two or three blocks must be restored at a time. It is local institutions that will be there for the long haul and that will be most responsive to the evolving needs and opportunities presented.

- *Focus on strengths and impact and be S.M.A.R.T.*: In medium- to long-term disaster rebuilding efforts, it is critical to focus on and connect strengths. One helpful framework is to view the recovery and rebuilding work as S.M.A.R.T.:
  - **Specific** — The work has to be specific and designed to eliminate contaminants in housing.
  - **Measurable** — There need to be clear benchmarks and targets for reclaiming housing.
  - **Achievable** — There needs to be sufficient training, safety equipment, and individuals and enterprises to clean up homes on a large scale in order to restore portions of neighborhoods that can become organic, functioning communities.

- **Results-oriented** — This is determined by the number of structures (residential, commercial, schools, etc.) that are reclaimed and returned to their best use.
- **Time-bound** — Some of the rebuilding strategies will take a long time, while reclaiming houses that are structurally and environmentally safe is a more immediate opportunity that is time-bound, once the training and support begin in earnest.

- *Link strategy/techniques to larger cross-sectoral opportunities*: A strong case can be made that restoring and rebuilding healthy homes contributes in many ways to larger strategies of repopulation and community stabilization. However, there is not a "silver bullet" solution for revitalizing the neighborhoods of New Orleans. Healthy homes alone cannot stabilize working-class neighborhoods without functioning public utilities, schools, transportation, commercial nodes, etc. This work has to be coordinated and supported by public-sector officials.
- *Build awareness and communicate regularly*: It is essential to build awareness of progress and momentum by communicating it through multiple information and communication channels, from flyers and church notices to press releases, radio announcements, and public service announcements on television. Communication must be undertaken on a regular, sustained basis.
- *Assume that government contributions and relationships will be uneven*: Governmental units and programs can be quite different, and government officials face major challenges in coordinating their initiatives. Some government programs and resources will be relevant and helpful, but others will not. Advocates must be strategic about when to wait and when to move forward in the face of these differences and potential difficulties among various levels of government. Organizations can always ask for forgiveness for exceeding boundaries after they have done something positive and important.
- *Maximize resources from government and private insurance*: Individuals and organizations were extremely generous with their money and time in the aftermath of Hurricanes Katrina and Rita. Yet these contributions still pale in comparison to the potential resources individuals can receive from the federal government. But funding for assistance to affected residents, as well as for cleanup and recovery, should not displace funding for prior and continuing social needs. The hurricane disasters dramatically illuminated the extent of poverty, a severe shortage of

decent affordable housing, and the substandard housing conditions in which many Americans live. It is neither fair nor sensible to exacerbate these crises for the rest of the country by using disaster relief spending as an excuse to further cut domestic discretionary spending. Spending priorities must ensure basic dignity and fairness for all Americans. All efforts, from advocacy for more government resources to applying for an array of programs, should be exhausted before turning to philanthropy, nonprofits, and others. Philanthropic and nonprofit resources can be very catalytic in terms of advancing significant rebuilding opportunities, including cleaning up structurally sound housing, but the federal government and the insurance industry must realize that it will take immense resources of the type that only government and industry can provide in order to reclaim New Orleans and the Gulf Coast.

- *Insist on fairness*: Landlords and homeowners will not be able to make needed repairs unless financial institutions, including insurance and mortgage companies, meet their corporate and civic responsibilities to assist their customers. Insurance companies should meet their obligations to policyholders with timely and fair payment of claims, and should cover the full range of damage from both the wind and rain brought by the hurricanes. Because many residents have lost their jobs, mortgage companies should accommodate home owners' and landlords' need to defer payments and adjust payment schedules without engendering adverse credit consequences. Federal and state officials should vigilantly oversee these financial institutions and protect the rights of consumers. Statutes regarding federal disaster-relief programs need to fairly address the needs of low-income renters. The long-term assistance programs presently are weighted in favor of owner-occupants, without equal opportunity for renters to either receive compensation for their personal property losses or regain their financial footing. Local governments should help rental property owners meet their responsibilities to repair properties and allow tenants back as soon as possible.

- *Provide needed training*: Free healthy homes training should be provided to homeowners, landlords, and contractors. Because the scale of the cleanup, repair, and rehab effort in the Gulf region is unprecedented, well-intentioned but untrained contractors and workers are flocking to the area. Moreover, many low-income homeowners will have no choice but to do the work themselves. All of these individuals need training in safe work practices around mold and other hazards in order to protect themselves and residents, and to avoid leaving behind, exacerbating, or even creating hazards that will put residents at risk over the long term.

- *Look for economic opportunities for residents and others*: Thousands of jobs have been temporarily lost, but there is great economic opportunity and job-creation potential in the rebuilding of New Orleans. The cleanup of housing, renovation of buildings, and re-landscaping are all labor-intensive, providing income and employment opportunities. Self-employment, or what is viewed as microenterprise, is one of the fastest expanding job sectors across the nation, and there are a growing number of technical assistance and financial resources available. Another good example are small business development centers (SBDCs), which are usually affiliated with a university. They offer help with business issues ranging from billing to marketing to management, and could be of real value to start-up businesses in the region. Workers who take on the dangerous job of cleanup and recovery are entitled to fair wages and to vigorous enforcement of health and safety standards.
- *Enforce federal laws that provide for local employment and contracting preferences*: Local individuals and companies should be given priority in rebuilding and restoration projects. When HUD funding is used for rebuilding, Section 3 of the Housing and Urban Development Act of 1968 provides for employment and contracting preferences for local low-income residents and the businesses that employ them. Also, the Stafford Act of 1993 (PL 100–707, amended in 2000), a federal law enacted to set rules for federal assistance after major disasters, requires that preferences be given "to the extent feasible and practical" to local organizations, firms, or individuals when federal funds are spent "for debris clearance, distribution of supplies, reconstruction, and other major disaster or emergency assistance activities."
- *Focus on relationships with important community institutions*: Schools, churches, chambers of commerce, commercial centers, and transportation nodes are good examples of visible and important community institutions to partner with in the cleanup of indoor and outdoor environmental hazards in New Orleans. By May 2006, ACORN was working with several neighborhood schools to serve as a locus for the rebuilding process.

A Strategy for Saving Low-Income and Working-Class Housing and Communities

Resources for rebuilding housing in low-income and working-class New Orleans-area communities affected by Katrina's and Rita's floods and winds have been very slow to materialize as of May 2006. Salvageable homes continue to sit empty and further deteriorate. As noted above, without community action to spur safe reoccupancy and rebuilding, the restoration of some communities may be delayed for years, or may never happen at all. Early land use planning proposals posed this threat in a dramatic fashion by recommending that homes in neighborhoods not able to prove they can come back to life within four months be forcibly transferred to a redevelopment authority and the communities converted to parks or wetlands. Additional threats to neighborhood viability may emerge as the political process unfolds. There is a desperate need for an affordable and pragmatic approach that will allow residents to reclaim, preserve, and repair structurally sound homes and begin safe and healthy long-term rebuilding and recovery in working-class neighborhoods within a reasonable period of time.

However, before anything can be done to prepare flood-affected homes for repair and re-occupancy, residents and contractors need to be equipped with sufficient knowledge, skills, and appropriate tools to protect their health and safety in the face of well-documented indoor and outdoor environmental health hazards. Training and appropriate personal protective equipment are urgently needed to help prevent exposure of workers and occupants to toxic substances that have been documented in the sludge left in homes and yards and from astronomically high indoor mold levels.

Several local community, housing, and environmental organizations; individual property owners and their contractors; and volunteers from throughout the country are already beginning to preserve and rebuild thousands of homes in low-income and working-class New Orleans area neighborhoods. By May 2006, ACORN volunteers and returning residents had already decontaminated and stabilized more than 1,000 homes in New Orleans. Several other environmental and community development organizations have made substantial efforts to provide some basic personal protective equipment and safety instructions to workers beginning to restore homes. Unfortunately, most returning residents and many contractors and workers have received little or no training or information about safe work practices and are not using appropriate protective equipment.

A practical and affordable approach to building the capacity for safe and healthy rebuilding has three major elements: (1) providing basic training and ongoing technical assistance to residents, volunteers, contractors, and others on how to safely clean up and stabilize their homes (and providing personal protective equipment for trainees); (2) delivering more in-depth training to people who renovate, weatherize, maintain, manage, or supervise older houses regarding safe, practical, effective, and affordable techniques to restore and maintain basic housing systems, surfaces, windows, and doors; and (3) training and assisting community-based leaders, public health professionals, and local elected officials to conduct environmental hazard assessments for lead, mold, and other environmental hazards, and to use their findings to advocate for needed environmental cleanup. Below, we describe in greater detail these three types of interrelated training to support safe, large-scale salvage and restoration of New Orleans' housing.

Safe and Healthy Home Salvage Training

Training in safely decontaminating and stabilizing structurally sound but flood-damaged homes that have mold, lead, and other major contaminants is the cornerstone of all future efforts to restore and rebuild affordable housing in New Orleans, and it could significantly increase the number of structurally sound homes that can be salvaged. A short (two- or three-hour) course should be made widely available to returning homeowners and rental property owners who are doing their own work, to contractors and laborers working for property owners, and to volunteers recruited by local organizations to assist with cleanup and salvage.

Workers need to learn how to work in a safe manner that protects them from dangerous exposure to mold, carbon monoxide, lead, a range of toxins in dried sludge, and other hazards. Workers and occupants need to be aware that clothing, furniture, food, appliances, carpeting, and wallboard contaminated with mold or toxins cannot be adequately cleaned and will have to be thrown out. In areas like New Orleans and neighboring parishes, where floodwaters carrying toxic sediments, bacteria, and raw sewage entered homes, structural components of homes may also be contaminated with mold, toxic sludge, and other hazardous substance residues. Training should include how to remove all belongings and building components that are contaminated with mold and other environmental hazards, how to treat remaining building materials to kill mold and prevent future mold growth, how to dry out homes, and how to protect homes from additional rain and water intrusion.

People returning to clean and stabilize homes also need easy-to-use materials and equipment to enable them to work safely. Each trainee should be provided a "Home Salvage Safety Kit" containing personal protective equipment and basic tools. The kits should include: appropriate respirators (N-100 or more protective); other protective garments such as disposable gloves, booties, safety goggles, and Tyvek suits; two five-gallon buckets; a water mister; an environmentally safe mold killing/prevention substance; a small first-aid kit with eye wash and soap; heavy-duty towels and rags; trash bags; basic hand tools; health and safety fact sheets; an instruction booklet; and other useful supplies.

With very limited resources, several local organizations have already attempted to fill this need. ACORN began in December 2005 to provide some basic safety training and supplies to returning residents and volunteers working to decontaminate and stabilize homes in New Orleans. In fall 2005, the Louisiana Environmental Action Network, working with Louisiana Physicians for Social Responsibility, began to provide some basic safety supplies and instructions to returning residents and workers in the wider New Orleans metropolitan area. Southern Mutual Help Association, working with Oxfam America, has undertaken a similar effort, mainly in rural communities. In January 2006, the People's Hurricane Relief Fund began distributing a pamphlet about toxic substances found in sediment in several New Orleans locations and how people can protect themselves from exposures as they return home. Such efforts need to be supported by formal and sustainable training programs that can be replicated wherever community-based organizations or local institutions (schools, churches, chambers of commerce, etc.) are positioned to serve as the anchor—and perhaps in other locales in other parts of Louisiana, Texas, and Mississippi. Trainees will need followup monitoring, support, and technical assistance.

Healthy Home Repair and Maintenance Training

A second type of more in-depth training in healthy home repair is needed for workers who will be doing extensive repairs and ongoing maintenance in homes that are salvageable. This training should be designed to teach practical, effective, and affordable strategies and techniques to make and keep homes safe and healthy for partial or total occupancy, while protecting workers, occupants, buildings, and the environment. The curriculum should focus on low-cost priority measures to be conducted in a salvaged structure, and guide contractors in staging the restoration of basic systems, surfaces, windows, and doors as repair funds become available.

Trainees should learn about how a house works and interacts with its occupants. They also should learn how to analyze the causes, quantify the risks, and remediate a broad range of interrelated residential environmental problems, including lead hazards, asthma triggers, carbon monoxide risks, air quality problems, and injury hazards. Moreover, trainees should learn about laws, policies, programs, and resources that can either hinder or support healthy homes restoration and maintenance, and they should discuss strategies for transforming the current approach to home repair and maintenance from one that is centralized, reactive, and fragmented to one that is community-based, preventative, and holistic.

The audience for this training should be contractors and their employees, including day laborers hired by contractors on an ad hoc basis, who will make extensive repairs to properties that have already been secured, cleaned out, dried out, and decontaminated. It also should be delivered to people who weatherize, manage, supervise, or maintain older houses. This training could be delivered through local universities, community colleges, and trade schools, as well as in locations where workers are living.

Grassroots Home Hazard Assessment and Advocacy Training

There is a great need for evacuees and government officials to have valid information about possible health risks in and around homes and other structures. Environmental hazards must be assessed before salvage work begins, not only to help protect workers and occupants from health hazards, but also to help determine which homes can be safely remediated and reoccupied.

A third type of training is needed to teach members of local grassroots organizations how to assess homes and yards affected by flooding for priority environmental health hazards (mold, deteriorated lead-based paint, carbon monoxide hazards, contamination with toxic chemicals and materials, pest infestations, etc.), how to assess homes for structural damage and injury hazards, and how to interpret and use results of these assessments to advocate for appropriate, protective levels of environmental cleanup and safety.

Because an unprecedented amount of toxic sludge was deposited on such wide swaths of land by floodwaters that inundated Gulf communities, the yards of residential dwellings, and especially play areas, must be evaluated to determine the extent of contamination and to plan for needed cleanup. While EPA, the State of Louisiana, university researchers, and some environmental organizations (such as Southern Mutual Help Association, Physicians for Social Responsibility–Louisiana, Louisiana Bucket Brigade, and NRDC) have conducted considerable ambient environmental sampling, very little environmental assessment has been performed inside homes. Misinformation and a lack of hazard-specific information continue to provide officials and others with justification for keeping neighborhoods closed and discourage displaced residents from returning home to assess and secure their homes and begin repairs.

Trained residents working through local community, housing, and environmental organizations are ideally suited to conduct assessments of health hazards in homes, in partnership with government agencies and local experts. Because community residents have more trusted relationships with their neighbors than do outside contractors or government officials, they will be better able to convince other residents to make their homes available for environmental assessments. Moreover, they have the credibility needed to effectively communicate to occupants the results of these assessments and the necessary action steps.

Residents can be trained quickly and equipped with simple, yet rigorous, assessment protocols that have been validated by researchers and practitioners. Local environmental groups and scientific experts from universities should be included in the assessment and cleanup strategies for yards and play areas in order to ensure transparency and accountability to community residents.

During the past four years, the Alliance for Healthy Homes Community Environmental Hazard Resources Center (www.cehrc.org) has provided a new generation of low-tech, low-cost housing hazard assessment protocols, materials, tools, and training to local healthy housing advocacy organizations in more than a dozen cities in the U.S., including New Orleans. These hazard assessment tools rely to the maximum extent possible on existing accepted protocols, methodologies, and technologies. They have been reviewed both by technical experts to ensure reliability and by community members to ensure clarity. The Alliance's partners assessed more than 3,200 homes for lead paint hazards, mold and moisture problems, pest infestations, and other environmental health hazards. These hazard assessment strategies can be adapted to fit the needs of post-hurricane homes and communities.

More importantly, though, trainees need to learn how to use hazard assessment results to advocate for needed environmental cleanup and decontamination and for expanded health and safety training for workers—just as many of the Alliance's local healthy homes partners in other cities successfully used the results of their home assessments to advocate successfully for policy solutions or increased funding to address unhealthy housing.

Trainees will need post-training monitoring and technical assistance. Other needs include stipends for hazard investigators, supplies, moisture meters, carbon monoxide monitors, and lab analysis of samples.

Conclusion

The devastation from Hurricanes Katrina and Rita visually and graphically underscored the impact of race and class in urban, suburban, and rural communities in the Gulf Coast region, most notably in New Orleans. Thousands of salvageable homes in low-income and largely minority sections of New Orleans remain vacant, with the risk of being bulldozed. This contrasts sharply with middle- and upper-income communities in New

Orleans and surrounding parishes where the housing is being stabilized and reoccupied.

Reclaiming structurally sound housing through safe, practical, and affordable healthy homes techniques will provide an important jump-start for reoccupying dwellings in flood-impacted neighborhoods. Community residents (home owners, volunteers, entrepreneurs, leaders, etc.) are best equipped to shape decisions about recovery and rebuilding of neighborhoods and communities where they have a huge stake.

If there is a silver lining to widespread hurricane destruction, it is the opportunity to repair, rehab, and rebuild homes to higher standards that protect occupant health and better withstand high winds and very moist conditions. The cleanup, repair, and rehab of salvageable homes, as well as the construction of replacement homes, should use construction standards, building materials, and methods that will ensure a healthy living environment for occupants and the durability of the home. Old, dilapidated housing that may be unhealthy can be replaced with new, healthier, more energy-efficient housing that is a good investment for lenders, insurers, and owners. The good news is that cleaning up housing is a practical, affordable, and safe strategy for helping to repopulate low- and moderate-income African-American communities. This approach will only succeed in the context of national, state, and local political resolve to prevent New Orleans and other communities from becoming "ghost towns" and "historical amusement parks."

References

Alliance for Healthy Homes. 2005. Lead Hazards and Other Housing-Based Health Hazards In Ten High-Risk Inner City Communities.

Brown, David. 2005. New Orleans Soil Poses Hazard. *Washington Post*: A11. December 15.

Brown, Matthew. 2005. NO Area Declared Safe to Live In. *New Orleans Times-Picayune*. December 10.

Centers for Disease Control and Prevention. 2004. Cancer Burden Data Fact Sheet: Louisiana. http://www.cdc.gov/cancer/CancerBurden/la.htm.

Knickerbocker, Brad. 2005. Tests on post-Katrina muck yield little consensus on risk. *Christian Science Monitor*. December 8.

Louisiana Department of Health and Hospitals, Office of Public Health, State Center for Health Statistics. 2003. Louisiana Health Report Card.

Natural Resources Defense Council. 2005. Press Releases. http://www.nrdc.org/media/pressReleases.

Physicians for Social Responsibility. 2004. Linking Chronic Disease and the Environment.

CHAPTER 9

A New Kind of Medical Disaster in the United States

EVANGELINE (VANGY) FRANKLIN

Pre-Katrina New Orleans: A Community Already at Risk

A recent Urban Institute report (Zuckerman and Coughlin 2006) concluded:

> Although Hurricane Katrina created many health problems, a wide range of indicators suggests that Louisiana had poor health status even before the storm hit. According to the United Health Foundation's 2004 State Health Rankings, for example, Louisiana ranked lowest overall in the country.... . It numbered among one of the five worst states for infant mortality, cancer deaths, prevalence of smoking, and premature deaths ... Louisianans also had among the nation's highest rates of cardiovascular deaths, motor vehicle deaths, occupational fatalities, infectious diseases, and violent crime.

Pre-Katrina New Orleans was a majority Black city with extreme levels of poverty, resulting in a de facto caste system of health care—a situation of course not unique to that city or state (Satcher and Rubens 2006). Our nation's health care system continues to provide unequal treatment for the poor, the uneducated, the homeless, the immigrant, the uninsured, and others who are disenfranchised (Institute of Medicine 2003; Franklin, Hall and Burris 2005)

While disparities in health services have long been a problem in New Orleans, the situation has worsened in recent years. Beginning in 2004, state cutbacks in funding for the only state charity hospital system in the nation led to dramatic reductions in ambulatory care services for the poorest residents. Closures of the Walk-In Ambulatory Care Clinic W-16 at the Medical Center of Louisiana at New Orleans (formerly known as Charity Hospital—which for generations had been appropriately used for non-emergency medical problems and available whether a patient had insurance or not) and the emergency room at Bywater Hospital (formerly St. Claude General Hospital) reduced access to nonemergency care for the city's uninsured and underinsured by more than two-thirds. Prior to closures, these facilities handled nearly 56,000 individual visits annually, mostly sourced from zip codes 70117 and 70119, neighborhoods of the city's poorest people. With the removal of these health care options, those in need of free care began to show up where they could find the easiest remaining source of care on demand and without charge—notably, emergency rooms, which became increasingly congested. It became a huge challenge for the system to assist patients to transition to stable alternative sources of primary and specialty care, and paying for that care once found. This situation has been disruptive, to say the least, and has created a significant challenge for the Charity ER system and other emergency rooms in New Orleans.

Poor health status in pre-Katrina New Orleans and elsewhere in Louisiana reflected more than disparities in the health care system. It is also the result of individual and community factors, such as ingrained behaviors regarding eating and exercise, language barriers, levels of education, community crime rates, employment status and income level, cultural and regional traditions, family values and attitudes, environmental and political factors—all of which contribute to poor overall health and worsening health disparities. In the case of New Orleans, many of the city's critical assets are also its tragic flaws when it comes to health. After all, in New Orleans we have a popular saying found—and practiced—everywhere: *"Laissez les bontemps rouler!"* ("Let the good times roll!")

Unfortunately, the city's fabled cuisine features high-calorie, high-cholesterol, and refined sugar dishes (big breakfasts with eggs, grits, bacon and biscuits; fried shrimp, fried oysters, fried catfish, hot sausage "po'boy" sandwiches slathered with mayonnaise; confections of pecans, butter, sugar, and cream known as "pralines"; bread pudding made with leftover French bread, eggs, cream, sugar, and spices, topped with a rum or whiskey sauce). Louisiana, and the South in general, have led the nation in obesity and the health problems connected with that condition: diabetes, hypertension, and cardiovascular diseases. Beyond the attractive cuisine is the relaxed environment and behaviors that can lead to substance abuse, poor judgment in sexual activity, drinking, and smoking, to name a few. In the case of unprotected sex, serious communicable medical problems (like HIV) are taken back home, in and out of the city and state.

The city's employment structure is a factor as well. Essentially, New Orleans is a port city with an economy also based on tourism. The level of education required for these jobs and the benefits attached to them have been comparatively low, and generally there is poor understanding by employees of how to use health benefits most beneficially. Additionally, New Orleans' historical lack of a manufacturing sector has prevented the development of a strong labor movement with its demands for health care.

Thus, even prior to Katrina, a grim picture of the health status of a poor, predominantly African-American city emerges, demonstrating the challenge of breaking a multi-generational cycle through aggressively engaging in a plan that targets the disparities of health status by race and class.

Post-Katrina New Orleans
Damage to the Health Infrastructure

Following Katrina, over 75% of the city was affected by floodwater that had become brackish from ocean surge and contaminated with sewage, dead bodies, polluted household chemicals, lead-based paint, and vehicular fluids. That water could not naturally recede in the heat of the summer for three weeks.

In that flood plain are the homes and offices of many health care providers. The health care delivery system—in the form of hospitals, doctors' offices, nursing homes, labs, x-ray facilities, treatment facilities, behavioral health facilities, supplies, vehicles, medical records, pharmacies, equipment, supplies, drugs, and medical records—virtually vanished for nearly all New Orleanians, public and private, white and black, rich and poor.

Most of New Orleans' hospitals are located in the center of the city and thus were damaged or flooded as a result of the disaster, and so over half of all hospital beds in Louisiana and one of two Level 1 Trauma Centers were lost due to their location in New Orleans. By November, three months after Katrina, only three hospitals were fully functioning in the Greater New Orleans area—none of which was in the city of New Orleans. Immediately post Katrina, only one New Orleans hospital (Touro Hospital) had reopened its doors, and only for emergency room patients (Connolly 2005a; Barringer 2005). Three hospitals in adjacent Jefferson Parish were operational, but their ERs were overwhelmed with those who had stayed in the Parish or relocated there from devastated areas. The care that was offered was free of charge. Some hospital beds were available through the Combat Support Hospital (successor to MASH—Mobile Army Surgical Hospitals) and the USS Comfort, a floating hospital supported by the Navy. Only two of the nine New Orleans Health Department clinic sites were operational. The clinics of Excelth, Inc. and Daughters of Charity were all destroyed. The medical records of all of these clinics were destroyed by flooding. Most pharmacies in New Orleans were also destroyed, and government shipments were delayed. Numerous nursing homes and assisted and independent living facilities were also located in the flooded area and were rendered uninhabitable, making their population trapped at their evacuation location unable to return home. Ambulatory health care facilities were also badly depleted in the aftermath of Katrina, with many facilities sustaining damage sufficient to render the facilities unusable for medical purposes. Because of this, a substantial number of health care workers had relocated following the storm and could not return because there was no place for them to live and no place to work. Moreover, many patients in New Orleans could not pay for their care. It is reasonable to anticipate that the vast majority of health care workers facing this situation may choose not to return for some time, or possibly ever.

The Diaspora

With most New Orleanians' homes and small businesses across all socioeconomic groups and professions completely devastated from floodwaters, most residents were unable to return after evacuation. They had been separated from their family and pets, and were unable to get clear and reliable information about their status or the situation in the city of New Orleans.

This resulted in a diaspora of massive proportions. Under the civil authority rules, people—including those who had evacuated to locations outside of New Orleans before the storm—could not return. Those who had remained in New Orleans and were at the Superdome or the Convention Center could not stay for any length of time and were transferred by bus to Dallas, Houston, and San Antonio, from where they dispersed further.

Many who had evacuated needed some kind of medical and/or behavioral health care and had only a general idea of what their medical problems were and the medications and therapies needed to remain medically stable. But there was no one in New Orleans at their provider's office to pull a file which in the vast majority of cases had probably been destroyed or rendered inaccessible by flood. In fact, for several weeks there was no ability whatsoever to communicate with phone numbers in the 504 area code.

As an evacuee to Dallas, I personally learned what that community had to do to assist and support evacuees. As a result of the destruction wreaked by Katrina, many receiving communities had to rapidly establish shelters that included some emergency medical and social service operations for the large influx of New Orleanians, regardless of their arrival time in these cities. Patients needed to refill medications, find new doctors to care for their chronic illnesses, deal with mental trauma (Nossiter 2005; Connolly 2005b), and find new emergency rooms and hospitals when they suddenly became medically or emotionally unstable. Those living in a shelter had to locate a new place to live and find new social services, schools for their children, and, if possible, employment. Medical facilities, mental health facilities, social services, and providers of all types rapidly became overwhelmed. As shelters became overcrowded, patients frequently were transported, without their consent, to other shelters. During this process, families were separated, increasing the stress of the situation.

It became clear in the days following this mass evacuation that the vast majority of the citizenry seeking medicines, medical care, and behavioral health interventions for chronic and acute problems could no longer depend on having access to the information that resided in their doctor's office or at the hospitals. Most of their paper medical records were either under water or had become wet and moldy in the humid environment. Patients were completely displaced from their physicians and other health care providers. Suddenly, communities with large and small numbers of evacuees had a medical community strained to do the right thing, but with mostly unhelpful or inaccurate oral histories from patients, and thus unable to understand their problems and attempt to continue medications. And there was no one to call to pull the medical records of some of the sickest displaced Americans, white or black; no one in oncology to call to get cell counts, reactions to chemotherapy, and the monitoring studies that go along with the treatment; no surgical notes describing the anatomy of a procedure; no radiation notes indicating the total number of rads given to a lymphoma; no x-ray films to review; no one to call at the academic medical center transplant program to find out the correct name, schedule, or the source of the experimental transplant drug for the renal transplant patient evacuated from his home via the Superdome and now in the Reunion Center Shelter medical van in Dallas. New Orleanians scattered through the U.S. were required to reconstruct their medical histories from memory—lay memory at that. And the professionals who previously cared for these patients had lost their homes, offices, jobs, and the hospitals they practice in. And of course, records had been destroyed.

The Immediate Help

During the post-evacuation period, New Orleans was occupied by a variety of military personnel who were valiantly providing a variety of services, including health care (Townsend 2006). The few doctors who remained in the city were working under first-responder and disaster situations with the military medical personnel to make certain that minimum care was being provided to working military personnel and citizens left behind in less-damaged parts of the city.

Aside from immediate and long-term mold and the lack of water, food, shelter, and sanitation facilities, there was concern that the prolonged flooding might lead to an outbreak of health problems in many neighborhoods among the remaining population. In addition to dehydration and food poisoning, there was the potential for communicable disease outbreaks of diarrhea and respiratory illness, all related to the growing contamination of food and drinking water supplies in the area. After dewatering and house-to-house searches for dead bodies and animals, public health concerns centered around acute environmental hazards related to houses standing in water for several weeks (mold, bacteria, concealed rodents, snakes, and alligators). This was combined with ruptured sewage lines, refuse, structural instability, debris, the lack of sanitary water (what water they had was usable only for flushing toilets), as well as a lack of gas and electricity. As the dewatering of the city proceeded, it became evident that a massive assessment of all infrastructural components was required to protect the health and safety of the citizenry. Martial law was imposed, and citizens were prevented from returning. Before the hurricane, government health officials had prepared to respond, and the Centers for Disease Control and Prevention (CDC) began sending medical emergency supplies to locations near the worst-hit area within 48 hours after landfall. The New Orleans Health Department directed the state and CDC personnel in developing a surveillance tool to help keep track of potential outbreaks.

National Guard, military, and U.S. Public Health Service personnel who appeared in New Orleans on their mission assignments convened regular meetings of the available medical provider leadership to assess the state of physical and human assets. The availability of vaccines and emergency services were considered key first accomplishments. Few local services were able to open, and care was augmented by the military and out-of-state volunteers permitted to provide care under an executive order by Governor Blanco.

Supplies shipped by CDC's Strategic National Stockpile and other private relief organizations provided pharmaceuticals. CDC's supplies served an estimated 30 acute care hospitals south of Interstate Highway 10, and volunteers organized around its "contingency stations" to become temporary stand-ins for hospitals, warehouses, and distribution facilities damaged by the storm.

Within days after landfall, medical authorities established contingency treatment facilities for over 10,000 people, and plans to treat thousands more were developing. In some cases, partnerships with commercial medical suppliers, shipping companies, and support services companies ensured that evolving medical needs could be met within days or even hours.

There was concern that the chemical plants and refineries in the area could have released pollutants into the floodwaters. People who suffer from allergies or chronic respiratory disorders, such as asthma, were susceptible to health complications due to toxic mold and airborne irritants, leading to what some health officials have dubbed "Katrina Cough." On September 6, it was reported that *Escherichia coli* (*E. coli*) had been detected at unsafe levels in the waters that flooded the city. The CDC reported on September 7 that five people had died of bacterial infection from drinking water contaminated with *Vibrio vulnificus*, a bacterium from the Gulf of Mexico. Wide outbreaks of severe infectious diseases such as cholera and dysentery were not considered likely because such illnesses are not endemic in the United States. And, despite attempts at surveillance, it was impossible to determine how many people needed medical care, but there was a clear sense shared by many that it was a large number.

Health Recovery Week at the Audubon Zoo, February 6–12, 2006

In early November 2005, I was assigned by Dr. Kevin Stephens, Director of the New Orleans Health Department, to be Project Manager of an ambitious outdoor primary care center that was eventually incorporated into "Health Recovery Week." The goal was in part to empower patients with their own health information in the case of future evacuation. The health information collected then could be loaded onto a portable digital device so that patients could be directed to followup care. Kyle Park, Communications Specialist and Chief of Logistics for the SNS Delivery in the Dallas/Fort Worth Regions of the Texas Department of Social and Health Services, was brought in to blend the clinical side with the IT side. This collaborative opportunity was supported by the Morehouse Medical College Hurricane Recovery Center, Remote Area Medical Volunteers, Intel Corporation, the American Academy of Family Physicians, Solventus, Inc., and local medical practitioners to provide health care and behavioral health and social service information on a first-come/first-serve basis. At the end of the event, patients would receive an electronic record that they could give to any physician, local or remote. More than a simple health screening, participants were offered full office services, including lab tests, Pap tests, and follow-up appointments. Patients were quickly given critical and abnormal test results so treatment could be sought. Mental health providers circulated throughout the crowd to help identify those with special behavioral needs and to guide patients to the appropriate locations. Volunteers participated from local colleges and universities (Xavier, Dillard, University of New Orleans, Tulane, and Louisiana State University) and local safety-net clinics. Many of the practitioners, most of whom were from out of state, said they had never seen the level of disease present in the patients coming to the event. It also documented the vast scope of need in the city and surrounding areas.

Over 5,000 citizens (some from as far away as Baton Rouge and Mississippi) attended the event and were provided dental, medical, and optical care, including free glasses (over 1,300 pairs of eyeglasses were dispensed) and 30 days of whatever prescriptions they needed (over 4,000 prescriptions were dispensed). On leaving, they had available to them a portable health device CD-ROM or USB memory drive with their health information. The event revealed that patients wanted their health information in this format. All clinical and nonclinical staff of the New Orleans Health Department participated in the event and trained on the software. Many patients became volunteers themselves.

It is likely that the dental and optical portions of this event will be repeated during hurricane season. Hurricane Recovery Week has evolved into Project Prepare 2006, which will be an ongoing project to provide portable health records to anyone requesting to have their health information preserved for emergency purposes. As part of this process, I coined a new saying in the New Orleans tradition: *"Laissez la bonne santé rouler!"* ("Let the good health roll!"). It is written on red and white t-shirts that continually remind everyone of our purpose and goal.

The Rebuilding

New Orleans is faced with a repopulation of returning and new residents. No doubt there are physicians among those inhabitants of the city applying for permits to rebuild their homes and offices. But physicians need hospitals, support facilities, labs, x-ray units, and pharmacies to provide any level of medical care. These facilities will likely return, but not anytime soon. Layoffs had occurred in the City of New Orleans work force (Health Department staff for its clinics went from 250 to 72), as well as in the school system (of course, this resulted in large numbers of persons losing their insurance). Monies for various health programs were shifted out of the city at the same time the rate of persons returning was increasing. Despite the increase in the number of public clinics open in all of Louisiana's Office of Public Health Region 1 (Orleans, Jefferson, St. Bernard, and Plaquemines Parishes), an analysis of office and hospital locations in flooded areas confirmed by Internet registries indicated that only 15 to 20% of private physicians had returned to practice by early Spring 2006. Many patients did not know where their doctors were and were not looking for replacements of those valuable relationships. There were virtually no dentists practicing at all. Two organizations are currently allowed to funnel in volunteer medical staff, clinical assets, and pharmaceutical donations for the distribution of medication to those without insurance.

The New Safety Net

Despite our recognition that race, gender, and class structure health disparities, disasters do not make these distinctions. It is how we prepare for and respond to those disasters that will express our dedication to the equal treatment of all people. The extensive disruptions in the New Orleans economy, altered living conditions, and the desire and ability of individuals to return to or to become new residents of the city will have a great impact on the future demographics of New Orleans. The city is already filled with a mix of strangers—many non-English-speaking—and newly unemployed neighbors, while some neighborhoods have permanently lost families because opportunities seemed better elsewhere. Exact changes cannot be predicted at this writing and would be speculation at best. But with the likelihood that a vast proportion of physicians will not be returning to a city that has less and less cash and insurance to pay for health care (from personal conversations, I know that many displaced physicians are planning to move their offices to more distant locations), there are concerns about reconstructing a safety net that must care for a large—albeit, different—mix of patients.

It is reasonable to assume that many of the public health concerns documented in the August 2005 unpublished report I co-authored for the New Orleans Health Department, "Getting People Healthy in New Orleans" (Franklin, Hall, and Burris 2005), will continue to exist post-Katrina, although perhaps in different geographic clusters and rates. The citizens returning to New Orleans and its new citizens who will come to this "frontier town" with new kinds of employment opportunities will require a health care delivery system that addresses probably the same medical problems but with more diverse, culturally competent service. We must also remember, and try to address, the longstanding health problems that have plagued our traditional population in an economy that now pays more for the same unskilled jobs that characterize groups with health disparities.

Personal Empowerment and Health Technology

American medical culture is characterized by resistance to a truly patient-centric model. Standard organized medical practice for all patients, from small to large groups, urban and rural, private and public safety-net providers, is largely driven by the traditional physician-centric model based on paper medical records housed in the provider's office (on shelves which usually stand on the floor). Even a small amount of standing water lasting for many weeks in hot weather will ruin charts on the shelves. Paper medical records could be lost forever by flood, fire or other forms of destruction. Personal ownership of a portable health record allows patients to view records themselves and have them available 24 hours a day for visits to other doctors—by appointment, when arriving unconscious at an emergency room, when traveling, or during evacuation. Ideally, the key elements of a portable health record should be:

- Password protection to avoid unauthorized access to the device
- Appropriate disclaimers and instructions for use
- Disease and status of stability as documented by certain lab tests
- Medications/therapy for those diseases and compliance patterns
- Previous electrocardiogram and radiologic image (x-ray, echocardiogram, ultrasound, and heart catheterization)
- Implanted devices, transplanted organs, etc.
- Names, emails, and phone numbers of treating physicians
- Names, emails, and phone numbers of experimental drug or chemotherapy vendors
- Next of kin and emergency contacts
- Dates of when the information was input and then changed

This disaster provided an opportunity to make sweeping change toward the improvement and preservation of health via inexpensive information technology models and, as a secondary outcome, to decrease the medical errors that have been documented in many studies. There is agreement among health leaders in the greater New Orleans area that this information technology is critical and will help them greatly in subsequent hurricane seasons.

Conclusion

There are some very disturbing weaknesses in our health care system that Katrina has underscored. However, the hurricane also exposed some new opportunities. Katrina provided us with a worst-case scenario to see how fragmented and unprepared our entire health care delivery system is when disaster strikes. In addition, Katrina also demonstrated both how fragile the communication tether is between health care providers and their patients regarding essential information and our medical system's overall inefficiency during normal times. A vast number of patients, emotionally paralyzed by the loss of their homes, family members, pets, and memories, were sent to distant, unknown cities.

Hurricane season is an annual event in New Orleans. What we need to learn for that next time, whether it be a hurricane or any type of disaster, in New Orleans or anywhere, can be summarized as follows:

- Mass evacuations should follow certain procedural standards created beforehand. These standards should predict as well as possible where relocation will occur, so as to prepare temporary shelter facilities and appropriate medical services in those locales.
- As much as possible, provide current and accurate information to those impacted by the disaster.
- Take into full account mental as well as physical health problems that disasters and forced displacement produce.
- "Health Recovery Events" of the type organized in New Orleans are effective short-term stopgaps.
- Deliver to patients portable health records and encourage physicians to institute compatible electronic medical records systems as widely as possible.
- In order to restore post-disaster medical facilities, establish systems which will assure the "safety net," create inducements for medical workers to return, and ensure the replacement of support services.

This chapter was written in May 2006, a month prior to the onset of New Orleans' annual hurricane season. There is no doubt that we have had a steep and rapid learning curve with lessons to take from and to contribute to the management of many kinds of disasters. Continued and sustained improvement must be the goal of all charged with this responsibility, which includes the personally empowered individual.

References

Barringer, Felicity. 2006. Long After Storm, Shortages Overwhelm N.O.s Few Hospitals. *New York Times*. January 23.
Connolly, Ceci. 2005a. N.O. Health Care Another Katrina Casualty. *Washington Post*. November 25.
_____ 2005b. Katrina's Emotional Damage Lingers. *Washington Post*. December 7.
Franklin, Evangeline, Patrick Hall, and Nancy Burris. 2005. Getting People Healthy in New Orleans, Vols. 1 and 2. New Orleans Health Department. Unpublished. August.
Institute of Medicine. 2003. *Unequal Treatment: Confronting Racial and Ethnic Disparities in Healthcare*. Smedley, Brian D. Adrienne Y. Stith, and Alan R. Nelson, eds. Washington, DC: National Academies Press.
Nossiter, Adam. 2005. Hurricane Takes a Further Toll: Suicides Up. *New York Times*. December 27.
Satcher, David and Pamies Rubens J. 2006. *Multicultural Medicine and Health Disparities*. McGraw Hill.
Townsend, Frances Fragos. 2006. The Federal Response to Hurricane Katrina: Lessons Learned. The White House. February. http://www.whitehouse.gov/reports/katrina-lessons-learned/.
Zuckerman, Stephen and Teresa Coughlin. 2006. After Katrina: Rebuilding Opportunity and Equity into the *New* New Orleans. Initial Health Policy Responses to Hurricane Katrina and Possible Next Steps. The Urban Institute. February.

CHAPTER **10**

Double Jeopardy
Public Education in New Orleans
Before and After the Storm

MICHAEL CASSERLY

Two days after Hurricane Katrina landed its devastating blow on New Orleans, two managing directors of the firm handling the finances and operations of the city's public schools waded through the muddy waters flooding the school district's administration offices. They did so to rescue data tapes that they would need to pay district teachers and administrators who had fled the city to escape Katrina and its terrible aftermath.

The firm was Alvarez & Marsal, which the State of Louisiana had hired in June 2005 to overhaul the financial affairs and operations of the faltering school district. With the information from the rescued data tapes in hand, Alvarez & Marsal then paid district staff members via Western Union one of the last regular paychecks they were likely to see. In many ways, this action could be considered the final chapter in the story of a school district that many observers believe was one of the worst in the nation.

Indeed, the compelling reality is that New Orleans and its schoolchildren were victimized twice—once before the storm hit on August 29 and again afterwards—in a kind of double jeopardy for some of the nation's poorest students. Before Katrina's onslaught, the children of New Orleans were isolated racially, economically, academically, and politically in public schools that were financed inadequately, maintained poorly, and governed ineptly. After the storm, the city and its schoolchildren were subjected to bureaucratic delays, racial squabbling, and political hostility, a dynamic that could have been predicted easily from decades of neglect, indifference, incompetence, corruption, and inaction. Unfortunately, some of the same ingredients exist in other cities awaiting their own "Katrinas," dreading the time when their own levees will break (Ladson-Billings 2006).

A Pattern of Underachievement

Before anyone even had heard of Hurricane Katrina, the New Orleans public schools were among the poorest-performing of any of the nation's urban public school systems. The district's student achievement levels were low, and its reputation for integrity was questionable at best. About 75% of the city's schools were in academic warning status and 35% did not make "adequate yearly progress" in 2005 under the provisions of the federal No Child Left Behind (NCLB) Act.

In the spring of 2005, the last testing cycle before Hurricane Katrina devastated the city, only 36% of New Orleans' third-graders scored above national averages (composite score) on the Iowa Test of Basic Skills, a nationally normed standardized test (Council of the Great City Schools 2006). Thirty-eight percent of fifth-graders scored above their peers nationally on the test, as did 32% of sixth-graders, 31% of seventh-graders, and 32% of ninth-graders—all very low achievement rates. (See Table 10.1.)

In addition, only 44% of the district's fourth-graders scored at or above *basic* levels on the state's English Language Arts (ELA) test—the Louisiana Educational Assessment Program (LEAP)—and just 26% of eighth-graders did. Math scores were little better, with 41% and 30% of fourth- and eighth-graders, respectively, attaining the state's basic benchmarks—a level of

Table 10.1 Average Percentile Ranks (Composites) of New Orleans Students on the Iowa Test of Basic Skills (ITBS), compared with Statewide Averages

	Grade	2000	2001	2002	2003	2004	2005
New Orleans	3	25	28	27	33	35	36
Louisiana	3	47	50	50	55	57	57
New Orleans	5	25	38	33	39	40	38
Louisiana	5	46	52	51	56	57	59
New Orleans	6	27	30	33	27	28	32
Louisiana	6	47	48	51	44	46	47
New Orleans	7	25	25	27	28	30	31
Louisiana	7	46	47	47	48	48	49
New Orleans	9	29	39	33	32	33	32
Louisiana	9	46	50	48	47	48	49

Table 10.2. Percentages of New Orleans Students Scoring at or above *Basic* Levels on the LEAP in English Language Arts (ELA) and Math, compared with Statewide Percentages

	Grade	2000	2001	2002	2003	2004	2005	Δ
				ELA				
New Orleans	4	33	38	31	38	40	44	+11
Louisiana	4	55	59	57	61	60	64	+9
New Orleans	8	29	21	22	22	22	26	-3
Louisiana	8	54	51	48	52	47	50	-4
				Math				
New Orleans	4	27	30	25	35	33	41	+14
Louisiana	4	49	54	50	60	53	61	+12
New Orleans	8	22	17	15	20	29	30	+8
Louisiana	8	47	46	41	47	53	51	+4

attainment one notch below what is required under No Child Left Behind. (See Table 10.2.)

By the time the district's students were in tenth grade, only 40% were scoring at basic levels in English language arts and 39% were scoring at the same level in math. (See Table 10.3.) And at the eleventh and twelfth grades, district students who aspired to go to college were scoring about four points lower than the national average on the ACT, a college entrance examination. In fact, students in only one high school in the city scored higher on the ACT than the national average. Most New Orleans' high school students, even among those who wanted to further their education, were scoring at or below 15—a level too low to gain admittance to a competitive college or university.

In general, the city's African-American students also performed at levels well below their African-American peers statewide. Some 43% of New

Table 10.3. Percentages of New Orleans Students Scoring at or above *Basic* Levels on the Louisiana Graduate Exit Exam (GEE) in English Language Arts (ELA) and Math, Compared with Statewide Percentages

	Grade	2000	2001	2002	2003	2004	2005	Δ
				ELA				
New Orleans	10	NA	32	30	29	35	40	+8
Louisiana	10	NA	56	52	53	60	61	+5
				Math				
New Orleans	10	NA	27	21	33	38	39	+12
Louisiana	10	NA	51	47	59	61	62	+11

Orleans' African-American fourth-grade students scored at or above basic levels on the state reading test, but 52% of African-American fourth-graders statewide scored at or above basic levels on the reading assessment. Likewise, 25% of the city's African-American eighth-graders scored above basic levels in reading, but 33% did so statewide. Gaps between African-American students in New Orleans and statewide in math were similar to those in reading.

Students in the New Orleans public schools had seen some gains since 2000, however, as one can see from the first two tables presented above. These modest gains might be attributed to Superintendent Anthony Amato's introduction of prescriptive reading programs such as "Success for All" and "Direct Instruction." But the academic gains were not much larger than those seen statewide, suggesting that the city's instructional programs were not adding much to what district students might have gained anyway. The result was that the children in New Orleans were attaining academic proficiency at rates that were only one-half those of students statewide—a serious indictment in a state where scores on the National Assessment of Educational Progress (NAEP) are well below national averages in reading and math.

Demographic Trends

In many ways, the students in New Orleans public schools were not like students elsewhere in Louisiana, much less students nationwide. Before Katrina hit, some 93.4% of the school district's students were African-American, 1.2% were Hispanic, 3.5% were white, and 1.9% were Asian-American and "other." Statewide, the student population was 47.8% African-American, 1.7% Hispanic, 48.5% white, and 2.0% Asian-American and "other." Nationally, the percentages for the four groups were 17.3, 17.8, 59.5, and 5.5, respectively.

Students in New Orleans also were substantially poorer than were students in Louisiana as a whole and those across the nation. Some 80% of the city's public school students were poor enough to be eligible for a federal free or reduced price lunch subsidy, compared with 60.7% of students statewide and 35.2% of students nationally.

Overall, before Katrina hit, the New Orleans public schools enrolled about 9.6% of the state's public school students, but approximately 18.8% of its African-American students and about 15% of its low-income students. These proportions translated into an enrollment that was more than twice as poor and about five times as black as that of the average school system nationwide. In this respect, the New Orleans school district was similar to other big-city public school systems, particularly those enrolling disproportionately large numbers of African-American students (e.g., Detroit, Washington, D.C., Atlanta, Memphis, Baltimore, Cleveland, and St. Louis).

Many urban school systems, including New Orleans, have lost significant numbers of students over the decades. The New Orleans public schools had an enrollment of some 110,000 students in the 1970-1971 school year, compared with approximately 55,000 when the schools opened in the days before Hurricane Katrina hit. In the intervening years, the school district became almost exclusively African-American and poor as young families left the city or fled traditional public schools for private schools or, in more recent years, for charter schools, public and private. The numbers tell the story: Thirty-five years ago, 69.5% of students in the New Orleans school district were African-American and 36% of the district's students were eligible for a free or reduced priced lunch; before Katrina hit, those proportions had jumped to 93.4% and 80%, respectively, as noted above.

In contrast, private schools in New Orleans enrolled about 30% of the city's school-aged population before the storm, and more than one-half of these schools were predominantly white. However, about one-third of the private schools were almost exclusively African-American.

The Consequences of Disinvestment

Well before Katrina lurked on the horizon, the State of Louisiana had largely disinvested in the New Orleans public schools. The school district, in fact, received less money from the state than one would have expected based on the size of the city's public school enrollment, meaning that the additional needs brought to the schoolhouse door by the city's children often went unfunded and unmet.

The results of this disinvestment were not difficult to see. The district's pupil/teacher ratio was higher than the national average, as was the ratio of pupil/guidance counselors and other student support personnel. Fewer city teachers had advanced degrees. Spending per pupil was below the national average, class sizes were larger, and the condition of the city's public school buildings was among the worst anywhere. The lack of investment doubtless contributed to the district's poor academic performance and spurred the exodus of students from the school system.

The toll that such demographic and financial conditions take on a city school system such as New Orleans' is devastating. One can see it in any number of cities across the country. Enrollment declines bring substantial decreases in revenues, which, in turn, result in the loss of personnel and talent. At the same time, the increasing percentages of high-needs poor children present schools with instructional challenges and discipline issues that overwhelm teachers and administrators, hastening the outflow of middle-class parents and students. School districts such as New Orleans' also are seen as the provider of last resort for health care, nutrition, clothing, parent-care, and other services, as city governments strain to serve the needs of a poorer population and sometimes use the schools to hire friends, relatives, or others who are otherwise unemployed or unemployable and are not necessarily qualified to teach children or run school operations. The consequence of these accumulating factors is a gradual lowering of academic standards, exacerbated by the bigotry of low expectations regarding the performance of students of color.[1]

Problem Upon Problem

This maelstrom in New Orleans has spun ever faster over the last decade with the decay of the regular system, the emergence of private schools, and the arrival of charter schools—schools that many saw as "private" schools at public expense. The regular school system, for its part, began to implode as the quality of instruction declined, operations worsened, facilities deteriorated, and some observers charged or suspected that unscrupulous staff, vendors, and others sacked the district to enrich themselves.

By 2001, when then-superintendent Alphonse Davis, a retired Marine Corps colonel, took the reins of the district's operations, the school system was largely dysfunctional: The district's personnel office was seriously broken; the transportation system was being misused; technology was nonexistent or out of date; and student achievement was at an all-time low.

The Human Resources department epitomized this systemwide dysfunction. The department lacked any strategic direction, goals, standards, or benchmarks by which to measure its progress, evaluate its work, or hold itself accountable for results (Council of the Great City Schools 2001). Employees across the system often were paid late because personnel data were not being entered into the department's antiquated computers in a timely fashion. Teaching and administrative staff positions were being filled well after the start of the school year because recruitment efforts started too late in the previous school year or were nonexistent. Department administrators were not able to identify staff vacancies at critical times in the school year. The system employed large numbers of uncertified teachers. Much of the district's record-keeping was maintained on paper. Operating procedures were not documented. Few personnel staff members were trained on Human Resources' computer systems. And the district was employing far more people than would be expected for a school system of its size.

The district's transportation system was also in poor shape (Council of the Great City Schools 2002). In addition to student transportation, the department handled everything from food delivery to maintenance, mail delivery, and materials distribution. The unit was seriously hampered by poor interdepartmental communications and collaboration, outdated equipment and policies, inadequate facilities, a weak organizational structure, nonexistent technology, insufficient supervisory staff, and the absence of strategic planning. Moreover, the department lacked any kind of database to determine who was eligible for transportation and who was not. The fact that principals could set their own bell times contributed to the inefficiency of the entire system. Purchases did not require competitive bidding. Bus drivers determined their own routes. Few controls of overtime pay were in place. And district employees sometimes provided field trips to outside groups without permission. They also failed to charge them for transportation services.

Poor technology, in fact, impeded the entire operation of the school district. No clear reporting lines existed in the technology offices; the middle-management structure was inadequate; serious morale problems afflicted staff; and the district's management information systems were in disarray. Moreover, staff training on technical systems was weak; the management information systems were largely unused; relations with vendors were inappropriate; and the district generally lacked standards for the purchase of computer hardware and software.

Finally, the school district's financial operations were of questionable integrity. Few controls on the general ledger were put into place; reconciliations within the sub-ledgers were not being made; expenditures were not being posted properly; the district sometimes was unable to close its books in a timely fashion; thousands of purchase orders were open, making it impossible to determine the accuracy of the district's budget; and internal controls on expenditures were weak. Overall, the district spent far more than it took in—for years.

By the time that Anthony Amato was on the job as superintendent in 2003, he summoned the Federal Bureau of Investigation to look into suspicions of fraud, abuse, and cronyism. (Some 20 people have been indicted to date.) And the district was receiving negative national press attention on NBC's "Fleecing of America" segment.

The State of Louisiana eventually stepped in. It gave Amato special powers in June 2004 to handle affairs, sign contracts, set budgets, shuffle personnel, and hire and fire staff without school board interference—something that critics had accused the board of for some years (Maggi 2004). Later, in 2005, the state retained the New York-based corporate turn-around firm of Alvarez & Marsal to help clean up the district's finances and run its operations. But the elected school board squeezed out Amato anyway and replaced him with Acting Superintendent Ora Watson, who Amato had brought to the city from Dallas. Then, Katrina hit.

Katrina and Its Aftermath

Along with wrecking large sections of the city and displacing its population, the hurricane literally demolished the school district. Approximately 50 of the system's 120 schools sustained severe damage from both wind and flooding, many beyond repair, including some of the city's most beautiful and historic structures. Another 38 or so schools suffered moderate damage, and about 30 to 32 schools suffered light to no damage (Ritea 2005).

The small number of schools suffering light damage were mostly in areas of the city that saw little or no flooding, such as Algiers, parts of the West Bank, and the Garden district, although every corner of the district was touched. O. Perry Walker, Henderson, Harte, Eisenhower, Lusher, Fischer, McMain, and Walker schools, for example, saw windows blown out, rain and glazing damage, downed trees, roof leakage, ceiling tile and penetration problems, but little else. But what was clear to inspectors was that the buildings that had sustained only moderate storm damage were in very poor condition, not just because of the hurricane but also because of years of neglect. Paint was peeling, fire code violations were common, exit signs were missing or broken, panic bars on doors were jammed, and windows were boarded up with plywood.

In the chaotic days during and immediately following the hurricane, the school district also lost some 300 of its buses as residents attempted to flee the city or used the vans for housing and as authorities commandeered the vehicles to close off freeway entrances or evacuate residents. (Governor Blanco had signed an executive order on September 7 allowing the National Guard to seize the buses to evacuate residents.) Many of the buses were eventually flooded, vandalized, stolen, or driven to distant cities—resulting in the complete loss of the school system's transportation capacity. And the district's some 7,500 employees scattered near and far, along with the rest of New Orleans' citizenry.

Alvarez & Marsal and the American Federation of Teachers set up hotlines, websites, and a relief fund within days of the storm to locate staff members in order to pay them; and the Council of the Great City Schools marshaled building engineers from other big-city school districts across the country to conduct an initial assessment of what the New Orleans school district had left to work with (Council of the Great City Schools 2005). The majority of the district's most damaged schools were in the same neighborhoods that sustained the worst overall destruction: the Ninth Ward, Lakeview, St. Bernard, and other areas.

The school board, an elected body, convened its first meeting following the onslaught of Hurricane Katrina in Baton Rouge on September 15. The meeting began with statements of determination by the members to work together to rebuild the school system, which was by then deeply in debt. The solidarity quickly disintegrated, however, when what turned out to be a contentious resolution failed on a close vote. Under the resolution, Acting Superintendent Ora Watson, who was African-American, would be replaced by Bill Roberti, a managing director of Alvarez & Marsal, and white. State officials, who supported the resolution, had heard enough of the rhetoric and the squabbling, and moved after the meeting to initiate legislation with the Governor and the legislature to strip the local school board of much of its remaining powers.

In the meantime, a budding effort in Washington emerged to fashion a response to the storm. Within a month of Katrina, Congress approved two huge emergency appropriations, but nearly all of the funds were earmarked for the Federal Emergency Management Agency (FEMA) to begin rebuilding the city's infrastructure—as is typical in cases of such disasters. However, the U.S. Senate Health, Education, Labor and Pensions Committee, led by Senators Mike Enzi (R-WY) and Edward Kennedy (D-MA), heard testimony on September 6 and September 8 from the Council of the Great City Schools and others, who described FEMA's spotty record in addressing the educational needs of schools and schoolchildren in past disasters and proposed a separate pot of resources solely for schools and colleges. The committee immediately began writing legislation that would aid schools receiving students from the storm-damaged areas and provide immediate direct assistance to schools that were damaged.

The U.S. Department of Education, for its part, moved rather quickly, convening a large meeting of interest groups on September 7 and proposing its own package on September 16 of some $2.6 billion in school aid, including some $488 million in aid to private schools (U.S. Department of Education 2005). The Enzi-Kennedy bill and the Administration's proposal were then combined, but because of squabbling over the details and bureaucratic foot-dragging, it took until December 30 for Congress to finalize the legislation and the President to sign it into law (Hurricane Education Recovery Act 2005). The measure provided $750 million for schools in Louisiana, Mississippi, Texas, and Alabama directly affected by Hurricanes Katrina and Rita; $645 million for schools across the country that had taken in students displaced by the storms; and $5 million to supplement the McKinney-Vento Homeless Education Act.

The Louisiana state legislature, in the interim, did indeed go into session in November and moved to seize public schools in New Orleans that had failed to achieve at state averages (34 schools) or that had not passed the state's accountability standards (68 schools). By the end of its 17-day special session, the state legislature—with bipartisan support—had approved Governor Blanco's proposal to shift responsibility from the city to the state for operating 102 of New Orleans' 117 schools (Tonin 2006). (Before Katrina hit, the state had seized five city schools because of their poor performance and hired outside groups to run them.) As a result of this legislative action, New Orleans' traditional school district, left intact because of state constitutional requirements, was restricted to just eight regular schools and five charter schools—all higher-performing schools. The remaining schools were scheduled for chartering or were swept into the state's "recovery" district if they were considered as failing.

Opposition to the plan came predominantly from members of the New Orleans delegation to the state legislature, who voiced concern that the citizenry was not included in the broad overhaul, and the city's teachers union, which argued that the legislation would effectively strip the teachers of their collective bargaining agreement (Maggi 2005a). This latter concern was not unfounded, as the district's teachers were furloughed in the weeks immediately following Katrina, and their right to return to the system on a seniority basis was replaced by state authority to hire and place teachers in the schools it had seized. The United Teachers of New Orleans then filed suit, but many observers view the union's pleading as a lost cause. As of mid-May 2006, the state court has not issued any dispositive ruling.

The union currently represents only 300 public school employees in the city, and teachers in most public charter schools are on year-to-year contracts without collective bargaining leverage and are required to pass a grammar and math test before being hired. Schools still subject to the union contract are required to give first priority to teachers who worked in the system pre-Katrina (Ritea 2006c).

Scattered to the Four Winds

Data on where students from New Orleans went after the storm are hard to come by, but in the weeks following the hurricanes, the U.S. Department of Education estimated that some 372,000 students—preschool though college—were displaced from the states hit by the storms. The state of Louisiana estimated that some 105,000 of its students were dislocated by the storm and were not attending their home schools (Jacobson 2006). Texas has indicated that it received some 40,200 out-of-state students as a result of both Katrina and Rita; Georgia was accommodating 10,300 students;

and Florida had absorbed 5,600. Reports from around the country indicated that students from the Gulf region appeared in such far-flung school systems as Anchorage, Alaska, in the days immediately following the hurricanes. Many students migrated to the homes of family members across the country, but others were evacuated by FEMA and other authorities to cities like Houston, Memphis, Dallas, and Atlanta.

The Houston Independent School District eventually absorbed some 7,000 evacuees at its high point in November, 2005, and serves about 5,800 students in the spring of 2006. Many students and their families were housed at either the Astrodome or the Brown Convention Center when they first arrived; others found hotel space or lived with relatives or in shelters. A number of families did not immediately enroll their children in school after coming to the city, as some were unsure how long they were staying and others simply did not want to let the kids out of their sight. In the end, students enrolled in over 200 of the district's 305 schools—mostly on the west, central, and south sides of the city—and came without academic, discipline, immunization, or health records of any kind. The district devoted considerable time and effort administering diagnostic tests and interviewing parents to determine grade status and special needs, and hired over 200 new teachers to accommodate the new arrivals.

Many—if not most—children were found to be significantly behind their peers academically, but others ended up thriving in their new schools. Problems caused by the loss of records were minimized because most public school data in Louisiana were kept on a state database that was not affected by the storm. The state of Texas, however, waived immunization and other rules for the first month to allow school officials to create their own records. The number of overcrowded classrooms in Houston jumped to 732 on February 3, 2006, from 547 the same time the year before; and Adequate Yearly Progress rules under No Child Left Behind were redefined—although not waived—for the spring 2006 testing cycle. Until those test results are available in the summer of 2006, it won't be clear what impact the new students had on the average performance of their new schools.

Preliminary results from the spring 2006 administration of the Texas Assessment of Knowledge and Skills (TAKS), however, indicate that young Hurricane Katrina refugees living in the state scored significantly worse than Texas children. Only 58% of evacuees in third grade passed the reading portion of the test, compared with 89% of state students (Weber 2006). State and local officials attributed the poor performance to the ineffective schools in Louisiana in general and in New Orleans specifically; to the ordeal that students experienced being uprooted from their original schools and homes; to the fact that some students were probably assigned to the wrong grades when they arrived in Texas; and to the disruptive effect on students of moving midyear to new classrooms, teachers, classmates, curriculum, and materials.

The process for both students and schools, all in all, has had its moments of glory and its days of despair. There have been the usual bureaucratic problems, culture shock, and poor placements. Some families were unhappy with where their children were placed. There were problems as students were subjected to different state standards and new high school graduation requirements. And there were mix-ups and screw-ups galore. But, by and large, the receiving schools in Houston and elsewhere across the country took in students with open arms and little promise that they would be either fully reimbursed or thanked for their efforts. To date, neither has arrived in great abundance.

Reopening the Schools

Schools in New Orleans—both public and private—began to reopen in October and November 2005 in the least damaged areas of the city. The first to open were a parochial school, St. Andrew the Apostle, and two charters, Milestone Sabis Academy and the James Singleton Charter School. (Zehr 2005). The first regular district school opened on November 28—Ben Franklin Elementary School. In all, 18 public schools were open by January 31, 2006; three were regular public schools (enrolling about 2,300 students), five were charters operated under the aegis of the elected school board (enrolling some 1,900 students), two were charters overseen by the state (with capacity for about 850 students); five were charters operated under the Algiers Charter Authority (enrolling about 3,500 students), and three were charters that were low-performing and part of the "recovery" district (with capacity of about 1,600 students). Each charter school was given authority to hire its own staff, handle its budget, and set curriculum. Some 12,000–13,000 students were expected by the end of June 2006; upwards of 25,000 by the reopening of schools in September 2006; and as many as 35,000-40,000 students by the start of the 2007-2008 school year.

The traditional school system, meanwhile, struggles to keep its head above water. The school board moved to charter as many schools under its control as possible, partly as a way to keep the district's mounting debt away from the few schools that were able to open independently. But part of the chartering was spurred by the advocacy of charter school proponents on the school board and part was due to the availability of $20.9 million in federal aid for new or expanding charter schools that the district was hoping to access.

The district's financial condition can only be described as dire. Its *ad valoreum* tax base was wiped out by the storm, and the district has received only limited sales tax revenue and $29 million in insurance proceeds to date. The New Orleans Public Schools, in fact, had not received a single dollar in reimbursements from FEMA as of February 16 to repair buildings damaged by the storm. It also had not received any federal charter school aid, any of its regular federal funding for the current school year, and limited use of its carryover funds—although the district was approved for a community disaster loan of about $20 million. The district is reeling from over $530 million in debt, including $265 million in bonded indebtedness, $120 million in unemployment benefits, $125 million in FEMA insurance penalties, and the $20 million loan amount. For all intents and purposes, the traditional school district has evolved into a liquidating entity with the responsibility of closing the books on a system with little control of its schools.

The district's personnel problems also continue to mount. On December 28, the district's benefits provider, Coventry Health Care of Louisiana, moved to terminate the school system's health insurance coverage, saying that it could no longer afford to protect the district's workers. And Civil District Court Judge Kern Reese blocked the firing of the district's 7,500 employees, arguing that they had not received the proper 60-day notification of their terminations (Ritea 2006b).

The state, which is facing its own revenue problems and had to cut about $64 million from its school aid formula (Maggi 2005b), has no immediate plans to open most of the recovery schools under its control until sufficient demand exists and it can identify independent providers to operate them. The state superintendent of schools, Cecil Picard, has indicated that he has no interest in running the schools that his agency had just helped to seize, but instead would put the work out to bid (Ritea 2006a; Louisiana Department of Education 2006a). The National Association of Charter School Authorizers announced on February 16 that it had been hired by the state to select and oversee the recovery schools that would be opened as charters. Forty-four organizations had applied to run the schools in New Orleans as of March 23 (NACSA 2006).

For the moment, the state appears to be squirreling away a substantial portion of the funds ($28 million of $100 million in first-round grants) that Congress approved for storm-impacted districts in order to open its own recovery schools, while dribbling out just enough money—only $5.6 million in first-round federal hurricane aid—to the New Orleans schools to keep them out of bankruptcy. (The state would assume the school district's debt if the system failed financially.)

The U.S. Department of Education, for its part, seems loathe, in the opinion of some, to help the system get back on its feet, preferring instead to devote its energies and resources to charter and private schools.

On a related front, in mid-fall 2005, New Orleans Mayor Ray Nagin moved to establish a broad citywide commission to plan and coordinate the rebuilding of the city. The result was the Bring New Orleans Back Commission. Tulane University President Scott Cowan heads the commission's education task force, which represents public and private interests across the city. The U.S. Department of Education arranged for the task force's staff work to be handled by the Boston Consulting Group. And the Broad and Gates Foundations provided the funding.

The task force, which was under considerable national and local pressure to remake the old school system, solicited ideas and recommendations from a broad group of people, including the state-appointed superintendent of the Oakland (CA) public schools, leaders of the Norfolk (VA) public schools, Cambridge Education, the Rand Corporation, the U.S. Department of Education, the Council of the Great City Schools, and an array of professors, activists, and architects from inside and outside the city. The task force also conducted an online survey of 4,000 parents and teachers from the New Orleans school system.

In December 2005, the Bring New Orleans Back Commission's education task force set forth a proposal that envisioned an "Educational Network Model"—a loosely coupled system of charter schools, privately managed schools, and traditional public school, each operated by a "network manager," under the aegis of a school board appointed by the governor and the mayor rather than an elected board (Bring New Orleans Back Commission 2006). The mayor and the broader citywide commission gave the plan their approval at their January 17 meeting this year. The state, however, voiced little support for the proposal, even though it did not release a draft plan of its own—short of indicating that it may charter the schools or contract them out—until May 8. A state plan is due by June 2006.

Looking Ahead

The school district, for the meantime, is struggling to plot out a future. It signed off on the Bring New Orleans Back plan in principle, but played a limited role in its design and remains uncertain what it means for the traditional school system. The school board expects to devote most of its next two years trying to keep the schools under its control above state averages, lest they also be swept into the recovery district; paying off debt and avoiding additional financial entanglements; and resolving remaining personnel problems. The board presently is engaged in resetting its goals and redesigning its structure and organization; replacing its Acting Superintendent, who has agreed to step aside; and articulating what it can accomplish over the next several years. The school board has agreed that it will step down in 2008 if it cannot meet its academic goals and pay off its debts.

As of January 5, the district was operating with a central office staff of about 68 people. Most of these staff members are instructional, finance, revenue, payroll, benefits, IT, and facilities specialists working with the Acting Superintendent and Alvarez & Marsal to clean up payments to vendors for bills incurred before the storm and to solve payroll and benefits problems (Alvarez & Marsal 2006).

The district's biggest challenge, however, lies in the unpredictability of its future. Citizens are trickling back into the city in numbers that are far smaller than New Orleans' pre-Katrina population. No one is sure what sections of town are likely to be resettled first. And no one is sure what the new residents will look like or be skilled at doing. Already it is clear that many—possibly most—of the city's poorest residents will not be coming back. They will not have the financial wherewithal to do so, and it is not apparent that they are wanted. The parents of many previous students of the New Orleans schools also may find that their educational prospects are better elsewhere. Anecdotal reports suggest that many parents who fled in the wake of Katrina are more satisfied with the public education their children are getting in their new cities than they were in New Orleans.

Nonetheless, there *is* some reason for cautious optimism. Political leaders at all levels and advocates nationally saw an opportunity in the disaster to start all over again and create a system of public education in the city that was second to none. One heard this goal from U.S. Secretary of Education Margaret Spellings, Governor Blanco, Mayor Nagin, State Superintendent Picard, Tulane University President Cowan, Acting School Superintendent Watson, turn-around expert Roberti, and many others locally and nationally. Sometimes other agendas hid behind the grand intent; sometimes the motives were pure. Either way, local leaders have been able to marshal an impressive braintrust to rethink the system and come up with a plan for a network of schools. Moreover, some of the new charter schools have infused new blood and enthusiasm into the public education promise of the city. And a number of private and public interests have committed small amounts of new resources in an effort to remake the schools of New Orleans.

But one can also see flashing yellow lights on the horizon. The preliminary plans for remaking the city's public schools were designed by people who were substantially different in hue from educational decision-makers before the storm, a touchy issue in these still-racially-sensitive times. The proposal to replace the currently elected school board with an appointed school board, for instance, is bound to exacerbate concerns among community activists and parents that the schools, along with other city agencies, are being highjacked by alien forces.

Moreover, the new plans for a network of schools are grounded in assumptions that have not been well tested elsewhere. The nearest try-out of a similar conceptualization of educational reform is found in Philadelphia, but it is not clear that Philadelphia's blend of regular, charter, and privately managed schools was responsible for the dramatic gains in student achievement that city has seen in its regular schools. The academic progress may have had more to do with the school district's instructional overhaul than its mixture of service providers. The network approach being proposed for New Orleans, while intuitively appealing to some, is a new paradigm for organizing the adults in the system but has little to do with the nature of the instruction provided in the classroom. And it presumes that all students and families are equally familiar with their new choices within the network and have equal ability to act on that familiarity.

The charter schools proposed by the state in its draft plan have similar problems. Nowhere in the state's proposals to date is there a vision for what instruction would look like in these schools (Louisiana Department of Education 2006b). The draft plan, instead, presents the state's rationale for governance and structural changes without saying much about how classroom instruction would be improved. It is also hard to conceptualize how the city would define public education when each of its schools—now mostly charters—were doing something different.

If the new balkanized system results in some of the same inequities that showed their ugly heads in the past, which is entirely possible, then the reforms will have failed, will have perpetuated the old racially identifiable disparities, and will have added to the nation's cynicism about the city and public education. All of this will not have occurred by design or conspiracy but by simple blindness about how a state and a school system can rig itself on behalf of the more privileged.

The most serious issue on the horizon, however, involves how poorly state and local authorities are working together and how little any of the existing plans—state and local—focus on classroom practice, quality teaching, and student achievement. State and local actors are often talking past one another about issues of power, money, and control—but not good instruction. The Bring New Orleans Back Commission has put together an intelligent plan, but it—like the draft state plan—omits a serious discussion of good teaching. The local school board and administration are having a hard time seeing where they fit and have but the flimsiest of notions about how to improve academic performance. The charter schools are on their own. And the state's hostility toward the city school district is palpable.

This enmity, distrust, and single-minded focus on adult issues are part of the reason why the city school system got into trouble in the first place and why it will continue having difficulty in the future if left unresolved.

It is hard to imagine that Hurricane Katrina could have had any other outcome than it did when it hit New Orleans. Poor and African-American children were too concentrated and isolated at the city's core when the storm struck for there to have been any other result than what Americans (some to their amazement) saw on their TV screens. But a nation as tolerant as this one is of its own inequities shouldn't have been surprised at the results of its indifference.

New Orleans is not the only city, however, in which our poorest children are concentrated and isolated in such a way. It is also not the only one where hostilities run so deep. And it is not the only one that embodies the nation's neglect of its poor. One can see the same pattern in many other cities across the country – if one is only willing to open one's eyes. And, in other cities, we run the same risk of double jeopardy whatever the next storm, wherever the next levees.

References

Alvarez & Marsal. 2006. Orleans Parish School Board Planning Meeting. January 5.

Bring New Orleans Back Commission. 2006. Rebuilding and Transforming: A Plan for Improving Public Education in New Orleans. New Orleans.

Council of the Great City Schools. 2001. *Rebuilding Human Resources in the New Orleans Public Schools.* Washington, D.C.

_____ 2002. *Improving Transportation Systems in the New Orleans Public Schools.* Washington, D.C.

_____ 2005. *Assessment of Hurricane Katrina Damage to New Orleans Public School Facilities.* Washington, D.C.

_____ 2006. *Beating the Odds: A City-by-City Analysis of Student Performance and Achievement Gaps on State Assessments.* Washington, D.C.

Greater New Orleans Education Foundation. 1999. Unpublished Survey Results Conducted for the New Orleans Public Schools.

Hurricane Education Recovery Act. 2005. U.S. Congress, PL 109-48.

Jacobson, Linda. 2006. Hurricanes' Aftermath is Ongoing. *Education Week.* February 1.

Ladson-Billings, Gloria. 2006. Now They're Wet: Hurricane Katrina as Metaphor for Social and Educational Neglect. *Voices in Urban Education.* Winter.

Louisiana Department of Education. 2006a. Type 5 Charter School—Request for Application, Applications Being Accepted for Providers to Take Over Failing Schools. Baton Rouge. http://www.doe.state.la.us.

_____ 2006b. Recovery School District: Legislatively Required Plan. May 8.

Maggi, Laura. 2004. Blanco Signs Bill Bolstering Amato; New Orleans Schools Designated 'In Crisis.' *The New Orleans Times Picayune.* June 11.

_____ 2005a. State to Run Orleans Schools. *The New Orleans Times Picayune.* November 23.

_____ 2005b. $64 Million in School Spending Cut. *The New Orleans Times Picayune.* November 22.

National Association of Charter School Authorizers (NACSA). 2006. Louisiana Department of Education Receives 44 Charter Applications for New Orleans. March 23.

Ritea, Steve. 2005. Schools in Disarray. *The New Orleans Times Picayune.* November 20.

_____ 2006a. La. Won't Run N.O. Schools by Itself. *The New Orleans Times Picayune.* January 3.

_____ 2006b. Court Delays Orleans School Firings. *The New Orleans Times Picayune*. February 1.

_____ 2006c. N.O. Teachers Union Loses Its Force in Storm's Wake. *The New Orleans Times Picayune*. March 5.

Tonin, J. 2006. New Orleans Charter Network Gets Under Way. *Education Week*. January 18.

U.S. Department of Education. 2005. New Support for Families and Areas Affected by Hurricane Katrina. Press Release. Washington, D.C.

Weber, Paul. 2006. Katrina refugees score lower on tests. *Associated Press*. March 24.

Zehr, Mary Ann. 2005. Catholic Schools Reopening After Katrina. *Education Week*. October 12.

Endnotes

1. A poll conducted by the Greater New Orleans Education Foundation found that 25% of the city's parents thought that African-American students were inherently less capable of performing academically as well as non-African-American students (Greater New Orleans Education Foundation 1999).

CHAPTER 11

An Old Economy for the "New" New Orleans?

Post-Hurricane Katrina Economic Development Efforts

ROBERT K. WHELAN

Over one million people in the New Orleans metropolitan region evacuated from Hurricane Katrina in August 2005. As they evacuated, personal safety was their highest short-term priority. Once they had survived the storm, people worried about their homes. Would they have a standing home, and what would be its physical condition—flooded, roofless, etc? Another great concern was employment. Upon their return, would people have jobs? Would employers—both large and small—continue in business? If so, would that be in New Orleans, somewhere else in the metro region, or in some other part of the country? In what ways, good and bad, might the local economy change?

This chapter considers economic development efforts in New Orleans in the immediate aftermath of Hurricane Katrina. The chapter begins with a review of the economic situation before the storm. The local economy was highly polarized, with some professional people doing very well and a much larger number of people employed in low-wage jobs. This discussion is followed by a consideration of the problems faced by businesses—especially small businesses—after the storm. Then, job prospects in the region are examined. Many different ideas have been presented and discussed in the brief time since the storm. Some of them are reviewed, with particular attention to the work of New Orleans Mayor Ray Nagin's Bring Back New Orleans Commission and Louisiana Governor Kathleen Blanco's Louisiana Recovery Authority. A concluding section assesses likely outcomes.

The New Orleans Economy Pre-Katrina

The New Orleans metropolitan region contains eight parishes (counties), with 1.3 million residents counted in the 2000 Census. The City of New Orleans' population was 485,000. In addition to the central city, neighboring Jefferson Parish had 455,000 residents and was beginning to exhibit the characteristics of an older suburb. St. Tammany Parish, north of Lake Pontchartrain, had close to 200,000 residents and was the major growth center. A December 2005 estimate done for the Bring Back New Orleans Commission has New Orleans at 134,400, Jefferson Parish at 375,000 (a 17% decrease), and St. Tammany at 280,000. A report by the RAND Gulf States Policy Institute estimated the city's population at 155,000 in March 2006. RAND analysts forecast a rise to 198,000 by September 2006, and a further increase to 272,000 by September of 2008. This last figure is slightly more than half the pre-Katrina population (RAND 2006).

The racial composition of New Orleans contrasts sharply with that of its suburban neighborhoods. In the 2000 Census, two-thirds of the city's population was African-American, while almost 75% of the suburban population in the Metropolitan Statistical Area (MSA) was white. Again, no one knows the precise nature of changes since the storms, but clearly, at present, New Orleans has a population that is now more white and more Hispanic than before the storms. Meanwhile, the African-American population declined—both absolutely and relatively.

The racial polarization is compounded by class polarization. As of the 2000 Census, the central city itself had a higher median income than the suburbs. This is unusual. It indicates that quite a number of people were doing very well. While the high-income people were mainly white professionals, a substantial number of middle-class African Americans were in this group. At the same time, a much larger group of people were hard-core poor. In 2000, 28% of the city's residents lived in poverty, with a high percentage of African Americans in this category.

This situation is, of course, hardly unique to New Orleans. In many ways, New Orleans' population and economy in the latter part of the twentieth century resembled that of older, "Rust Belt" cities in the Northeast and Midwest, such as Buffalo, Cleveland, and Pittsburgh. Although it is geographically part of the Sunbelt, New Orleans has not experienced the growth of Atlanta, Dallas, or Phoenix.

Traditionally, the New Orleans economy had a tripartite base: the port, oil and related industries, and tourism. Employment growth in New Orleans was stagnant over the last two decades of the twentieth century. There were slightly fewer jobs in 1997 than there were in 1977. The city registered substantial job losses in port-related industries and manufacturing. Containerization and other technology-driven processes led to the displacement of 8,900 workers. Manufacturing, which never employed a large part of the New Orleans workforce, saw a 50% decline. As the city lost jobs in these areas, it gained jobs in health care, tourism-related industries, business services, legal services, social services, and education (Whelan, Gladstone, and Hirth 2002).

One way to glimpse the local economy quickly is by considering the largest private employers as of 2000. The largest private employer in the metro area is Litton Avondale, a shipbuilding firm. An aerospace firm, Lockheed Martin, is the sixth largest employer. The top ten private employers include a university (Tulane), a health care firm (Ochsner), a casino (Harrah's), two utilities (phone and electric), a restaurant chain headquartered in the area (Copeland's-Popeyes), and a vacuum cleaner manufacturer. There are no oil companies on the current list, although there were in the 1990 Census.

In the latter part of the twentieth century, some industries saw an increase in real earnings. These included oil and gas, legal services, and tourism. Port-related industries and manufacturing evidenced earnings declines.

In 2001, Greater New Orleans, Inc., the regional economic development agency in the regional chamber of commerce, identified ten existing and emerging industry clusters in the region for attraction and retention strategies. These clusters included: manufacturing (food processing, shipbuilding, aerospace, petrochemical, and machinery), maritime, construction, repair services, information services and technology, biomedical research and development, media production/entertainment, tourism, health care, and warehousing distribution. Workforce plans and policies for the region emphasize targeting these clusters.

In 2001, Greater New Orleans, Inc. suggested a focus on six occupational clusters in which the region had a comparative advantage: maritime, medical, oil and gas, petrochemical and refining, shipbuilding, and tourism (Whelan, Gladstone, and Hirth 2002).

Before Hurricane Katrina, the problems of racially-related poverty seemed especially intractable in the New Orleans area. No one has easy answers for the problems of a substantial underclass in an urban economy that was not especially dynamic. Organizations with excellent track records in other U.S. urban areas have not succeeded in New Orleans. The Annie E. Casey Foundation has sponsored workforce development efforts in many urban areas. In New Orleans, they funded the New Orleans Jobs Initiative (NOJI), a major collaborative effort to provide job opportunities, but the Foundation has been frustrated by the slow pace of its New Orleans efforts, in contrast to other cities.

Another example is the efforts of the Local Initiatives Support Corporation (LISC) to build housing in New Orleans. LISC came to New Orleans in 1993 after considerable success with its nonconfrontational strategy in other cities. In their analysis of the early years of this effort, Ross Gittell and Avis Vidal (1998:66) note that "city officials were preoccupied with controversies concerning riverboat gambling and expansion of access to the harbor, and the city lacked a low-income housing strategy." Moreover, Gittell and Vidal observed that "the local government was perceived as paternalistic and corrupt, and there was widespread skepticism that this could be changed. Consequently, accountability and expectations of community development in the city were low" (Gittell and Vidal 1998:67). LISC pulled out of the New Orleans area after a decade of trying to build housing, with little to show for its efforts.

Problems Faced By Businesses

Obviously, one fundamental problem faced by businesses after Hurricane Katrina is the housing of employees. A majority of the housing stock in New Orleans was damaged or destroyed in the storms. The same is true in Plaquemines and St. Bernard Parishes. A substantial minority of homes on the East Bank of Jefferson Parish was flooded. While problems in St. Tammany Parish resulted from storm surge only, the impacts were considerable by normal standards. 40–45% of housing units in the city of Slidell were flooded. Overall, the result is a severe shortage of housing in the region.

There is widespread recognition of the existence of evacuees and their problems. Many people are living with relatives and friends in the region. Again, there is recognition that many are living in trailers—FEMA or otherwise. These may be on their own properties or in a trailer "park." Many people are living in tents, on their own property, or in other public and private locations.

There has been a huge job loss in the region. The metropolitan area lost more than 200,000 jobs in the wake of the storm. The unemployment rate in the New Orleans area was 17.5% in November of 2005. The comparable figure in November of 2004 was 4.6%. Health care, and leisure and hospitality, two of the pillars of the local economy, were especially hard-hit. The December 2005 rate did, however, fall to 8.2%. By April of 2006, the rate fell to 5.1%, as opposed to 4.1% a year ago.

It is difficult to find precise figures, but it is clear that there is a substantial housing need—both short-term and long-term. Business groups, such as the Greater New Orleans, Inc. Task Force on Housing, have called for an expedited approval process for temporary housing. The reality, however, is that very little is being done to expedite the provision of temporary housing. There are numerous stories of FEMA trailers sitting in various locations within the region, with release to local authorities delayed for obscure reasons. When FEMA trailers are released, further delays occur. In New Orleans, a trailer must pass electrical inspection. With city budget cutbacks after the storms, there are only two inspectors for the entire city. Larger trailer sites inevitably face NIMBY-ism. Proposals to house private- and public-sector employees in trailers have encountered opposition in the suburban parishes. Such opposition is not confined to the suburbs. Since Hurricane Katrina, the New Orleans City Council and Mayor Nagin fought over potential trailer sites on several occasions.

Long-term proposals will encounter the same kind of opposition. Groups of every political persuasion have urged the city to follow mixed-use, mixed-income processes in rebuilding. Specific development proposals were slow to emerge, with the only major one in the fall of 2005 coming from KB Homes. This upscale California housing firm proposed building 20,000 new homes on the West Bank of Jefferson Parish; their average house price nationwide is around $275,000 (Thomas 2005). While building these homes would help to ease the shortage, it would help only middle- and upper-income people. And moreover, proposals of this magnitude typically face significant opposition from homeowner groups.

On an individual basis, there are several reasons why businesses may be slow to rebuild. It took months before FEMA gave clear guidance to any affected jurisdiction. No one knew whether he or she would be allowed to rebuild, and if so, to what height they had to rebuild to qualify for federal flood insurance. This affects businesses in the same way it affects individuals. It has long been said that New Orleans was an undercapitalized community. Major development projects were funded by outside capital. In recent years, many of the local banks merged with larger national (and even international) banks. The New Orleans banking community was very conservative traditionally, in terms of its lending processes. Again, will banks and mortgage companies support businesses as they try to rebuild? There is also the problem of insurance. Two insurance companies that account for 57% of the homeowners' business in the state—State Farm and Allstate—are not writing new policies. A state-sponsored option is available, but is more costly (Mowbray 2005).

Small businesses face problems different in kind and degree from large multinational conglomerates. Most small businesses had only enough cash on hand to sustain themselves for 60–90 days. The federal and state governments provide bridge funding for short term sustenance of businesses. In the aftermath of Hurricane Katrina, many businesses that applied could not get the assistance in a timely fashion. The same is true of Small Business Administration (SBA) loans. A January 2006 *Washington Post* report said that 1,891 business loans had been approved in Louisiana, but more than 23,000 businesses had applied for loans. The article dramatized the situation with the plight of Hubig's Pies, a popular local institution in a mixed-use neighborhood, still waiting for a needed decision (Babcock 2006). Hubig's Pies eventually received the money, and resumed business. Many small businesses were not so fortunate.

The allocations of contracts and government bidding processes have been criticized after Hurricane Katrina. Many cleanup and construction contracts went to firms from Texas and Arkansas. Louisiana is not known for a highly skilled, highly educated labor force. But it does have plenty of firms and individuals who wanted to work in the rebuilding process. More recently, the City of New Orleans' bidding processes have been criticized. In one case, a local uniform company lost out to a Kentucky company in a police department contract bid. While the city saved $160,000 on the bid, the use of a local company would have kept money—and perhaps jobs—in the community (White 2005).

Larger companies face different kinds of problems. Some of the city's biggest employers (Shell, Freeport McMoRan) have returned employees to the city. Others are waiting for housing, and resolution of the levee situation, before making a decision. The city's biggest problems seem to be with its utility providers. Bell South and Chevron are moving jobs out of the city, although the jobs are relocating to Covington in St. Tammany Parish, and to Baton Rouge, and thus aren't leaving the region. A bigger problem exists with Entergy, the company that provides New Orleans' electricity and gas. As a result of the costs of the storm and the lack of cash flow, Entergy New Orleans declared bankruptcy. A federal bailout was requested, citing the precedent of Consolidated Edison in New York City after 9/11. Entergy's request was denied. The City may have to take over the utility. In the meantime, resumption of service to many areas of New Orleans has been slow.

Business confidence in the area is perhaps even more important than the confidence of individual homeowners. The state of the levee system is integral to the restoration of business confidence. The Army Corps of Engineers repeatedly told New Orleanians over the years that the city enjoyed protection from a Category 3 hurricane. At the time of its landing, Katrina was a Category 3 storm. Storm surge breached the Industrial Canal and the 17th Street Canal. Governor Blanco, Mayor Nagin, and other public officials made the levee system the highest priority in rebuilding. The repair of levees is proceeding more slowly than expected. For example, as of May 2006, an Army Corps of Engineers project to armor the levees still awaits approval. Repairs will not be finished by the 2006 hurricane season. Longer-range plans include protection from Category 5 storms and coastal restoration. Ultimately, these projects, if undertaken, will involve larger monetary outlays.

In discussing business relocation, the issue of remaining within the region or moving out of the region entirely is critical. Many companies relocated to higher ground north of Lake Pontchartrain. A growth corridor has emerged, extending along Interstate 12—from the state capitol in Baton Rouge (now the largest city in the state) to Slidell in East St. Tammany Parish. Chevron and Shell, mentioned above, both relocated employees north of the lake. One estimate shows that 700 displaced businesses and out-of-stock contractors applied for occupational licenses in St. Tammany Parish alone in the three months after the storms. These include attorneys, barbers, insurance companies, and health care services (Gordon 2005).

Job Prospects

In the short run, job prospects exist in certain occupational categories. The largest job gains reported in the November 2005 employment figures were in construction and in trade and transportation. These reflect the region's need for workers in the cleanup and renovation of damaged properties. Debris haulers and drivers are included in the transportation category.

An examination of *New Orleans Times-Picayune* want ads in December 2005 shows that construction workers and drivers are in high demand. Many restaurants remain closed because they cannot find the staff needed for operation. This is evidenced by the fact that fast-food chains are offering substantial signing bonuses ($6,500, e.g.) for workers who commit to 18–24 months. Despite many layoffs and closings of medical facilities, there is still a strong demand for medical professionals in the few facilities that are open. Skilled workers of all types are in demand.

Over the last two decades, there has been a concern over the "brain drain" from Louisiana. At least since the administration of former Governor Buddy Roemer (1988–1992), the state government has been aware of the problem. In brief, Louisiana has lost young educated professionals to other parts of the United States. Periodically, some policymakers will raise the question: How can we bring these talented people back to New Orleans and to Louisiana?

Some examples of people who left Louisiana are Dean Baquet, editor of the *Los Angeles Times*, Walter Isaacson, former head of CNN, and jazz musician Wynton Marsalis (the latter two are working directly with the Governor's and Mayor's rebuilding efforts). Thousands of professionals who have been trained in Louisiana colleges and universities are part of the exodus.

Let me offer a small personal example. In the College of Urban and Public Affairs at the University of New Orleans, we grant Master's degrees in Public Administration and Urban and Regional Planning. From our perspective, it is unfortunate that most administrative and professional jobs in Louisiana's state and local governments do not require a Master's degree in public administration (or a Master's degree in a related field, such as business). Many people in these positions have practical experience and political connections, but lack professional credentials. Some of our students work for the federal government, and leave because of transfer to other locations, especially Washington and regional headquarters cities. Others would prefer to stay. City planners with Master's degrees are offered starting salaries below those of entry-level schoolteachers and police personnel by New Orleans and other local governments. These problems (lack of professionalism, poor pay and benefits) are often the case in public- and private sector positions in many fields. Thus, we have the "brain drain."

Hurricane Katrina exacerbated this problem. Thousands of professionals from the region were relocated by their employers. Others lost jobs, or gave them up as they relocated. In these situations, it is middle-class professionals with technical and entrepreneurial skills who will most easily find employment elsewhere. There needs to be a plan to bring them back. As of May 2006, there was not a hint of this.

Let me illustrate the difference between low-skilled and professional demand, as follows: Low-skilled jobs are in demand. If you want to work as a retail clerk, waiter or waitress, or as a fast-food employee, you can easily find work. You may even receive a bonus. On the other hand, think of the public school teachers in Orleans Parish. There were 4,857 teachers in Orleans Parish in 2003–2004 (GNODC 2005). In addition, there were 2,000–3,000 other school employees. Almost all of these were laid off after the storm. Teachers' average salary was not great ($38,251) (http://la.aft. org/005270/), but it was full-time professional employment, with a pension, health benefits, and summer vacation. There was an enormous job loss, particularly in the African-American middle class. Many of these professionals have found employment in other places.

People without education and skills face a different set of problems. Many may find work in the "new" New Orleans. However, they need a place to live, as noted above. Moreover, poor people rely on public transportation. As of May 2006, the Regional Transit Authority operates 27 bus routes and 2 streetcar routes, as opposed to 62 bus routes and 3 streetcar routes before the storm. FEMA is currently providing operating funds which are scheduled to run out on June 30, 2006, presenting another difficult fiscal situation for the city. People without skills will find it more difficult to find employment in regional centers of the service-based, high-technology economy, such as Atlanta and Dallas.

Job prospects must be placed into the context of statewide plans. The state's economic development plan, "Vision 2020," was adopted in 1999. The plan has three major goals. The first is to recreate the state as a "learning enterprise"—to make lifelong learning a goal for all citizens and businesses. The second is to emphasize the "culture of innovation." The idea is to make the state innovative and "globally competitive" in high-technology fields. The third is to be one of the top ten states in the country by 2020, as measured by a number of quality of life indicators (Louisiana Economic Development Council 2003).

These were ambitious goals before Hurricane Katrina. Per capita income in the state, as of 2003, was low, with the state ranking 43rd of 50. Average wages were low. Both figures were slightly over 80% of the national average. 17% of the state's residents lived in poverty. This ranked Louisiana as 46th. Education levels were also low, with many lacking in the skills necessary for a technology-based economy (Louisiana Economic Development Council 2005).

The state had adopted the strategy of cluster development for its economic policies. However, the storms wreaked havoc on many of the state's targeted clusters. Oil and gas facilities, such as rigs and refineries, were damaged and destroyed. Many other industries were devastated by flooding and other storm damage. Agricultural crops were destroyed. Many of these targeted clusters are especially hurt by the "brain drain" noted above. The people with the highest skill levels are the most likely to find good jobs elsewhere.

Perhaps the greatest danger is that the issues of job creation, attraction, and retention will be lost amidst a great number of concerns. On a daily basis, the levee system is a focus of attention. The Mayor and Governor are hearing from returned home owners who are rebuilding and from evacuees who want to return. There are so many issues that the task of job development may be overwhelmed by other concerns. Moreover, the state and city have been criticized for not having specific plans to deal with recovery from Hurricane Katrina. In both the city and state, there are significant existing plans for economic and workforce development. These plans may need to be modified in light of Hurricane Katrina, but they could be ignored altogether.

Options for Economic Recovery

In the aftermath of the storm, many governmental, policy, and activist groups have offered possible courses of action for economic recovery. Although they have different political orientations, a great deal of common ground exists. First, recovery should be undertaken with sustainable development. The environmental destruction caused by the petrochemical industry in the river parishes north of New Orleans and the coastal erosion caused by the oil and gas industry should not be repeated in the future. Many of the planners working in the city stress the need for mass transit and for "smart growth" development. Second, recovery should aim for a more balanced economy. The New Orleans regional economy has always depended on a few industries; future development should be more diverse and equitable.

State and Local Policies

The Louisiana Recovery Authority (LRA) is a 33-member body appointed by Governor Kathleen Blanco. It is charged with identifying and prioritizing short- and long-term needs in the recovery process. As a planning and coordinating body, it is working with FEMA in distributing federal money for recovery. Given its regionwide scope and its collaboration with FEMA, it may be the most important body in post-Katrina economic development.

In developing ideas for recovery, the LRA has been influenced by PolicyLink, a national, nonprofit organization promoting equitable economic development. PolicyLink also seeks the inclusion of low-income persons and people of color in development policymaking. In the Gulf Coast rebuilding efforts, PolicyLink is the representative of Living City, a collaboration of leading foundations and banks (e.g., Annie E. Casey, Rockefeller, MacArthur, Ford, J.P. Morgan Chase, Bank of America, Deutsche Bank).

The PolicyLink-LRA nexus is clear. Indeed, the LRA's draft principles to guide long-term recovery planning are virtually identical to PolicyLink's "Ten Points to Guide Rebuilding in the Gulf Coast Region." These planning guidelines emphasize the redevelopment of New Orleans and other devastated areas as mixed-income communities. In general, equitable development is stressed. Two points are of particular salience to this chapter: (1) "the creation of wealth-building opportunities to effectively address poverty," including jobs with "wages sufficient to lift people out of poverty, and small business development"; and (2) creating jobs that go first to local residents and businesses in the rebuilding process. This includes investment in "massive" job training as necessary (Louisiana Katrina Recovery 2005).

The LRA has 13 task forces that work with recovery teams of state government administrators. One of those task forces is Economic and

Workforce Development, whose chairman is a jewelry manufacturer from Lafayette. The vice-chair is an African-American woman from New Orleans who is past president of the state AFL-CIO. The task force had several short-term goals: expediting bridge loans and SBA loans, getting access to federal contracts for Louisiana firms, providing transportation to workplaces for employees, job-training programs for recovery (as well as existing economic efforts), and rebuilding of the fishing industry, which has been greatly damaged by the storm.

At the local level, in early October 2005, Mayor Ray Nagin urged creation of a casino district in downtown New Orleans. The Mayor thought this might jump-start the local economy. Nagin's thought was to allow seven hotels with more than 500 rooms each in the downtown area to open casinos. This would have required a change in the state's arrangement with Harrah's, the sole land-based casino downtown. The idea was a nonstarter, and was immediately shot down by the Governor, business leaders, and the local media. No one, however, came forward with an alternative for a potentially speedy recovery.

The Bring Back New Orleans Commission is a 17-member body appointed by Mayor Ray Nagin. The Commission sees itself as taking the lead role in the rebuilding effort. Many believe that New Orleans suffers from a lack of unity in the recovery process. The multiplicity of commissions is one example of this, although the Nagin Commission says it will ultimately report to, and coordinate with, the LRA.

The Bring Back New Orleans Commission has sought advice from a number of national groups. In particular, the Urban Land Institute (ULI), a nonprofit organization based in Washington, representing land use and real estate development interests, was brought in for a planning consultation. The ULI's recommendations included a "smaller footprint for the city" (i.e., not necessarily rebuilding all neighborhoods) and included the following language:

> The city should be rebuilt in a strategic manner. Areas that sustained minimal damage should be encouraged to begin rebuilding immediately, while those with more extensive damage will need to evaluate the feasibility of reinvestment first and then proceed expeditiously in a manner that will ensure the health and safety of the residents of each neighborhood (ULI 2005:13).

The Commission backed away from this recommendation very quickly. Commission members are basically representatives of the New Orleans business community, and they clearly have their own ideas, based upon years of experience.

The Bring Back New Orleans Commission has seven subcommittees, one of which is economic development. The chairs of that committee are the president of the local economic development agency and the president of the local utility company. The latter was probably an unfortunate choice, given the company's well-publicized difficulties, with trips to Washington taking him away from New Orleans.

The economic development subcommittee's mission statement is "to assure an open, inclusive and vibrant business community that will create livable wages and higher-salaried jobs to our qualified citizens" (Bring Back New Orleans Commission website 2005). The committee wants to bring businesses back to New Orleans, as well as to retain and expand existing businesses. The committee's main activity is to develop a plan to help businesses rebuild. The subcommittee issued their report in January 2006. The plan stressed restoration of the city's economic base, emphasizing industries that were the base of the economy before Katrina. The subcommittee recommended provision of worker housing, tax incentives for businesses, developing worker-training programs, and beginning a marketing campaign. Its vision also included new industries that might emerge from rebuilding (e.g., housing).

A third effort is that of Lieutenant Governor Mitch Landrieu. In Louisiana, the Lieutenant Governor is the chief executive of the state's Department of Culture, Recreation and Tourism. Landrieu's "Louisiana Rebirth Plan" is more focused, given the narrower scope of his concerns. The strategic plan, released after Hurricane Katrina, has four main points: (1) rebuilding Louisiana as a top tourist attraction; (2) making the cultural economy the engine of economic and social rebirth; (3) building better lives and livelihoods for all Louisianans; and (4) doing this with high performance standards, accountability, and ethical behavior (Louisiana Department of Culture, Recreation and Tourism 2005). Although he is not credited, the influence of Richard Florida's ideas on the "creative class" is evident (Florida 2002, 2005). To implement the plan, Landrieu will have a public relations campaign as one part. A foundation has been established for needy artists, musicians, and writers. Landrieu offered the state parks as a place for temporary housing after the storm (Website of Lieutenant Governor Mitch Landrieu, 2005).

In looking at state and local policies, we must briefly discuss state and local politics. Nagin was elected Mayor in 2002 as a political outsider, a political novice who headed the local cable television company. Blanco was elected Governor in 2003. Nagin, a Democrat, endorsed Representative Bobby Jindal, Blanco's Republican opponent in the campaign. There is no love lost between the two. Much of their time since the storms has been spent on justifying their actions before, during, and immediately after the hurricane.

Landrieu is the son of former New Orleans Mayor and U.S. HUD Secretary "Moon" Landrieu, and younger brother of U.S. Senator Mary Landrieu. He has been very visible since the hurricane. At a conference sponsored by the American Institute of Architects and the American Planning Association in November 2005, Landrieu upstaged the Governor, with a dramatic speech calling for one commission and one unified point of view when going to Washington seeking funds. He wound up in second place in the April 22 New Orleans mayoral primary, but in a result that surprised many observers, lost to Ray Nagin in the May 20 run-off election, despite receiving the support of the third-place primary candidate.

Federal Policies

The major federal legislation affecting post-Katrina economic recovery is the Gulf Opportunity (GO) Zones Act, passed by Congress in December of 2005. GO Zones affect an area extending from Florida to Texas impacted by the 2005 hurricane season. A key provision allows businesses to depreciate 50% of the cost of new property investments. Major purchases, such as real estate and computer systems, are included in this. GO Zones also allow for tax-exempt bond authority to help rebuild the infrastructure. The act also permits the issuance of tax-exempt bonds for housing projects. Another provision allows public utilities to write off disaster loans. Some observers think that Entergy could get as much as $60 million from this provision. While this is not as much as their requested bailout figure, $60 million would help their financial situation.

Congressional reactions during the legislative process were predictable. Democrats noted that most businesses would reopen without these incentives. Republicans feared the cost of the legislation, which would add to an already substantial federal debt. Academic literature on state enterprise zones questions the effectiveness of these efforts (Peters and Fisher 2002). They are frequently criticized for subsidizing activity that would have occurred anyway and for diminishing the tax base.

Two other bills have potential impact on regional economic recovery. One is the supplemental spending bill, passed in the closing days of the 2005 congressional session, for repair and strengthening of the levee system. The impact of this legislation is not that great in direct terms, but, indirectly, it has profound effects on business and individual decisions to rebuild within the region. The second is another supplemental request for $4.2 billion in federal aid, which is before Congress as of May 2006. This money will implement Governor Blanco's and the Louisiana Recovery Authority's The Road Home housing program. Under the program, eligible home owners can receive up to $150,000 in relief through federal funds.

All affected citizens who meet the damage requirement will be eligible. The program will begin with partial funding, in anticipation of future funding. If Congress fails to fund this, the state will revise its plans.

Nongovernmental Ideas: Interest Groups, Professional Organizations, Think Tanks

Hurricane Katrina brought responses from people and groups throughout the United States, and from many foreign countries.

The Association of Community Organizations for Reform Now (ACORN) has been active in several New Orleans neighborhoods for the last two decades. It is a grassroots group, with its constituency in lower- and moderate-income communities. ACORN's proposals for rebuilding include the need for "sufficient, living-wage employment." In terms of jobs, ACORN's proposal includes "first-source hiring agreements with living-wage requirements and employment priority for area residents. These jobs should include health insurance, adequate health and safety standards, and union organizing rights" (ACORN 2005:1-2). In November 2005, ACORN sponsored a Community Forum on Rebuilding New Orleans in conjunction with academic planners from around the country. They have also been especially concerned with the problems of citizens displaced to other parts of the region and with the environmental safety of their neighborhoods. Their concerns about jobs have not been addressed.

The Louisiana chapter of The Sierra Club, a national environmental conservation organization, has issued a statement of "Seven Principles for Rebuilding the Gulf Coast" (available at www.louisiana.sierraclub.org). One of the principles is "Invest in the Local Workforce and Economy." They stress the need to use local workers and local businesses in rebuilding, keeping up wages, equal opportunity, and safety provisions. As one might expect, they are also concerned about the environmental impacts of the cleanup. The Sierra Club's involvement is indicative of a widespread consensus that exists on equitable, sustainable redevelopment.

The American Institute of Architects and the American Planning Association are the professional organizations that sponsored the Louisiana Recovery and Rebuilding Conference in November 2005, in conjunction with the Governor's Louisiana Recovery Authority. This conference was facilitated by America Speaks, a Washington-based organization that uses modern technology to organize meetings that engage the participants. After presentations by national experts in the field of economic development, conference participants broke into groups to discuss the issues. The group consensus was for the promotion of inclusive sustainable economic growth, including:

1. "A diverse economy ... supported by respect for the region's historic character and innovative funding strategies. A foundation for growth, including quality education, job training, housing, and transportation."
2. "Equity that includes living wages and career tracks, benefits to everyone in the region, and long-term economic opportunity" (Louisiana Recovery and Rebuilding Conference 2005:1–2).

The conference organizers did an excellent job of bringing together 600 people, and achieving a large degree of consensus on the rebuilding process. It must also be noted that architects have had a more substantial role than planners in the rebuilding process thus far, although planners are becoming more involved as actual neighborhood rebuilding begins.

The Brookings Institution's Metropolitan Policy Program has stepped up with an outstanding response to Hurricane Katrina with its October 2005 report, *New Orleans after the Storm*. Many Brookings recommendations focused on improving the regional economy. A short-term idea is to put New Orleanians back to work by giving local businesses and workers priority in the short run. Over the long run, Brookings calls for plans to develop the industry clusters in the region and for rebuilding the area's universities. Brookings also recognizes the need to revamp the regional workforce system. Workers need to be better linked to jobs, and their report calls for creation of "a coordinated, regional workforce development system to streamline education, training and workforce demands" (Brookings Institution 2005). Brookings continues to have an impact, as its report card on the recovery process is issued and publicized on a regular basis.

Governor Blanco has brought a number of world-renowned planners and architects into Louisiana to work with the Recovery Authority in developing a long-term vision. These include Peter Calthorpe, Andres Duany, Elizabeth Plater-Zybek, and other proponents of the "New Urbanism." In particular, Calthorpe is known for designing neighborhoods with housing located in close proximity to jobs, public transit, and shopping. The LRA team's schedule includes meetings with citizens statewide. Their innovative ideas and calls for new building codes and regulations clash with Louisiana's "laissez faire" attitude toward planning. Indeed, many of the parishes in the Katrina-Rita recovery lack planning and zoning ordinances.

Conclusion

Before Hurricane Katrina, the New Orleans economy suffered from fundamental problems — a large poor population lacking basic skills, a lack of a diverse base, and a general lack of opportunity and dynamism.

Since the storms, many ideas for rebuilding the local economy have been presented. Many of these ideas have merit. Still, it is very difficult to be optimistic about this vital aspect of the rebuilding process, for several reasons.

First, economic development does not seem to be a high priority at this point. Most public and media discussion of the Bring Back New Orleans Commission's recommendations focuses on the physical development aspects of rebuilding. Physical development was the first BBNOC committee to report. Its somewhat controversial recommendations commanded media attention for days and continue to do so. Subsequent committee reports were relegated to the inside pages of the newspaper. The economic development committee was last to report. Its recommendations did not even merit a separate article in the paper, but were buried in a story about the Mayor's planning efforts. Similarly, the early efforts of the LRA focus on physical development. Economic development may become a high priority, but it is not high on governmental agendas now.

Second, many believe in the idea of a "city-region"—or at least in the idea of a city acting as a base for its regional hinterland. No one is approaching economic development from a regional perspective. St. Tammany Parish and Baton Rouge may now be the motors of the regional economy. This reality is not being taken into account. The Mississippi Gulf Coast is a major part of the regional economy. FEMA administers Louisiana through the Dallas office, Mississippi through the Atlanta office. There is no evidence of multistate efforts (Louisiana, Mississippi, Alabama, Texas) to rebuild the regional economy.

Third, there is a significant lack of vision in the political and business leadership. Both the Mayor and the Governor are inexperienced political leaders. The most visionary leaders in history would be challenged by the magnitude of this disaster. The Mayor's Commission represents the people and interests who ran the New Orleans economy before the storms. The extent of their vision is to restore the status quo ante. Wynton Marsalis is the one exception to this, and he has brought forward interesting ideas in the music and cultural area. His ideas include the development of community-based cultural conditions and facilities, and the improvement of cultural and arts education in such areas as music, literature, music, art, and architecture. No previous public report had discussed the need to keep traditions such as Mardi Gras Indians alive. The Governor's authority is well-connected politically, but thus far seems committed to more of the usual in economic development. If jobs and people are going to return to the region, some creative thinking is necessary.

The New Orleans economy lacked dynamism before Hurricane Katrina. The port no longer provided the number of jobs it once did. Oil and gas industries employment was cyclical, with office jobs moved to Houston headquarters often. Tourism had never recovered from the post-9/11 downturn. As noted above, New Orleans leaders want to bring the economy back to what it was before the storm. This is a large order. Businesses face many problems in re-opening. To this point, local businesses are more likely to re-open than are national businesses or chains. Individual job prospects are bright only at the lower end of the employment scale. There are good ideas for recovery. At this point, they have not been implemented, and there is no likely prospect for the adoption of new approaches to the New Orleans economy in the near future.

References

Association of Community Organizations for Reform Now. 2005. *ACORN Proposal for Hurricane Katrina Recovery and Rebuilding.* http://www.acorn.org.
Babcock, Charles. 2006. New Orleans Pies Can't Wait for SBA. *Washington Post*: D01. January 5.
Bring New Orleans Back Commission. 2005. http://bringneworleansback.org.
Brookings Institution, Metropolitan Policy Program. 2005. *New Orleans After the Storm: Lessons from the Past, a Plan for the Future.* Washington, D.C. Brookings Institution. http://www.brookings.edu/metro.
Florida, Richard. 2002. *The Rise of the Creative Class And How It's Transforming Work, Leisure, Community and Everyday Life.* New York: Basic Books.
Florida, Richard. 2005. *Cities and the Creative Class.* New York: Routledge.
Gittell, Ross and Avis Vidal. 1998. *Community Organizing: Building Social Capital as a Development Strategy.* Thousand Oaks, CA: Sage.
Gordon, Meghan. 2005. St. Bernard Firms Move to North Shore. *New Orleans Times-Picayune*: A-10. December 4.
Greater New Orleans Date Center. 2005. http://www.gnodc.org.
Louisiana Department of Cultural, Recreation and Tourism. http://www.crt.state.la.us.
_____ 2005. *Louisiana Rebirth Plan.* http://www.crt.state.la.us/LouisianaRebirthPlan.
Louisiana Economic Development Council. 2005. *Action Plan.*
_____ 2003. *Vision 2020 Plan.*
Louisiana Katrina Recovery. 2005. Overview of Community Driven Statewide Recovery Planning Process.
Louisiana Recovery and Rebuilding Conference. 2005. *Preliminary Report; Day Two.*
Louisiana Recovery Authority. 2006. Governor, LRA, Legislature stand united in Louisiana's Housing Recovery. April 26. http://www.lra.louisiana.gov.
Mowbray, Rebecca. 2005. Insurance moratorium making home sales difficult. *New Orleans Times-Picayune*. December 22. http://www.nola.com.
Peters, Alan H. and Peter S. Fisher. 2002. *State Enterprise Zone Programs: How Have They Worked?* Kalamazoo: W.E. Upjohn Institute for Employment Research.
PolicyLink. 2005. Ten points to guide rebuilding in the Gulf Coast Region. http://www.policylink.org/EquitableRenewal.
RAND Gulf States Policy Institute. 2006. RAND Study Estimates New Orleans Population to Climb to About 272,000 in 2008. News release March 15. http://www.rand.org.
Russell, Gordon. 2006. New Orleans population is coming back more quickly than expected. *New Orleans Times-Picayune*: p. 1. January 1.
Thomas, Greg. 2005. 20,000 New Homes Planned for West Jeff. *New Orleans Times-Picayune*: p. 1. December 6.
Urban Land Institute. 2005. A Strategy for Rebuilding New Orleans. November. http://www.uli.org.
Whelan, Robert K., David L. Gladstone, and Trisha Hirth. 2002. Building a Workforce Development System in New Orleans. The College of Urban and Public Affairs, University of New Orleans.
White, Jaquetta. 2005. Low-bid policies hurt local firms. *New Orleans Times-Picayune*: C8. December 13.

CHAPTER 12

From Poverty to Prosperity

The Critical Role of Financial Institutions

JOHN TAYLOR AND JOSH SILVER

Ultimately, only the historians of the future will be able to accurately assess the level of our national response to the catastrophe resulting from Hurricane Katrina in the Gulf region. Were the government and the private sector timely in their responses? Were those responses adequate? Most of the commentary to date has focused on the role and resources of federal, state, and local governments. The stakeholders, however, have not given much consideration to how geographical areas devastated by Hurricane Katrina, particularly areas of concentrated poverty, must receive substantial private-sector investment in order to realize wholesale economic gain.

Simply put, for any metropolitan or regional economy to succeed, private sector financing must play a significant role. Bank loans and financial institution investment and equity capital will make the difference between a rapid and broad revitalization effort versus a slow rebuilding or even outright failure in regenerating the economy of the Gulf region.

The only way for a region to eradicate poverty is to build wealth and prosperity through access to capital and credit. The root causes of poverty—poor-paying jobs, inferior education, and a dearth of affordable housing—are combated through economic development, development of affordable housing, and small business creation. Private-sector lending and investment make home ownership and economic development possible.

Corporate, philanthropic, and government resources will be maximized if they are used to leverage private-sector capital for rebuilding the Gulf region. Federal, state, and local policies and fair lending regulations ought to be strengthened so as to facilitate the role of the private financial services sector.

This chapter makes the case that banks and other financial institutions are central to recovering from disasters of all sorts and combating long-term poverty. For banks to realize their full potential, however, they must make significant changes in their marketing, underwriting, and branching presence in minority and working-class communities. The chapter describes race and income disparities in home lending, small business lending, and branching in the Gulf region before the hurricanes. For any sustainable recovery to occur, the rebuilding effort must orient the financial industry towards a new era of equitable lending and investing in order to reduce disparities and increase access to credit and capital for working-class and minority neighborhoods. Strengthened Community Reinvestment Act (CRA) and fair lending laws are instrumental in re-orienting banks and savings and loans. CRA is currently undergoing changes, some good, others bad, from this perspective.

As well as describing necessary changes in CRA and fair lending regulations, the chapter outlines a range of short-term policies, including forbearance, as well as longer-term policies that must be developed. The chapter asserts that only a comprehensive planning effort that calls upon the private sector to provide most of the financing will succeed in housing the hundreds of thousands of displaced families, restoring the financial condition of thousands of small businesses, and repairing the region's damaged infrastructure.

Inequalities in Lending Before the Hurricanes

Before the devastation of Hurricanes Katrina and Rita, a less visible hurricane of economic injustice had been afflicting working-class and minority communities in the Gulf region and elsewhere for decades. This economic injustice hurricane is the practice of redlining, or the refusal by banks to make loans to creditworthy residents of minority and working-class neighborhoods. Redlining devastates neighborhoods by making it very difficult for residents to obtain loans to buy homes, repair homes, purchase small businesses, or expand existing small businesses. When a neighborhood is systematically redlined and access to credit is restricted, property values decline, people with means move out, small businesses close, and those who remain in the neighborhood experience increasing unemployment and poverty.

The inverse of redlining is reinvestment. In 1977, Congress passed CRA, imposing an affirmative and continuing obligation on banks to meet the credit and deposit needs of the communities in which they are chartered, including low- and moderate-income communities. CRA's affirmative obligation and the empowerment of communities has dramatically increased lending in working-class and minority neighborhoods across the country in the last couple of decades. In response to their CRA obligations, a number of lenders found that establishing branches, issuing loans, and making investments in minority and lower-income neighborhoods was profitable. Yet, despite the increase in lending, stark inequalities in lending remained in the Gulf region as well as nationally.

Home Lending: Inequalities in Access and Price

Lending disparities by race and income remain stubborn and persistent. Inequalities in home lending include differential access to loans and the tendency for minorities to receive higher-cost loans than whites.

Prime or market-rate loans are loans made at prevailing interest rates to borrowers with good credit histories. Subprime or high-cost loans, in contrast, are loans with rates higher than prevailing rates made to borrowers with credit blemishes. The higher rates compensate lenders for the added risks of lending to borrowers with poor credit histories. While responsible subprime lending serves credit needs, public policy concerns arise when certain groups in the population receive a disproportionate number of high-cost loans. When subprime lending crowds out prime lending in traditionally underserved communities, price discrimination and other predatory and deceptive practices become more likely, as residents have fewer product choices.

In an earlier report, *The Broken Credit System*, the National Community Reinvestment Coalition (NCRC) obtained creditworthiness data on a one-time basis and combined it with 2001 Home Mortgage Disclosure Act (HMDA) data. We found that after controlling for creditworthiness, housing characteristics, and economic conditions, the number of subprime loans increased markedly in minority and elderly neighborhoods in ten large metropolitan areas. Our study revealing pricing disparities while controlling for creditworthiness was consistent with an analysis conducted by Federal Reserve economists (Calem, Gillen, and Wachter 2004).

NCRC has also found that fair lending disparities are particularly striking in the southern United States. In a report released in the spring of 2005—*Fair Lending Disparities by Race, Income, and Gender*—NCRC discovered that the 20 metropolitan areas with the greatest inequalities in market-rate and high-cost lending to African Americans were concentrated in southern states and Gulf region states, including Alabama,

Louisiana, South Carolina, North Carolina, and Georgia. For example, 2003 HMDA data revealed that out of 331 metropolitan areas in the country, New Orleans had the tenth worst level of inequality in market rate and high-cost lending to African Americans. In New Orleans, high-cost lenders issued 43.8% of their home loans to African Americans while market-rate lenders made just 11.5% of their home loans to African Americans.

The most recent HMDA data (for 2004, released in the summer of 2005) reveal a persistence of unequal access to market-rate loans for Gulf region residents. The data also demonstrate that without dramatically reducing the inequalities, the prospects for long-term rebuilding are dim. If lenders do not close the gap in the portion of market-rate loans received by minority and lower-income residents, rebuilding becomes much more difficult, since tens of thousands of families will not receive loans at all or will receive very costly loans.

Government assistance cannot reach the scale that will be necessary to extend loans to the tens of thousands of families that need financing. Public-sector housing programs and subsidies are quite commendable, but they have not been operated at the scale necessary to reach the great majority in need. According to the Department of Housing and Urban Development's strategic plan, the HOME program operates on a $1.7 billion yearly budget and assists about 25,600 new homebuyers annually (HUD 2003). The HMDA data shows that FHA-guaranteed loans reached 69,115 low-income and 205,312 moderate-income homebuyers during 2004. In contrast, banks and mortgage companies issued 309,383 nonguaranteed, conventional home purchase loans to low-income homebuyers and 998,626 home purchase loans to moderate-income homebuyers during 2004.

As these data reveal, government programs make significant contributions, but private-sector lending to low- and moderate-borrowers operates at a much larger volume. Public-sector programs are unlikely to step up their production to match the need for home purchase loans during normal times or in response to disasters. Yet, despite the much higher private-sector loan volumes, significant disparities by race and income persist. The public sector has a vital role in encouraging and mandating that the private sector eliminate these disparities.

Figure 12.1 reveals that in 2004, African Americans received just 15% of market-rate loans, although they comprised 34% of New Orleans' metropolitan statistical area (the city and surrounding suburbs) households. In contrast, market-rate lenders issued 81% of their loans to whites, but whites were only 63% of metropolitan area households.[1]

High-cost lending trends are the mirror opposite of market-rate lending trends. High-cost lenders made 47% of their loans to African Americans during 2004, but African Americans were just 34% of metropolitan area

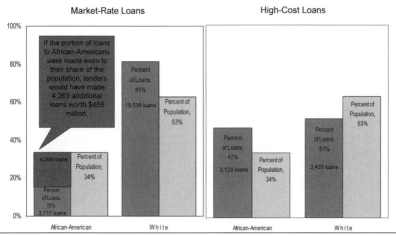

Figure 12.1 Home Lending Disparities by Race in Metro New Orleans, 2004

households. Whites received a portion of high-cost loans (51%) that was smaller than their portion of the area's households (63%).

If these racial inequalities in lending are significantly reduced, market-rate lending to African Americans could increase by thousands of loans and hundreds of millions of dollars. Instead of issuing 15% of their loans (or 3,717 loans) to African Americans, let us suppose that market-rate lenders made 34% of their loans to African Americans (the African-American percentage of households in the New Orleans metropolitan area). African-American borrowers then would have received 4,269 additional market-rate home loans, worth $458 million, more than doubling the number of loans to African Americans.

This example is not meant to assert that the portion of market-rate loans can be made consistent with the portion of African-American households overnight. But it illustrates that possibilities exist to substantially increase market-rate lending to African Americans if lenders, community groups, and public officials work together to reduce the stubborn and persistent lending disparities. In the context of rebuilding the Gulf region, preventing the reappearance of these large lending inequalities becomes a paramount public policy concern.

Inequalities also exist in lending to borrowers of different income levels, as shown in Figure 12.2. In 2004, market-rate lenders issued 25% of their loans to low- and moderate-income borrowers, who constituted about 41% of New Orleans metropolitan area households. In contrast, market-rate lenders made 75% of their loans to middle- and upper-income borrowers, who made up just 59% of the area's households. (High-cost lending exhibited a curious pattern, with the portion of high-cost loans to low- and

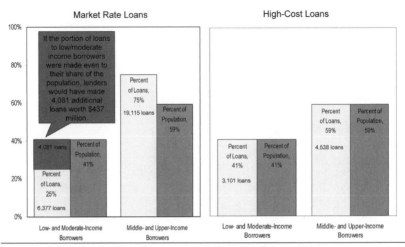

Figure 12.2 Home Lending Disparities by Income in Metro New Orleans, 2004

moderate-income borrowers being exactly equal to the portion of households that had low and moderate incomes. The same pattern applied to middle- and upper-income borrowers.)

Again, if the inequalities in market-rate lending could be reduced, low- and moderate-income borrowers could receive thousands more loans. If the portion of market-rate loans to low- and moderate-income borrowers is made equal to the portion of households that are low- and moderate-income, the number of loans to those borrowers would increase by 4,081, providing $437 million in additional loan dollars.

Granted, there are significant barriers to closing the lending gap to low- and moderate-income borrowers, including higher debt-to-income ratios. Nevertheless, the available evidence suggests that market failures and discrimination contribute to the lending gaps, meaning that a significant portion of the gap could be closed with market-rate loans that are safe and sound. Rebuilding efforts must include efforts to close these lending gaps so that the Gulf region can attain a sustainable recovery based on increases in affordable, market-rate lending to traditionally underserved populations.

Inequalities in Small Business Lending

Market failure and discrimination contribute to inequalities by race and gender in small business lending as well as home lending. A rebuilding effort in the Gulf region must overcome the persistence of these failures if access to credit is to increase significantly for minority- and women-owned small businesses as well as small businesses located in minority and working-class neighborhoods.

The research generally concludes that discrimination occurs in certain loan markets and against certain small business borrowers. Using data from the Survey of Small Business Finances (SSBF), Mitchell and Pearce (2005) construct variables that reflect the degree of market concentration and variables that capture characteristics of the small businesses, including gender, ethnicity, creditworthiness, history of bankruptcy, and asset levels. They find that, after controlling for market and business characteristics, African- American and Hispanic business owners are less likely to have bank transaction loans than whites.

Similarly, Cavaluzzo, Cavaluzzo, and Wolken (2001) assess the likelihood of discrimination when controlling for multiple other factors. Supplementing SSBF data with creditworthiness data obtained from Dun and Bradstreet, they examined the connections among demographic characteristics of small business borrowers, market concentration, and the ability to access credit. A series of regression analyses revealed that increases in market concentration result in African Americans and females being more likely to experience denials of loan applications. Additionally, results show that African Americans and females are more likely to have unmet credit needs (as measured by a reluctance to apply because of possibilities of discrimination or actual rejection) when market concentration increases. After rigorously testing their models, Cavaluzzo, Cavaluzzo, and Wolken conclude that gender and race discrimination cannot be dismissed when assessing differences in credit application and denial rates. Moreover, their study suggests that consolidation and increasing market concentration can exacerbate discriminatory behavior.

In the Gulf region, as elsewhere across the country, federal regulatory agencies must take steps to promote a competitive lending marketplace offering a range of products, in order to protect against lending discrimination and/or significant fair lending disparities. NCRC's data analysis of the small business loans reveals striking inequalities in the Gulf region. During 2004, CRA-covered lenders issued 19,068 loans to the 50,288 small businesses located in minority neighborhoods (neighborhoods where more than 50% of the residents were minority) in Mississippi, as shown in Figure 12.3. Dividing the number of loans by the number of small businesses reveals that banks made loans to 38% of the small businesses in minority neighborhoods. In contrast, banks issued loans to 51% of the small businesses in predominantly white neighborhoods. If lenders had reached 51% of the small businesses in minority neighborhoods, just as they did in white communities, they would have made 6,588 additional loans worth $307 million to small businesses in Mississippi's minority communities during 2004.

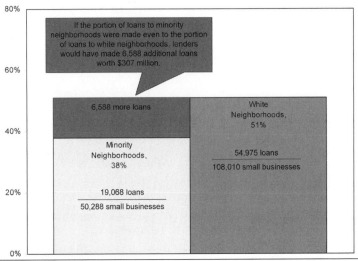

Figure 12.3 Percent of Businesses in Minority and White Neighborhoods in Mississippi that Received Loans in 2004

Inequalities in small business lending are slightly greater by income of neighborhood than by race of neighborhood. Figure 12.4 reveals that CRA-covered lenders issued 14,190 loans to 41,142 small businesses in low- and moderate-income neighborhoods in Mississippi during 2004 (that is, to 34% of the small businesses located in these neighborhoods). On the other hand, banks issued loans to 51% of the small businesses in

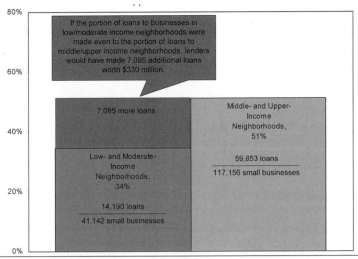

Figure 12.4 Percent of Businesses in Low/Moderate Income and Middle/Upper Income Neighborhoods in Mississippi that Received Loans in 2004

middle- and upper-income neighborhoods. If lenders reached the same percent of small businesses in low- and moderate-income neighborhoods as in middle- and upper-income neighborhoods, they would have issued 7,095 additional loans to small businesses worth $330 million in low- and moderate-income neighborhoods in Mississippi during 2004.

Even before the storm, economic inequality in small business lending was raging in Mississippi, and a Herculean effort would have been needed to eradicate these disparities. After the storm, an even greater effort is required to make sure that the credit needs of all small businesses are equitably met. While the private sector is the source of much of the inequalities, only the private sector has the resources to reduce, if not eliminate, the inequalities. The public sector does not have the resources to make the necessary loans to the small businesses in traditionally overlooked neighborhoods. For example, loans guaranteed by the Small Business Administration constituted only about 1% of the publicly reported small business loans (NCRC forthcoming). But the public sector has an important role to play in prodding the private sector to address these inequalities and make capitalism thrive in all communities by equitably meeting credit needs.

Inequalities in Bank Branching

Research has found that bank branches are critical to bolstering equity in lending, but significant disparities in branch location by race and income of neighborhood existed before the Gulf region hurricanes. In order to achieve a new era of equality and revitalization, the rebuilding in the Gulf region must address inequalities in bank branch location.

Bank branches are generally found to boost small business lending. A significant amount of small business lending, particularly for the smallest business, still features personal interaction between the loan officer and small business borrower at bank branches. Frame, Srinivasan, and Woosley (2001) report that the number of bank branches increases the share of small business loans in a bank's portfolio. Immergluck and Smith (2001) report that their research in Chicago reveals that banks with the highest percentage of their branches in low- and moderate-income census tracts make the highest percentage of their loans in these tracts, while banks with the lowest percentage of branches in low- and moderate-income tracts make the lowest percentage of their loans in these tracts. Squires and O'Connor (1999) came to similar conclusions in Milwaukee.

Even though home lending has become more automated and much home lending occurs over the phone, bank branches nevertheless reduce disparities in home lending just as with small business lending. A recent study by Federal Reserve economists revealed that banks exhibited fewer disparities in high-cost home lending to minorities when they conducted

Table 12.1 City of New Orleans Bank Branch Analysis, 2003

	Number of Branches	Percent of Branches	Number of Households	Percent of Households
Low- and Moderate-Income Neighborhoods	60	43.48	96,989	51.49
Middle- and Upper-Income Neighborhoods	78	56.52	91,376	48.51
Total	138		188,365	
Substantially Minority Neighborhoods	70	50.72	137,447	72.97
Substantially Non-Minority Neighborhoods	68	49.28	50,918	27.03
Total	138		188,365	

their home lending through branches than when they used brokers outside of their branch networks (Avery, Canner, and Cook 2005).

Despite the great benefits of bank branches, too many minority and working-class communities do not have an equitable share of them. New Orleans is a case in point. Before the hurricanes, bank branching by income and race of neighborhood was strikingly unequal there. Table 12.1 shows that 60 of the 138 branches (or 43.5%) were in low- and moderate-income neighborhoods, although 51.5% of the city's households resided in such neighborhoods. The mismatch was even worse by race of neighborhood. Just over 50% of New Orleans' bank branches were in substantially minority neighborhoods, but 73% of the city's households lived in those neighborhoods. In contrast, 49.3% of the bank branches were in predominantly white neighborhoods that were home to just 27% of the city's households. As an extreme example, the predominantly minority and lower-income Lower 9th Ward and St. Claude neighborhoods have just one bank branch, while bank branches are clustered around the tourist hub in the French Quarter and in predominantly white neighborhoods across the city (see Maps 12.1 and 12.2). Banks can make a powerful difference in building wealth and increasing access to fairly priced credit if they locate more bank branches in neighborhoods like the Lower 9th as New Orleans rebuilds.

Comprehensive Planning with Financial Institutions as the Engines for Recovery

In the wake of the hurricanes, media accounts have focused public attention towards government and charities as the entities that will lead the rebuilding of the Gulf region. While government has an important leadership

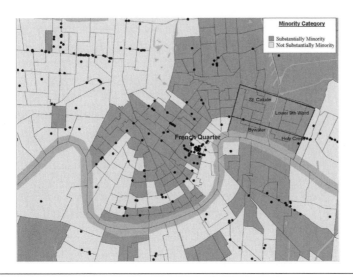

Map 12.1 Bank Branches in the City of New Orleans by Minority Level.

Map 12.2 Bank Branches in the City of New Orleans by Income.

role, relying on government alone to finance and plan the recovery will doom rebuilding to failure. The federal and state governments have neither the capacity nor the will to effectively finance the rebuilding on their own. Private-sector financial institutions have the resources and the obligation to finance the recovery and rebuild in a manner that overcomes the vestiges of redlining and discrimination in lending. Government has a vital role to play in directing and prodding lending institutions to finance an equitable and effective recovery.

There are two aspects of recovery that government financing alone will fail to completely address: assisting the hundreds of thousands of displaced families and business owners, and overcoming the patterns of fair lending inequalities. Media accounts focus on the first need, which is understandable, since the magnitude of displacement was overwhelming. However, more public attention needs to be directed at overcoming fair lending inequalities, since recovery efforts will not be sustainable if unequal access to credit and capital is not significantly overcome as well.

The displacement caused by Hurricane Katrina is on a scale that is unprecedented for any similar hurricane, and perhaps any disaster in United States history. Reports indicated that in Louisiana alone as many as 205,000 homes were destroyed and 35,000 were damaged (*Washington Post* 2005a). About 2 million families have been displaced by the hurricanes, and 1.6 million families have been approved for FEMA hurricane assistance. Of these, 800,000 households have received cash aid, and 519,000 families have received rental assistance (Hsu 2005). But what happens to these families after their temporary FEMA assistance runs out?

In response to this calamity, federal long-term assistance has varied from slow to inadequate. The Department of Housing and Urban Development (HUD) announced a program that would pay one year's worth of mortgage payments for upwards of 20,000 families (HUD 2005a). Financing would also be made available to repair homes. While this may be a good start, it pales in comparison with the hundreds of thousands of home owners lacking adequate home or flood insurance and in desperate need of financing or forbearance on their mortgage payments.

The Small Business Administration's (SBA) tepid response led *The Washington Post* (2005b) to dub the agency the Slow Business Administration. By early December 2005, the SBA had received 37,214 applications for small business disaster loans, but had approved only 2,127. It also set up an expedited program called GO (Gulf Opportunity) loans, but through the first week of December had approved only 10 of these loans

The SBA's disaster home lending program has been nothing short of a disaster. *The New York Times* (Eaton and Nixon 2005) documents that through the middle of December 2005, the SBA received 276,000 applications for emergency home loans, rejected 82% of the applications, and approved just 17,463 loans. To make matters worse, the approval patterns mirror the sad pattern of redlining. Of the loans approved, 47% were for families in affluent communities, while just 7% were for families residing in poor neighborhoods. A government disaster loan program should overcome the legacy of redlining, not exacerbate redlining.

So far, the federal response appears to be nothing more than quickly cobbling together ad hoc home and small business loan programs that cannot adequately respond to the overwhelming need for forbearance, new mortgage loans, and small business and home repair loans. Instead of reacting in an uncoordinated fashion, the federal government and state governments need to have comprehensive planning mechanisms in place that effectively estimate needs and then marshal government and private sector resources to meet those needs.

The first step for a comprehensive plan is conducting a thorough needs assessment. The assessment should include how many families need forbearance or loan modifications; how many owner and rental units were destroyed beyond repair; and how many units can be repaired. On the small business side, the needs assessment should include how many small businesses need loans to cover their cash flow requirements; how many small businesses can be repaired; and how many small businesses are beyond repair and need to be rebuilt.

After a tally has been developed estimating the number of modified and new loans that are needed, the second step in the planning process is to assess how much private- and public-sector resources will be allocated to the lending effort. In order to maximize the amount of available financing, the comprehensive plan should assume that the private sector will be meeting most of the needs for credit and capital. For starters, the plan can inventory how many loans are outstanding, in how many cases these outstanding loans can be restructured, and if dollars for repair needs can be added to the loans. The private sector should be asked to make as many unsubsidized loans as possible so as to maximize the leveraging of government subsidies. When government subsidies or insurance are required to assume risk, the planning effort should assess how to stretch the subsidies or insurance so as to reach as many families and small businesses as possible. These "shallow" subsidies should be used first so as to stretch government funding. Direct government lending programs should be used only when shallow subsidies cannot cover risk and motivate the private sector to make loans.

A comprehensive plan also needs to consider infrastructure and institutional issues. Should new structures involving banks and government agencies be created to make loans in areas suffering considerable amounts of devastation and loss of infrastructure? In other geographical areas not suffering the same degree of physical destruction, can a substantial amount of the lending be conducted through banks? The SBA was assuming its traditional role as a direct provider of disaster loans after Hurricane Katrina, although a number of banks were asking the SBA to empower them to directly provide subsidized disaster loans. The banks were asserting that they could operate the programs quicker and more efficiently than the SBA, which in the weeks after the hurricanes was scurrying around trying to hire loan officers from banks on a short-term basis (Reosti 2005).

After a major disaster like Hurricane Katrina, the federal response must be of the magnitude of the Marshall Plan or the GI Bill. The critical difference, however, between the current response and the historical responses is that most of the financing now needs to come from the private sector. The new era of Marshall Plans after a disaster must strategically employ government subsidies and guarantees to leverage private-sector financing that is exponentially greater than the public-sector recovery funding.

The current recovery efforts run the risk of lifting pockets of the Gulf region out of devastation, but leaving large swaths of the region economically devastated and impoverished for decades to come. Unless the course of disaster recovery changes dramatically, the impoverished and destroyed areas are likely to be those that were poor before the hurricanes.

Tools in a Comprehensive Recovery Plan—Short-Term

In the aftermath of Hurricane Katrina, the first questions involved survival: Where were the Gulf region's families and small businesses? Did they flee or did they ride out the storm? Did they still have their jobs? Soon after these questions were answered, another dilemma became apparent: Did these families have the means to pay their mortgages, and did they have houses left for which to pay mortgages?

A series of short-term and immediate crises present themselves after a devastating disaster. One such crisis is the real possibility of massive foreclosures. Freddie Mac (the Federal Home Loan Mortgage Corp.) issued guidelines requiring financial institutions with which it did business to suspend mortgage payments for 90 days (Freddie Mac 2005). Fannie Mae (the Federal National Mortgage Association) allowed lenders to suspend mortgage payments for 90 days (Fannie Mae 2005). The actions of Freddie Mac and Fannie Mae had a profound influence on lenders and other financial institutions because in any given year these two institutions purchase almost half the mortgage loans made by banks.

After the initial 90-day forbearance period expired in early December 2005, the federal bank regulators issued supplemental guidelines encouraging banks to work with residents on additional forbearance plans (FFIEC 2005). Some large lenders, such as Washington Mutual and Wells Fargo, responded by announcing an additional 90-day forbearance period (Carrns 2005). Freddie Mac required financial institutions with which it did business to suspend foreclosure proceedings through February 2006, which amounted to a second 90-day forbearance period (Freddie Mac 2005). HUD also announced a foreclosure moratorium on FHA mortgages through February 2006 (Department of Housing and Urban Development 2005b). However, there were disturbing reports that some high-cost lenders were demanding immediate payment after the initial 90-day forbearance period had expired and were threatening borrowers with foreclosure (Walsh 2005; Shenn 2005). In addition, early data suggest a looming problem with foreclosures. The *Los Angeles Times* reported that in Mississippi and Louisiana, respectively, 17.4% and 24.6% of mortgage borrowers were one payment behind; by contrast, the national figure was 4.4% (Gold 2005).

None of the stakeholders, including federal agencies, lenders, Fannie Mae, and Freddie Mac, have devised mechanisms to adequately deal with the real possibilities of widespread foreclosures affecting tens of thousands of people after forbearance periods expire. Freddie Mac and HUD responded commendably by establishing six-month forbearance periods, but their actions did not cover all mortgage loans, nor in many cases is a six-month period adequate for borrowers to get re-established financially. Banks are in a dilemma because nonperforming loans threaten their safety and soundness. And, in many cases, if banks foreclose, they will be acquiring physically damaged property whose future value is uncertain.

While forbearance is an immediate short-term issue, it also has profound longer-term consequences. If a mechanism can be devised that keeps consumers and lenders whole for extended periods after disasters, the amount of private-sector or public-sector subsidies needed to modify loans or extend new loans to cover missed payments could be dramatically reduced. Perhaps FDIC insurance for deposits is a model that can be adapted for disasters. The government could lead in the development of a public-private sector insurance fund available to protect homeowners, owners of rental property, and lending institutions from losses associated with foreclosures after a disaster.

Flood insurance is an existing mechanism designed to deal with disasters, but the scope of Hurricane Katrina threatens to render flood insurance coverage inadequate, particularly for the families that were incorrectly advised that they do not need flood insurance (Mullins 2005). According to industry sources, about 80,000–100,000 homeowners in areas devastated by Hurricane Katrina lacked flood insurance (Gold 2005). Not only are private insurance companies retreating from coastal areas (Hsu 2006), but the back-up federal flood insurance program also is inadequate (Drew and Treaster 2006). Perhaps the flood insurance programs could be kept in place for areas that are obvious flood plains, but another insurance mechanism could be developed that covers broader geographies. A nominal fee imposed on mortgage loans, paid by lenders, could develop a large enough pool of funds for such an insurance program.

Another short-term but highly significant issue after disasters involves the impact of missed mortgage or credit card payments on the creditworthiness of consumers. It is manifestly unfair for consumers to suffer significant decreases on their credit scores (which are numerical representations of their creditworthiness) if they missed loan payments due to financial hardship, job loss, and destruction of their homes at the hands of Hurricane Katrina. So far, the federal regulatory agencies and Fannie Mae and Freddie Mac have encouraged lending institutions to not penalize consumers for missed loan payments and to refrain from reporting any missed payment information to credit bureaus (the entities that develop credit scores) until conditions stabilize and the borrower can be reasonably expected to repay (Office of the Comptroller of the Currency 2005). But clearer guidance is needed regarding the length of time after disasters during which consumer credit scores are not negatively impacted. Lower credit scores significantly increase the possibilities that loan applications will be denied or that applicants will only qualify for higher-cost loans. Negative credit scores impacts consumers, home owners, and small business owners alike.

Tools in the Comprehensive Planning Effort—Medium- and Longer-Term

For the medium and longer term, a vital tool for the rebuilding effort in the Gulf region is vigorous enforcement of the Community Reinvestment Act. As noted above, CRA imposes an affirmative and continual obligation on banks and thrifts to meet the credit and deposit needs of low- and moderate-income borrowers and communities. Not only does CRA outlaw redlining, but it imposes an affirmative obligation on these financial institutions to aggressively seek out lending and investment opportunities in low- and moderate-income neighborhoods. A law that requires affirmatively meeting credit needs is well tailored for responding to disasters.

Banks and thrifts undergo CRA exams every few years that assess how many loans, investments, and services they make available to low- and moderate-income borrowers and communities. Banks of various asset sizes and with different specialties (retail versus wholesale institutions, for example) undergo different types of CRA exams on different timetables (see www.ncrc.org for more information). Banks receive ratings that reflect the quantity and responsiveness of their loans, investments, and services to low- and moderate-income communities. The exams and data on their home and small business lending activity are publicly available.

Community groups and members of the general public can comment on bank CRA exams and comment on banks' CRA performance when they submit applications for regulatory approval of mergers. The public availability of CRA exams and the public participation in the CRA process have increased the accountability of lending institutions, which has led to far more loans and investments in minority and low- and moderate-income communities (Bostic and Robinson 2003; The Joint Center for Housing Studies 2002).

Recently, the federal banking agencies have made changes to the CRA regulations and have addressed issues related to CRA points for banks financing disaster recovery efforts. Banks will now receive CRA points on their exams for community development loans and investments that assist designated disaster areas to recover economically by attracting and retaining businesses, home owners, and residents. The regulators established a one-year lag period after expiration of the official designation of disaster status, during which CRA points will be awarded for bank loans and investments. Moreover, the federal CRA examiners will award more CRA points for community development loans and investments that primarily benefit low- and moderate-income borrowers and communities rather than upper-income communities recovering from disasters. Banks will also receive CRA points if they finance projects assisting the recovery of low- and moderate-income neighborhoods damaged by the disaster or benefiting low- and moderate-income families that have evacuated damaged areas and are resettling in new localities (*Federal Register* 2005).

These new aspects of CRA regulations targeted towards disaster areas are promising. The potential of the changes, however, will not be completely realized unless they are implemented rigorously in a manner that maximizes the benefits to low- and moderate-income communities. CRA exams will be vital to determining the long-term benefits of the changes to the CRA regulations. If CRA examiners generously award CRA points to projects in disaster areas that would have occurred anyway, such as downtown development, and do not provide long-term jobs or other real benefits to low- and moderate-income people, then the new disaster-related regulation provisions will not be that helpful. On the other hand, if CRA examiners focus the new aspects of the regulations towards motivating banks to rebuild neighborhoods like New Orleans' Lower 9th Ward—projects that may not have been otherwise done except for the CRA prodding—then the new changes will be enormously beneficial.

The key to whether the recent CRA regulatory changes will substantially benefit low- and moderate-income individuals and communities recovering from disasters is heightened oversight by the general public and the Congress. CRA and federal banking law provide critical opportunities for community organizations and the general public to comment on bank CRA performance during CRA exams, merger applications, or at any time. (Banks must keep public comments on their CRA performance in their public files for three years.) If the public is active in commenting on banks' CRA performance, the chances increase that CRA examiners will conduct vigorous exams and that banks will significantly increase their lending and investing to low- and moderate-income families recovering from disasters. On the other hand, if CRA examiners and banks themselves operate quietly without public scrutiny, CRA exams have a tendency to become rubber-stamp documents that give a pass to banks making minimal efforts to serve low- and moderate-income communities. In this vein, Congress has an important role in conducting oversight hearings, on at least an annual basis, to review CRA exams for a sample of banks of different sizes. Oversight hearings should also ask tough questions about how and why CRA examiners awarded banks CRA points for various lending and investment programs, including bank community development financing after disasters.

The recent regulatory changes are just the beginnings of what needs to be done to change the CRA law and regulations in order to maximize safe and sound lending and investing in low- and moderate-income communities. Currently, CRA exams are incomplete in their scope. They scrutinize lending and investing activity in low- and moderate-income communities but do not explicitly evaluate financing in minority communities.

CRA exams generally confine their scrutiny to areas around bank branches, although banks now are making considerable numbers of loans through brokers and correspondents outside of their branch networks. If CRA is to ensure that credit needs of all communities are met, including communities afflicted by disasters receiving bank loans through brokers, then CRA must mandate rigorous exams of all geographical areas in which banks make significant numbers of loans.

Data disclosure remains incomplete and has also been cut back by other recent changes in the CRA regulations. In particular, CRA small business data are not sufficiently detailed and resemble the home loan data of 15 years ago, before Congress and the federal agencies significantly improved home loan data collection. In particular, the general public does not have information on the race and gender of the small business borrower, although the race and gender of the home loan borrower are publicly reported. Congress must pass the bill proposed by Representative Jim McGovern (D-MA) that would require the disclosure of the race and gender of the small business borrower. The federal regulators actually deleted small business loan disclosure requirements for mid-size banks (those with assets between $250 million and $1 billion). These banks are important small business lenders in medium-sized cities and rural areas that characterize the Gulf region. Restoring and augmenting data disclosure will aid the region's recovery. Publicly exposing continuing disparities in home and small business lending will motivate lenders to take additional steps to reduce the disparities and increase their lending to traditionally underserved populations.

Lastly and importantly, the reach of CRA throughout the financial industry needs to be expanded. CRA applies to only banks and thrifts. It needs to be applied to large credit unions, independent mortgage companies, insurance firms, and securities companies. If CRA were expanded, it would cover trillions of additional dollars in the financial industry. Its power to contribute to comprehensive plans for disaster recovery would increase exponentially. Moreover, a strong CRA applying across the financial industry would ensure that minorities and low- and moderate-income communities were the center of recovery efforts, instead of being left out once again.

Conclusion

Recovering from disasters, combating concentrated poverty, and successfully revitalizing redlined communities requires the leadership of the public sector but the financial commitment of the private sector. The public imagination, fueled by media reports, assumes that the public sector and charities will take care of rebuilding the Gulf region. This is an outdated paradigm that is not feasible politically or economically. Private-sector financial institutions, including banks and nonbank financial institutions, have the resources and the obligation to finance a sustainable regional recovery.

The financial sector, while contributing some to the rebuilding of the devastated Gulf region, has yet to address the inequalities between minorities and whites that were magnified by the hurricane's damage. Yet, the legacy of redlining and discrimination motivated Congress three decades ago to impose an affirmative and continual obligation on banks and thrifts to meet the credit and deposit needs of low- and moderate-income families and communities. CRA has led banks to substantially increase their loans, investments, and services to minority and low- and moderate-income communities. However, much work remains to be done to rectify persistent inequalities in the Gulf region and across the country, as demonstrated by the data presented in this chapter. A renewed effort to vigorously enforce CRA and equitably implement the recent regulatory changes to CRA so that it will direct financing to areas afflicted by disasters is the key to financing broad-based recovery that includes populations normally left out. The amount of credit and capital available to minority and working-class communities would increase exponentially if CRA is expanded to include nonbank financial institutions. Further, there is a critical need to encourage other financial institutions, such as pension fund managers and securities companies, to make more capital available to lower-income micro-economies.

This chapter has also argued that developing comprehensive planning mechanisms will mean the difference between ad hoc efforts doomed to failure and sustainable recovery after disasters. The response to Hurricane Katrina demonstrated that the federal government lacked advance planning capabilities and infrastructure that would have made possible a rapid and equitable response to the devastation of the hurricanes. In order to effectively meet future disasters, the federal and state governments must develop agencies and infrastructure that rapidly meet immediate needs for shelter and food. The federal government must also establish mechanisms, whether they are additional insurance funds or some other arrangement, that offer suitably long loan forbearance periods after such disasters.

The federal and state governments must establish planning mechanisms that quickly estimate needs for home, small business, and economic development loans and investments. After public agencies have estimated these needs, they must work through the institutional arrangements they have with the private sector. Banks and other financial institutions must make the great majority of needed loans and investments, while federal agencies provide subsidies and risk-sharing guarantees when necessary. Only in this manner will the recovery effort be broad-based and equitable.

Government-led comprehensive planning is required to deal with disasters because needs are immediate and overwhelming. But comprehensive planning will achieve long-term recovery only if government agencies, philanthropies, corporations, financial institutions, and nonprofit organizations work in an intentional and collaborative manner to impact areas of concentrated poverty. In addition, long-term recovery depends upon the rigorous enforcement of CRA and the fair lending laws in order to motivate financial institutions to assume their roles of financier of the recovery. Capitalism works only when all communities have access to credit and capital, whether they are recovering from disaster and/or trying to escape concentrated poverty.

References

Avery, Robert B., Glenn B. Canner, and Robert E. Cook. 2005. New Information Reported under HMDA and Its Application in Fair Lending Enforcement. *Federal Reserve Bulletin* (Summer): 344–394.

Bostic, Raphael and Breck Robinson. 2003. Do CRA Agreements Increase Lending? *Real Estate Economics* 31(1): 23–51.

Calem, Paul S., Kevin Gillen, and Susan Wachter. 2004. Neighborhood Patterns of Subprime Lending: Evidence from Disparate Cities. *Housing Policy Debate* 15(3): 603–622.

Carrns, Ann. 2005. Banks Extend Mortgage Deferrals For Gulf Coast Hurricane Victims. *Wall Street Journal*: A16. December 12.

Cavaluzzo, Ken S., Linda C.Cavaluzzo, and John D. Wolken. 2001. Competition, Small Business Financing, and Discrimination: Evidence From a New Survey. *Journal of Business.*

Department of Housing and Urban Development. 2003. HUD Strategic Plan FY 2003-2008. http://www.hud.gov/offices/cfo/reports/03strategic.pdf.

_____ 2005a. HUD Announces Mortgage Assistance for Disaster Victims. December 5. http://www.hud.gov/news/.

_____ 2005b. HUD Extends Foreclosure Moratorium for FHA-Insured Homeowners in Hurricane Affected Areas: Additional Relief Granted to Victims of Katrina and Rita. November 23. http://www.hud.gov/news/release.cfm?content=pr05-161.cfm.

Drew, Christopher and Joseph R. Treaster. 2006. Politics Stalls Plan to Bolster Flood Coverage. *New York Times.* May 15.

Eaton, Leslie and Ron Nixon. 2005. Loans to Homeowners Along Gulf Coast Lag. *New York Times.* December 15.

Fannie Mae. 2005. Fannie Mae Announces Mortgage Relief for Hurricane Rita Victims. September 26. http://www.fanniemae.com/newsreleases/2005/3616.jhtml?p=Media&s=News+Releases.

Federal Financial Institutions Examination Council. 2005. Agencies Encourage Insured Depository Institutions to Continue Efforts to Meet the Financial Needs of Customers Recovering from the Aftermath of Hurricane Katrina. Press Release. November 30. http://www.ffiec.gov.

Federal Register. 2005. Vol. 70, No. 147, August 2, pp. 44256–44270 and Vol. 70, No. 217, Thursday, November 10, p. 68450.

Frame, W. Scott, Aruna Srinivasan, and Lynn Woosley. 2001. The Effects of Credit Scoring on Small Business Lending. *Journal of Money, Credit, and Banking* 33 (3): 813–825.

Freddie Mac. 2005. Bulletin: All Freddie Mac Sellers and Services. November 30.

Gold, Scott. 2005. Waning Days of Grace for New Orleans Homeowners. *Los Angeles Times.* December 26.

Hsu, Spencer S. 2005. FEMA Official Criticizes Trailer Plan for Evacuees: Lump-Sum Payments to Victims Urged. *Washington Post.* December 9.

Hsu, Spencer S. 2006. Insurers Retreat from Coasts. *Washington Post.* April 30.

Immergluck, Dan and Geoff Smith. 2001. *Bigger, Faster...But Better? How Changes in the Financial Services Industry Affect Small Business Lending in Urban Areas.* Chicago: Woodstock Institute.

Mitchell, Karylyn and Douglas K. Pearce. 2005. *Availability of Financing to Small Firms using the Survey of Small Business Finance.* Washington, DC: Small Business Administration. May.

Mullins, Luke. 2005. Baker Pitches Bill: Agency to Buy Storm-Hit Property. *American Banker.* October 21.

National Community Reinvestment Coalition. Forthcoming study for the Appalachian Regional Commission on small business lending.

Office of the Comptroller of the Currency. 2005. OCC Information Related to Hurricane Katrina. November 28. http://www.occ.gov/hurricaneQA.htm#Credit.

Reosti, John. 2005. Gulf Storms' Demand Has SBA Seeking Bank Help. *American Banker.* November 4.

Shenn, Jody. 2005. Prepayment Fees Latest Issue in Gulf. *American Banker.* December 23.

Squires, Gregory D. and Sally O'Connor. 1999. *Access to Capital: Milwaukee's Continuing Small Business Lending Gaps.* Milwaukee: University of Wisconsin-Milwaukee.

The Joint Center for Housing Studies. 2002. *The 25th Anniversary of the Community Reinvestment Act: Access to Capital in an Evolving Financial Services System.* Cambridge: Harvard University. http://www.jchs.harvard.edu/publications/pubs_year.htm.

Walsh, Bill. 2005. More Bad News at a Bad Time: Subprime Lenders are Getting Nasty. *The New Orleans Times-Picayune*. December 11.

Washington Post. 2005a. The Great Default. December 8.

_____ 2005b. Slow Business Administration. December 9. A-30.

Endnotes

1. NCRC uses CRA Wiz, produced by PCi Corporation (http://www.pciwiz.com/) to analyze HMDA, CRA, small business data, and Census data.

CHAPTER 13

The Role of Local Organizing

House-to-House with Boots on the Ground

WADE RATHKE AND BEULAH LABOISTRIE

A Generator Kicks in on Jourdan Avenue on New Year's Eve

At midnight on New Year's Eve, four families stood in front of their houses on Jourdan Avenue in the deepest part of the now infamous Lower 9th Ward of New Orleans. The fog was everywhere as it collected from the Mississippi River only blocks away and from the Industrial Canal a mere few feet away from what was left of a limping and failed levee. With them were ACORN (Association of Community Organizations for Reform Now) organizers and leaders who had worked to see this night come after four months of fighting all comers since the storms. After Katrina, the entire area had increasingly been written off, seeming to go down for the count time after time, yet now it was spiritedly bouncing back.

The weather was not cold, but it was wet and damp. Near midnight, when elsewhere in the city fireworks traditionally lit up the sky, the families nodded silently as ACORN Services turned the crank on a generator at the back of a panel truck with "ACORN Mobile Action Center" painted on its side. Suddenly there were lights—and life—everywhere in four Jourdan Avenue houses. These were the first houses revived in an area inexplicably barred from entry by armed National Guardsmen and New Orleans Police barricades. This section of the Lower 9th Ward had been near one of the several breaks in the Industrial Canal, and water had poured through in sudden and lethal waves, obliterating houses, families, and everything else in its way.

The factors that brought these first families back home on New Year's Eve speak to the critical fight being waged by grassroots organizations trying to bring New Orleans back. It speaks to the critical role that must be played by local organizers in the reconstruction and the fight to obtain a future for communities where low- and moderate-income families, especially African-American ones, live and work.

Running from the Storm

ACORN has operated its national headquarters from New Orleans since 1978 after opening its New Orleans office in 1975. In its 30+ years, New Orleans ACORN built an organization of 9,000 dues-paying families rooted in virtually every part of the city. New Orleans ACORN had played a strong role at every level of local social, economic, and political life for years, leading efforts to raise the minimum wage, winning lead abatement, reviving abandoned houses, increasing home ownership, and engaging neighborhood improvements and participation at every level.

Suddenly, at the ebb of the storm, ACORN found itself unmoored from its members, its offices, its staff, and every landmark along the way. A disproportionate number of the over 480,000 residents who now became part of the great New Orleans diaspora were the low- and moderate-income ACORN families and their neighbors in communities throughout the city.

This was a city with a long history of hurricanes, with names like past generations of Hollywood starlets—Betsy and Camille particularly— names not common now, but on every tongue around 40 years ago. People were veterans. They didn't cut and run when the storm hit. Most people did end up leaving, though others were caught, not so much in the storm, but in the unexpected floods as the levees collapsed. So for hundreds of thousands of people, most dramatically in the Superdome and Convention Center, but most prosaically everywhere else, there was suddenly a "city in exile." People had just the clothes on their back for a couple of days on the road, and were now trapped outside of the storm line, unable to return for some indeterminate amount of time, glued to television news, Google maps, and newspapers, trying to divine the amount of water that might be in their bedrooms.

People and Property

Local organizing starts on the block and moves from house to house as families come together in the neighborhood or unit to unit in buildings and housing projects. People come and go due to a whole variety of reasons—work, welfare, whatever—but the address is there, and the family leaving will be replaced by another one, not so unlike the one before, moving in behind them. Years of organizing produces lists on turn-out, meetings, issues, phone calls, fundraisers, dues payers, and sundry other categories. A database pushes them all together in categories that allow leaders to survey, committees to call and assemble, and organizers to constantly massage and visit.

Then, overnight, it was washed away. And, just as suddenly, community organizers for whom it is *all about people* were also caught in the paradox of having depended, perhaps too much, on property, with populations defined as much by physical space as by personal contact. The addresses may still exist or they may have washed away. Phones no longer operated, rendering hundreds of call and walk lists immediately useless. Cell phone towers were down and would be so for months. Lower-income people rarely had e-mail addresses before the storm. Almost any tool used in the past to connect people with each other suddenly became useless. For ACORN, as one example, the real answer to the riddle of how one finds 9,000 families is that you cannot. Amazingly, however, the several thousand members who were paying their dues by bank draft in New Orleans have been totally steadfast, without one cancellation!

This problem affected every level of public life. Elections were delayed due to the inability to locate the citizens in the diaspora. Red Cross lists have been either spotty or nonexistent. FEMA has refused to release names and addresses to any private or public authorities because of privacy rights guarantees, and one doubts that they have any information other than the address of residents to which they sent checks.

The collapse of many social networks in the absence of communication and the ways in which people were still able to reach out to others is one of the most interesting—and unexamined—phenomena rising from Katrina, and is likely to still play a huge role in whether or not the city can come back from this tragedy. Yet the mobilization to rebuild social and community networks is huge. A Chevron retiree meeting had double the normal attendance at its first meeting three months after the storms. A community garden club trying to meet for the first time in a Gentilly neighborhood had a record crowd and drew attendance from as far away as Lafayette and Baton Rouge. In December 2005, new member sign-ups in New Orleans led ACORN nationally and surged, responding to ACORN's leadership on the ground and their struggles to reclaim their neighborhoods.

Faith-based organizations faced perhaps more difficult challenges. Without direct memberships, except through religious institutions per se, their gatekeeper was the priest, nun, or pastor of the physical institution. When these institutions were washed away, frequently the clerics were gone with them. The Methodists had 60 pastors in New Orleans who were left churchless. Reverend Fred Luther, pastor of the 7,000-member Franklin Avenue Baptist Church, the largest African-American congregation in the local Southern Baptist denomination, had to preach from Birmingham and throughout the South, and the doors were shuttered until after Thanksgiving 2005, when the first cleanup efforts began. In New York City, I ran into a Muslim imam whose mosque was located several blocks from our office. He said he would be stuck there for quite a long time.

The crisis faced by faith-based community organizations like People Improving Communities through Organizing (PICO) and the Industrial Areas Foundation (IAF), both of which had affiliates in the New Orleans area, was acute. Their support and their base were institutional. When the congregations washed away, the institutions no longer existed, and neither did the base under them. PICO in particular joined with ACORN during the crisis and worked on several important events. PICO also managed to assemble several meetings of its pastoral base in Washington, where it witnessed and lobbied effectively. The IAF reached out in a rare collaborative gesture, offering to follow ACORN's lead on issues around housing and mortgage financing. In an act of solidarity, the Gameliel Foundation, which does not organize specifically in the New Orleans area, was generous in its financial support for ACORN's Hurricane Recovery and Rebuilding Fund. The challenge faced by all community organizing efforts is captured in the irony that in a time when people most need a voice and are called on to act, the obstacles faced by the scattering of so many people diluted the voices when they most needed to be heard.

Other local community-based institutions fared no better. Unions were decimated. The strongest, United Teachers of New Orleans, faces termination of 7,500 public school workers' jobs. Construction and trade locals are merging with their Baton Rouge counterparts, since they either cannot fill job calls because their members are scattered or face the loss of their traditional contractors and therefore work. Local 100 of the Service Employees has faced layoffs of City workers, garbage workers, transportation workers, and janitorial workers. The nonprofit sector was devastated. The Zoo, Aquarium, United Way, and Catholic Charities, all of which had been forces in the community, find themselves in deep restructuring and experiencing massive layoffs. Ironically, as the demand for services has increased, the suppliers of social services have collapsed.

What worked? Nothing well! But some things have taught us lessons for the future.

New Orleans ACORN was able to set up the technology to send out text messages to otherwise inoperable cell numbers and received 200 replies from all around the country. Text messaging works even when normal cell service collapses. Who knew? Immediately moving a message board on the ACORN website (www.acorn.org) allowed people to reach out to each other. The website also became a rallying spot, attracting offers of help and support.

Given the collapse of local institutions and infrastructure, the value of national organizations, networks, and relationships in supporting local work acquired tremendous importance. In ACORN's case, having offices throughout the region suddenly took on new meaning, because it meant that there were offices, leaders, and organizers in what had suddenly become the evacuation route of the diaspora—not only in Louisiana, but also in Little Rock, Dallas, San Antonio, Atlanta, Birmingham, and Houston. As buses pulled into the Astrodome in Houston for example, ACORN members waving ACORN flags and wearing ACORN t-shirts were able to quickly identify members from New Orleans caught in the crises. Parachuting a dozen housing counselors into Houston from the ACORN Housing Corporation meant that we could handle the myriad issues around mortgages, credit, and daily concerns that people now suddenly found themselves confronting. Similarly, Scott Reed of PICO told us that he and many of their national network staff had been dispatched to Louisiana to support their affiliates in the aftermath of the storm. The IAF worked hard to leverage its historic presence in Texas cities to connect to evacuee efforts, particularly in Houston.

The backbone and heart of a membership organization like ACORN was demonstrated as thousands of members from every office called, volunteering to take in brother and sister members if they somehow showed up in this or that city, whether San Francisco, Vancouver, New York, or points in between. The generosity of the requests was overwhelming and heartwarming. The membership immediately understood it was about people, not property, and responded accordingly. As hard as it was to locate New Orleans ACORN members around the country, it was easy to find ACORN members in all of our cities who had opened their homes. At an organizing committee meeting in Houston shortly after the storms, 12 of 15 people present reported that they had Katrina survivors living with them at the time. New Orleans people have been located by simply going door-to-door in some lower- and moderate-income neighborhoods in Houston, Dallas, Atlanta, and Little Rock. Big issues and policies all boiled down quickly to person-to-person human needs and responses. Not a lesson exactly, but a reminder that is invaluable.

Surprisingly, the day-to-day requests created a tension not easily resolved between the "home" team and the "away" team. New Orleans ACORN wanted to see families allowed a voice and a way to come home, which was readily supported. At the same time, sitting in a shelter, members wanted to get out of a public facility immediately, regardless of the location. Balancing the New Orleans demand of the *right of return*, while at the same time demanding adequate care now in the "host location," continues to be a policy paradox and pressure point between well-meaning, yet contentious, interests.

The City of Houston, under Mayor Bill White, stood as an interesting organizing contrast to Mayor Kip Holden of East Baton Rouge Parish. Hardly a week had passed since Katrina made landfall when Mayor White stood in front of a crowd of New Orleans evacuees and supporters from Houston ACORN at a September 9th Town Hall Meeting—prepared with specific proposals and resources to address the immediate demands he knew he would hear about, including housing and food cards for host families. Throughout the crisis, White seemed to bend over backward to accommodate every demand and *keep* the Katrina survivors in his city. In daily 8:00 A.M. meetings that included ACORN, business leaders, and other civic authorities, White would crack the whip to move goods and services to evacuees, with speed and efficiency being the first premium, ahead of equity. Without waiting for FEMA, the City of Houston stood behind one-year rental commitments to fill the city's backlog of vacancies through the apartment association, where 9,000 units had stood open before the hurricanes. Hundreds of our members have told us how hard it is to come home until they have "spent" the year of rent provided by the City.

On the other hand, Baton Rouge, which had even more refugees than Houston, seemed virtually to resent the intrusion, the traffic, and everything but the sudden income from so many additional residents. There was no outreach or welcome or real assistance. The location of the first FEMA trailer park on the outskirts of East Baton Rouge Parish in Baker, far from jobs and transportation services, was emblematic of the problems there. Inevitably, putting people at the center of these plans depends on the strength and capacity of local organizing—and, it turns out, local government as well. The weakness of our New Orleans city government was crippling, but we learned interesting lessons from our neighbors.

Doing What Had to be Done

As the community imploded, there was virtually no area of its operation that did not collapse and require citizen action and intervention. The infrastructure's demise was transparent, like looking at a skeletal x-ray. Quickly, for example, there were no schools, and therefore no children. Then there were no charter schools because children were the ultimate source of money; and then, before one knew it, one could telescope the future for five years because the charters could not be re-evaluated until the end of such a period, when once again people would be able to vote. Over and over again in New Orleans, we see institutions stripped bare. The organizing response was different in every case. Here are some examples from the ACORN experience:

- *Mortgage and Credit Issues:* ACORN and the ACORN Housing Corporation (AHC) began making calls immediately after the storm surge to prime and subprime mortgage-holders in order to first secure a 90-day forbearance period and then an additional extension into 2006. Most large companies quickly agreed, even on the subprime side, led by Ameriquest. Scofflaws like Ocwen Mortgage and Homecoming Mortgage that attempted to skirt the agreements or add on prepayment penalties were immediate targets and folded quickly. The problem was huge and real: Where people owed mortgages and had been outside of the flood plain, but were now underwater with levee failure, how would they satisfy the mortgage, maintain their credit, and start over? Where would mortgage-holders settle, while allowing a family's credit scores to be maintained at pre-Katrina levels, giving them the opportunity to either rebuild or start over? When ten AHC housing and loan counselors arrived at the Houston Astrodome and Convention Center to assist the ten already on the ground, they were inundated with questions that will continue to be asked for months and years after the storm, which all swirl around these basic realities and uncertainties. Interestingly, HUD initially requested a multimillion-dollar proposal from AHC to provide a similar set of services throughout the evacuee footprint, but then quickly reneged, saying only that they were budgeted out and that FEMA would not support such services to evacuees. Within weeks of the storms, ACORN officials met with a top officer of one of the world's largest banks the day after it had written off more than $200 million in the Katrina footprint, about the problem of land-banking and mortgage and loan problems in the recovery and rebuilding. He frankly replied that because they did not have much of an investment in the area, he had not really given the problem any thought. It was sobering to find one of the world's unique disasters simply part of the mundane background noise of New York. These will be issues for years.

- *Organizing Survivors:* An ongoing organizing challenge has been to create organization and support for evacuees from city to city. There are few states that have not received evacuees, but the overwhelming concentrations are in Louisiana, Texas, Arkansas, Georgia, and elsewhere in the south. The IAF was active early on in Houston, seeking to mobilize support in that city around resources for the shelters. PICO and its Louisiana affiliates organized an early meeting in Baton Rouge of hundreds from its statewide church network to demand action from Governor Blanco. ACORN initially began by organizing "town hall" meetings in over 30 cities around the country, from California to New York, but largely in the Katrina evacuee trail. In Delaware, ACORN demanded a new emergency evacuation plan. In Portland, ACORN won opening of the shelters on a 24-hour basis. These town hall meetings focused on examining how the issues of race and class played out in these cities, compared to what people were seeing and experiencing in New Orleans. The meetings in Texas, Georgia, Arkansas, and Mississippi laid the groundwork for building the ACORN Katrina Survivors Association. In Houston, a meeting of over 300 evacuees launched the efforts there. In Baton Rouge, meetings were held with hundreds within days of the storm. The vast depopulation of New Orleans was met with a surge in other cities, and organizers and leaders, particularly those who understood the issues because of local relationships and national networks, responded quickly and aggressively.

- *Meeting Immediate Issues:* FEMA has been a moving target in many early campaigns. New Orleans in the early period was more of a "federal" city than Washington, DC. FEMA ran the show and paid the bills, from picking up garbage to street clearance to the individual checks that made it possible to both run and then stay away from the city. The National Guard provided the early security for the city and its vast and vacant acreage. A critical role has been played by lawyers, particularly Bill Quigley and his associates at the Loyola University Law Clinic, who filed, with ACORN and other groups as plaintiffs, to win early halts to tenant evictions and to bulldozing certain neighborhoods, and produced other procedural victories that were critical in winning the time to create the space for organizational work. Houston ACORN led two large direct actions of frustrated evacuees at the regional FEMA headquarters to win support of faster housing assistance. Dallas and San Antonio ACORN similarly pushed for housing guarantees on the same basis created by the Houston initiative in advance of the FEMA stall. Actions by groups of all descriptions have pushed FEMA steadily on the issue of providing trailers for temporary housing in the neighborhoods. Initially, FEMA had proposed virtually permanent relocations in neighboring states and throughout the diaspora, but fairly quickly direct community action on one hand and the rapidly worn-out welcome from our neighbors led a slow movement back to locations as near to home as possible in neighborhood parks, lots, front yards, side alleys, and anywhere else a trailer might fit. The provision of vouchers and support for hotel rooms has been an interesting struggle. FEMA has announced several dates for evictions, and thus far had to retract its threats every single time. Actions by evacuees in all of the cities have produced results here. The problem with FEMA as a target is that by definition it is an emergency and temporary presence, no matter how powerful, and therefore operates from the premise that it can run from accountability with impunity.

- *Making a Plan for the Rebuilding:* It quickly became clear that residents of many of the devastated communities were desperate to begin rebuilding and return home, but lacked the information and tools to evaluate the nuts and bolts of how to achieve these goals. They were also standing in a gale-force wind whipped up by developers, the local newspaper, and others that were sending the message that it was foolhardy to return and that bulldozing whole neighborhoods was the real solution. The ACORN Community Forum on Rebuilding New Orleans, held at the LSU Conference Center on November 7–8, 2005, and cosponsored by the LSU School of Art and Design, the Pratt Center in New York City, and the Cornell University Planning Department, brought together 50 top experts around the country in engineering, disaster planning, architecture, job creation, and urban planning, paired with 50 survivors from New Orleans. Thousands more participated via webcast (www.acorn/katrina.org) in 30 cities around the country where evacuees were living. The overwhelming professional opinion that emerged from the forum was that the heart of the problem was levee failure which resulted from poor design and construction, and that it could be repaired to meet security needs in all neighborhoods. The overwhelming opinion from residents is that they wanted a voice, they wanted the right to return, and they wanted help in rebuilding their homes and lives in New Orleans. Partnerships for the future were constructed to make plans, particularly in four key areas that were the subject of the forum: New Orleans East, the 9th Ward, Gentilly, and Upper Carrollton-Hollygrove.

- *Campaigning on the Right to Return:* Within this mandate, the project beginning at the aftermath of the storms and likely to continue for many years in the future revolves around winning the right of return for residents. The overriding concern has been to secure a voice for residents in and outside of New Orleans about their issues and needs around returning. The first issue related to actions by FEMA officials in Texas and Louisiana and had to do with the pace and progress of relief efforts. The need for FEMA-provided trailers *in* the city has been central to allowing people to return to jobs that may still remain in the city, and access to homes that desperately need constant attention and repair. Preventing further deterioration of the housing stock has also been an overarching concern. One issue concerned the provision of "blue tarps" by FEMA for use as temporary cover for damaged roofs. Amazingly, it turned out that, at the same time that 50,000 tarps had been provided along the Gulf Coast, there were only 7,000 in New Orleans. Research done by ACORN found that FEMA subcontractors were not able to tarp roofs of slate or asbestos tile, both of which are ubiquitous in the older housing stock of New Orleans, leading ACORN to demand a change in standards. It became clear quickly that a program to support the "right to return" was essential. The ACORN Clean-Out and Demonstration Project sprang from this concern and the earlier community forum. If clusters of homes could be assembled in the four targeted areas that were among the hardest hit, and we could prove that houses could be cleaned out, saved, and prepared for rebuilding for residents at a reasonable price—which we set at $2,500 per property—then at the ground level we could offset the grandiose visions of destruction being promoted by so many businesses, developers, and conservative forces. The ACORN Project focused on a goal of 1,000 houses, and within weeks, soaring demand and constant lines in the Elysian Fields headquarters as the office re-opened made us revise the program to 2,000 homes, assuming resources could be found. Volunteers were recruited both locally and from college campuses, including University of Connecticut, Sarah Lawrence, Cornell, Columbia, and now hundreds of young people from Tulane, Xavier, and other local institutions as they return to the city.

- *Taking the Fight on the Road:* One of the constant demands of citizens which has emerged at one community meeting after another inside and outside of the city has been to "speak truth to power." Within a month or so of the storms, a delegation of PICO ministers went to Washington, DC to meet with the Louisiana congressional delegation. Similarly, ACORN dispatched survivors from Baton Rouge, Houston, Dallas, and Little Rock to Washington and to one expert conference after another to express their emotions (including rage) and offer ideas for addressing the disaster. In February 2006, ACORN led a delegation of 400 survivors to Washington to hearings sponsored by Senator Mary Landrieu and a number of individual Congresspeople. This list does not include hundreds of other meetings, conferences, press calls, neighborhood tours, and all manner of activity where in many cases ACORN members are the only people on the ground and in the community who can speak to and represent life—and the struggle to live—in the city today. Local organizing in many ways has become the social fabric tying together a far-flung people, their homes, and their hopes for their community.

House to House

During the ACORN Community Forum on Rebuilding New Orleans, several things became crystal-clear. One was that the levees had failed, in one of the engineers' words, because "everything that could go wrong did go wrong." There were structural, design, and construction flaws in the levees. They had not been overtopped, they had been undermined. This was something that could be fixed to an acceptable level, and if that was achieved, then, with other adaptations, communities could be habitable again—all of the communities.

Despite the fact that a confluence of natural forces and human frailties combined to flood the city in the *aftermath* of the hurricane itself, these events offered opportunities for assorted special interests to attempt to achieve what they had sought *before* the storm, using the storm as rationalization for their advocacy. Developers, "new urbanists," the whiter, richer "Disneyland by the River" advocates, school "reformers," good government wonks, the hospitality interests, and the financial interests on Poydras Avenue could all push forward in the void created by the storm to advance ideas that had been disregarded and vetoed in the past. Slum clearance would have a place in public policy again. Near-town public housing projects like Lafitte and Iberville could finally be captured for mixed-use, upper-income developments because of their proximity to the

French Quarter, as long advocated by developer Press Kabacoff. Schools could be seized in the name of the crisis. As James Reiss, a prominent Uptown voice, indicated to the *Wall Street Journal*, this was the opportunity to create a whiter and richer city. Reiss, to everyone's shock, became a member of Mayor Nagin's committee reviewing recovery, which has led this whitewashing effort under the leadership of mega-developer Joe Canizaro. If this is reminiscent of anything, it is the same strategy used by President Bush in exploiting the tragedy of 9/11 to pursue a grudge match war in Iraq. This has become the policy of non sequitur. Such a program could also win by default, because no action, and no resources, meant that nothing would happen. Developers would be able to come in and buy up the properties from hapless owners and landlords for a pittance. Unless we could prove that people could and would rebuild these houses in these areas, that would be the future. To counter such policy initiatives created in boardrooms, behind government halls and ivy walls, could only be trumped on the ground, house by house.

Here the order of the chicken and the egg was clear. Any rebuilding first depended on stopping the deterioration from the flood-ravished homes from advancing further through inaction. No repairs on the roofs meant more water damage from the topside in New Orleans' heavy rainfalls. The city's humidity also meant that unless the houses were opened up, aired out, and treated now, mold would take over and make the repairs either prohibitive or small-scale biohazards for the returning residents. If families trying to come home to their properties could be married to some ability to stave off further damage, then rebuilding would be possible. It would take a grassroots effort, but the grassroots were in one place and the properties were in another.

ACORN had some advantages. The creation of the ACORN Institute's Hurricane Recovery and Rebuilding Fund meant that we had some immediate resources we could make available to prime the pump. Individuals had pitched in more than $300,000 on the Internet. Our partners in housing and lending programs and other ventures had contributed more than a million dollars. One key donor invested a critical million into the organizing program to contact the survivors. Other foundations, large and small, contributed additional resources to assist ACORN's headquarters to be reconstructed so that we would be back in full-scale operations quickly. The Catholic Campaign for Human Development and similar church-based programs pitched in to support offices in the impacted areas. The Tides Foundation made an appeal through their Shelter Fund to support the ACORN Clean-Out and Demonstration Project.

ACORN also had people to do the work, and do it well, quickly, and as cheaply as possible because of its network of contacts and experience in housing development in New York, Phoenix, and Chicago. Most critically, ACORN also knew the people who wanted to come home. The investment in increased organizing capacity in Louisiana and Texas, as well as the growing ACORN survivors' network, meant that we were in touch with hundreds and thousands of families who were looking to come home and needed a hand to help make it there. The goal of cleaning out more than 1,000 houses by the end of March 2006 in four critical areas—9th Ward, New Orleans East, Upper Carrollton-Hollygrove, and Gentilly—seems well within reach if the resources become available. Each house clean-out costs $2,500. In the first month, 200 houses were done, and ACORN is scrambling to raise the millions and prove our point: Houses can be rebuilt, people want to come home, and the city can live again. Others are less happy, and the reasons are clear. City inspectors, police, and others stop the ACORN vehicles regularly now as small pockets begin to establish larger beachheads and then expand rapidly into small cores, proving that the neighbors and the neighborhoods can make it.

Fight for the Future!

In the muddle of "non sequitur" policy making, nothing has become more freighted with both conflict and importance than the question of a "shrinking footprint" for the city. Mayor Ray Nagin appointed a committee to advise him on a host of subjects, not only about rebuilding but about other flashpoints for various elites in the city. The consultant hired by big-time developer Joe Canizaro, the Mayor's Committee Chair, was the Urban Land Institute, which he had previously chaired. What is at stake now has become more obvious with the revelation of the Urban Land Institute's report. The ULI recommendations to the Mayor's Come Home Committee have earned the controversy they have stirred for reasons both simple and complex. At the simplest level, they are arguing for a staged developmental process in which the highest ground is privileged over the rest of the city, and they are doing so with a *noblesse oblige* attitude, which amounts to a cavalier cynicism. In a poor and financially strapped city, their recommendations are transparent. There is *no* money for one stage of development, much less three. Their argument that properties should be purchased at pre-Katrina prices is purely gratuitous. All of that is mere subterfuge, fooling few, but allowing developers and elites camouflage for their agendas. Their recommendations become clearer as one examines their fundamental anti-democratic bias. The ULI does not want the citizens to vote on these plans, fearing the outcome will be less than perfect planning. Furthermore, they want to continue the program of post-Katrina authoritarianism, which has destroyed the public school system and created the largest charter school system in the country. They want to have the finances of the city and its redevelopment taken out of the hands of public officials and put in an unaccountable body. The ULI and its gang really don't like New Orleans as they understand it, and see the city, its citizens, and its culture as much of a problem as the ravages of the storm. Members of the ACORN Katrina Survivors Association struck a responsive chord when they turned out to denounce the ULI plan at each stop of the national tour of hearings conducted by the Bring Back New Orleans Commission.

Months of fighting have proven that there is deep grassroots resistance to the developers, their bulldozers, and their tract house dreams. The endorsement by any elected official of such a blatant land grab would guarantee a quick exit from elected office. Instead, there is now a dangerous dare on the table—part bluff and part brass. Communities, and the home owners and renters living there, would have a year, maybe two or three, to see what kind of progress can be made in any area anywhere in the city to try and rebuild and come back. The developers and big shots would then determine by an unknown set of standards whether an area has demonstrated that it is coming back or not. Presumably, part of the measurement will be the simple one: Are people living there? Joe Canizaro argued earlier in the process that the communities that make it should be supported and the neighborhoods that don't should be bought out and essentially "cashed out" for the cost of their effort.

Looking forward from 2006, the fight seems clear, even if grossly unfair. If we can prove that our neighborhoods can be rebuilt where they are, and the way people want them, then we win, which means that we get to live in New Orleans, too. But whether we like the deal or not, we have no choice but to play, because the stakes are essentially "winner take all," and fortunately, every house counts, and it will be a house-to-house battle. We are now winning, even against the odds. But we are only winning in the neighborhood, not in the public debate. Finally, the more boots we can put on the ground, the better our chances of success.

Today, the fight is still rearguard. Every day our crews with ACORN Services and our organizers doing the clean-outs are also advising home owners of what they need to do in order to prove that their house was less than 50% damaged, and therefore eligible for repair—and insurance! Every day we are forced to measure the progress in inches while trying to travel miles. On the one hand, we are buoyed by the constant offers of help from architects, planners, lawyers, students, filmmakers, and others who want to help the citizens and save the city, while on the other, we still count the areas without electricity and gas in miles. We have ceased to believe that telephones are anything other than quaint rarities. We venture to the

West Bank or Metairie and look at all the activity of the city the way it was, as if we were foreigners now traveling in a strange land.

For the 5–10 houses now being saved by the project every day or the 1,000 or 2,000 we hope to handle in the Demonstration Project, we realize there are 100,000 that need the same work. Meanwhile, years will be spent begging, borrowing, and stealing the resources for these houses. If these houses are saved, then where does the money come from for the next steps: rebuilding the sealed and protected shell up to the point where a family can move back in again? There the deck is stacked once again, but the current round has to be won in order to get to that next high-stakes pot.

The actual recommendations to Mayor Ray Nagin cut the timeline for determination to a four-month planning process in 13 individual districts, some of which still have virtually no residents, to determine the plans for people to return. This part of the process appears to have no hope of success given the unrealistic mission and preposterous timeline. The committee additionally recommended that no building permits be issued during the period in order to try and stop continued development. The Mayor was quickly forced to abandon that recommendation, and the City Council unanimously passed a resolution continuing to demand that *all* areas of the city be rebuilt.

In some ways there is now a face-off between one elite faction drawing castles in the air against ground troops of determined residents in one neighborhood after another sticking to their ground and facing the future and forcing the planners' mirage to be reshaped in the light of the residents' homes and stubborn, determined vision. Grassroots efforts in Lakeview, a white, upper-middle-income redoubt, have forced the Mayor's hand as he tries to find a future. A similar gritty effort in New Orleans East organized around the Maria Goleta Parish, without a working church but with the strong support of the local chapter of All Congregations Together, the PICO affiliate, inspires the same hope, along with all of the other efforts in different communities.

Vote by Vote

There is only one equalizer, and here local organizing has the opportunity to finally level the playing field, though again the odds are long.

Elections, for local, state, and federal offices, despite fierce voter anger, likely will not produce seismic differences in the players because the field is weak, underfunded, and confused. This is obviously not a normal situation.

Demographically, New Orleans was around two-thirds African-American, and new estimates are that the city may be less than one-third African-American. The actual outcome of the elections over the next several years may rise and fall on the power of the absentee ballots case by evacuees in cities around the country, and their willingness to continue to see themselves as New Orleanians. Once again, this is where the other side of the ACORN coin toss lands heads-up, because it allows the fight to be waged on a different battleground outside of the usual boundaries of normal elections. If New Orleans voters can be found and mobilized for these elections, particularly in Houston, Dallas, Atlanta, and other large evacuee locations, then the political reality will not be just located on the high ground away from the flooding, but also on the low ground where New Orleans once thrived. Politicians would be forced to campaign on their abilities to bring people home, not their willingness to kowtow to developers, tourism moguls, and Uptown wannabes. Leveraging the ability to get to voters where there are no lists, mailing addresses, phone numbers, or even televisions, against the best package of programs, policies, and resources that will help a family and its community rebuild their homes and neighborhoods, could give ACORN and its allies a real opportunity to finally win back the city.

There is going to continue to be a constant tug of war between interests, both of class and race, over the future of the city. This impact will not be limited solely to New Orleans. Jefferson Parish will face the same post-Katrina election impact in two years. Governor Blanco will win or lose her 2007 re-election effort based on the long shadow of the storm. Senator Mary Landrieu would be difficult to re-elect if there is no longer a New Orleans with an overwhelmingly African-American and Democratic voting bloc. Everything changed, but at the same time, the demand to return, the demand for a voice, and the rising expectations of government will mean that there will be no easy way to predict elections or the shape of the electorate for quite some time. This may not be what the business elites and financial forces want, but it will be the reality in New Orleans, south Louisiana, and therefore much of the rest of the state for a long, long time.

When you are moving from house to house, family to family, neighborhood to neighborhood with boots on the ground, what finally makes the difference may not be the money, may not be the planners, may not be the FEMA maps, insurance dollars, but the strength of new and existing organizations that are moving forward daily to meet a special situation and circumstance. The people are moving with their gloves on to rebuild the city, but when it comes to protecting their homes and community, there is every reason to believe that in the coming years, the gloves are coming off.

Thank goodness!

CHAPTER 14

Rebuilding a Tortured Past or Creating a Model Future
The Limits and Potentials of Plannng

PETER MARCUSE

A story in *The Wall Street Journal* (September 8, 2005) right after Katrina sets the stage:

Despite the disaster that has overwhelmed New Orleans, the city's monied, mostly white elite is hanging on and maneuvering to play a role in the recovery when the floodwaters of Katrina are gone. "New Orleans is ready to be rebuilt. Let's start right here," says Mr. O'Dwyer, standing in his expansive kitchen, next to a counter covered with a jumble of weaponry and electric wires.

A few blocks from Mr. O'Dwyer, in an exclusive gated community known as Audubon Place, is the home of James Reiss, descendent of an old-line Uptown family. He fled Hurricane Katrina just before the storm and returned soon afterward by private helicopter. Mr. Reiss became wealthy as a supplier of electronic systems to shipbuilders, and he serves in Mayor Nagin's administration as chairman of the city's Regional Transit Authority. When New Orleans descended into a spiral of looting and anarchy, Mr. Reiss helicoptered in an Israeli security company to guard his Audubon Place house and those of his neighbors.

He says he has been in contact with about 40 other New Orleans business leaders since the storm. Tomorrow, he says, he and some of those leaders plan to be in Dallas, meeting with Mr. Nagin to begin mapping out a future for the city.

The power elite of New Orleans—whether they are still in the city or have moved temporarily to enclaves such as Destin, Fla., and Vail, Colo.—insist the remade city won't simply restore the old order. New Orleans before the flood was burdened by a teeming underclass, substandard schools and a high crime rate. The city has few corporate headquarters.

The new city must be something very different, Mr. Reiss says, with better services and fewer poor people. "Those who want to see this city rebuilt want to see it done in a completely different way: demographically, geographically and politically," he says. "I'm not just speaking for myself here. The way we've been living is not going to happen again, or we're out."…

So the "monied, mostly white elite" is "mapping out a future for the city." That is not consistent with how democratic planning should be done. Is there a better way?

The argument of this chapter is simple:

- A massive planning effort is required to deal both with the causes and the consequences of the disaster that followed Katrina.
- The principle guiding the planning effort should not simply be subservience to the desires of the "monied, mostly white, elite," sweeping the area's past problems under the table and its poorer residents out the door.
- The principles guiding that planning effort should be based on a process that provides: (1) democratic participation, and (2) equitable distribution of costs and benefits.
- The resources needed to implement such planning will also be massive, and should largely come from the federal government.
- The Congressional Black Caucus' Recovery Bill is thus far the closest to confronting the requirements of that process.

And beyond New Orleans:

- The goal should not be restoration of the status quo before Katrina, but rather moving towards making the cities and region affected a model of what American communities should and could be.

The State of Present Planning

The desires of the "power elite," or at least a substantial part of it, have been discussed in detail elsewhere, including editorial pages from *The New York Times* to *The Nation,* and criticized as an effort to rebuild the city with "fewer poor people," meaning also fewer African Americans, solidifying by policy what Katrina did by force. Few of us involved professionally or politically in planning would like to see that approach dignified by the name of planning. Mapping out a better future for the city, not accepting the inequalities and injustices of a backward-looking elite, is what good planning, in theory, is about.

But going from theory to practice can be very hard. What planning, and professional planners, can contribute to improving city life is very much dependent, in the first place, on who is in charge of the planning. The cast of characters in the Gulf Coast is broad. It now includes, at least formally, Mississippi Governor Haley Barbour's Commission on Recovery, Rebuilding and Renewal; Mayor Nagin's Bring Back New Orleans Commission; Governor Blanco's Louisiana Recovery Authority; and a committee of the New Orleans City Council. And each has its consultants, some paid, some volunteer. Each city in the region, of course, has its own land use regulations, and most have city planning commissions, or at least zoning boards, that have jurisdiction to a varying extent over land uses within their borders. The opportunities of planners to do planning ought to be tremendous—as the need for planning certainly is.

The American Planning Association (APA) and its professional affiliate, the American Institute of Certified Planners (AICP), certainly see the problems of post-Katrina planning as a direct challenge to the profession to show its worth. And various groups in the planning field have not hesitated to go to the Gulf Coast and develop plans for reconstruction. Perhaps most important, in terms at least of their formal connections with the governmental machinery, are the Urban Land Institute (ULI) and the Committee for a New Urbanism (CNU). All devote considerable attention to preservation of historic structures and espouse principles of equity and environmental sustainability. APA's involvement, as might be expected, is strong on the role of planning, applying established tools to the new situation. The ULI, as might be expected, is development-oriented, and sees casino development as a necessary linchpin for that purpose. The CNU proposals, as might again be expected, recommend concentrated, well-designed, suburban-type development in both reconstruction and new construction. Other proposals are more focused on housing provision, as those developed with ACORN (the Association of Community Organizations for Reform Now) are, or concentrate on engineering to protect against hurricanes and floods (e.g., levees, construction minimizing impacts if flooding occurs, such as houses on stilts or shotgun houses), planning for hurricane and flooding protection and impact minimization, or transitional measures (e.g., pre-fab housing).

Yet, in real life, it is not professional planners who make the planning decisions, who "map out the future for the city." Power in New Orleans and the Gulf Coast lies, in general, primarily with the monied, mostly white elite, those at the top of the hierarchies of class and race. But it lies not only with those elites at the local level; it lies also with their parallels nationally, and indeed internationally: the multinational oil companies piping oil out of the Gulf and through pipelines in the Gulf wetlands to refineries on the coast; the shipping firms using the ports and the inland waterways, most of all the Mississippi River; the casino owners, hotel chains, and entertainment impresarios thriving on the tourist industry; and the real estate owners and developers whose land ownership and land use patterns are so directly involved in what happens. All these have interests that include the local, the national, and the international in various mixes.

Of course, these holders of power do not act unrestrained. It is rare that any are as blunt as Mr. O'Dwyer's *Wall Street Journal*-quoted comments. They are aware that others, the local and state political leadership in particular, have a stake in what happens, and have some ability to influence its results. And in turn there is some recognition that those who elect that political leadership must also be taken into account—the voters, who comprise citizens of different classes and races. Towards the bottom of the totem pole, but also of necessary concern, are those who provide the labor to make the area's businesses function: the dockworkers, the waiters and chambermaids, the croupiers, the social service providers needed to keep the workforce going, the teachers, the police and fire personnel needed for public safety, the construction workers. And at the bottom of the list are the foreign workers, sometimes undocumented, who in fact are being brought in increasing numbers to do some of the necessary labor, from oyster-shucking to construction.

Given this unequal distribution of power—and it is widely acknowledged that New Orleans is one of the most polarized communities in the country—what can professional planners contribute to the decisions the planning process is supposed to help frame?

Planners are not a homogeneous group, and there are many different approaches within planning theory to what planning is, ought to be, or can be. But, four approaches relevant here can be separated out:

- **Realistic Planning**: Planners can be realists, accept the prevailing distribution of power, and devote themselves to making the results that the powerful desire flow more smoothly and efficiently in the areas in which planners conventionally have influence: land use regulations, zoning, environmental requirements, transportation routes, building codes. To take casino development as an example, a realistic planning approach simply acknowledges the power of the interests involved and their aim to produce a profit from their operations. Planning is then used to optimize access to the casinos, provide parking, choose attractive locations, etc.

- **Compromise Planning**: Planners can try to bring people together and forge compromises that, as far as possible, satisfy the parties. Such planning frequently refers to "stakeholders" as the key participants in decision-making, often treating all stakeholders as equal, and attempts to mediate any conflicts among them and achieve an objective at least minimally acceptable to all. In the casino case, a compromise planning approach would try to bring casino owners and their immediate neighbors together—in the Gulf case perhaps together also with representatives of environmental groups, of other tourist-related businesses, and of municipal (hence taxing) authorities—to forge an acceptable plan.

- **Ameliorative Planning**: Planners can try to produce plans that, within the limits of the calculated possible, produce the best results and ameliorate the worst results, judging best and worst in terms of their own values and the ethics of the profession. Those ethics, in the Codes of the APA and the AICP, speak of "serving the public interest," "dealing fairly with all participants," and "expanding choice and opportunity for all persons, recognizing a special responsibility to plan for the needs of the disadvantaged and to promote racial and economic integration" (American Planning Association 1992; American Institute of Certified Planners 2005). In the casino case, it might mean minimizing the adverse environmental impact of casino development, making sure the casinos do not preempt all the waterfront to the exclusion of public access, and pushing for affordability in housing, all with the tools available to planners and within the limitations of what the existing distribution of power makes possible.

- **Advocacy Planning:** Planners can examine the existing distribution of power and decide to cast their lot with those who have the least power, specifically with those who have the least access to professional planning services, and become their advocates. Rather than seeking an elusive public interest, they would dedicate themselves to the service of underrepresented groups as their clients, making as their objective insertion into the planning process the defense of these groups' interests. In the casino case, it might mean working with organizations of poorer residents and "minority" groups pressing to maximize affordable housing, public access to the waterfront, provision of living-wage jobs, without concern for protecting the interests of casino owners/developers, assuming those interests will be well represented elsewhere in the planning process.

All of these approaches have been represented in the Gulf Coast discussions. Planners working for casino interests, for instance, see themselves as simply being realistic about what will happen. Some academically-based planners, and to a significant extent the CNU, are simply concerned to bring people together, compromising among diverse interests, and getting implementation underway, although there is always a presence of their own values and goals in the background (or in the foreground, as with the CNU's new urbanism ideology). The ULI groups, while basically development-oriented—as is the ULI itself—seek to ameliorate the negative aspects of development wherever possible. The APA includes both the compromise and the ameliorative viewpoints. Advocacy-oriented planners are a minority among those involved, although ACORN has pulled together support from a number of quarters, including the Planners Network (a three-decades-old national organization of progressive urban planners) and some academically-based planning teachers and students.

All of these approaches, however, see themselves constrained by the existing distribution of power, whether they simply accept it or try to influence it at the margins as they go along. Looking beyond the limitations of the power status quo in favor of what is seen as ideally desirable in each approach, plausibly, as utopian planning, although it continues in a line of thinking that has always been present within the long history of planning. In the best of the utopian tradition, ideals are developed that are based on moral values but link to ingredients of the present order, hopeful experiments, demands, groups, or organizations whose desires are not constrained by the apparently possible. It could be argued that all "good" planning should begin with such a view of what the ideal would be, then go on to see how closely it could be achieved and what parts might have to be surrendered, given the prevailing realities of power and influence. The approach might be called "ambitious planning," and the values it seeks to implement are those of social justice.

- **Ambitious planning:** Planners would not expect that an ideal socially just planning process and result is immediately attainable, but would rather commit to a plan that is clear on what ultimately the most desirable process might be, and then to try to come as close to it as possible. They would then seek to approach the results such a process would hypothetically produce. Moving from such an ideal to professional practice would obviously involve at least an understanding of what the realistic constraints are, what ameliorative measures are immediately practicable, what compromises are necessary along the way, and, most of all, what advocacy, community organizing, and direct confrontation with power relationships should be considered. The gap between what is practicable and what is desirable would be constantly exposed.

Ambitious, socially committed planning would feature three overriding principles, already expressed in the profession's Code of Ethics:

- Planning should be **democratic** (which is complex, but doable if the will is there);
- Planning should be **equitable** (which involves both justice and adequacy, and requires redistribution);
- Planning should be **practical**, and thus resource-conscious (which involves political organization and a focus on the federal government, the only level where real redistribution can take place), but pursue a long-term vision of a truly desired result.

In the casino case, this might mean looking at alternatives both to casinos as an economic motor and to casinos as a use of waterfront and high-amenity locations, allowing casinos only if they are democratically approved (other alternatives being on the table) and if their benefits are equitably shared within the community.

How, then, would an ambitious, socially-oriented planning program aim to fulfill these principles?

Democracy in Decision-Making

All of those affected should be involved in the decision-making process. Everyone and his or her brother/sister is beginning to make suggestions as to what should be done, long-term, to New Orleans and the Gulf Coast— from House Speaker Dennis Hastert suggesting abandoning the city to President Bush talking of immediately starting the reconstruction. Planners are taken by the idea of regional approaches, although the difficult issues of participation that would be involved in such planning are clear. Yet little positive has emerged on how such a planning process might be concretely undertaken; frequently, handpicked representatives of stakeholders are assembled for advice that can be either accepted or rejected by those actually making decisions. And those affected but not present—i.e., the hundreds of thousands displaced by the Katrina and Rita—are rarely even considered stakeholders in the discussions. One solution to that particular aspect of the problem might be to make the planning process people-rather than place-based: Ask those displaced where they might want to live, and consider relocation planning (perhaps even on a national basis) as much a part of the planning process as in-place reconstruction.[1]

Try this thought experiment. Take the estimated $32 billion needed to "rebuild" New Orleans in a sustainable fashion (the estimates vary widely, but for this purpose that is unimportant). Divide it by the population injured by Katrina—say, 500,000. That's $64,000 each, $128,000 per (conservative) household average. Give each household that money. Would the levees be rebuilt? Would a new town be founded? Would the risk of staying be taken, minimum repairs made, and the money used to buy cars for the car-less, send children to college, bring families out of poverty? Or would the money be used to start a new life elsewhere?

Democracy here really has two aspects: individual and collective. It means each individual should be able to have his or her individual preferences respected so far as is possible within the framework of collective decisions collectively arrived at. In the case of New Orleans, it means, in the first place, that the choice, for those displaced, of whether to return or not must be left to each household. In order for that to be a realistic choice, compensation for loss should not depend on whether the household moves back to the city or not; it should be based on person, not place.

It means, in the second place, that a process must be devised which allows for collective decisions about major issues. There is substantial experience in how to promote participation in planning. Normally, it involves providing full information to all affected; opportunities for discussion with planners and policymakers; outreach to make sure involvement is broad; hearings, meetings, consultations, charettes, focus groups, and "Listening to the People" sessions—ultimately, fully democratic voting arrangements. In the Katrina case, however, these requirements, difficult as they are to implement under normal circumstances, are thrice compounded by the dispersion of those affected, the limited resources available for ensuring participation, and the inequalities in the way available resources are distributed. And that is largely an organizational question.

There are now a number of efforts to organize and give the poor of New Orleans a direct voice in replanning the city. They face major obstacles: not only an elite that has very different ideas from theirs (see the *Wall Street Journal* quote above), but a federal government not known for its concern with equity, and a constituency that is largely dispersed at the moment and thus hard to organize. They, and their allies, need the political muscle to win the major role in replanning New Orleans that a democratic process would require.[2]

There are grounds for some pessimism. The planning being implemented as of mid-2006 seems to be in the hands of giant global engineering firms, including Bechtel National Inc. of San Francisco and Fluor Corporation of Aliso Viejo, California (Lipton 2005). But some innovative suggestions for the use of newer technologies could be a big help in doing much more: email listservs, discussion sites on the web, teleconferencing, etc. The addresses of almost all in the diaspora are known, if only through FEMA applications, and their involvement, as well as their support for efforts to help them organize, can be pushed much further than has been the case to date.

Equity in Distribution of Costs and Benefits

Focus resources on economic development for the poor. Federal involvement in rebuilding after Katrina has obvious economic development implications, and, in view of the lamenting about poverty and racism generally featured in those efforts today, a focus on how federal expenditures could contribute to reducing poverty, rather than just compensating for it, would be in order. That would involve a variety of programs:[3] paying decent wages on all reconstruction work; combining hiring with job training where needed; seeking out employment opportunities for the unemployed; planning infrastructure investment so as to foster the best job creation possibilities; and targeting subsidies where job creation possibilities are most promising.

More generally, many planners and planning organizations see casinos, and tourism in general, as the major economic development machine for the Gulf region. The ULI proposals, for instance, go in this direction, and many political leaders see the tax revenues from tourist-related activities as central to meeting their needs. But this view is not based on any in-depth analysis of the alternatives: where else investment might go, with what costs and what benefits — specifically, how the majority of those in the region (the poor and lower-income households, African Americans and Hispanics, immigrants and noncitizens) would be benefited. If economic development increases the gap between the wealthy — including investors, speculators, and land owners — and the majority of the residents, it is not equitable development.

Beyond equity, adequacy of support: A safety net and beyond is needed. The country is wealthy enough to be able to guarantee all its citizens, not only a safety net that keeps them above starvation and homelessness, but a standard of living appropriate to live a life with human decency and the potential for self-fulfillment. Economic development, with benefits shared equitably, is a step in this direction: Provisions such as minimum wage laws, living-wage laws (Gertner 2006), health and safety standards in employment and housing, fair labor standards, the right to organize, and protection from discharge or eviction without fault—all can contribute to this goal.

Face up to the distributional trade-off issue. Risk assessment is a large field, and means are largely available to give at least working assessments of the risks associated with various kinds of disasters, and of the likely consequences of each level of risk. Some basic principles that should be applied are obvious: Put human lives above property damage, aid to the poor above compensation to the well-off. To draw policy/planning conclusions from a risk assessment, trade-offs have to be assessed. For any given risk, they involve at least three estimates: The damage (in human lives—how measured? property damage vs. social damage, etc.); the cost of avoidance or prevention; and the benefit to be gained by using preventive measures prior to the likely disaster. In each case, there are distributional questions involved, value judgments implicitly or explicitly made. What values should be used in comparing human lives to economic benefits? Economic benefits are not distributionally neutral and cannot simply be averaged over a population. What's good for "the city" will have different impacts on different groups within the city. And that pertains to both benefits and costs: Both are unequally distributed by class, race, gender.

The compensation issue. Presumably, substantial sums will be made available to help repair the damages and compensate for the loss of life after Katrina. The approach used after 9/11 offers both good and bad ideas. The basic assumption was that government should absorb the entire loss incurred by anyone who lost relatives or dependents, or property or income. It is an interesting challenge to try to formulate clearly to what circumstances that policy should be applied. We speak generally of "disasters," but is this only a matter of scale? (But what scale: 1,000 persons? 500? x dollars, or x lives?) Of "avoidability?" (But any disaster could have been avoided if those affected had not been in its way.) Of "natural" rather than manmade disasters? (But no disaster is entirely natural, as the title of this volume asserts.) The damage of Katrina is at the less debatable end of the spectrum of possibilities. The broad coverage of the response to 9/11 should apply there, too.

On the other hand, the Victims Compensation Commission established after 9/11[4] determined that compensation for loss of life should be based on earning capacity lost, following the rules of tort law. That means the survivors of those with high income received more than those with low income, hardly an equitable result. Likewise, large property owners received more than small property owners, and owners in general were compensated where tenants were not. Where justice lies here is not an easy question, but the 9/11 solution evades it; it reflects no search for an equitable distribution of compensation. An equitable rule would start with the recognition that all damages are not alike. Some business losses were covered by insurance. Many knew the risks they were assuming, were able to cover themselves against prospective loss, and have questionable claims for public assistance (distribution of emergency aid is in a different category). In general, one might differentiate between those who were exposed as a matter of a calculated risk and for a calculated profit, and those who were there simply because they had no choice, economically or socially. The most obvious analogy in the Katrina case is the discrepancy in the handling of losses to owners, judged by the value of the property lost, and to tenants, whose interest in a particular place they may have lived in for many years is disregarded. In economic terms, exchange values are regarded, but use values are not. That discrepancy is made even worse by the practice of granting loans based on standard measures of good credit. When 82% of all SBA loan applicants are turned down for inadequate credit or income (*The New York Times*, December 21, A38), something is seriously wrong.

Again, there are grounds for pessimism. The Administration initially decided to suspend the Davis-Bacon Act on post-Katrina reconstruction projects, a law that requires construction jobs funded by federal dollars to pay a prevailing wage (in New Orleans, $9/hour). Even that is below the level that would lift a family of four above the poverty line. It took substantial pressure to get the Administration to reverse itself, but its attitude is a taste of its approach to the problems. At its very best, the Administration's proposals might simply reproduce in place a social order conceded to be inequitable and undesirable. At worst, they would lead to "fewer poor people," in Mr. Reiss' phrase, simply by excluding them from participation entirely.

How Practical Can Such Planning Be?

Substantial—primarily, federal—government resources are essential. The resources for most of the recovery effort must come from government, not private profit-driven sources. Disaster recovery is not a job for the private sector. It was by permitting the market to establish land uses and locations that nature's hurricane was converted to a manmade disaster. It was the private sector's market-led polarization of incomes and the reflection of private discriminatory patterns in governmental actions that led to the racially- and class-skewed negative impact of Katrina. What's needed now is action, and resources, that will undo and compensate for what the private sector, acting through the market, did. This is no reflection on the private sector—it is doing what it is supposed to be doing, producing development that is profitable, not producing equity or distributing resources based on need. That is not to say that the private sector has no role to play. The private sector is able to move more swiftly, and more flexibly, than government, under many circumstances. Not all circumstances, of course: Military rescue operations, for example, may be more swiftly carried out and better coordinated than private operations, given their high technological level, their back-up resources, and the manpower available to them. The issue of when private firms can do a better job than direct government work is a complex one (Sclar 2000), and it is not here suggested that all work should be done directly by government employees or agencies.

However, where private sector action is appropriate, direct government regulation is a sine qua non. The profit motive should not be allowed to dictate what is done: where, for whom, or how. Provisions like the Davis-Bacon Act regulating wages on government building contracts; moratoriums on foreclosure and eviction; Community Reinvestment Act requirements for investment in what the private sector considers higher-risk areas; perhaps excess profits taxes or limits on speculation — all are necessary to make the private sector function in an optimal manner from a social point of view. Health and building code provisions are other long-recognized examples of necessary government regulation. And of course land use planning is inevitably a governmental function. None of these regulations denigrate the private sector; they simply recognize the different motivating forces behind private and public action.

But beyond regulation, direct government resources—whether in money subsidies, contracted or direct labor, or materials or land—are necessary where private households' resources are inadequate to achieve a decent standard of living for themselves. The need for a social safety net is widely recognized, and after a disaster like that which followed Katrina, only government can guarantee it. The private sector, perhaps nudged on by government, may delay foreclosure when a mortgage is unpaid by a family that has lost its home, but the private sector will not replace that home. As well, only if work will produce a profit for the employer will it provide the jobs with which income can be earned to make mortgage payments. Certainly, the private sector should be encouraged to find and take opportunities to make money and thus provide jobs, but if it does not, it is unreasonable to expect mortgage lenders to forgive mortgages or extend payments indefinitely. Given the levels of poverty among those affected by the disaster, the need for additional resources is inescapable, and can only be met by government.

Beyond aid to individuals, the large-scale public works required in any serious reconstruction effort are necessarily public responsibilities. No one is suggesting that the private sector pay for the levees needed to protect New Orleans, nor for the canals or the drainage of low-lying areas or the restoration of wetlands. It has indeed been suggested that the oil companies and other large commercial enterprises benefiting from such public works contribute to their costs, and the billions of dollars made by oil and shipping companies as a result of the ability to raise prices after the disaster would suggest the fairness of such a requirement. But it would have to be enforced by government. The private sector will not volunteer to pay.

"Government" in this case means the federal government, both for subsidies and for regulation. Only the federal level of government has the necessary resources for the job. The resources of the cities involved are inadequate to deal with the catastrophe, as are the resources of the states involved. The City of New Orleans had to lay off 3,000 City employees in the aftermath of the disaster, and state governments are similarly strapped. Mississippi is the poorest state in the country, Louisiana the fourth poorest. Simply on this account, the biggest share of governmental support must come from the national government. Further, only at the national level can a real socially-oriented redistribution of resources take place; decentralization of fiscal responsibility is inherently regressive in tendency. The national government must make the needed resources available. Decisions as to allocation should be made democratically; and resources should be directed to the local level (local in terms of those affected, not those in place after Katrina). As to regulation, the susceptibility of local regulation to private business pressures was well known in cities like New Orleans before Katrina. Any improvement in practices should logically—if not always successfully—be expected from the federal government. At least more people are watching.

Don't slough off public responsibilities to private entities. That certainly goes for privatizing planning or land use controls, or reconstruction and relief efforts. Essentially, firms like Halliburton and Bechtel should not be directing the process (Dreier 2005). But it applies to nonprofit groups too. The Red Cross and the Salvation Army and countless voluntary and charitable organizations have contributed mightily to helping out in the present emergency. It has long been public policy in the United States to try to maximize the role of private nonprofits, at least in the social service sector. But there is a growing disquiet, more visible in Europe than here, that such policies lead to an abdication of public responsibility and are motivated by efforts to hold down public costs, and taxes, rather than to provide better or more efficient services. There is an ideological component to the encouragement of private charitable contributions for disaster relief as a substitute for public responsibility, linked to opposition to raising taxes for the same purpose. Yet public disaster relief and planning are classic arguments for an active public sector.

Conclusion: The Congressional Black Caucus Effort

Can all this be put together? What's needed is a massive planning effort,[5] based on principles of democracy and equity, with the resources to implement it. What are the possibilities?

As of this writing (mid-May 2006), the closest to a plan that tries to meet the requirements of democracy and equity and provide the resources to implement them is to be found in the legislation introduced by Congressman Mel Watt (D-NC) and the 42 members of the Congressional Black Caucus (CBC), a bill that now has 91 co-sponsors (http://thomas. loc.gov/cgi-bin/query/z?c109:H.R.4197:).[6] It operates at the level of government—the federal—essential for obtaining the necessary resources. It is really a plan—in the best sense of the word—with implementation elements. There are other proposals as well, from ACORN, from the ULI and the CNU (with all their shortcomings), from PolicyLink (Reardon 2006),[7] from various academic and professional studios, and from individuals. But the CBC proposal—the Hurricane Katrina Recovery, Reclamation, Restoration, Reconstruction and Reunion Act of 2005 (H.R. 4197 of the 109th Congress)—is the most comprehensive, concrete, and detailed example of what a group at the center of government, concerned both with democracy and with equity, and knowledgeable about the distribution of power, thinks is feasible. It places the reconstruction issues squarely in their political context, and is practical insofar as (and only insofar as) there is political organization behind it.[8]

Examining their bill also permits a comparison with what a more ambitious proposal might eventually look like. Table 14.1 summarizes the bill. It provides for a Victims Compensation Board, to return to their previous economic status those families who lost members in the disaster. It deals with the return of residents to their prior locations; with the related problems of health; and with the provision of funding for community development through existing government agencies. It expands educational funding; deals with voting rights; modifies provisions regulating financing; adds funding to the Small Business Administration with a focus on job creation; and concludes with a call to the President to plan for the elimination of poverty in the United States. It is detailed in authorizing funds where needed for each of these purposes.

The bill of course was prepared in the context of a conservative Congress and a conservative Executive, whose expected additional spending for the war in Iraq in 2006 substantially exceeds the amount bruited about as the maximum to be made available for Katrina relief ($85 billion as of mid-2006). Yet the provision of over $30 billion (albeit out of the $62 billion already authorized in the immediate aftermath of the hurricanes) to

Katrina-related expenditures in the Defense Reauthorization Budget Bill passed in December 2005 is seen by staff of the CBC as implementing some of the portions of its bill, and the CBC plans to continue its pressure to push its objectives in the next Congress. The bill deliberately avoids establishing any new administrative structure, so as to avoid charges of merely expanding big government.

It is understandable that the bill, given its context, is not more ambitious. Yet it may be worthwhile to explore what a more ambitious (if less immediately realistic) set of provisions might be. The bill itself, after all, calls for the President, within six months, to come up with a plan to eliminate poverty in the United States by the year 2015—not an immediately likely prospect. Some of the following proposals might in fact become realistic, as negotiations progress and the political climate changes. Others may be useful as longer-term goals to be kept in play for the future. In any event, a vision of future possibilities can be useful as a stimulus to explore what more can be done in the present.

Consider, then, the following points that might be provided for by federal legislation:

- To require a minimum wage (better yet: a living wage) fixed at or above the poverty line, and indexed to inflation.
- To require and fund a program for replanning the affected cities, with a detailed resident participation requirement.
- To amend existing programs, such as the Community Development Block Grant, those of the Small Business Administration and the Department of Labor, and others relevant to issues of implementation of the Act's goals, so as to conform with those goals.
- To develop and fund specific outreach and educational programs for effective citizen participation in voting, and to provide for channels whereby noncitizen interests can be represented in or with electoral bodies.
- To fund a public works program, on the New Deal model, aimed not simply at restoring the status quo ante, but meeting specified levels of adequacy for infrastructure.
- To provide rehousing subsidies—as grants or loans (depending on the recipient's circumstances)—in order to permit evacuees, former tenants, and home owners to obtain adequate housing on the private market.
- To require the establishment of regional planning, and, where needed, regional operating agencies, with jurisdiction over all supra-local public services, including, but not limited to,

transportation, economic development, major land uses, environmental protection, water supply, and, of course, flood protection.

- To regulate the major activities impacting susceptibility to hurricane damage, including oil drilling, transportation, and waterfront real estate development.
- To impose an excess profits tax on all firms having contracts for reconstruction or directly benefiting from public reconstruction efforts, and impose criminal penalties for profiteering.
- To provide compensation for victims based on needs, rather than on losses, in order to correct the inequities resulting from application of the rules of the Victims Compensation Board established after 9/11.

An even more ambitious bill might add these provisions:

- To guarantee every resident a right to a minimum standard of health, safety, and welfare, with standards set at a given percentage of average national levels, and provisions for enforcement of such rights by individuals or class action. (Discussions regarding a right to housing [Bratt, Stone, and Hartman 2006] might provide guidance.)
- To provide for comprehensive health insurance for all residents.
- To set up a new implementation structure that would be locally based, although bound by federal minimum standards as established in the bill, with provision for democratically selected minimum representation of the most affected groups by race/ethnicity, income, and gender.

Table 14.1 juxtaposes some of these suggestions against the existing structure of H.R. 4197, highlighting what the bill accomplishes and what is not included.

The CBC bill comes as close to a comprehensive approach to the Katrina-related problems as anything now on the table in Washington, although it does not provide details on long-term goals or the needed planning processes. It was written while still awaiting the formulation of a comprehensive and long-range plan for prevention and reconstruction, a plan not yet produced by any local or state level of government or any private or voluntary group. It therefore also refrains from calling for any specific total sum for reconstruction; it pushes for what is immediately needed. Even at that, it goes well beyond what is provided by the Administration's Katrina provisions in the Defense Reauthorization Bill, which the CBC sees as a first step in providing what is needed—indeed, a first step that does not

Table 14.1 H.R. 4197 and Beyond

Title	H.R. 4197	Further Possible Provisions
I	Compensation to victims to return them to pre-Katrina status.	Pre-Katrina status was below poverty level for many residents. Many were unemployed, had health problems, inadequate educations. Equity would require a level of redistribution that would raise the floor to be an adequate standard of living for all.
II	Planning for the return of residents to prior locations, with protection of their health.	Democracy would require a provision for replanning of the city, with resident participation required in the process, rather than freezing existing unsatisfactory patterns.
III	Supplementation of existing health, welfare, and unemployment benefits for victims.	The occasion might be used for a pilot project of comprehensive single-payer health care coverage at adequate levels.
IV	Limited funding for public housing and additional funding for existing CDBG programs, and adequate funding for rental assistance vouchers. Gives HUD funds for capacity-building for nonprofit community development corporations and housing development corporations.	The creation of a right to housing, and provision for the estimated cost of providing adequate and affordable housing for all. More explicit capacity-building assistance to grassroots groups with support for organizing work. Priorities for CDBG funds should make it clear that low-income communities should be assisted first.
V	Supplemental funding for existing educational programs at all levels.	Standards should be set for what a comprehensive education program might be.
VI	Requires absentee ballots and funds election equipment.	Should fund outreach to the diaspora.
VII	Facilitates financial transactions to overcome credit obstacles for victims, with limited additional funding.	Should review and improve existing mechanisms, add grants, and provide full needed funding.
VIII	Expands SBA and related programs, primarily loans, and imposes other job-related requirements on private-sector firms.	A general living-wage requirement should be provided, along with a public works program on New Deal model.

Table 14.1 (continued) H.R. 4197 and Beyond

Title	H.R. 4197	Further Possible Provisions
IX	Tax credits for builders and owners of housing, not tenants, and for providers of low-income rental housing.	Credits should go to tenants as well as home owners and rental property owners, and should be deeper and broader. As in IV, a right to housing and a goal of complete coverage to those in need.
X, XI	Exemption from Katrina-related bankruptcy restrictions; miscellaneous provisions reimbursing nonprofits rendering certain services.	General support for active community-based nonprofits with support for necessary grassroots provision of services and advocacy.
XII	Expresses that the President should present within 6 months a plan to eradicate poverty in the United States within 10 years.	Should include such a plan for Katrina-affected areas today.
	Not included.	Causes should be analyzed by an independent commission.
	Not included.	Regional planning issues should be confronted, including location of economic activities on and off shore.
	Not included.	Funding from tax on oil revenues.
	Not included.	Regulation of environmentally impacting economic activities: oil drilling, shipping, casinos, and tourist development.
	Not included.	Examination of costs and benefits of levee construction vs. alternatives.
	Not included.	An excess profits tax on all firms doing recovery work, and criminal penalties for profiteering.

add new money but stays within the original $62 billion authorized by Congress immediately after Katrina.

The bill is a good one, far better than anything else pending in Congress as of spring 2006. The even more ambitious provisions suggested above are clearly ideal—indeed, they appear as utopian in today's circumstances. It is conventional in disaster relief programs to limit recovery assistance so that recipients are not better off, just not worse off, than before the disaster. But that is not a logical goal for planning: restore the status quo ante. Restoring the status quo in this case would mean reproducing an unjust, inequitable, and unsustainable state of affairs. As one woman told Senator Barrack Obama: "We had nothing before the hurricane. Now we got less than nothing."

Getting her back to nothing is hardly a desirable objective. Certainly, in terms of doing what needs to be done to prevent a recurrence of the disaster, the status quo ante is inadequate. That is widely recognized, and underlies the goal of providing defenses against a Category 5 hurricane, not just a Category 3, as (in theory at least) the present system provides. It is also widely recognized that many practices—having to do with oil drilling and pipelines, the filling in of wetlands, development and land use practices—cannot continue as they were before, or another hurricane will produce another disaster. But is the goal of restoring a condition in which 29.7% of the population was under the poverty line, including well over 30% of the African-American population; in which the level of segregation was among the highest in the country; in which casinos were a dominant user of waterfront and river locations; in which educational facilities were grossly unequal in funding and achievement—is that a worthy goal of planning in the United States today?

Clearly, addressing the root causes of the disaster following Katrina and pursuing truly democratic and equitable goals in the rebuilding may well place recipients in a better position, comparatively, than others in the country, at least temporarily. Might that not indeed be desirable, with equity requiring not that those in the Gulf Coast be brought to the average of others, but that others be brought up to the higher standard? One magazine has already suggested that "New Orleans could become the nation's classroom" (*The Nation*, 2006:5). Could not, indeed, the reaction to the disaster that followed Katrina be to rebuild the affected communities as models of what should be in all communities, and to treat individuals as they should be treated all over the land? Isn't that the ambition that good, socially-oriented planning would have? Or is it only to reproduce with government assistance the inequitable and unsustainable situation that existed before the disaster?

References

American Institute of Certified Planners. 2005. Code of Ethics and Professional Conduct. Adopted March 19, 2005; effective June 1, 2005. http://www.planning.ethics/.

American Planning Association. 1992. Ethical Principles in Planning. Adopted May 1992. http://www.planning.org/ethics/ethics/html.

Dreier, Peter. 2005. Katrina in Perspective: The disaster raises key questions about the role of government in American society. *Dissent*. September 14. http://www.dissentmagazine.org/.

Gertner, Jon. 2006. What Is a Living Wage? *New York Times Magazine*: 38ff. January 25.

Lipton, Eric. 2005. Rush to Set Up U.S. Housing for Survivors. *The New York Times*: p. 1. September 13.

Nation, The. 2006. January 2. Page 5.

Reardon, Kenneth M. 2006. The Shifting Landscape of New Orleans: While Planners and Developers Redraw the City Map, Displaced Residents Struggle to Have a Role. *Shelterforce* (Spring): 22-25,27.

Sclar, Elliott. 2000. *You Don't Always Get What You Pay For: The Economics of Privatization.* Ithaca, NY: Cornell University Press.

Endnotes

1. Mayor Nagin's Commission's recommendation—that reconstruction in low-lying residential areas be delayed a year to see what percent of their prior residents want to return to them—sounds reasonable, as based on the free choice of those affected, but is not. It creates a vicious circle: whether people want to return depends on what reconstruction plans are, so reconstruction plans can't wait to find out what people want. As the immediate reaction to it shows, many feel the Commission's proposal is a way of discouraging African-Americans from returning, thus "whitening" the city. If it were made clear from the outset that those returning could determine the direction of reconstruction in their communities, and get the resources needed for it, and if those then not wishing to return could have equal support in re-establishing themselves elsewhere, there might be real freedom of choice.

2. For a recent and relevant example of organization to protect an African-American community threatened by gentrification and by wetlands development in Gulfport, see Trisha Miller. "Crossing Muddy Waters: The Struggle to Preserve Historical Neighborhood along Mississippi's Gulf Coast." *Shelterforce*, July/August 2005, #142, pp. 8-11.

3. See Good Jobs First, Good Jobs New York, the Labor Community Advocacy Network to Rebuild New York, and Fiscal Policy Institute. An Open Letter from Civic Groups in New York on 9/11 and Katrina. September 15, 2005. For relevant ideas based on the New York post-9/11 experience, see Fiscal Policy Institute. An Open Letter from Civic Groups in New York on 9/11 and Katrina. Spetember 15, 2005 at http://www.Fiscalpolicy.org/openletterontherebuildingprocess.pdf at its web site.

4. As quoted at http://www.911injured.org/VCF/aboutvcf., the statement of purpose reads: "It is the purpose of this title to provide compensation to any individual (or relatives of a deceased individual) who was physically injured or killed as a result of the terrorist-related aircraft crashes of September 11, 2001. The Commissions work is archived at http://www.usdoj.gov/archive/victimcompensation. For the reaction of those benefiting from the Commission's work, see http://www.familiesofseptember11.org/include/viewfile.asp?vfile=./.%2fdocs%2fFOS11+VCF+FINAL+REPORT.pdf

5. As this article was being prepared for publication, a story in the The New York Times was headlined: "In New Orleans, Money Is Ready but a Plan Isn't" A comment on the limits of volunteer planning without power, given the absence of a formal democratic governance planning process? *The New York Times*, Adam Nossiter Published: June 18, 2006, available at http://www.nytimes.com/2006/06/18/us/nationalspecial/18orleans.html?_r=1&ex=1150776000&en=2ec5f582815c2985&ei=5087%0A&oref=slogin.

6. Paul Brathwaite, Executive director of the Congressional Black Caucus, was helpful in putting together some of the information on which the following discussion is based. He is of course in no way responsible for the interpretation or conclusions presented here.

7. Ten Points to Guide Rebuilding in the Gulf Coast Region, by PolicyLink, is an excellent set of proposals. It does not attempt to formulate them in as parts of legislation. http://www.policylink.org/EquitableRenewal.html.

8. As of this writing, the bill appears to be languishing before the House Subcommittee on Educational Reform, to which it was referred on March 27, 2006.

Contributors

Mary Frances Berry (mfberry@prodigy.net) is the Geraldine R. Segal Professor of American Social Thought and Professor of History at the University of Pennsylvania, where she teaches History of American Law and advises graduate students in Legal History and African American History. She was appointed by President Carter and confirmed by the Senate as a Commissioner on the U.S. Commission on Civil Rights. In 1993, President Clinton designated her Chairperson of the Commission. She was reappointed to a six-year term in January 1999. She resigned from the Commission on December 7, 2004. Dr. Berry was one of the founders of the Free South Africa Movement in the 1980s, which instigated protests at the South African Embassy in the successful struggle for democracy in South Africa. She was arrested and jailed several times in the cause. She was in Capetown on February 11, 1990 to meet Nelson Mandela upon his release from Robben Island. Dr. Berry was elected by her peers as a vice-president of the American Historical Association and President of the Organization of American Historians. She has received over 30 honorary doctoral degrees and numerous awards for her public service and scholarly activities, including the NAACP's Roy Wilkins Award and Image Award, the Rosa Parks Award of the Southern Christian Leadership Conference, the Ebony Magazine Black Achievement Award, the Hubert Humphrey Award of the Leadership Conference on Civil Rights, and the American Bar Association's Spirit of Excellence Award. She is one of the 75 women photographed for the book and national exhibition, "I Dream A World: Portraits of Black Women Who Changed America."

Michael Casserly (mcasserly@cgcs.org) has served as Executive Director of the Washington, D.C.-based Council of the Great City Schools since January 1992. Casserly also served as the organization's Director of Legislation and Research for 15 years before assuming his current position. As head of the urban school group, Casserly unified big-city schools nationwide around a vision of reform and improvement; launched an aggressive research program on trends in urban education; convened the first Education Summit of Big City Mayors and Superintendents; led the nation's largest urban school districts to volunteer for the National Assessment of Educational Progress (NAEP); led the first national study of common practices among the nation's fastest improving urban school districts; and launched national task forces on achievement gaps, leadership and governance, finance, professional development, and bilingual education. He is currently spearheading efforts to boost academic performance in the nation's big-city schools; strengthen management and operations; challenge inequitable state financing systems; and improve the public's image of urban education. He is a U.S. Army veteran and holds a Ph.D. from the University of Maryland and B.A. from Villanova University.

Sheila Crowley (sheila@nlihc.org) is the President and CEO of the Washington, DC-based National Low Income Housing Coalition, a membership organization dedicated solely to ending the affordable housing crisis in America. She also teaches social policy, social justice, legislative advocacy, and community organizing as an adjunct faculty member of the School of Social Work of Virginia Commonwealth University. She is a member of the Board of Directors of the National Housing Trust, the Poverty & Race Research Action Council, the Enterprise Foundation, the Technical Assistance Collaborative, and the Alliance for Healthy Homes. She was the 1996-1997 Social Work Congressional Fellow, where she served on the Democratic staff of the Housing Subcommittee of the United States Senate Banking Committee. From 1984-1992, she was the Executive Director of The Daily Planet, a multipurpose homeless service and advocacy organization in Richmond, Virginia. She was the founding director in 1979 of the YWCA Women's Advocacy Program in Richmond, the shelter and service program for battered women and their children. She is a founding member of the Virginians Against Domestic Violence, the Greater Richmond Coalition for the Homeless, and the Richmond Better Housing Coalition.

Evangeline Franklin (vangyfranklin@earthlink.net) M.D., MPH is the Director of Clinical Services and Employee Health of the City of New Orleans. During Hurricane Katrina, her responsibilities included being co-medical director of the Special Needs Shelter in the Superdome. She was evacuated to Dallas with her Superdome co-workers, where she worked with the public health organizations and the Centers for Disease Control and Prevention in the Convention Center and Reunion shelters. In her current position she is working with Health Department Director Kevin Stephens and Deputy Director Sandra Robinson to reestablish the City of New Orleans public health infrastructure. She is the author of *Getting People Healthy in New Orleans*, a comprehensive monograph that describes the state of health in New Orleans and the Health Department's agenda for change. Dr. Franklin's career includes working as health insurance plan medical director for Aetna and United Healthcare in Louisiana, director of urgent care, lab and xray services, and occupational medicine services at UniversityMEDNET, a large group practice in Cleveland, Ohio. She received her medical degree and masters in public health from Yale University. She has a board certification in internal medicine. Her home in Gentilly as well as many of her relatives' homes in New Orleans East were flooded by Katrina. She currently lives in New Orleans.

Margaret Morganroth Gullette (mgullette@msn.com) is a Resident Scholar with the Women's Studies Research Center at Brandeis University. She is the author of *Aged by Culture* (University of Chicago Press, 2004), *Declining to Decline: Cultural Combat and the Politics of the Midlife* (University Press of Virginia, 1997), and *Safe at Last in the Middle Years: The Invention of the Midlife Progress Novel* (University of California Press, 1988). Gullette has written for the *New York Times Magazine, Nation, Ms., Boston Globe, Miami Herald, womensenews, American Prospect, American Scholar,* and many scholarly and literary publications. She has been the recipient of NEH, ACLS, and Bunting Fellowships. An internationally known age critic, she lectures and has been interviewed frequently on the social construction of the midlife and similar issues related to age, gender, race, and class. She finds funding in her Sister City, San Juan del Sur, Nicaragua, for educational programs for hundreds of adults, which include two literacy projects for women and currently a free High School for Adults. She is also a member of PEN-America.

Brian Gumm (bgumm@afhh.org) has worked as the Washington, D.C.-based Alliance for Healthy Homes' writer and researcher since 2004. He works on a variety of projects, including the monthly *Alliance Alert*, the Alliance's website content, and integrated pest management and pesticide issues. He has a J.D. from the University of Wisconsin Law School and a B.S. in Environmental Policy from Northland College in Ashland, Wisconsin.

Chester Hartman (Chartman2@aol.com) is Director of Research for the Washington, D.C.-based Poverty & Race Research Action Council, for which he was founding Executive Director from 1990-2003. He is also founder and former Chair of The Planners Network, a national organization of progressive urban planners. He currently serves on the Long-Term Community Planning Task Force of Governor Blanco's Louisiana Recovery Authority. His most recent books are *City for Sale: The Transformation of San Francisco* (University of California Press, 2002); *Between Eminence and Notoriety: Four Decades of Radical Urban Planning* (Rutgers Center for Urban Policy Research, 2002); *A Right to Housing: Foundation for a New Social Agenda* (Temple University Press, 2006); and *Poverty & Race in America: The Emerging Agendas* (Lexington Books, 2006).

Heidi Hartmann (Heidi@iwpr.org) is the President of the Washington, DC-based Institute for Women's Policy Research, a scientific research organization she founded in 1987 to meet the need for women-centered, policy-oriented research. She is also a Research Professor at The George Washington University. Dr. Hartmann has published numerous articles in journals and books, and her work has been translated into more than a dozen languages. She lectures widely on women, economics, and public policy, frequently testifies before the U.S. Congress, and is often cited as an authority in various media outlets. She is a co-author of *Unnecessary Losses: Costs to Americans of the Lack of Family and Medical Leave*; *Survival at the Bottom: The Income Packages of Low-Income Families with Children*; and *Still A Man's Labor Market: The Long-Term Earnings Gap*. Prior to founding IWPR, Dr. Hartmann was on the faculties of Rutgers University and the New School for Social Research and worked at the National Research Council/National Academy of Sciences. In 1994, she was the recipient of a MacArthur Fellowship Award for her work in the field of women and economics. She is Vice-Chair of the National Council of Women's Organizations and co-editor of the *Journal of Women, Politics, and Policy*.

Hasan Kwame Jeffries (Jeffries.57@osu.edu) is an Assistant Professor in the History Department and the Kirwan Institute for the Study of Race and Ethnicity at The Ohio State University. His research and teaching focus on twentieth century African-American protest, particularly during the Civil Rights and Black Power eras. His published works include "Organizing for More than the Vote: The Political Radicalization of Local People in Lowndes County, Alabama, 1965-1966," which appears in *Groundwork: The Local Black Freedom Movement in America*. At present, he is completing a book project that investigates the freedom struggle in Lowndes County and the making of Black Power.

Avis Jones-DeWeever (jones-deweever@iwpr.org) is the Director of Poverty, Education, and Social Justice Programs at the Washington, D.C.-based Institute for Women's Policy Research. Her work examines the causes and consequences of poverty on the well-being of low-income women and families while identifying effective programmatic strategies that result in poverty reduction. Dr. Jones-DeWeever has authored or co-authored numerous publications, including "Before and After Welfare Reform: The Work and Well-Being of Low-Income Single Parent Families"; "When the Spirit Blooms: Acquiring Higher Education in the Context of Welfare Reform" (*Journal of Women, Politics, and Policy*); and "Saving Ourselves: African American Women and the HIV/AIDS Crisis" (*Harvard Journal of African American Public Policy*). A highly sought-after speaker, Dr. Jones-DeWeever's policy perspectives have been distributed through a variety of media outlets, including CNN, *ABC News Now*, National Public Radio, BBC Radio International, and the *New York Times*. Her areas of expertise include poverty in urban communities, inequality of educational opportunity, and the impact of welfare reform on women and communities of color.

Beulah Labostrie (laacorn@acorn.org) has been the President of Louisiana ACORN for more than a decade and has been active in the organization in New Orleans virtually since its founding in the city in 1975. She has led the organization and its 9,000 members in their community campaigns, living-wage battles, fights for lead abatement, and numerous other efforts. She is also active in the National Baptist Convention. She raised seven children in New Orleans. She lived in the Fairgrounds neighborhood and was flooded by the storm and is currently living in Kenner with one of her daughters.

Jane Malone (JMalone@AFHH.org) joined the Washington, D.C.-based Alliance to End Childhood Lead Poisoning (since renamed the Alliance for Healthy Homes) in 1988. She has worked on efforts to implement federal lead-safe housing policies and directed *Building Blocks for Primary Prevention: Protecting Children from Lead-Based Paint Hazards*, a CDC-funded effort to describe innovative and promising strategies to prevent childhood lead poisoning. Malone works on federal, state, and local policymaking related to housing and environmental health hazards, and provides technical assistance to agencies and advocates regarding effective policy choices.

Before her move to Washington, D.C., Malone worked on housing policy, public education, and other issues affecting low-income communities in neighborhood-level, citywide, and statewide arenas for more than 20 years. Among other accomplishments, she co-authored multiple reports focused on housing-related needs and resources across the Common-wealth of Pennsylvania and in the City of Philadelphia, and led the reform of Philadelphia's $36 million homeless program. Malone studied sociology, social work, and city planning at the University of Pennsylvania.

Peter Marcuse (pm35@columbia.edu) is a lawyer and planner who is Pro-fessor of Urban Planning at Columbia University. He has also taught in West and East Germany, Australia, the Union of South Africa, Canada, Austria, and Brazil. He has written extensively on housing, urban develop-ment, the history of planning, the ethics of planning, racial segregation, and globalization. His most recent books are (with Ronald van Kempen) *Globalizing Cities: A New Spatial Order?* (Blackwell, 1999) and *Of States and Cities: The Partitioning of Urban Space* (Oxford University Press, 2002). He is currently much involved in the debates about the redevelopment of lower Manhattan after the September 11 attacks and the implications of the so-called "war on terrorism" on urban development globally. His most recent work has been on issues of sustainability, the role of the state in housing development in less developed countries, and on globalism as an extension of Edward Said's concept of Orientalism. He has been President of the Los Angeles City Planning Commission and chaired the Housing Committee of Community Board #9, Manhattan, in New York City.

Daniel W. Newhart (dnewhart05@yahoo.com) is a graduate research associate at the Kirwan Institute for the Study of Race and Ethnicity at The Ohio State University. He has a B.A. in Philosophy as well as a B.A. in Psychology from Purdue University. He recently received an M.A. in Higher Education Administration at Ohio State and is currently a Ph.D. candidate in the College of Education at Ohio State. His research focuses on whether "color-blind racism" is affected by service-learning pedagogy in higher education.

john a. powell (powel008@yahoo.com) is an internationally recognized authority in the areas of civil rights, civil liberties, and issues relating to race, ethnicity, poverty, and the law. He is the Executive Director of the Kirwan Institute for the Study of Race and Ethnicity at The Ohio State University. He also holds the Williams Chair in Civil Rights and Civil Liberties at Ohio State's Moritz College of Law. He has written extensively on racial justice and regionalism, concentrated poverty and urban sprawl, the link between housing and school segregation, opportunity-based housing, gentrification, disparities in the criminal justice system, voting rights, affirmative action in the United States, South Africa and Brazil, and racial and ethnic identity and the current demographic shift.

Michael Powers (michaelppowers@gmail.com) is a researcher in the Economic Policy Department at the Center for American Progress in Washington, D.C. where he focuses primarily on federal tax and budget issues. He has contributed to numerous analyses, including reports on budget reconciliation, complexity in the tax code, and the demographic characteristics of the regions devastated by Hurricane Katrina. His writings include "Budget Deficit Disorder," an article assessing the inability of conservative political leaders to control the budget deficit. In 2004, he worked at the Democratic Caucuses in Iowa for the Gephardt campaign, conducting GOTV activities and overseeing the Drake University Caucus. He attended The George Washington University, where he studied health policy, the history of the progressive movement, and the American political system and graduated Summa Cum Laude in 2005 with a B.S. in Public Health.

Gene B. Preuss (PreussG@uhd.edu) is Associate Professor of History at the University of Houston-Downtown, where he teaches African-American, Mexican-American, and the history of ethnic minorities in America. His research focuses on the history of public education. He conducted numerous interviews and assisted with the development of oral history projects at the Southwest Collection/Special Collection Libraries at Texas Tech University, and worked on the Lyndon Baines Johnson Space Center's Oral History Project. He is a moderator on H-Oralhist, an H-NET discussion list.

Wade Rathke (chieforg@acorn.org) is the founder of ACORN—the Association of Community Organizations for Reform Now—and has been its Chief Organizer for more than 35 years. The national organization is headquartered in New Orleans, and he has been part of the ACORN team responding to the cataclysmic changes being wrought since the storm and helping direct the fight day to day. The ACORN headquarters are in Fauborg Marigny on Elysian Fields Avenue. Rathke and his family live in the Bywater neighborhood. Both areas were fortunate to not be flooded.

Ralph Scott (rscott@afhh.org), Community Projects Director at the Washington, D.C.-based Alliance for Healthy Homes, joined the staff in 1997 to help build the capacity of the organization, as well as of state and local advocacy organizations and national stakeholders to work collaboratively on lead poisoning prevention. Scott currently anchors the Alliance's advocacy work with grassroots groups. He has worked as a community organizer on housing and tenants' rights issues since 1979, most recently with New Jersey Citizen Action as their Lead Poisoning Project Director. Prior to that, he helped found, and worked as an organizer for, the Lead Elimination Action Drive, a Chicago coalition of community and health groups. Scott holds a B.A. in Mathematics from the University of Chicago.

Josh Silver (jsilver@ncrc.org) is Vice President of Research and Policy of the Washington, DC-based National Community Reinvestment Coalition. He develops NCRC's policy positions, writes congressional testimony, and produces research studies on community reinvestment and the role of financial institutions. Major NCRC reports co-authored by Silver are "The Broken Credit System: Discrimination and Unequal Access to Affordable Loans by Race and Age," "The Performance of GSEs at the Metropolitan Level," "America's Best and Worst Lenders," and "CRA Commitments." In his technical advisory role, Silver helps community organizations devise neighborhood reinvestment strategies and interpret HMDA and CRA data on lending activity. Silver was a policy analyst at The Urban Institute for five years before coming to NCRC. He has 16 years experience in the housing and community development field.

Gregory D. Squires (squires@gwu.edu) is a Professor of Sociology, and Public Policy and Public Administration, and Chair of the Department of Sociology at The George Washington University. He is a member of the Board of Directors of the Woodstock Institute, the Advisory Board of the John Marshall Law School Fair Housing Legal Support Center in Chicago, and the Social Science Advisory Board of the Poverty & Race Research Action Council. He has served as a consultant for civil rights organizations around the country, including HUD and the National Fair Housing Alliance, and as a member of the Federal Reserve Board's Consumer Advisory Council. He has written for several academic journals and general interest publications, including *Housing Policy Debate, Urban Studies, Social Science Quarterly, Urban Affairs Review, Journal of Urban Affairs, New York Times*, and *Washington Post*. His recent books include *Urban Sprawl* (Urban Institute Press, 2002), *Organizing Access to Capital* (Temple University Press, 2003), *Why the Poor Pay More: How to Stop Predatory Lending* (Praeger,

2004), and *Privileged Places: Race, Residence, and the Structure of Opportunity* (with Charis E. Kubrin, Lynne Rienner, 2006).

Alan H. Stein (astein@csufresno.edu) is presently on faculty at California State University, Fresno in the Madden Library. He was Head of the Louisiana Division, City Archives and Special Collections at the New Orleans Public Library from 2004-2005 and was elected as a member of the Metropolitan Leadership Forum, City of New Orleans, just prior to Hurricane Katrina. Stein serves on the Education and Program Committees of the Oral History Association, and is Vice-Chair and Chair-Elect (2006-07) of the Society of American Archivists' Labor Archives Roundtable. He is also on the board of the Consortium of Oral History Educators and is a contributor to *Preparing the Next Generation of Oral Historians: An Anthology of Oral History Education*, edited by Barry A. Lanman and Laura M. Wendling, to be published by AltaMira Press in 2007.

Eric Stiens (estiens@gmail.com) is a research associate with the Kirwan Institute for the Study of Race and Ethnicity at The Ohio State University. Formerly, he worked with john powell at the Institute on Race and Poverty at the University of Minnesota. He has a B.A. in Sociology from Macalester College and is currently an M.S.W. candidate studying community development at Washington University in St. Louis.

John Taylor (jtaylor@ncrc.org) is President and CEO of the Washington, D.C.-based National Community Reinvestment Coalition. Raised in the housing projects of Boston and trained as an attorney, he has worked for more than 25 years in the field of economic justice. He has been the recipient of numerous local, state, and national awards, including the Martin Luther King, Jr. Peace Award, a United States Congress Citation/proclamation (twice), the State of Massachusetts *Award for Excellence in Community Economic Development*, and a Presidential appointment to the CDFI Fund. Taylor recently was appointed to the board of directors of the Rainbow Push Coalition and the Leadership Conference for Civil Rights. He has also served on several other national boards, including the Consumer Advisory Council of the Federal Reserve Bank Board, The Fannie Mae Housing Impact Division, and the Freddie Mac Housing Advisory Board. He has appeared on ABC's *Nightline*, CBS, Fox News, CNN, CSPAN, in the *New York Times, Washington Post, Chicago Tribune,* and hundreds of other print, television, and radio media. Taylor has also testified before numerous congressional committees, both in the U.S. Senate and the House of Representatives.

Robert K. Whelan (rkwhelan@uno.edu) is Freeport McMoran Professor of Urban and Public Affairs at the University of New Orleans. He is co-author of *Urban Politics and Policy in a Bureaucratic Age*, and has authored and co-authored many book chapters and articles. Dr. Whelan chairs the Planning and Zoning Commission in the city of Slidell, Louisiana. His main research interests are metropolitan governance and citizen participation, in New Orleans and in Quebec.

Robert O. Zdenek (rozdenek@afhh.org), DPA, is Executive Director of the Washington, D.C.-based Alliance for Healthy Homes, the leading national advocacy and technical support organization for helping to eliminate environmental hazards in low-income housing. Prior to heading the Alliance, he was Principal of Robert Zdenek Associates, a consulting firm that worked with over 30 national, regional, and local clients between 2002 and 2005, including serving as Senior Consultant for two years to the U.S. Department of HHS/Office of Community Services. Other major professional roles include serving as Vice President of Community Building at United Way of America; President of United Way of Somerset County (NJ); Director of Economic Development at New Community Corporation; Senior Associate at the Annie E. Casey Foundation; and long-time President of the National Congress for Community Economic Development. He has written extensively on community economic development topics and co-authored a book with Carol Steinbach titled *Managing Your CDC: Leadership Strategies for Changing Times*. Zdenek has served on over 15 boards of directors. Currently he serves as Vice President, National Housing Institute, and as a board member for Manna Ventures and Leadership Committee, National Disability Institute and Global Urban Development. He has a doctorate in Public Administration from the University of Southern California and is adjunct faculty at the Robert J. Milano Graduate School of Management and Urban Policy at New School University. He is a frequent speaker and columnist.

Index